URBAN AMERICA
From Downtown to No Town

D0143188

URBAN AMERICA
From Downtown to No Town

David R. Goldfield
Virginia Polytechnic Institute
and State University

Blaine A. Brownell
University of Alabama
in Birmingham

Houghton Mifflin Company   **Boston**
Dallas   Geneva, Illinois
Hopewell, New Jersey
Palo Alto   London

For the children of the city

Copyright © 1979 by Houghton Mifflin Company.
All rights reserved. No part of this work may be reproduced
or transmitted in any form or by any means, electronic or
mechanical, including photocopying and recording, or by
any information storage or retrieval system, without permission in writing from the publisher.

Printed in the U.S.A.

Library of Congress Catalog Card Number: 78-69562

ISBN: 0-395-27397-8

CONTENTS

Preface   ix

Introduction. The City: People, Space, and Time   1
A System of Cities □ Urban Ecology □ Urban Forms
in American History

I.
GENESIS   22

1. An Act of Faith: The Planting of Cities   25
God, Glory, and Gold □ Spanish and French
Settlement □ English Settlements in New England
□ Philadelphia and New York □ Settlements in the
Chesapeake and Southern Colonies □ Patterns of
Colonial Urban Growth

2. On the Waterfront: The Cluster Economy   41
Agriculture, Commerce, and Colonial Towns
□ The Waterfront □ The Atlantic Trade
□ New Crops and New Markets □ The Workings of
International Commerce □ Urban Growth in the
Backcountry □ Merchants and Artisans

3. All Sorts of Opinions: Colonial Urban Society and Politics   62

Social Structure □ Family, Church, and Tavern
□ Poverty and Social Disorder □ Political Community

4. Maturing Cities   81

Problems and Responses □ The Changing Face of
Colonial Cities □ Urbanity □ Revolution

II.
MARKET PLACE   98

5. Re-creation: The Planting of Cities   100

Urbanmania in the West □ Eastern Cities in the West
□ Paris on the Potomac

6. "The Goddess of Christianity": The Economy of the Market Place 109

The Tortuous Journey of Trade □ The Entrepre-
neurs: Marketplace Engineers □ The Song of Steam:
Marketplace Technology □ The Business Revolution:
Organizing the City for Profit □ The National
Market Place

7. Society in the Market Place: A New Spatial Order   134

The Shape of Things to Come: The New Market
Place □ The Residential City: Preference and Tech-
nology □ Space and Class □ Spatial Reflections of
Work and Ethnicity □ The Separate and Separating
Urban Societies

8. The Business of Government and Services   166

Advancing Political Technology □ Urban Services:
Policy Reflections of Economic Objectives □ The
Caring City: The Provision of Social Services □ The
Esthetic City: The Provision of Environmental Ser-
vices □ The City as a Way of Life: Reflections from
the Market Place

III.
RADIAL CENTER   198

9. The Economy of the Radial Center   202

Radiant Centers and Radial Suburbs □ The City
Beautiful □ The City Efficient □ The Garden City

□ Twilight's First Gleaming: Steel-Driving Cities
□ Working Is Not a Living: Labor in the Industrial
City □ A Woman's Work . . . □ The Workers' Response

10. Yearning to Breathe Free: Urban Society and the Great Migrations   243

The Foreigners □ Ethnic Space: The Neighborhood
□ Making It □ The Blacks □ Racial Space: The Ghetto
□ Helping the Other Half: Poverty and Its Relief
□ Ward Heelers and Mornin' Glories: Urban Politics
in a Diverse Society

IV.
VITAL FRINGE   296

11. Urban Society: Cells and Fortresses   307

New Morals, New Music, New Negroes, New Heroes,
Old Values □ Old Frustrations and Old Divisions
□ Suburban Fortresses and City Cells

12. Urban Economy: Technology and Efficiency   332

Bigger Is Better: Cities in the National Economy
□ National Urban Technology □ The Suburban
Migration: Searching for a Lost Eden Through
a Windshield

13. Urban Politics and Public Policy: With Friends Like These . . .   355

New Political Technology and Old Results: The
Search for Order □ City Planning: The Politics of
Space □ Cities Become National Policy: Depression
and War □ Housing and Urban Redevelopment:
A Policy Gone Astray □ Urban Transportation
Policies: Cities Taken for a Ride

14. Beyond the Fringe: Downtown and No Town   382

The Urbanization of Suburbia □ The Suburbanization of the Cities: Back to the Basics □ The Rise of
No Town: A New Type of City

Suggestions for Further Reading   407

Index   419

PREFACE

"From downtown to no town" succinctly describes the development of the
American city from the colonial beginnings to the last quarter of the twentieth century. The phrase implies no value judgment but is merely a statement about space. One of the themes of this book is space—specifically,
spatial relationships within and between cities.

Most urban histories of the United States have emphasized politics or
social patterns. Without neglecting these important elements, we have chosen to focus on space, since the physical arrangement of the city in space
reflects in a very tangible and visible way the shifts and the significance of
social, economic, and political patterns. More than any other aspect of
urban development, the use of space allows us to "read" cities for the
secrets they contain. Behind every suburban enclave or shopping center,
every freeway plunging into the central core or ramshackle neighborhood
clinging to the railroad tracks, lie changing economic realities, political
decisions and values, and the efforts of people to succeed or merely to
survive.

Space, then, is the thread that ties together the elements of this book.
The book falls into four main parts, each covering a period of American
history and centering on the "form" of urban place that was dominant in
that particular period. These four forms are the *cluster*, the *market place*, the
radial center, and the *vital fringe*, characteristic, respectively, of the colonial

period, the early nineteenth century, the late nineteenth and early twentieth centuries, and the period since 1920 or so. In dealing with such a complex phenomenon as urbanization in as large a country as the United States, we cannot be too precise. But these urban forms generally reflect stages in an evolutionary process and reveal, in their characteristics, the relationships between patterns of economic activity, political organization, institutional development, social life, and spatial arrangement. Each form receives roughly equal treatment. We believe that urban development is a cumulative process, with each era building on the previous one and no one period more important than any other.

We have attempted in this book to tell "whole" the story of cities in the United States, at least so far as this is possible in a space of some four hundred pages. We have sought to provide a synthesis of what has been learned about the history of the American city in an original framework that makes sense, that stresses the most important elements in the urbanization process. The book is, necessarily, interdisciplinary. It draws on the work not only of historians but also of geographers, economists, sociologists, political scientists, and city planners. It is simply not possible to understand urbanization from the perspective of a single discipline and perhaps historians are in a particularly good position to build some bridges among these various perspectives. We have tried to build sturdy bridges without using the finicky tools of jargon and specialized terminology. We have no illusions that this book will be acceptable to all, or that it will be the last word on this fascinating and difficult subject. But we believe it is the first genuinely comprehensive, interdisciplinary history of urban America.

We have also tried to include much more information on cities in the southern and western regions of the country, and on small and medium-sized cities, than is usually provided in American urban histories. New York, Boston, and Chicago are indeed as important as their size and notoriety suggest, but three dominant foci in the American urban network do not fully explain the character of that network. In many ways, the largest cities constitute exceptions rather than the rule, and in any event life in Peoria, Nashville, and Phoenix was often quite different from that in Manhattan or along Halsted Street.

We have written this book in the conviction that an understanding of the development of cities in the United States—an understanding of the urbanization process—not only offers its own interest and revelations but is absolutely crucial to the formation of wise and effective urban policies for the present and future. All too often, policymakers and citizens act on superficial and simplistic assumptions about what is "natural" or inevitable in city development, and these assumptions become self-fulfilling prophecies. Certainly, a study of our urban past reveals strong currents that we can expect to flow into the future. But it also reveals that the most "natural" law of urbanization is change, and that any efforts to guide that change must be based on thorough knowledge as well as the inevitable good intentions and unspoken fears, and on a realization of the complexity of the urban mechanism and the problems of tinkering with one aspect while ignoring other, more fundamental elements. We hope this book in some small way helps others to shape a better urban future for us all.

Finally, we alert the reader to another conviction: We both love the city. We hope that at the end of this book, you will savor the city as we do. We have exposed here the city's problems, past and present, to be sure, but we hope that our faith that it represents a positive, invigorating, and essential environment will be shared and realized.

A text, in many respects, is a synthesis of other people's work. We are indebted to the numerous historians, geographers, sociologists, and planners whose ideas have been incorporated into this book. Our acknowledgment of specific scholars appears in the notes at the end of each chapter. As the work has unfolded we have benefited from the valuable insights and advice of a quartet of noted urbanists: Kenneth T. Jackson of Columbia University, James B. Lane of Indiana University at Gary, James F. Richardson of the University of Akron, and Bruce Stave of the University of Connecticut. To the extent to which they wish to accept the final product, this is their work, too.

We have been fortunate to receive superb cooperation from an array of colleagues and support personnel. Specifically, Gordon Bechanan, Director of Libraries at Virginia Tech, and Katy Wilson, in charge of interlibrary loan, provided books and articles (some quite obscure) for our digestion. Boo Brubaker, Louise Oliver, Christy Seaborn, Terry Stover, and Patricia Wade wore out several Virginia Tech typewriters and some eyes typing this manuscript. Evia D. Wilson and Joyce Shackleford of the University of Alabama in Birmingham, and Eiko Tsukamoto of Hiroshima University, Japan, endured similar deprivations to get the manuscript completed on time. Leonard J. Simutis, friend, colleague, supporter, and Dean at Virginia Tech, is still all four after a year of fending off students who were asking why Dr. Goldfield was locked up in his office. Finally, Mardi Brownell deserves special thanks for being there at the right times with encouragement, advice, and lasagna.

D. G.
B. B.

Introduction.
The City:
People, Space, and Time

Like the Bible, this book begins with Genesis. Lest we be accused of sacrilege or, at the very least, of delusions of grandeur, let us explain that the allusion is appropriate for two reasons. First, in America, city building was an act of faith. Whether the object of that faith was God, as it was in colonial New England, or economic gain, as it was almost everywhere else, the history of the development of American cities is, essentially, a history of the men and women who molded their cities' destinies and who in turn were shaped by those destinies. The city builders were the prophets of their time. Like the Biblical prophets, they envisioned the kingdom of heaven on earth but frequently had to settle for something less, all the while struggling to attain grace. The hope for urban America is that, historically, we have always been striving toward this better vision. Second, Genesis signifies the beginning. In a sense, the process we call civilization began with urbanization. Perhaps the first cities existed in the Mesopotamian basin, that "cradle of civilization," some forty centuries before Christ. Similarly, American civilization and American cities have grown together.

It is the story of that growth that concerns us here. Specifically, we are concerned with "the process of city building over time."[1] The process is illuminated when we look at the changes in spatial order within the city and examine the ways these changes affect the lives of the city's residents; it is also illuminated when we look at the city's relationship with other cities and

1

with the nation. In short, we will be studying the changing internal structure of the city and its changing external relations.

This is not, of course, the first attempt to explain the process of American urban growth, though historians have only recently begun to shift emphasis from case studies and from the analysis of one particular aspect of the urban environment to examination of the broader question of how cities grow. Geographers and sociologists, on the other hand, have been grappling with the question of process for at least half a century. They have developed a body of theory designed to explain both the city's changing external relations and the city's internal structure. The theories should serve as convenient reference points for our study of the urbanization process, rather than as a mirror of what actually happened. Most models tend to idealize reality and are frequently bound, quite understandably, by the era in which they were formulated.

A System of Cities

The historians' emphasis on case studies and on particular aspects of the urban environment sometimes leaves the impression that cities are independent entities floating somewhere in space and time but with little connection to their immediate surroundings, to other cities, or to the nation. Cities are not, of course, islands. In 1933, Walter Christaller, a German geographer, constructed his *central place theory* around the fact that cities often exist as central points for the territory surrounding them. He noted that cities depend on their hinterlands for food and raw materials, while they provide, in turn, processed goods, markets, and a variety of services for the surrounding area. Moving from the example of a single city and its surrounding countryside, Christaller theorized that if the rural population is equally distributed throughout a region or country, a pattern of equally spaced cities will result, with each city serving as the heart of a hinterland or trade area. Christaller drew these hinterlands as hexagons, since these six-sided figures connect with each other without overlapping, as is shown in Figure I.1.

Not all towns or cities are necessarily central places, which are defined as those towns and cities that provide economic, social, administrative, and transportation services for a surrounding territory. And, of course, cities vary in size and serve different functions. Larger cities exist as central places for larger hinterlands, and some cities dominate whole regions and even nations. Christaller believed that the location of cities is directly related to their size, the functions they perform, and the areas they serve.

Christaller developed a ranking of cities from the smallest and simplest

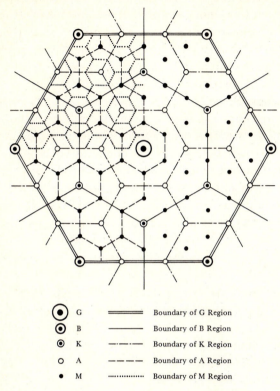

	G		Boundary of G Region
	B		Boundary of B Region
	K		Boundary of K Region
	A		Boundary of A Region
	M		Boundary of M Region

Community (Region)	Population	Miles Apart	Tributary Population	Service Area (In Square Miles)
Market town (M)	1,000	5	3,500	17
Township center (A)	2,000	9	11,000	50
County seat (K)	4,000	15	35,000	160
District city (B)	10,000	25	100,000	470
State capital (G)	30,000	45	350,000	1,500
Provincial head city	100,000	75	1,000,000	4,200
Capital city	500,000	135	3,500,000	13,000

Figure I.1 Christaller's Hexagonal Network of Urban Places. (From Ralph Thomlinson, *Urban Structure: The Social and Spatial Character of Cities* [New York: Random House, 1969], p. 128)

to the largest and most complex (See Figure I.1.) This *urban hierarchy* ranged from the small market town with a population of 1,000, which served a 17-square-mile territory containing 3,500 people, to capital cities serving vast areas with populations numbering in the millions. The specific sizes in the hierarchy are less important than the basic concept: As urban places increase in size, they also increase in the number and variety of functions they perform and the economic activities and services they contain. Thus, Christaller's "district city" performs all the economic and cultural functions of the market town, the township center, and the county seat and contains all of their hinterlands within its own.

Christaller intended his theory not as an actual description of the way things always are, but as a means of understanding relationships among urban location, size, and function. Obviously, rural populations are rarely distributed evenly over a whole region (though this may be the case in small areas), and the presence of important topographical and geographical features like mountain ranges, rivers, lakes, and deserts alters patterns of population distribution considerably. Likewise, the presence of a major transportation route such as a railroad or highway can create a linear population pattern rather than a circular or hexagonal one. But cities do serve as central places for surrounding territory, even within metropolitan regions; they are generally arranged in a hierarchy of size and function; and, taken together, they fashion larger urban networks. All of these facts are most important in any study of the development of cities in the United States.

We can get a very general idea of the nature of any urban system and the relationships among different cities in a system by employing the *rank-size rule* and by examining the *rank order* of cities over time. Simply stated, the rank-size rule is $M = RS,$ where M is the size of the population of the largest (most populated) city in the region or nation (for example, Chicago in the Midwest), R is the population rank of each city, and S is the population size of any given city. Thus, the second largest city in the urban system or network should, ideally, have half the population of the largest city, and the fifteenth largest city should contain one-fifteenth the population of the largest city. This "ideal" rank-size distribution of cities is rarely encountered and is most typical of developed, industrialized societies in which cities exist in all size ranges and categories of the urban hierarchy. In developing areas, the rank-size distribution is often characterized by one or two very large and dominant urban areas, or *primate cities,* and a large number of smaller cities of roughly the same size.

The urban network illustrated in Figure I.2a is clearly dominated by a single city, and the fourth largest and twelfth largest cities are about the same size. This type of distribution of cities on the rank-order scale is most likely to be encountered in an underdeveloped or developing society. In Figure I.2b, on the other hand, the distribution of cities is more even: A genuine hierarchy of urban places exists in this case, which is most typical of a developed urban society. A comparison of rank-order distribution of

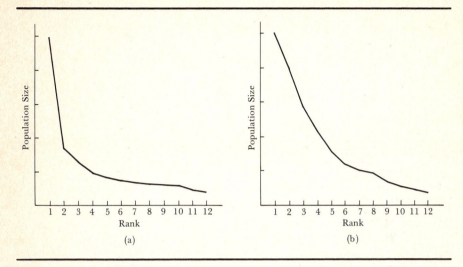

Figure I.2   Rank-Order Scales: (a) Dominance of One City, (b) a Hierarchy of Dominance

cities in the United States between 1800 and 1950 offers an example of this change in distribution type that occurs with social development. (See Figure I.3.) In the mid-nineteenth century the distribution was not very even, and a single urban area (New York City) dominated the urban pattern. By 1950 cities of varying sizes were distributed all along the range from the largest to the smallest and much more closely approached conformity to the rank-size rule.

We can also tell something about the process of urban growth by examining *rank-order stability* within an urban network. If the ranks of, say, the twenty largest cities fluctuate greatly—for example, if the second largest city drops to eighth place and the eleventh largest city rises to third place in the space of a single decade—a situation of rapid urban development usually exists. If, however, there is little change in the rank order of cities in a region or nation over time, then growth is not as pronounced or the cities in the network have clearly established their positions and their relationships to each other. Like central place theory, these rank-size tests are useful in understanding certain theoretical relationships among cities, but they are the beginning rather than the final step in the analysis of urban systems.

Economics plays a substantial role in determining location, whether of cities or individual business enterprises. And a basic economic factor is the relationship between price and distance, which determines the "range" of a good or service. The business that can produce or sell a product at the

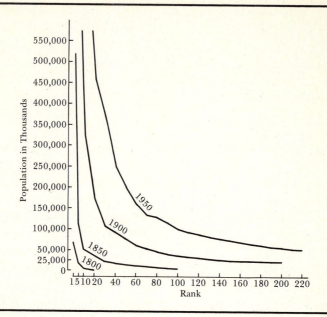

Figure I.3   Rank-Size Relations of United States Cities, 1800–1950. (From Ralph Thomlinson, *Urban Structure: The Social and Spatial Character of Cities* [New York: Random House, 1969] p. 138)

lowest price over the greatest distance will consequently enjoy the most favorable competitive position and the largest market. The city that offers the least expensive services and products over the widest area achieves a similar dominance in its competition with other urban areas. Generally, "location theory" can be applied in a variety of situations—from the study of cities within regions to the study of businesses within cities.

A number of factors affect the initial cost or price of a good or service: labor, raw materials, overhead, and other operating expenses. The most important factor influencing the distance or range of a good or service is transportation cost. A factory that produces an item at a very low initial cost but has no access to efficient and inexpensive transportation can serve only a fairly small market area.

In Figure I.4 we have an example of three equally spaced cities that produce or sell goods at the same initial price. Since all three cities have identical transportation costs, the increase of price with distance occurs at the same rate for all three. Since the cities are separated by a distance greater than the distance over which any of them can economically transport goods or services, their trade territories—or market areas—do not overlap. So long as these basic economic conditions prevail, the three cities will not compete with each other but will continue to serve small and distinct hinterlands. This was, in fact, the pattern that prevailed in portions of the Midwest in the early nineteenth century. Small, isolated towns containing grain mills served separate hinterlands, providing processing for agricultural products and other goods and services for the immediately surrounding area.

Figure I.5 illustrates an entirely different situation with a different set of economic circumstances. Cities 2 and 3 produce or sell goods and services at a lower initial cost or price than city 1. But both cities 3 and 1 have either fairly expensive transportation costs or limited transportation services, so the market areas they serve are constricted. City 2, on the other hand, not only has the benefit of a competitive initial price, but also has access to much better and less expensive transportation. The price of its goods and services thus rises much less steeply with distance, and the territory it serves is much greater. The hinterland of city 2 is so great, in fact, that it cuts into the trade territory of both cities 1 and 3. Within the overlapping areas represented in Figure I.5, a good or service could be procured at the same rate from city 2 as it could from the nearby city, even though the distance to city 2 is much greater. Unless cities 1 and 3 can reduce their initial prices and greatly improve their access to inexpensive transportation, they are destined to hold secondary positions in this urban region.

Figure I.4   Market Area of Cities with Similar Production and Transportation Costs

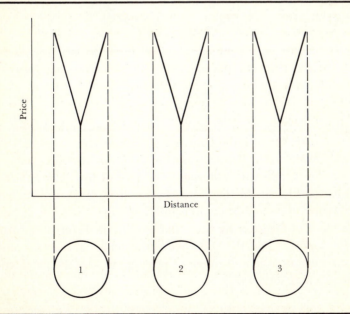

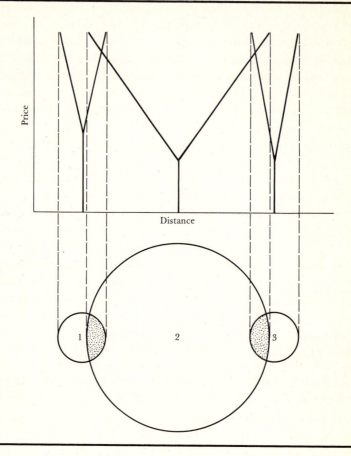

Figure I.5   Market Area of Cities with Different Production and Transportation
Costs

The practical consequences of the price-distance relationship are reflected in history. Cities in the United States were almost invariably located
as close as possible to the best transportation routes, with access to markets,
population flows, and raw materials. The fate of towns by-passed by the
railroad is well known. In the hierarchy of cities, market towns serving a
limited territory have a distinct place and have persisted for long periods in
this function. But the growing cities that were in the forefront of American
urban development had the edge over other cities in transportation, the
flow of information, the movement of population, and the production and
sale of goods and services.

Urban Ecology

Growing cities change not only in their relation to other members of the urban system, but in the relations that exist within themselves as well. *Urban ecology*—the system of spatial relationships in the urban environment—reflects a city's stage of growth and the lives of its residents. By discerning the ecological pattern of a city, then, it is possible to learn a great deal more about that city than just the space it occupies.

The city is a complex mechanism—a web of social activities, economic functions, mobility patterns, and lifestyles, all arrayed in space. Ecology is the study of the interrelationships among objects or beings within an environment or system. First applied to investigations of plants and animals, and later popularized by the environmental movement, ecological thinking is also very prominent in efforts to understand the process of urban growth. For cities not only exist within urban systems, but also are themselves complex systems of activity. The "human ecology" pioneered by Robert E. Park, Ernest W. Burgess, and others at the University of Chicago in the 1920s became an important foundation for much of modern urban sociology.

From the standpoint of human, or urban, ecology, the city is like a biological ecosystem composed of a complex variety of interrelated elements. The challenge for the ecologists was to understand how these elements function and to identify the regular patterns involved. Of particular importance were patterns of social interaction. "The city is not," Park wrote, ". . . merely a physical mechanism and an artificial construction. It is involved in the vital processes of the people who compose it; it is a product of nature, and particularly human nature."[2] The spatial organization of the city reflects the social order. According to Park, "most if not all cultural changes in society will be correlated with changes in its territorial organization, and every change in the territorial and occupational distribution of the population will effect changes in the existing culture."[3] The ecologists viewed the city as a product of human nature, divided into a number of "natural areas," such as vice districts, immigrant colonies, upper-income enclaves, fancy shopping areas, and industrial suburbs. (See Figure I.6.) These areas were "natural" in the sense that they were the results of ecological forces at work within the system. As cities grew, these areas changed in character and shifted in relationship to each other. Increased physical distance meant increased social separation in most cases, and urban dwellers came to function not within the city as a whole but within various distinct parts of it. Thus, social patterns were etched in space.

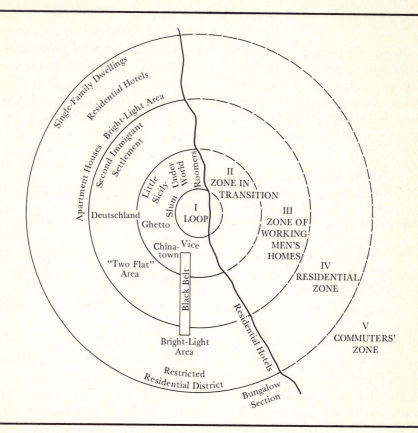

Figure I.6   Natural Areas of the City, According to a 1932 Scheme by Burgess. (American Sociological Association)

The model is based on the fact that socioeconomic status tended to rise with distance from the core, and the dynamic element of the theory was provided by the constant growth of the city from the center outward. Like ripples in a pool, business activities pressed upon the lower-class residential districts close to the center, and the better residential areas gave way to lower- or middle-class occupancy as the more affluent citizens moved further from the center. (See Figure I.7a.)

Much of the *concentric zone theory,* as it is called, rings true, but it applied only in the most general way to Chicago at a particular point in history. Some of the city's very best residences lay in the "Gold Coast" area just north of the central business district, and much development proceeded along radial transit lines rather than in a circular pattern. The application of the model to other cities also posed problems, especially because physical barriers like mountains or lakes, areas with poor drainage, or large blocks of private, undeveloped land could wrench the circles out of shape. And the theory obviously neither portrayed nor explained the very different structural patterns of the preindustrial city or the automobile-dominated metropolis of the 1970s. But this concept stimulated others to improve upon it.

The *sector* or *wedge theory* of urban structure was advanced by Homer Hoyt in the 1930s. Hoyt based his theory on block data collected in sixty-four cities. His principal interest was housing, and he discovered that the

Figure I.7   Rival Models of Urban Growth. (Reprinted from *The Nature of Cities* by Chauncy D. Harris and Edward L. Ullman in volume no. 242 of *The Annals* of the American Academy of Political and Social Science © November, 1945, pp. 7–17)

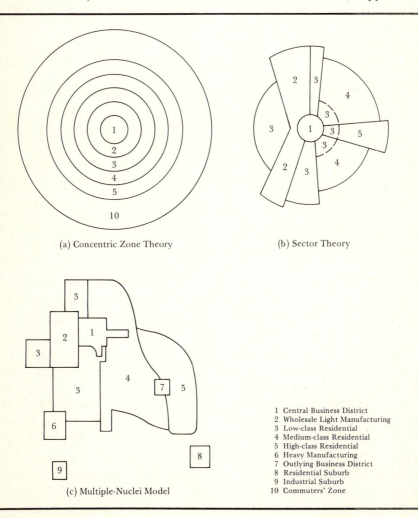

(a) Concentric Zone Theory

(b) Sector Theory

(c) Multiple-Nuclei Model

1 Central Business District
2 Wholesale Light Manufacturing
3 Low-class Residential
4 Medium-class Residential
5 High-class Residential
6 Heavy Manufacturing
7 Outlying Business District
8 Residential Suburb
9 Industrial Suburb
10 Commuters' Zone

location of various rent (or income) areas does not conform to the concentric zone model. Upper-class or "fashionable" residential districts radiate outward from the city core in sectors or wedges along transportation lines, not like ripples in a pool. (See Figure I.7b.) High-rent residential areas move in a regular pattern toward high ground and open country and tend to pull other high- and medium-rent residential and commercial development in their direction. According to Hoyt, "if one sector of the city first develops as a high, medium, or low residential area, it will tend to retain that character for long distances as the sector is extended outward through the process of the city's growth."[4]

Hoyt's model is based on the location of residential areas, but it obviously contains many of the features of Burgess's concentric zone theory. Among other things, the sector model assumes outward population growth and commercial development from the central business district. It further assumes that urban growth proceeds by the transition of neighborhoods from one class of urban dwellers to another (though Hoyt did show that this transition occurs over a long period of time and that areas originally created for low-income occupancy may never experience this transition at all). In the period in which Hoyt developed his theory, radii of transportation lines—whether railroads or highways—constituted the matrix upon which residential development occurred; but the center-to-periphery pattern of this matrix would be changed significantly by the full impact of the motor vehicle in later years.

In the 1940s two other observers, Chauncy D. Harris and Edward L. Ullman, modified both the concentric zone and the sector models of urban structure. Urban land uses develop, they argued, not from a single core, but from a number of smaller, distinct centers, or nuclei. This *multiple-nuclei model* posits the existence, often from the very earliest days of a city's growth, of specialized commercial, industrial, and residential districts that attract similar or complementary land uses and activities. (See Figure I.7c.) The central business district contains the most concentrated retail commercial activity in the city, but a heavy manufacturing area may be located on the urban outskirts rather than in a belt near the downtown section, and smaller business centers exist to serve outlying residential communities. In addition, the Harris-Ullman model contains suburbs and satellite communities that are set apart from the city proper but lie within the metropolitan area.[5]

The multiple-nuclei theory recognizes that certain land uses serve as magnets for others; high-class residential areas, for example, attract high- and medium-rent land uses. And the reverse is also true. Certain land uses—like manufacturing—tend to repel other land uses—like high-class residential—and these areas are usually separated by a considerable distance.

In some respects, these three models are quite different, ranging from the ripple effect of the concentric zone theory to the organization of the city around many separate points. But in other ways they are very similar. All were developed in the first half of the twentieth century with particular application for American cities; all assume the outward growth and development of the city; and all are based on the division of the city into areas of different land use. Most importantly, all three models point to relationships between location and socioeconomic realities. For the historian, they are the products of people seeking to understand their cities in a particular era as well as the means of analyzing the urban fabric.

Urban Forms in American History

Growth models tend to obscure distinctions among cities. Every city is somehow unique. Urban differences are sometimes pronounced, sometimes muted; but all cities, great or small, contain different populations, develop at different rates, cover different terrain, and respond to varying challenges and problems. This endless variety makes it very dangerous to talk about "cities" as one phenomenon existing in slightly different forms. To know one city is definitely not to know them all. To understand urban life in New York City does not automatically make one privy to the mysteries of Omaha.

Cities also change over time, sometimes with great rapidity. The distance from the small bands of settlers clustered in the seventeenth-century wilderness to the twentieth-century urban agglomeration along the northeastern seaboard is not only a span of centuries but also an awesome leap in social experience.

Cities do, however, share a number of common characteristics and develop in similar ways over the broad sweep of history. Certain patterns of growth and arrangement are more characteristic of some periods than of others, just as certain tools and processes are dominant in general technological epochs. In a way, we must seek these shared characteristics and broad patterns of change before we can begin to appreciate and comprehend the variety. The exception demands a rule.

This book is organized around four basic urban forms. Although the dates associated with each form serve as convenient reference points rather than as definitive boundaries (there is considerable overlap between urban forms), each of these forms was generally dominant at a different stage in United States history.

1. *The cluster* (the period of genesis to 1790). Cities in America were European settlements, newcomers to the world's urban tradition, having risen in the seventeenth and eighteenth centuries on the farthest fringes of

established European society. But they were very much a part of the world urbanization process and cannot be understood in isolation from this larger story or from their own origins. They also shared certain features with other urban areas. Some early American towns, like Plymouth and Jamestown, were walled in the European pattern. Others, like Mobile, Jacksonville, New Amsterdam (later New York City), and St. Louis were organized around fortresses and resembled earlier towns in France, Ireland, and other parts of Europe. Like their forebears, they provided protection and sites for trade.

Residents in these early communities clustered in the city center. (See Figure I.8.) In fact, downtown was the city, and most land uses, including

Figure I.8   Cluster

Table I.1   Rank-Size of America's Twenty Largest Cities, 1790

Rank	Previous Rank	City	Population (Thousands)	Rank	Previous Rank	City	Population (Thousands)
1		New York	33.1	11		Portsmouth, N.H.	4.7
2		Philadelphia	28.5	12		Brooklyn, N.Y.	4.4
3		Boston	18.3	13		New Haven, Ct.	4.4
4		Charleston, S.C.	16.3	14		Taunton, Mass.	3.8
5		Baltimore	13.5	15		Richmond, Va.	3.7
6		Salem, Mass.	7.9	16		Albany, N.Y.	3.4
7		Newport, R.I.	6.7	17		New Bedford, Mass.	3.3
8		Providence, R.I.	6.3	18		Beverly, Mass.	3.2
9		Gloucester, Mass.	5.3	19		Norfolk, Va.	2.9
10		Newburyport, Mass.	4.8	20		Petersburg, Va.	2.8

Source: Most figures are from James Vance, Jr., "Cities in the Shaping of the American Nation," *Journal of Geography* 17 (January 1976), 43. Population figure for Philadelphia is from Sam Bass Warner, Jr., *Private City: Philadelphia in Three Periods of Its Growth* (Philadelphia: University of Pennsylvania Press, 1968), p. 3

some light agricultural uses, were located there. Given the needs for protecting inhabitants and facilitating commerce and social intercourse, and the technological limitations of the time, this type of settlement pattern is understandable..

The leading colonial cities in terms of population reflect the importance of a coastal location. (See Table I.1, which gives data for the early postcolonial period.) Merchants in these cities developed a transatlantic pattern of trade. Once established, these entrepreneurs felt secure enough to reach out into their own hinterlands as they had reached out across the Atlantic.

The merchants not only built an urban economy, but they also played a major role in ordering the life of their city, from making fire regulations to influencing public opinion. Indeed, the desire for economic expansion and security prompted some of the most heated pre-Revolutionary debates. Though natural forces like geography and topography may have dictated the urban form in the early years of settlement, the merchant was responsible for the growth and style of the colonial city.

2. *The market place* (1790 to 1870). Building on a commercial economic base, the merchants took the colonial city into a period of unprecedented population growth. The application of steam technology enabled cities to expand their economic spheres. The leading cities of the period were those that were able to take advantage of the technology, the cities on navigable waterways. The coastal cities continued to dominate, but interior ports like Cincinnati, Richmond, and Pittsburgh achieved prominence as well. (See Table I.2.) The development of industrial technology accounted for the rise of several New England cities. The major spatial development within the urban system, however, was the formation of a national economy centered at New York, which became the primate city of the new national urban system.

Within the city, economic growth had caused the expansion of downtown, the sorting out by location of some economic activities, and the development of some fairly distinctive residential districts reflecting a social stratification in urban society, though considerable spatial interaction still occurred. (See Figure I.9.) The city was still quite small (one and a half to two miles square, usually), even though newer transportation technologies had been developed. Despite the relatively small space, a great deal of movement occurred both within the city and to and from the city. Transiency and geographic mobility were common themes of mid-nineteenth-century urban life as populations ebbed and flowed between neighborhoods and between cities. Ethnic and racial diversity increased and, with them, tensions. Merchants attempted to order this volatile situation through more extensive utilization of local government. The market place still defined the economic focus and the leadership.

Table I.2   Rank-Size of America's Twenty Largest Cities, 1830

Rank	Previous Rank	City	Population (Thousands)	Rank	Previous Rank	City	Population (Thousands)
1	1	New York	202.5	11	8	Providence	16.8
2	5	Baltimore	80.6	12	15	Richmond	16.0
3	2	Philadelphia	80.4	13	—	Pittsburgh	15.3
4	3	Boston	61.3	14	6	Salem	13.8
5	—	New Orleans	46.0	15	—	Portland, Me.	12.5
6	4	Charleston, S.C.	30.2	16	—	Troy, N.Y.	11.5
7	—	Cincinnati	24.8	17	—	Newark, N.J.	10.9
8	16	Albany	24.2	18	—	Louisville, Ky.	10.3
9	13	Brooklyn	20.5	19	13	New Haven	10.1
10	—	Washington, D.C.	18.8	20	19	Norfolk	9.8

Source: Compiled from U.S. Bureau of the Census, *Sixteenth Census, 1940, Population,* I: *Number of Inhabitants* (Washington, D.C.: Government Printing Office, 1942), pp. 32–33.

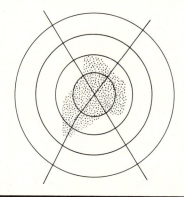

Figure I.9   Market Place

3. *The radial center* (1870 to 1920). New York, which had dominated the urban system at the beginning of the period, shared more of its power by the end. The regionalization of the American urban system had begun, and cities such as Chicago, St. Louis, and eventually San Francisco achieved regional economic supremacy and a growing national parity with New York. (See Tables I.3 and I.4.) A city's position in the urban hierarchy was not identical with its rank-size. Economic base was a significant factor in determining the extent of a city's economic sphere of influence, which determined its position in the hierarchy. Industrial cities tended to fare

Table I.3   Rank-Size of America's Twenty Largest Cities, 1870

Rank	Previous Rank	City	Population (Thousands)	Rank	Previous Rank	City	Population (Thousands)
1	1	New York	942.3	11	13	Pittsburgh	139.3
2	3	Philadelphia	674.0	12	—	Buffalo	117.7
3	13	Brooklyn	420.0	13	10	Washington, D.C.	109.2
4	—	St. Louis	310.9	14	17	Newark	105.1
5	—	Chicago	299.0	15	18	Louisville	100.8
6	2	Baltimore	267.4	16	—	Cleveland	92.8
7	4	Boston	250.5	17	—	Detroit	79.6
8	7	Cincinnati	216.2	18	—	Milwaukee	71.4
9	5	New Orleans	191.4	19	11	Providence	68.9
10	—	San Francisco	149.5	20	12	Richmond	51.0

Source: Compiled from U.S. Bureau of the Census, *Sixteenth Census, 1940, Population,* I: *Number of Inhabitants* (Washington, D.C.: Government Printing Office, 1942), pp. 32–33.

Table I.4   Rank-Size of America's Twenty Largest Cities, 1920

Rank	Previous Rank	City	Population (Thousands)	Rank	Previous Rank	City	Population (Thousands)
1	1	New York[a]	5,620.0	11	12	Buffalo	506.8
2	5	Chicago	2,701.7	12	10	San Francisco	506.7
3	2	Philadelphia	1,823.8	13	18	Milwaukee	457.1
4	17	Detroit	993.7	14	13	Washington, D.C.	437.6
5	16	Cleveland	796.8	15	14	Newark	414.5
6	4	St. Louis	772.9	16	8	Cincinnati	401.2
7	7	Boston	748.0	17	9	New Orleans	387.2
8	6	Baltimore	733.8	18	—	Minneapolis	380.6
9	11	Pittsburgh	588.3	19	—	Kansas City, Mo.	324.4
10	—	Los Angeles	576.7	20	—	Jersey City, N.J.	298.1

[a]Included Brooklyn after 1898.

Source: Compiled from U.S. Bureau of the Census, *Sixteenth Census, 1940, Population,* I: *Number of Inhabitants* (Washington, D.C.: Government Printing Office, 1942), pp. 32–33.

more poorly economically than their size would indicate, while cities emphasizing insurance, finance, and commerce were more wide ranging in their economic contacts. Though historians have referred to this period as the age of the industrial city, other types of cities carried off a greater share of the national economic booty. Finally, as this discussion implies, a degree

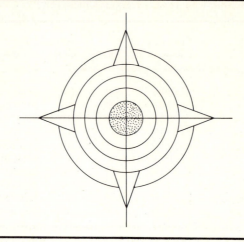

Figure I.10   Radial Center

of urban specialization was developing, with particular cities serving particular functions.

The internal structure of the city was characterized by significant spatial expansion, typically along transportation routes radiating from the city center. (See Figure I.10.) Growing affluence, the tremendous influx of racial and ethnic groups into the city center, and improved transportation technology spurred the move outward. As the city expanded, it became segregated. Downtown areas became primarily retail, wholesale, and financial; some small industry clung to its edges, but larger industries moved to the periphery for more and cheaper space, and residential neighborhoods became more clearly defined by economic, racial, and ethnic status. This should not imply that urbanites were locked into specific spatial and social situations. They were not. Residential mobility continued and, depending on the city's economic growth and age and the particular ethnic group, social mobility occurred as well, though much less frequently than geographic mobility. Reformers sought to alleviate the problems inherent in the spatial separation while ensuring the continuation of this spatial order.

4. *The vital fringe* (1920 to the present). The regionalization that had begun in the previous period continued, though today New York and Chicago still have a shaky hold on the national economy, as they had a century ago. (See Table I.5.) The most significant development in the national urban system involved the emergence of southern and western cities as centers of regional dominance. Specialization also accelerated as industrial cities began

Table I.5   Rank-Size of America's Twenty Largest Cities, 1970

Rank	Previous Rank	City	Population (Thousands)	Rank	Previous Rank	City	Population (Thousands)
1	1	New York	7,894.8	11	—	Indianapolis	744.6
2	2	Chicago	3,366.9	12	13	Milwaukee	717.6
3	10	Los Angeles	2,816.0	13	12	San Francisco	715.6
4	3	Philadelphia	1,948.6	14	—	San Diego	696.7
5	4	Detroit	1,511.4	15	—	San Antonio	654.1
6	—	Houston	1,232.8	16	7	Boston	641.0
7	8	Baltimore	905.7	17	—	Memphis	623.5
8	—	Dallas	844.4	18	6	St. Louis	622.2
9	14	Washington, D.C.	756.5	19	17	New Orleans	593.4
10	5	Cleveland	750.9	20	—	Phoenix	582.0

Source: Compiled from U.S. Bureau of the Census, *Nineteenth Census, 1970, Number of Inhabitants,* Table 13 of reports for individual states.

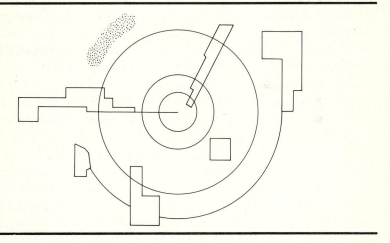

Figure I.11   Vital Fringe

to decline, and cities dependent on service activities—finance, real estate, insurance, and administration—increased in importance or held their own until 1970. This change reflected the changes in the national economy— from commercial to industrial to service—over the past two centuries. In addition, natural advantages such as climate and topography appeared as determinants of urban growth, much as geographic location had influenced urbanization during the first period of settlement.

The geographic expansion of the city accelerated to such a degree that the suburb frequently became the locus of regional political power and population. (See Figure I.11.) Again, transportation technology, affluence, and the presence of ethnic and racial elements in large numbers in the cities hastened this outward movement. A new featured player, the federal government, enhanced fringe settlement with an array of post–World War II policies to stimulate the national economy. Commercial nuclei multiplied throughout suburbia, weakening the traditional economic dominance of downtown. Spatial segregation solidified, if anything, as black and Hispanic ghettos expanded, wedging their way out toward the urban periphery. On several occasions in the 1960s, low-income neighborhoods rebelled against the economic and social consequences of this spatial segregation, but their rebellions were unsuccessful in weakening the spatial patterns developed over centuries.

Urban settlement has now spread over much of the country. With the decline of cities, population is more evenly distributed throughout the urban region, and the traditional spatial conception of the city—a core and a periphery—is being replaced by a view of clusters of roughly equal density constituting a city. Newer cities in the South and West present this spaced-out appearance so different from the spatial organization of cities that evolved from pedestrian downtowns more than two centuries ago. The era of no town has begun.

Yet there are indications that the pedestrian emphasis, along with the downtown itself, is undergoing a revival. The spirit of community possessed by the earliest cluster settlements is being rekindled in the modern city's version of the cluster—the residential neighborhood. It may be that downtown and no town will get along just fine.

Within the framework of these four urban forms, we will describe the social, economic, and political elements that affected and continue to affect the urban process. The impacts of these elements vary from period to period, so our coverage will vary as well. Although it is usual for urban texts to offer a definition of the city, in the course of our description we will offer a statement more of approach than of definition. Urban growth is a process, and process implies change. Definitions of the city based upon size or function limit the possibilities of what a city may be, since the urban process has altered both the size and the function of cities over time. We view the city, with historian Roy Lubove, as "a physical container within which complex human and institutional relationships are established, and essential maintenance functions performed."[6] Let us begin to fill the container.

Notes

1. Roy Lubove, "The Urbanization Process: An Approach to Historical Research," *Journal of the American Institute of Planners,* 33 (January 1967), 33.

2. Robert E. Park, "The City: Suggestions for the Investigation of Human Behavior in the Urban Environment" in Robert E. Park, Ernest W. Burgess, et al., eds., *The City* (Chicago: University of Chicago Press, 1925), p. 1.

3. Robert E. Park, *Human Communities* (New York: Free Press, 1952), p. 14.

4. For the complete statement of this theory, see Homer Hoyt, *The Structure and Growth of Residential Neighborhoods in American Cities* (Washington, D.C.: U.S. Federal Housing Administration, 1939). The sentence quoted is from page 76 of Hoyt's work.

5. See Chauncy D. Harris and Edward L. Ullman, "The Nature of Cities," *The Annals of the American Academy of Political and Social Science,* 242 (November 1945), 7–17.

6. Lubove, "The Urbanization Process," p. 33.

I.
GENESIS

Go to, let us build us a city and a tower . . . ; and let us make us a name, lest we be scattered abroad upon the face of the whole earth.

(Genesis 11 : 4)

Venturesome journeys in our own time are usually products of a marvelous technology. In the sixteenth and seventeenth centuries, they were trials of human endurance. Like modern space travel, transatlantic voyages were risk-filled flights into the unknown. We can only guess at the inner reactions of these Old World voyagers as they confronted the New after months at sea, with a seemingly endless wilderness lying before them. When the Plymouth settlers landed in 1620, as William Bradford recalled, "they fell upon their knees and blessed the God of heaven, who had brought them over the vast and furious ocean, and delivered them from all the perils and miseries thereof, again to set their feet on the firm and stable earth, their proper element."[1]

The first impulse of most colonists was not to dash into the forest, but to gather in settlements near water for security and sustenance. Even the first intrepid explorers hailed from a complex European culture and social life based on institutions and the ways of groups rather than of individuals. Besides, the tractless wilderness was often dangerous and—certainly to the European mind—quite forbidding. Most early settlements were little more than collections of rude huts surrounded by wooden walls, never far from the ocean which stretched to native lands. But they served a purpose that was often repeated as the frontier eventually moved westward. In this sense, forays to the New World were urban from the beginning.

Down through the late seventeenth century, the dominant—or most typical—sort of urban place was a *cluster* (Figure I.8) rarely more than a mile across and containing no more than 6,000 people. Connected with the mother country by ship and with each other over water or rough roads, these small villages depended upon large cities for some basic necessities and for virtually all luxury or manufactured goods. Their economies were primarily *external*—that is, oriented to the resources of the outside world. Cluster dwellers, generally of very modest means and with few specialized skills, lived close together regardless of their respective stations in life. Buildings were simple, roads were poor, and services were very limited and informal. Streets were scavenged by pigs and other animals for the garbage thrown from houses. The slightest fire might easily turn into a catastrophe. Clusters were anchored to specific places or points—usually the waterfront, church, or plaza—that served as the symbolic core of town life.

As time passed, villages became towns, and towns became cities. Many clusters developed into *market places*. This was perhaps the major urban transition in the first two centuries of colonization in North America. Populations increased, economies grew and diversified, and formal institutions emerged. Little communities which seemed for all the world like peasant villages were sometimes transformed into the image of English provincial cities, while new towns sprang up far inland. The market place was the most prevalent type of urban settlement after the American Revolution, but its origins can be clearly traced to the development of the earliest colonial towns in the eighteenth century.

Notes

1. Samuel Eliot Morison, ed., *Of Plymouth Plantation, 1620–1647,* by William Bradford (New York: Knopf, 1952), p. 61.

1.
An Act of Faith:
The Planting of Cities

God, Glory, and Gold

Sustained European exploration of the Western Hemisphere was more than a century old by the time the Plymouth colonists put ashore. Before them had come the Spanish expeditions throughout the Americas and the founding of St. Augustine in 1565, the voyages of John Cabot along the northeastern seaboard, the Portuguese ventures in South America, Samuel de Champlain's missions to Canada, and the explorations culminating in the first English settlements in Roanoke in the 1580s and Jamestown in 1607.

Whether these efforts were made in the name of God, glory, or gold, all major colonial powers assumed that towns were necessary to exploit a new domain. Europeans brought to their colonies a respect for cities and a variety of notions concerning their design. They drew upon their culture and experience in laying out cities in forms that seemed suitable and necessary amid the challenges of a New World environment. As early as the thirteenth century, new territories in southern France, northern Spain, and areas of Ireland and Wales had been initially secured by the construction of *bastides*—small towns with gridiron street patterns and elaborate fortress walls. Not surprisingly, these provided one model for urban design in the virgin and often hostile territory of the Americas. The popularity of open public spaces in the Renaissance era also left a mark on early American towns, as did other European ideas, ranging from the modest residential square to the broad thoroughfares of imperial capitals. As in most other things, Europeans attempted to fashion the New World in their own cultural and even physical image.

European town-building in the New World, even with the many cultural differences, reflected some basic similarities. Urban places were generally distinguished from the rural or wilderness areas around them, either through the dramatic gesture of a wall or by more subtle means. This distinction was usually maintained even when town and countryside were designed to function together, as in the Spanish pueblo. Most settlements featured a major central point, and in some cases several interrelated points, intended to establish the character of the place and to facilitate its function. These were not formless, sprawling cities, but communities with a definite core and periphery, marked on the ground as well as in the mind. Many European towns built in America during this period contained some variant of the gridiron street pattern with regularly spaced blocks. This was a rule with many exceptions—from the strong axial design of Williamsburg to the meandering pattern of Boston—but it was nevertheless quite prominent. Finally, urban places seemed to take on particular significance for the colonists in an uncharted wilderness. In fact, they were much more than places. Within their boundaries resided not only colonists, but Old World traditions, habits, customs, and institutions—all of those things which quite literally represented civilization and the finest attainments of humankind. In early colonial days cities and towns were first of all shelters for colonists, but they were also shelters for European experience and aspirations.

Spanish and French Settlement

The Spanish were the first Europeans who sought to exploit the riches of the Americas on a broad scale. Santo Domingo, oldest existing city in the New World, was established in 1496, and St. Augustine was located on its present site in 1570. Spanish settlements were initially outposts from which expeditions into the interior were launched, but many were intended ultimately as expressions of Spanish power and empire. While other countries had some definite ideas about how towns should be constructed, the Spanish developed a system of formal rules and standards for town construction. In 1573 Philip II promulgated the Laws of the Indies, which contained procedures and regulations for town planning and settlement. These regulations were not especially innovative (mainly they formalized a number of common practices) and they were rarely followed precisely, but they provided an excellent glimpse into Spanish city-building notions.

Under the Laws of the Indies, a town plan allowing for orderly expansion in the future was to be drawn before any actual construction began. The major feature of the town was a plaza, located near the shore in coastal towns and at the center in inland cities. The dimensions of the plaza were specified—the length was to be at least one and a half times the width—and a series of arcades were to be built along the major and minor streets leading out from the plaza's edge. In most cases, a gridiron street pattern prevailed elsewhere in the town. The other central landmark was a church, placed either facing the plaza or dominating it from some elevated point at a distance. The emphasis on prior planning, major landmarks, and orderly development make the Laws of the Indies a most significant document in the history of city planning.

The Spanish also identified three principal types of cities on the basis of the purposes they served: *Missions* were religious outposts; *presidios* were military installations; and *pueblos* were civil settlements for trade and colonization. The Laws of the Indies applied only to the pueblos, but in fact the three orders were often mingled. The *presidios* at San Diego (1769), Monterey (1770), San Francisco (1776), and Santa Barbara (1782), for example, grew beyond their initial military character and served a variety of purposes. The pueblo was actually a town and the rural area immediately surrounding it. As with settlements in New England, land in the pueblo was often distributed in feudal patterns, with certain common lands reserved for the community as a whole.

The Spanish played a significant role in early North American town-building, but cities like Sante Fe (1609) and Pensacola (1698) were meager villages compared with the great, congested imperial cities of the Spanish domain in South and Central America, which dominated whole regions.

The French focused their attention on North America, founding the cities of Quebec and Montreal and sending traders and missionaries deep into the Mississippi Valley. The fortified outpost at Detroit, established in 1701, closely resembled the *bastide* towns of southern France. The original town was burned completely, however, and was later rebuilt by the Americans. Fort Duquesne, constructed on the present site of Pittsburgh, and St. Louis were also fortified settlements that did not significantly expand until after the Revolutionary War.

The most dramatic examples of French urban influence outside Canada are found along the Gulf Coast. The present site of Mobile was selected around 1710, and a city ten blocks long and five blocks wide, anchored to a parade ground along the water, was proposed. From Mobile, the French moved on to consider other possible town sites. To the west, along the winding course of the Mississippi River near the mouth, Jean Baptiste, sieur de Bienville, founded New Orleans in 1722. The Mississippi Delta hardly seemed a promising place for a great city, and the constant battle with rising water, the prevalence of tropical diseases, and the virtual isolation from other settlements shaped the early history of New Orleans. By 1727, however, the city contained almost a thousand people, and less than a century later—after periods of Spanish rule and British commercial dominance and after the advent of American control with the Louisiana Purchase of 1803—New Orleans became the commercial sieve for the commodities drained southward from the great Mississippi Basin.

Bienville's aspirations for New Orleans were not modest. The city was intended to be a great capital. The regular blocks were originally surrounded by a formal fortified wall, beyond which long, narrow plantations were laid out in the French manner in the low bayou country. (See Figure 1.1.) Eventually, the wall disappeared and avenues replaced it, as settlement moved inland and to the west. The focal point of Bienville's city was the *place d'armes,* a formal open ground now named Jackson Square, centered perfectly on the river and dominated by the city's principal church and later also by government buildings and the apartments of wealthy and prominent

Figure 1.1   Plan of New Orleans, 1764

The simple grid was to become the hallmark of American urban street patterns. (Belin, *Le Petit Atlas Maritime,* Olin Library, Cornell University)

citizens. This ensemble of structures, grouped around the modest square, has been called "the most important architectural plaza in the United States."[1]

English Settlements in New England

Along the Atlantic, English colonization and town building predominated. Jamestown, established by the Virginia Company of London in 1607, was the first permanent English settlement in North America, but its history, like that of its ill-begotten predecessors along the Carolina coast, was one of disease, hunger, and disaster. The wooden wall that surrounded it in the beginning was a clear throwback to medieval design. A few brick structures were erected outside the wall in later years, but the town was not destined to survive. Even the site itself has now been swallowed by the river.

The English town was transplanted most completely to the shores of New England. The first permanent settlement in the region was established by the Pilgrims at Plymouth in 1620. A much more significant colonization began in 1629, however, when the Puritans set out for their lands in Massachusetts Bay and founded the town of Boston a year later. The Puritans brought to New England not only the traditional notions of English and European town-planning, which emphasized security and order, but also a highly developed idea of community based on religion.

The Puritans sought not merely a more favorable climate for the practice of their religion, but also a base from which to cleanse the established English church of its corrupt elements. As John Winthrop declared on the voyage to America, "we must consider that we shall be as a city upon a hill, the eyes of all people are upon us."[2] What he had in mind was not a physical city, but a spiritual example so persuasive that it would reform the Church of England. The Puritans undertook an "errand into the wilderness"[3] to accomplish in a new world what they had been unable to perform at home. But this mission also entailed the building of physical cities—towns that reflected in their form the relationships that God had ordained among people.

The basic unit of Puritan settlement was the *plantation,* a grant of land from the Massachusetts Bay government. While the authorities did not mandate a particular pattern of urban design, certain common practices and Puritan religious notions dictated in all cases a tightly knit cluster. For the Puritans, the word of God was the means to salvation, and the individual congregation was the basic and virtually autonomous unit of religious worship. Therefore, the church—or meetinghouse—was the focal point of the New England town for most of the seventeenth century, and the presence of a minister to meet the spiritual needs of the community was considered a necessity. Land grants, for example, usually required that a minister reside in the settlement and that a church be established in any new settlement within a few years' time, or the grant would be rescinded. The Puritans believed that God is awesome, all-powerful, and ever-present, whereas people are weak, sinful, and unworthy, and require the means of grace and the nurture of a godly community to lead moral lives and to be saved from damnation. The sheep could not stray from the flock. The devil haunted the wilderness, and expulsion from the community was the ultimate penalty for disobedience and heresy. The Massachusetts General Court decreed in 1635 that no dwelling could be built more than half a mile from the meetinghouse in any new town. Though this ruling was repealed five years later, the concept continued to affect patterns of social thought and thus patterns of town building. Even Hester Prynne, condemned for adultery in Nathaniel Hawthorne's *The Scarlet Letter,* remained at the edge of the town.

New England was settled by groups who gathered in communities, not by individuals. The Puritans consciously structured the environment to promote proper moral behavior that would fulfill God's will. As the Rev. John Norton said in 1659, "Forms are essential without which things cannot be."[4] Town design was sometimes quite formal. One anonymous writer suggested that towns be ordered as six concentric circles within a six-mile square, with the meetinghouse at "the center of the whole circumference."[5] This was in itself an excellent comment on the Puritans' notion of a self-contained, organic community, wherein the spheres of work, family, property, and the inner self were all interrelated, centered on the church, and contained within the town.

Property was divided among inhabitants who had been admitted to the town. Those with greater wealth and status received the most and best land, but all received some. House lots were usually awarded first and were grouped along the principal roads and close to the meetinghouse. Then surrounding farm plots were allotted, again on the basis of position within the social hierarchy. Certain common lands were almost always retained by the community as a whole, especially for pasturage. In many cases, property ownership was denied to those who did not actually live in the settlement, and land that was neglected, abused, or abandoned would revert to the town. The whole aspect of the New England town conveyed a sense of order and shared purpose and a human scale that remain appealing even today. (See Figure 1.2.)

The size of New England towns was fairly limited, both by the desires of the inhabitants for compact settlement about a single meetinghouse and by the fixed amount of land awarded in the initial grant. Population expansion in the region thus resulted in the formation of new settlements rather than in

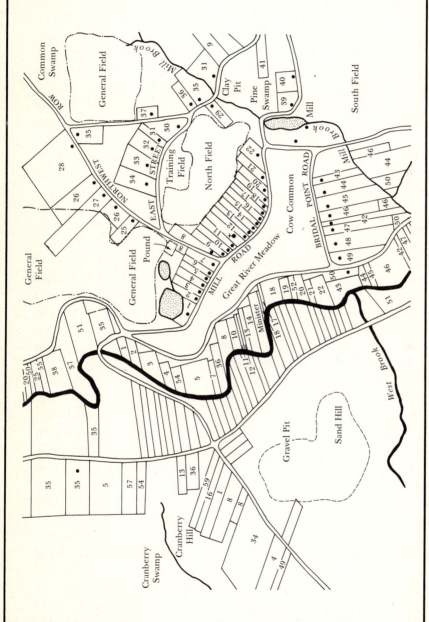

Figure 1.2   Plan of Sudbury, Massachusetts: The Village Center

A spatial arrangement designed to promote community spirit. Dots indicate dwellings; numbers indicate patterns of land ownership. (Copyright © 1963 by Wesleyan University. Reprinted from *Puritan Village: The Formation of a New England Town*, by Sumner Chilton Powell, by permission of Wesleyan University Press.)

the significant growth of existing towns. The first wave of town planting in New England began in the mid-1630s and extended well into the 1640s. Between 1634 and 1636, settlers from the original Massachusetts Bay towns founded the first four towns in Connecticut, and Roger Williams, the religious dissenter, left for Rhode Island to establish the town of Providence. Typically, the new towns were settled to accommodate the desires of new immigrants for land, but they were also established by groups from previously settled communities who disagreed with their former fellow citizens over some religious or political matter or who simply could not receive adequate amounts of land in the older town. Also, New England had its version of an American institution—the town promoter. John Winthrop, Jr., son of the great Puritan leader, arrived in Massachusetts Bay in 1631. Among other things, he organized a group of investors to support an ironworks, prospected for minerals, and eventually promoted and lived in four different towns: Boston, Ipswich, Saybrook, and New London. Individual towns appeared quite stable and resistent to change, but they consistently contributed to the formation of new settlements that took the word of God and English culture into the backcountry.

By the end of the seventeenth century, the strict settlement patterns had begun to disappear in New England. Home lots were often located by this time on outlying farming plots, rather than in a tight central group. In expanding towns the focal point shifted from the meetinghouse to the market or waterfront. These were spatial manifestations of significant changes in the region, and to some extent throughout the colonies. Church membership in New England had been dropping since the middle of the century, and ministers lamented the decline in religious piety and the rise in worldly attitudes and pursuits. The opportunities of commerce won out over the rewards of religion. In America, land was wealth, and the huge stretches of available land beyond the tight confines of the town beckoned overwhelmingly, especially when threats of Indian attack were removed. This supply of available land was, perhaps, more than anything else, the acid that wore away the solid structure of the New England town. Piety had given way to progress, and the implications for New England, and for America, were momentous.

Even in the 1640s, New England towns were not identical, and the differences among them were magnified as time passed. Some communities remained small, periodically sending some of their own to settle new areas. Other towns grew beyond a manageable size and were fragmented into several different communities, each with its own church. Some were agricultural villages, while others developed into important market centers, and still others, like Cambridge, became suburbs of a large city. None, however, could rival Boston in size or influence.

Boston was the dominant city of New England: "the center town and metropolis of this wilderness work," as Samuel Maverick expressed it.[6] Even though it consistently fed a stream of new migrants into the surrounding towns and colonies, its thriving market formed the economic base for the region by 1650, and its rising merchants and tradesmen signaled an end to John Winthrop's dream of a selfless, godly community. Situated on a marshy peninsula, Boston had two focal points located close together, the meeting-house and the market. As the seventeenth century wore on, the town dock expanded into a series of wharves that eventually ringed the major part of the city, the masts of the sailing ships challenging the height of majestic church spires. The great Common remained a central feature and was in fact the largest public park in America until the completion of Central Park in New York City some two centuries later. By the eighteenth century, Boston had spawned a dozen suburban towns and driven most agricultural pursuits off the peninsula altogether.

Philadelphia and New York

The tightly knit community pattern of New England generally declined in importance as one moved south into the other colonies. But towns were actively promoted just the same, both by British authorities who wanted to bring the new continent under firm control and by the colonists themselves who realized the importance of urban places for trade, security, government, and culture. Philadelphia, envisioned by William Penn almost immediately after he became proprietor of Pennsylvania in 1681, was one of the most impressive colonial cities. Penn intended his city as the crown for his new province and awarded a ten-acre tract in the "great town" to anyone who bought five hundred acres anywhere in the colony. Penn planned Philadelphia as a large and impressive, but also proportioned and orderly, city— a great but uncrowded center situated between the Schuylkill and Delaware rivers just north of their convergence. The gridiron street pattern was fashioned of ample blocks intended to distribute population and discourage the spread of fire. The original plan called for five main squares to relieve the severity of the grid, with one square lying near the city's core. (See Figure 1.3.) These were, in fact, the first dedicated public parks in America. Penn drew heavily on several English planning schemes, especially the plan drawn by Richard Newcourt for London after the great fire of 1666. By 1683 some eighty houses stood in Penn's city, and by the Revolution Philadelphia was,

by at least one modern estimate, the largest city in the colonies and the largest
in the British Empire except for London. The orginal plan was com-
promised and distorted, and the five parks were unable to compete with the
thriving waterfront as the real focus of the city. But Philadelphia was
perhaps the most widely admired and most frequently copied urban design
in the colonies. The five-square pattern was repeated in Raleigh, North
Carolina (1792), and Tallahassee, Florida (1824), and the single, central
square was evident in many midwestern towns and cities.

The first permanent settlement on Manhattan Island—and the first of
North America's major cities—was established around 1625 by the Dutch.
Within a generation, a four-cornered fort overlooked the harbor and a
fortress wall isolated New Amsterdam from the rest of the island to the
north. By 1660 the city was closely settled in various shaped blocks reminiscent of the typical medieval pattern, except for the broad avenue leading to
the fort from the main town gate. Appropriately, the wharf was the focus for
this outpost of one of the most developed commercial societies in the Old

Figure 1.3   Plan of Philadelphia, 1683

The relentless grid is Anglicized. (From John C. Lowber, *Ordinances of the City of
Philadelphia, 1812*, Olin Library, Cornell University)

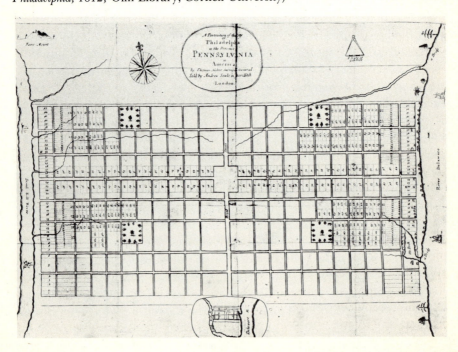

World. In 1664 the city fell bloodlessly into the hands of the British, after which it was renamed New York. A century later, the character and appearance of the town had changed considerably. The wall had come down, but Wall Street was etched for posterity in the city's structure. Houses and farms spread northward beyond the confines of the original settlement, already assuming the relentless gridiron pattern that became the official municipal policy of land division in the early nineteenth century. "This populous and well built Town," as one observer described it in 1753,[7] was the second-largest city in the colonies by the end of the colonial period and was superbly situated to outstrip all competitors in later years.

Settlements in the Chesapeake and Southern Colonies

From the time of the founding of Jamestown by the Virginia Company in 1607, British authorities had proposed urban settlements in the Chesapeake area, but, as the Reverend Hugh Jones wrote in 1724, "neither the interest nor inclinations of the Virginians induce them to cohabit in towns. . . ."[8] The statement was equally fitting for Maryland and the colonies farther south. Nevertheless, the Chesapeake area did contain urban places, and some of these were significant especially when considered from the standpoint of their design.

Annapolis, established in 1649, was another town that mirrored some of the plans proposed for London following the 1666 fire. Two ample circles containing the principal civic areas were joined to the rest of the city by radial avenues. The resulting angles created a variety of interesting shapes in a structure that was altogether different from the unidimensional gridiron. Located about two miles upriver from the Chesapeake Bay, Annapolis was an active trading center before the Revolution and one of the most interesting and urbane in the colonies.

Williamsburg, originally settled in 1633, was designated the state capital by the Virginia assembly in 1699 in legislation that included much specific information about the town's physical design, even including street names. Whereas Annapolis revolved around its central circles, the layout of Williamsburg was strongly axial, assuming its shape from the perfectly straight Duke of Gloucester Street. This main avenue connected the capitol building at one end with the College of William and Mary at the other. Along this spine the shops and residences of the community accumulated. Williamsburg was planned for a population of about 2,000, and a village it was. But this sleepy college town was periodically transformed into a bustling political hive when the assembly met, and the inns and coffee houses teemed with the people's representatives and assorted visitors. In Williamsburg, the main street, anchored at either end by major institutions, was itself the focal point.

Baltimore was founded in 1729 on the Patapsco River, an estuary of Chesapeake Bay. Initially growth was slow and Baltimore could be counted as but one among a dozen other promising tobacco ports in the area. But even though cargoes had to be transported some distance by wagon to and from the docks at Fells Point, Baltimore outdistanced most of its competitors, largely because it was able to tap the considerable resources in wheat and other grains in its hinterland. By 1776 the city contained some 6,800 residents.

Urban settlements were less numerous and more dispersed in the Carolinas and Georgia. Scarce populations were spread over a large territory devoted increasingly to farms and large-scale plantation agriculture. Charleston, established on its present site in 1680, dominated the best harbor between the Chesapeake Bay and the Gulf of Mexico. Like many other settlements, it was originally defined by a fortress wall. Though growth was modest at first, the city expanded considerably by the early eighteenth century, with population flowing beyond the wall. The proprietors had foreseen such an event and indicated a series of sections for eventual development outside the original cluster. Generally, their design was carried out. Charleston was the largest and most important city along the southern portion of the Atlantic seaboard. Towns and trading posts were planted in the interior and scattered along the coast, but none could rival Charleston in size or wealth. The Palmetto City was, in fact, one of the wealthiest in the colonies. It was also, however, the major colonial city most influenced by the economic and social consequences of black slavery.

Even farther south lay the city of Savannah—important not for its size or influence, but because it was framed in one of the most innovative and unusual plans in the American colonies. The city was established in 1733 by a group of English trustees led by James Oglethorpe. Like Penn in Pennsylvania, Oglethorpe was a man of great talent and firm conviction who impressed his spirit and will on his colony in its early years. Prohibiting slavery, keeping much of the land in the hands of the trustees, and recruiting settlers from all ranks of society (including prisoners) were among the most notable of Oglethorpe's actions. But perhaps the most remarkable was his design for Savannah.

The city was constructed of building-block units, or wards, each of which contained ten or a dozen house lots with an open square at the center. Since the city controlled surrounding lands (until these were used up in the nineteenth century), the expansion of Savannah could be easily regulated with the simple addition of wards as the need arose. This allowed for considerable expansion without formless sprawl and without detraction from the existing residential units or confusion of the established transportation pattern. Oglethorpe doubtless drew on a number of planning ideas in arriving at this scheme, but he and the other Georgia trustees probably were most impressed with the comfortable and urbane residential squares built in London in the late seventeenth and eighteenth centuries (such as the famous St. James's Square of 1684). Whatever the origins of the plan, it was unfortunately of no apparent influence anywhere else in the colonies. Savannah, however, remained a pleasant and orderly community for some time, at least until the mid-nineteenth century when growth began to get out of hand and the municipality no longer controlled the territories along its periphery.

Patterns of Colonial Urban Growth

The growth of colonial towns fluctuated with the waves of immigration and with the process of settling the backcountry. Through most of the seventeenth century, towns served as more-or-less secure outposts in the first stages of colonization. As transportation connections became more established with the Old World and as many areas along the seaboard were secured under European control, new towns were founded farther inland and more and more colonists set out to farm in more remote regions. Thus, the proportion of the total colonial population residing in the major Atlantic ports declined in the eighteenth century even as these cities grew more important in the development of the country. (For the pattern of settlement that obtained at the end of the century, see Figure 1.4.)

Settlement did not proceed evenly and consistently from east to west. The major cities were found along the Atlantic coast, and usually spawned a number of smaller outlying communities that were the nation's first suburbs. To the west, and in the more sparsely populated areas along the coast, small market centers developed, serving the immediately surrounding agricultural territory. Then there were the smallest settlements, scattered in the backcountry or on the edges of the hinterlands of other towns. Colonial urban places could, in fact, be arranged on a scale from the smallest to the largest and from the simplest to the most complex, and the colonies themselves could be pictured as composed of the various hinterlands carved out by towns and cities. The smallest places were often no more than mere villages with a meetinghouse or an inn, perhaps, but little else. At most, they served as collectors for nearby agricultural products. The

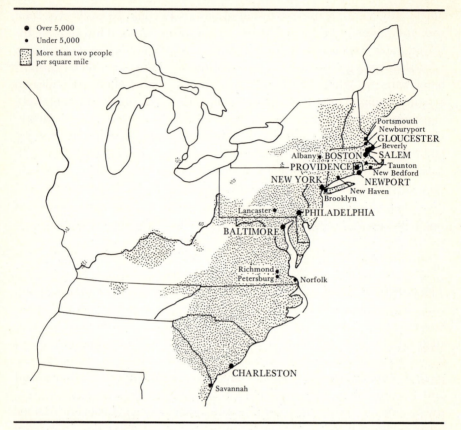

Figure 1.4   Urbanization and Spread of Population in the United States, 1790. (From *Cities and Immigrants: A Geography of Change in Nineteenth-Century America* by David Ward. Copyright © 1971 by Oxford University Press, Inc. Reprinted by permission.)

intermediate-sized towns usually provided markets for a limited trading territory and boasted at least some skilled artisans and perhaps some professional services. But the largest institutions, the most influential leaders, and the most highly skilled craftsmen were to be found in the major cities.

Judged by where most people lived, the American colonies could not be called primarily urban. But colonization itself would have been virtually impossible without urban places. Boston, Philadelphia and New York were truly dominant centers in this era, with Charleston playing a similar role in the South and with dozens of other cities cropping up in response to commercial opportunities or new population flows westward. By 1690 Boston contained more than 7,000 persons, and the five major seaboard cities

(Boston, Newport, New York, Philadelphia, and Charleston) accounted for a combined population of roughly 18,000. On the eve of the American Revolution, Philadelphia and New York had surpassed Boston in size, and the total number of inhabitants in these five cities was approaching 104,000. (See Table 1.1.) According to some modern estimates, Philadelphia ranked as the largest English city outside of London. But cities were more than just collections of population; they were crucibles of commerce, seats of government and colonial authority, and cores for the transmission of Old World cultures and values. Their presence made the penetration of the wilderness possible in a number of ways, if only because they provided the essential links between the Old World and the New. They were the hubs of a growing transportation and communications network that made the idea of an independent America, as a group of united states, plausible and perhaps possible by 1776.

North American cities were small compared with the great agglomerations to the south: Mexico City had some 70,000 inhabitants by 1750, and Lima, Peru, about 60,000. But these Spanish cities stood aloof from their surrounding regions. They were, more than anything else, symbols of Old World power and domination and administrative centers for colonial control. Boston, New York, Philadelphia, and other towns to the north, by contrast, grew in conjunction with their hinterlands and gradually evolved from fortified clusters into market places. They helped to shape the destiny of the country, and spawned dozens of newer towns that served similar functions on a smaller scale. All in all, the growth of towns in North America was an integral, and essential, part of the colonial experience.

Table 1.1   Population Growth in the Major Colonial Cities, 1690–1775

	1690	1720	1742	1760	1775	
Boston	7,000	12,000	16,382	15,631	16,000	
Charleston	1,100	3,500	6,800	8,000	12,000	
New York	3,900	7,000	11,000	18,000	25,000	
Newport	2,600	3,800	6,200	7,500	11,000	
Philadelphia	4,000	10,000	13,000	23,750	40,000	(23,750)[a]

[a]The first figure is Bridenbaugh's; the second, Warner's. Philadelphia's population of roughly 28,500 in 1790 suggests that Warner's more conservative figure is closer to the actual population total in 1775.

Sources: Carl Bridenbaugh, *Cities in the Wilderness: The First Century of Urban Life in America, 1625–1742*, 2nd ed. (New York: Putnam, 1964), pp. 6, 143, 303, and *Cities in Revolt: Urban Life in America: 1743–1776* (New York: Knopf, 1955), p. 216; and Sam Bass Warner, Jr., *The Private City: Philadelphia in Three Periods of Its Growth* (Philadelphia: University of Pennsylvania Press, 1968), p. 12.

Notes

1. Christopher Tunnard and Henry Hope Reed, *American Skyline: The Growth and Form of Our Cities and Towns* (New York: New American Library, 1953), p. 89.

2. Quoted in Perry Miller and Thomas H. Johnson, eds., *The Puritans: A Sourcebook of Their Writings,* 2 vols., rev. ed. (New York: Harper & Row, 1963), I, 199.

3. Perry Miller, *Errand into the Wilderness* (Cambridge, Mass.: Harvard University Press, 1956), p. 2.

4. Quoted in John R. Stilgoe, "The Puritan Townscape: Ideal and Reality," *Landscape,* 20 (Spring 1976), 3–7.

5. Quoted in *ibid.,* p. 7.

6. Quoted in Darrett B. Rutman, *Winthrop's Boston: Portrait of a Puritan Town, 1630–1649* (Chapel Hill: University of North Carolina Press, 1965), p. 241.

7. Quoted in Carl Bridenbaugh, *Cities in Revolt: Urban Life in America, 1743–1776* (New York: Capricorn, 1955), p. 3.

8. Quoted in John W. Reps, *Town Planning in Frontier America* (Princeton, N.J.: Princeton University Press, 1970), p. 113.

2.
On the Waterfront:
The Cluster Economy

Agriculture, Commerce, and Colonial Towns

They were farmers before they were traders. The early colonial communities, whether missions in Florida or compact communities in New England, were faced with the task of survival. Economic and spiritual supporters back home on the Continent or in England had little conception of the harsh wilderness that awaited their migrating brothers and sisters. The Virginia Company of London had sprinkled their Jamestown settlers with young gentry and able craftsmen but few farmers, and the bitter early years of the colony were due, in part, to its failure to produce food. Town builders on the New England, the Middle Atlantic, and later the southern urban frontiers learned from these early mistakes and made ample provisions for farm land to be cultivated in or near the new city.

New England settlements incorporated the distribution and cultivation of land into their community life. For well over a century, until these early towns began to run out of land, urban residents typically combined farming with another occupation. By 1682—the year that William Penn's plan for Philadelphia became a reality—it was an accepted maxim throughout the colonies and in Europe that farming and urban settlement should go hand in hand. The Philadelphia plan provided for "liberty lands" located beyond the city where urban residents holding town lots could choose land to farm. The success of the Philadelphia plan was reflected in James Oglethorpe's plan for Savannah a half-century later. Imitation of successful aspects of another plan, a common urban characteristic, was evident in the garden plots and larger farms that surrounded Savannah. Oglethorpe proposed a hierarchy of agricultural units, to which he gave considerable attention. As one contemporary observer described it:

Each Freeholder . . . has a Lott . . . beyond the Common of 5 Acres for a Garden. . . . Each Freeholder of the Tything [ten houses equaled one tything] has a Lott or Farm of 45 Acres. . . . Beyond . . . commence Lotts of 500 Acres; these are granted upon Terms of keeping 10 Servants.[1]

Self-sufficiency in terms of food production was a worthwhile goal for fledgling communities to pursue. The early colonial town builders, however, did not look on subsistence as a virtue. As soon as an adequate food supply seemed assured, their sights lifted from the gardens of their homes and the fields in the vicinity to the great Atlantic world. "I desire thee," wrote a Philadelphia Quaker to an English colleague scarcely after Penn's town was settled, "let us have a little trade together."[2]

The English gracefully accepted the offer for trade and went about the process of ensuring that the Atlantic commerce turned to their benefit. It was, after all, the age of mercantilism. The economic welfare of a nation, according to this doctrine, depended on commerce, and commerce should be controlled by the state for the benefit of all the people. Translated into the realities of seventeenth- and eighteenth-century commerce, this meant that colonies supplied the mother country with raw materials and foodstuffs while the mother country provided its colonial offspring with manufactured products. This economic relationship required colonial urban development.

In order to fulfill their mercantile objectives, the English believed that urban settlements, as focal points for commerce, credit, and royal supervision, were essential. In the seventeenth century, the personal objectives of the Puritans and William Penn, as well as the legacy of the Dutch, coincided with English desires to encourage the growth of towns. The southern colonies presented a different problem, and English policy sought unsuccessfully to generate towns in the South throughout the seventeenth century. Promised debt relief, tax credits, and town lots to attract prospective settlers, as well as a planned urban center for each county, were some of the proposals put forward as enticements to southern urban development. The overwhelming faith of the English and colonial lawmakers in their ability to legislate towns into existence underscored their general ignorance of the forces that inhibited and fostered urbanization in the mercantile age.

First, there was the problem of geography. Deep-water ports were essential for fulfilling the colonial part of the mercantile bargain. This requirement disqualified North Carolina from the urban sweepstakes. The wreckage of thousands of tons of vessels off the Outer Banks attests to the hidden shoals that lurk beneath the Carolina coast. What navigable rivers existed in the interior of the province flowed into South Carolina to benefit Charleston. The Chesapeake region, especially Virginia, was an example of too much of a good thing. The rivers in the region were navigable far into the interior, allowing ocean-going vessels to tie up at plantation landings to take on tobacco. The plantations themselves often functioned as centers for light manufacturing, labor supply, and provisions for the immediate hinterland. These functions were precisely the types of activities usually carried on by interior towns. Plantations stunted urban growth not only in the interior, but on the coast as well. Warehouses, merchants, factors, and the paraphernalia of Atlantic commerce were unnecessary in a society where individual planters provided these facilities. Beyond this, a substantial proportion of the population was composed of either indentured servants or slaves who lacked the capital resources necessary to fuel urban growth, and the planters themselves had much of their capital tied up in human labor.

Geography may have stifled urban development, but policy makers aggravated the impact of geography by an overzealous commitment to town building. One proposal put forth by the Virginia assembly late in the seventeenth century called for the creation of forty-five new towns in the province—a herculean task for even the most sophisticated central planning agency. The debate over the proposal also revealed that Crown and colony had different objectives with regard to the town-building scheme. Through these urban nodes the Crown hoped to focus and control trade—an impossible aim, given the highly individualized system of commerce that prevailed in the province at that time. The burgesses looked to towns as a means of extricating the province from some of the ill effects of mercantilism. The colonial lawmakers viewed the commercial concentration fostered by town life as a means of generating local manufacturing, thereby lessening dependence on England for manufactured products. The grandiose ideas and conflicting objectives ensured the doom of the proposal.

By 1700, the English had generally abandoned their efforts to create towns in the southern colonies. European wars, the immense profitability of the tobacco, rice, and indigo trades, and the maturation of urban centers elsewhere cooled the fires of town building. Ironically, a little more than a generation later, urban centers dotted the coastal and interior landscape of the South. Commerce would build the towns if geography and the English could not.

The Waterfront

They gathered at the river, or the bay, or the ocean. People, produce, and structures clustered at the waterfront, drawn by the magnet of commerce.

And commerce meant profits. The great cities of colonial America were great because of their participation in the mercantile system. The cities— Boston, Newport, New York, Philadelphia, Charleston, and later Baltimore—were strung out along the Atlantic coast like pearls threaded on a watery chain. They were truly gems to the London and Bristol merchants who sat in their countinghouses scarcely believing the profits emerging from these precious cities. The power of England, the wealth of her merchants, and the success of her colonies and subjects depended on the waterfront. There lay the heartbeat of empire.

Farm and city came together at the waterfront in the form of the urban market, the most visible example of the interrelationship of the two environments. The array of wares and food that stretched along the city's major thoroughfare for as long as a quarter of a mile provided an exciting variety for the urban shopper, who doubtless marveled at the fertility of the backcountry and the skills of local artisans on display.

The importance of the waterfront determined the shape of the colonial city. William Penn located Philadelphia with a sharp commercial eye. The Delaware River afforded a protected, yet accessible highway to the markets of Europe. Ships of the heaviest tonnage came to the port in all seasons, since the river water, being salty, rarely froze. Market Street, the city's major thoroughfare, began at the waterfront as Penn had planned it, but Penn's plans failed to account for the centripetal attraction of the river. The city hugged the waterfront with warehouses and wharves extending more than a mile along the shore. Philadelphia became a linear city as settlement in the eighteenth century rarely wandered more than half a mile from the river.

The affinity of Philadelphians for their river destroyed Penn's plans for a spacious, almost pastoral urban environment. Businesses and residences crowded along the river in a mixture of work and residence areas characteristic of the dense cities of medieval Europe. The marine trades and merchants spawned retail activities and artisans' workshops, all of which were packed into a narrow area. Noise, air pollution, and congestion forced those who could afford to leave to move to the suburbs, where the original conception of spaciousness could be temporarily revived. Benjamin Franklin, one of the city's more heralded citizens, captured the essence of turbulent waterfront life when he complained: "The din of the Market increases upon me; and that, with frequent interruptions, has, I find, made me say something twice over."[3] Franklin soon moved away from the river.

Penn's spacious blocks were divided and divided again. Alleys and small houses proliferated as the value of land came to be measured by the square foot rather than by the acre. People and produce still mingled near the wharves, but by 1750 the lure of the waterfront began to result in greater sorting out of land uses. A commercial district was forming, pushing residential uses away from the river as riverfront property became too expensive and undesirable for residential purposes.

The other pearls of the Atlantic experienced similar concentration of settlement at the waterfront, though the degree of differentiation and crowding was not as great as in Philadelphia, the most active colonial port by the time of the Revolution. In seventeenth-century Boston, for example, the homes of the leading merchants overlooked the wharves and warehouses of the harbor, though by 1775 many wealthy citizens had moved from this convenient location to the nearby towns of Roxbury and Cambridge.

The Atlantic Trade

The major source of this waterfront activity was, of course, the Atlantic trade. The extent of participation and of success in the trade depended on the ability of local merchants to market commodities desired by member nations of the Atlantic world. The English mercantilist system imposed continuous pressure on colonial merchants to find, process, and ship produce and goods in order to pay for the manufactured goods sent to colonial ports. Failure to do so resulted in an imbalance of trade, a strain on credit, and a blow to growth and prosperity. Waterfront activity, however noisy and noisome, was the gauge of a city's success or failure in the world of international commerce.

International commerce was a nerve-racking business. Merchants and their employees periodically paced the wharves checking the wind, chatting with customs officials, and hoping that the store of flour and grain warehoused nearby would not burn, rot, or be stolen before it could be loaded on their overdue vessel. The merchants shared similar troubles and thoughts. Suddenly declining or rising prices, new statutes, and messages bearing ill or good tidings were typical topics of conversation. Usually, the outcome of this furtive pacing and talking was good. Sometimes it was not, and the result could be personal or even general ruin. Uncertainty always lurked beneath the hubbub of activity on the waterfront. From the dock laborer to the sailmaker to the merchant—their future was closely bound to the blue Atlantic.

The numerous examples of urban failure probably troubled the minds of colonial city dwellers the most. Urbanization is not like fermentation. Cities do not necessarily continue to improve until they reach a state of perfection; rather, at almost any moment, a city can sour. While historians have generally concentrated on the urban success stories, there have been significant failures. The men and women down at the waterfront were by nature optimistic, or else they would have been back in Europe. They were well aware, however, of the capriciousness of fate. They could not make the wind blow gently, or replenish the soil, or alter a coastline. They knew their own and their city's fallibility. Failure had happened before.

There was New Haven, Connecticut. A medium-sized, uninspiring city today, its past held greater hopes. Settled as an outpost in the New England fur trade during the 1630s, New Haven's location at the mouth of the Quinnipiac River seemed critically important. The young settlement was to be the largest port between Boston and New Amsterdam. As local merchants readied the first great cargo of furs to be shipped directly to England, they hoped that this shipment would inaugurate an era of unequaled growth and prosperity. Alas, it was an ill wind that accompanied the vessel in its transatlantic journey. The ship never arrived at its destination, New Haven's merchants suffered severe financial misfortune, direct trade was never established with England, and the town sank back into a semirural condition. A visitor to the once-hopeful settlement in 1660 tersely recorded the scene: ". . . the land very barren, the Merchants either dead or come away, the rest gotten to their Farmes, The Towne is not so glorious as once it was."[4] New Haven revived in the nineteenth century as industrialization created new urban growth, but by then its pretensions to commercial pre-eminence were gone and it was merely another river city on the way from Boston to New York.

The redemption of New Haven after a long period of dormancy indicates the often cyclical nature of the urbanization process. To the citizens of the time, however, the decline seemed very real and permanent. Further south, another protometropolis took flight nearly a century later. Unlike New Haven, this town experienced a few moments in the limelight and then quickly expired, a victim of geography and of the insatiable appetite of the mercantile system.

London Town, Maryland, as the name implied, possessed considerable urban pretensions. Tobacco, that valuable commodity that struck delight and profit into merchants on both sides of the Atlantic, was responsible for the initial dream and temporary reality of London Town's presumptions. The intricate river system of the Chesapeake region produced numerous settlements like London Town, often only five miles apart but separated by watery barriers. A traveler from Williamsburg to Annapolis, for example, required at least twelve ferries to negotiate the 120 miles. A five-mile journey from London Town to Annapolis lasted more than an hour. The isolation of each settlement from the others enabled the towns to develop and market the produce from their own backcountry without significant danger of competition from neighboring communities.

London Town was especially blessed with fertile soil that produced high-quality and high-priced tobacco. A quality product plus increasing European demand for the weed attracted capital and merchants to the small community, and by 1720 a flourishing trade with England had developed. In late October, luffing sails and stately masts bobbed gracefully at the town's harbor as ships unloaded manufactured goods, luxury items, and wine in exchange for the precious tobacco. Unfortunately and suddenly, however, the waterfront activity ceased. The decline in tobacco prices in the 1740s induced the Maryland assembly to pass an inspection law to ensure that the colony's tobacco would compete favorably in the tight market with crops from the other colonies. To this end, the colony established government warehouses at designated inspection stations. The assembly overlooked London Town and the community shriveled and disappeared.

New Crops and New Markets

There were numerous New Havens and London Towns and no certainties in the Atlantic world. The search for marketable commodities and markets was a constant one for the waterfront denizens. Their ingenuity in seeking out these necessities in a mercantile world tells, in large part, the success stories of colonial urban America. Some of these stories will be narrated in the pages that follow, but for the stories in brief, see Figure 2.1.

The merchants in each colonial seaport were subject to the demands of colonial mercantilism. According to English mercantile law, the English colonies were to trade directly only with England. The objective of the Atlantic trade, from the English as well as the colonial viewpoint, was for colonials to secure a marketable commodity to exchange for England's manufactured goods. Without such a commodity, colonial merchants would be perpetually in debt to their English counterparts. The catch was that none of the colonial cities along the Atlantic seaboard could disgorge sufficient produce to pay for the articles shipped on the return voyage from England. It made sense, therefore, to seek out other markets where more favorable balances could be struck to pay for English cargoes. The ingenious merchants scoured the Atlantic world for legal and illegal trading partners. The merchants could and did rationalize that the alternative to illicit trade was penury. The presence of French and Dutch translators in urban countinghouses of the English colonies indicates how formalized the illegal trade had become by 1750.

Philadelphia affords a good opportunity to study the relationship between urbanization and international trade. Although the Quaker city was the last major seaport founded in the colonies, its merchants made up in

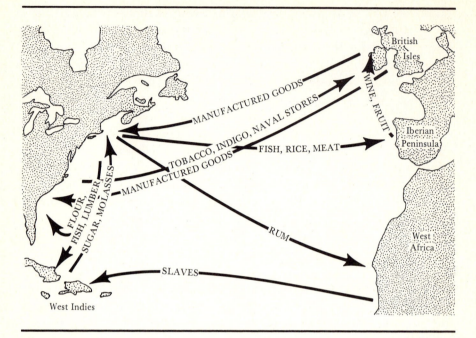

Figure 2.1   Colonial Trading Patterns. (From *Cities and Immigrants: A Geography of Change in Nineteenth-Century America* by David Ward. Copyright © 1971 by Oxford University Press, Inc. Reprinted by permission.)

aggressiveness what the city lacked in age. Almost immediately after its initial settlement in 1682, Philadelphia merchants began to erode Boston's monopoly of the carrying trade in the Middle Atlantic region. Here were two good rules for fledgling cities to follow: First, build and use your own ships. The shipbuilding industry had enabled Boston, for example, to carry away produce all along the Atlantic coast in its own ships. Although backed by a meager hinterland, Boston merchants grew wealthy serving as middlemen for other ports and investing wisely in shipbuilding. Besides, local captains, local crews, and local ships meant, ultimately, that profits from the voyage would be spent in the community. Second, establish commercial leadership in your own area. Merchants were impolite when it came to observing provincial boundaries. No trading area, no matter how far removed, was off limits. Before foraying wide and far, however, the home country must be secured: No hinterland meant no trade. It was a lesson that towns like New Haven, and later Newport, were to learn much to their distress.

The Quaker merchants began their Atlantic commerce modestly in 1690 by establishing a trade in horses and provisions with various Caribbean ports. In return, the merchants received rum, molasses, and sugar, which could either be shipped to England to settle the trade imbalance or distributed at other colonial ports for a profit that could be used in part to redress that same imbalance. Illustrated by the West Indies trade were a number of good commercial maxims. First, for a port with marginal commodities like horses and provisions (certainly few English merchants yearned for these items), it was essential to seek out markets with more attractive products. Second, despite the modest level of the initial trade, when Philadelphia's fertile hinterland began to produce wheat in the eighteenth century, the trade contacts made in the seventeenth century provided immediate entrees for wheat and its products. Finally, discovering new trade areas often led to further discoveries. Evidently, early Quaker captains became "lost" in the maze of islands and wandered onto Dutch and French West Indian shores—forbidden harbors according to English mercantile statutes. The Quaker captains undoubtedly felt at home in these foreign ports, however, because they probably met officers and crews from New York, Boston, and Charleston vessels. By the 1740s, the Dutch and French island ports of call were commonplace itineraries on sailing orders: "My order to you," wrote a Boston merchant to one of his captains in 1743, "is that you take the first wind and weather for sailing and proceed to the West Indies. You have Liberty to go to any of the English Islands, and if you think it Safe to any of the french Islands."[5]

By this time, Philadelphia had expanded her trade across the Atlantic. Wheat was the commercial catapult. Palatine (German) and Scotch-Irish immigrants sailed across the Atlantic highway to settle in the tolerant woods and fields of William Penn's plantation. Their diligent cultivation of wheat enabled Philadelphia merchants to feed a hungry Atlantic world whose appetite for wheat products had been sharpened by the incessant European warfare. Philadelphia merchants loaded Quaker ships with flour and bread bound for old trading partners in the Caribbean—and by 1775 the city exported more flour to these ports than did all the other colonies combined. The ships loaded with flour and bread sailed on to southern Europe and the Wine Islands, where the precious grain was exchanged for salt and wine—two more marketable commodities. The extent of the city's trade with southern Europe outdistanced that of all other colonial ports. Then the ships sailed on to England for the dry goods, woolens, and other manufactured products from the dismal factories of its crowded cities. To the end of the colonial period, Philadelphia merchants could not find a significant commodity to interest English merchants. But the resourcefulness of the merchants in seeking out new markets produced profits for themselves and growth for the city.

It was evident that wheat had played an important role in the Philadelphia success story, and this was another lesson for the rising Atlantic ports. The importance of finding a marketable commodity was such that urban merchants probed deep into the interior, braved icy waters, and invested in processing industries. In early Boston, the fur trade was a lucrative business. Since animals were a finite commodity and security on the fur frontier was generally absent, Boston merchants soon turned to other creatures—fish—to make their way in the Atlantic world. The merchants disposed of the fish in Spain and the Wine Islands, where profits were sufficient either in bills of exchange (the equivalent of cash) or in produce to pay for English manufactured products. While Philadelphia was able to live by bread alone, Boston merchants found fishing an arduous and marginal activity. So they turned to shipbuilding and the carrying trade to generate profits and finally to a widespread illicit trade.

The odyssey of Boston merchant Thomas Hancock's ships reveals the extent of that commerce in the 1740s. His vessels took fish to the West Indies, calling at British and at forbidden French ports to load molasses, then headed back to Boston to unload a portion of the cargo, and then proceeded to Holland—another prohibited port—to pick up European manufactured products. For Boston merchants with an unproductive hinterland at their backs and with rival colonial ports snipping at their carrying trade, the illegal cargo was one way of scratching profits out of the Atlantic trade. Though most of their commerce was within the bounds of mercantile propriety, that portion of their trade carried on outside the Empire provided essential profits for a seaport that had seen its commercial leadership pass to Philadelphia.

Farther south, Charleston merchants enjoyed a less difficult situation. The gentle breezes that blew along the wide waterfront promenade lent a leisurely, esthetic quality to this city that contrasted with the frenetic and crowded ports in the northern colonies. A closer inspection, however, revealed the same graceful ships, the same concerned merchants, and the same collection of trades and people associated with maritime endeavors. If there was less strain on the faces of Charleston's merchants, it was probably due to two commodities: rice and indigo.

These commodities were wheat and more to Charleston. In the industrial cities of northern Europe, rice had become almost a household necessity. From the 1720s until the Revolution, rice accounted for one-half to two-thirds of the total value of Charleston's exports. The value of rice and the volume of the trade allowed Charleston's merchants to trade directly with England. The crystal chandeliers and broadlooms that graced the interiors of spacious Charleston town houses were purchased with rice.

The city's merchants were not about to rest on their rice, however. The proximity of the Caribbean gave rise to a flourishing West Indian trade, not only in rice but also in naval stores, with molasses, rum, and slaves (from Jamaica and Barbados) as the return cargo. Equally important, ships from other colonial ports returning from the West Indies found the South Carolina port a convenient point to unload a portion of their cargoes for distribution throughout the Carolinas and Georgia.

New York merchants, unleashed from the constraints of the Dutch West India Company, which had monopolized trade at the port, secured trade connections with illegal ports and even with pirates in the early years of the eighteenth century. It was not until 1730, however, that New Yorkers were able to mount a local fleet to prevent Bostonians from carrying away the city's hinterland produce. By then, the fertile lands of the Hudson River Valley were producing wheat and livestock in sufficient quantities for New York merchants to sail the trade circuit of the Caribbean, southern Europe, and England. It was not until the Revolution, though, that New Yorkers were to seize on the advantage of their deep-water facilities and strategic location to build a commercial empire. The present still belonged to Philadelphia.

The Workings of International Commerce

As the Atlantic trade developed, the merchants on the waterfront widened their international connections. While the merchants bore the burdens of insecurity pretty much alone, they shared their profits with a number of different people who sought to ensure the smooth working of the ocean commerce. The colonial urban merchant, then, was merely one link in the chain of commercial command.

The factor was probably the merchant's most intimate and important partner in the Atlantic trade. It was on the factor that the merchant vented his rage for damaged cargoes or low prices and with this invaluable colleague that he shared the joys and profits of a good sale or a new market. The factor was an individual who performed services for the colonial merchants on a commission basis. In a typical arrangement, the factor sold a cargo for the merchant and sent the proceeds of the sale or another cargo to the merchant in return. The factor also provided valuable market information, though it was likely to be a little out of date by the time it reached the colonial merchant. In return for these services, the factor received a commission. In short, the factor was the merchant's eyes, ears, and purse abroad.

Factors also worked for English merchants. Resident factors in colonial ports were more typical in the southern colonies, where the valuable staple commodities of tobacco, rice, and indigo inspired English merchants to send agents (factors) to secure the best quality at the best price. These factors, acting at the behest of English merchants, often played a wider role than that of middleman for the staple trade. Their connections with England enabled them to secure capital for investment in colonial enterprises. Since colonial merchants were chronically short of liquid assets, this arrangement helped to stimulate urban growth in the southern colonies. English factors in Charleston, for example, financed the fur trade, which extended as far as a thousand miles into the interior. They also made Charleston a lucrative port for the slave trade by arranging the purchase of slaves for area planters.

The three major actors in the Atlantic trade—the colonial merchant, the factor, and the English merchant—were linked by a chain of credit. The chronic shortage of currency in colonial ports (there were no banks, and paper money issues were frowned upon) was one element in starting the urban merchant on a journey to secure credit to expand his business, pay for his imports, and remit to the farmers or agents in the backcountry. The continuing search for markets was, in part, an effort to secure coin and currency from foreign ports. This currency was especially important in paying for the English manufactured goods that no colonial city could seem to afford without ranging through the entire Atlantic world.

The English merchants who sold the manufactured products to the colonies eased the financial burden of the colonial merchants by extending them credit on the purchase for one year. In turn, the colonial merchants allowed retailers to whom they sold the imported goods one year to complete payment. Finally, the retailers allowed consumers one year to settle accounts.

The neat credit pyramid sometimes collapsed, however, and the colonial merchants were caught in the middle. The periodic financial depressions that afflicted the Atlantic world dislocated the credit arrangements. Consumers fell behind in their payments to retailers, who fell behind in their payments to the merchants. English creditors, whose far-flung enterprises required immediate cash flow in times of distress, called in their American debts. The consequences could be serious indeed for merchants who lacked sufficient reserve capital to stave off the English wolf. Here is where the search for markets and commodities reaped benefits.

The difficulties inherent in the credit system added yet another potential worry to those already faced by the colonial merchant. Because of their great expense, English imports were at the core of the problem. While colonial merchants had long sought to diversify their markets and products as a hedge against financial distress, they began increasingly by 1750 to get to the root of the problem by curtailing the volume of English imports. A severe cutback would seriously affect the colonial urban lifestyle, which by the mid-eighteenth century matched the best that English urban society offered in terms of variety and quality of manufactured goods. But a slight decrease seemed in order, especially since the British were reluctant to expand the local currency.

Colonial merchants began to funnel a portion of their profits into modest manufacturing enterprises. Boston, which faced a severe financial situation as its role as middleman diminished, began to manufacture and export furniture and shoes. Shipbuilding continued to expand as an investment outlet for merchants. Moreover, as Boston and other colonial cities grew, artisans, who composed from one-third to one-half of the population in some cities, began to manufacture products on a small scale for local consumption. Artisans who had heretofore produced only custom orders now began to manufacture wares for potential demand. Some colonial enterprises, like hat manufacturing, were so successful that Parliament passed laws designed to limit or prohibit them altogether. Enforcement of these laws was sporadic, however.

When a severe depression wracked the colonies following the Seven Years' War, merchants in several colonial cities formed organizations designed to develop manufacturing in order to reduce the cash outflow resulting from English imports. A group of New York merchants founded the Society for the Promotion of Arts, Agriculture, and Economy in 1765; seven years later the Society for Encouraging Manufactures formed in Charleston; and on the eve of the Revolution, leading merchants in Philadelphia organized the United Company of Philadelphia for Promoting American Manufactures. A diversified economy, including manufacturing as well as commerce, would not only stimulate urban growth by providing employment for numerous craftsmen, but would also keep local capital from leaving the city (though some merchants enjoyed plowing profits into land speculation rather than industry). Finally since self-sufficiency was the ultimate goal in the mercantilist philosophy, colonial merchants felt that there was no reason why they and their communities should not strive to attain that objective. Ultimately, they hoped, the products from these early industrial efforts would find their way to the waterfront to join the list of marketable commodities for overseas ports.

By 1775, the urban merchants held a sophisticated if somewhat cynical world view. Gone were the days when the major concern was catching a few animals in the forest or harvesting the backyard crop. The urban merchants and their cities were part of the great Atlantic mercantile world. It was a

world mined with numerous obstacles to success. Whether overlooking the
waterfront from his countinghouse or ruminating in the study of his comfortable town house far removed from the din of the docks, the merchant
was likely to be mulling over complex credit arrangements or mentally
searching for new markets and commodities and new opportunities for
investments. His ships traveled the Atlantic world: up and down the colonial
coast and to Newfoundland, the West Indies, the Wine Islands, the European continent, and the British Isles. And if the merchant was successful, he
appreciated the fact that the roots of his Atlantic world lay not in England
but in the hinterland, where settlers, produce, and ultimately towns fed the
hungry coastal cities. As the merchant paced the waterfront, the dirt highway out of town to the backcountry doubtless occupied a portion of his
thoughts.

Urban Growth in the Backcountry

Since the growth of the coastal city from wilderness to metropolis in the
colonial era was so startling, the more modest urbanization of the interior
has generally gone unnoticed. Yet the process of urbanization in the
backcountry towns is equally important. Not only did they provide important collecting points for hinterland produce, but they also served as
suppliers to settlers and places for settlers to meet, swap stories, and exchange information in relative security from Indian attack. In addition,
these settlements provided the coastal city with access to hinterland commodities so essential in the mercantile world.

Backcountry urbanization was a product of migration, geography, and
above all, nurture from the larger coastal metropolis—basically the same
features that generated growth in the Atlantic colonial cities. Surrounded by
wilderness, the hinterland's ties with the coastal plain were bound to be very
close. As urban outposts on an often inhospitable frontier, these interior
communities performed the dual function of making the backcountry more
civilized and enabling the coastal city to grow and attain wealth.

One such settlement was Camden, South Carolina, located 125 miles
northwest of Charleston along a major trade road to the backcountry fur
trade. While waterways formed the most convenient highways to most interior settlements, in the absence of nearby rivers, the functional old Indian
trails were heavily traveled. Another important interior settlement was Lancaster, Pennsylvania, located along the Great Philadelphia Wagon Road
used by migrants on their treks into the Valley of Virginia and the Carolina
Piedmont. The German and Scotch-Irish ancestors of current residents of
the area probably stopped at Lancaster to pick up supplies and spend a

restful night before moving on in the morning. Lancaster as a way station soon evolved into Lancaster as a trading center.

Performing the collector function was the primary value of the backcountry communities. In the eighteenth century, Virginia towns finally appeared along the rivers, gathering and warehousing tobacco grown in the area. Often these towns were essentially extensions of the plantations as planters owned grist mills, warehouses, and country stores. Dumfries and Colchester, downriver from Alexandria, and Leedstown and Hobbes Hole, down the Rappahannock from Fredericksburg, fed hogsheads and bushels to their larger upriver towns. In early New England the collecting function of the Connecticut River fur-trading towns like New Haven proved short-lived, but while it existed it enabled Boston merchants to invest capital from the trade in the shipbuilding industry.

Camden's merchant-farmers, benefiting from the collecting function, followed the lead of the coastal cities and began to cast about for a staple crop. Both rice and indigo were inappropriate for the soil of the area so wheat became the specialized crop, and the merchants erected mills to process wheat, which was then sent on to Charleston. The collection function was still prominent, but in the meantime, Camden had become a minor industrial center. It was by this time common for country wheat to be milled in collection settlements for shipment to the city.

With increased commercial and industrial activity came more buildings and increased population. Soon Camden began to follow the pattern of Lancaster by becoming an urban settlement in its own right: A sawmill, a circuit court, a warehouse, two meeting houses, a jail, and some fine residences had transformed a collection crossroads into a town, a genuine *central place* for a surrounding agricultural hinterland. Charleston merchants began to pay more attention to their profitable trading partner in the interior, and Camden entered its next phase of growth.

As Camden illustrates so well, urbanization had a multiplier effect, which generated a full-blown urban hierarchy by 1775. Dominated by the primary coastal center, the colonial system of cities linked together by roads and rivers developed the economic relationships that allowed the pearls of the Atlantic to maintain and increase their luminescence. Virginia's colonial urban development affords a good example of the complexities of this hierarchy, even in an overwhelmingly rural colony.

Communities like Alexandria, Norfolk, Richmond, and Petersburg, at the head of river navigation, were the primary market centers in the colony. Downriver, collection communities like those mentioned earlier developed. These towns, in turn, generated small crossroads settlements that might consist of only a warehouse and a general store but had potential for growth.

In addition to this urban hierarchy, several regional economies grouped around a major town developed in Virginia. There was the James River region with Norfolk and Richmond as its primary urban centers; the Potomac River region dominated by Alexandria, whose satellites pushed far into the Valley of Virginia; and the Rappahannock region, where Fredericksburg functioned as the major trade center.

The smaller size of the interior centers was an indication of their unequal economic relationship with the primary center on the coast, a relationship similar to the one that existed between the coastal seaport and London. The wheat-processing centers in Maryland, for example—Elkton, Charlestown, and Havre de Grace—enjoyed brief periods of growth until Baltimore merchants fanned out into the hinterland to capture an increasing share of the wheat trade, as Charleston's merchants had involved themselves in Camden's economic life. Larger towns like Newport, Rhode Island, also experienced growth limitations as both Boston and New York widened their spheres of influence.

"Urban imperialism" is an appropriate phrase to describe the pattern of the dominance of primary centers over interior settlements. Aggressive merchants from coastal cities realized that their fortunes in the Atlantic trade depended on the extent of their backcountry and the volume and value of the produce derived from it. It was common, therefore, for local merchants to open branch offices (actually stores) in the interior settlements. The managers of these stores secured the crop of the surrounding area, provided the farmer with implements, manufactured goods, and assorted baubles, and thereby drained the area of both produce and cash. Just as mercantilism created a trade imbalance between England and the colonial ports, so the interior trade favored the coastal city. The stakes involved in the backcountry trade were no less high merely because the commercial game was played in the woods, fields, rivers, and dirt roads, rather than in London countinghouses or tall ships on the great ocean. As one Philadelphia merchant put it: "It is a fact indisputably certain, that what port soever on this continent can acquire the greatest share of its inland commerce, must proportionately advance in riches and importance."[6]

When the rewards of urban imperialism are considered, it is not surprising that an intense competition developed among the coastal cities for dominance over ever-widening interior trading areas. Baltimore, for example, battled Philadelphia for control of the lucrative Middle Atlantic wheat trade. As inducements, Baltimore offered lower transportation costs over better roads and hence better prices for wheat and flour. On the other hand, Philadelphia merchants pointed to the extensive storage facilities and equally high prices paid for wheat and flour. This was the beginning of a long and often bitter rivalry between the two ports that reached a climax in the nineteenth century.

Merchants and Artisans

For the colonial merchant, it was not enough to seek out markets and commodities, blaze trails and towns in the interior, combat grasping rivals, and juggle the complex financial accounts of London merchants and backwoods farmers. The merchant, whether looking out to sea, down the road, or over his shoulder, had to make certain that his town was sufficiently organized to receive the bounty from the sea, river, and road. Wharves had to be clean and extensive, warehouses large and dry, and market days well regulated and convenient. Market days were particularly important because this is where farm and city met. The extent and profitability of the relationship depended on how the city managed the market.

Markets were conducted several times a week, and, as the city grew, market stalls appeared at more than one location to accommodate the citizens. Markets provided urban residents with food. As the city grew, its gardens and small farms could no longer produce sufficient food to feed a growing population. In 1691, New York City opened two markets at two separate locations and for two different functions: one for meat and one for fish and vegetables. These provisions were available Tuesday, Thursday, and Saturday from seven in the morning. The markets required strict regulations to protect consumers against damaged, rotten, or misrepresented produce. Merchants, who operated many of the stalls, also sought and received protection from itinerant hucksters who wandered about the city vending produce just purchased from the market.

Market days were colorful occasions. Farmers, merchants, and consumers converged on the stalls to shop, converse, and deal. The colonial seaports were street cities in that residents looked forward to leaving their crowded, ill-heated, and ill-ventilated homes for a walk on the street, whether for social or commercial purposes. Merchants enjoyed market days as an opportunity to meet new customers, discuss a grain shipment from the interior, talk about establishing a branch store in some interior locale, and converse about possible investments. This was the merchant's milieu: the street, the waterfront, and the market. Activity meant profits and profits meant growth and more profits.

As the merchant expanded his contacts across the Atlantic, into the backcountry, and beyond the neighborhood, the city was changing. The colonial urban economy had altered both the cityscape and the people who worked to support and generate economic progress. The change in the division of labor was probably the most evident consequence of the evolution of the colonial economy over the first century and a half of English colonization. The merchant, of course, remained the most important figure in the urban economy. He was, in essence, economic planner and decision maker for the community. In 1744 Governor George Thomas of Pennsylvania stated the obvious when he declared that Philadelphia "in some way or other depends upon the merchant, and if he cannot trade to advantage, it will soon be very sensibly felt by the whole."[7]

The merchant was important because, as we have seen, he performed a wide variety of tasks. He was an exporter, importer, wholesaler, retailer, purchasing agent, banker, attorney, and town builder. These roles involved significant profits and, of course, substantial risks. By 1750, however, the seaport economies had grown so extensive and in so many different directions that it was physically and mentally impossible for a merchant to wear all of these hats. The emergence of the retail function as a separate occupation was probably one of the more significant events in the urban division of labor. By this time most of the great merchants were strictly wholesalers, who supplied urban and backcountry retailers with manufactured products. Young merchants with ambition usually began their careers as retailers or factors, risking little of their own capital, while accumulating a stake to enter the Atlantic sweepstakes where there were profits and prestige.

Both the wholesaler and the retailer furthered the division of labor by specializing in certain commodities. Some merchants, for example, were primarily dry-goods importers. Artisans used their special skills to retail silverwork, furniture, or implements. The great merchant, though, still performed numerous jobs. Not until the nineteenth century would a more strict differentiation of occupation develop.

While merchants and cities shared the mutual benefits of expansion, other economic groups in society prospered in a similar, if less ostentatious, manner. The urban artisans performed valuable economic functions in the growing seaport cities. Although their contacts were much more parochial than those of the merchants, the artisans enabled the city to broaden its economic base in the constant drive to diminish dependence on England.

Artisans were numerous in the northern seaport city and constituted from one-third to one-half of the employed population by the time of the Revolution. There were such large numbers of artisans for several reasons. First, the weakness of guilds—those craft organizations that tightly regulated membership and price in Old World cities—made entry into the artisan class open to any ambitious individual. Second, the traditional apprenticeship period, sometimes lasting as long as seven years, gradually shortened in the face of rising demand for skilled labor in the colonial city. Third, the crafts generally fared well in the urban economy—so much so that a diligent artisan could hope realistically for upward mobility. The attractiveness of a prosperous future doubtless encouraged many young men who lacked the influential connections and education to enter the merchant ranks immediately. Finally, the rapidly advancing population of the colonial cities coupled with an increased standard of living generated a significant consumer appetite.

The importance of artisans to the urban economy may be judged by a brief catalog of some of the more common tasks they performed. Most artisans worked alone, perhaps on occasion with one or two apprentices. If colonial urban America was a nation of shopkeepers, it was the artisan who kept shop, usually displaying the fruits of his labor in the front, while his work and living areas were to the rear of the shop. Coopers, for example, showcased barrels and kegs, essential for packing flour, fish, and beer. The waterfront gave rise, even more directly, to the occupation of sailmaker, carpenter, and smith. On a less dramatic, though equally important level, urban housewives relied on the neighborhood baker for their daily bread. In addition, since ovens were usually a luxury in most colonial homes, bakers sometimes branched into the food-service business by offering the use of their ovens for local residents to prepare their dinners. Finally, the baker also participated indirectly in export business by turning flour into bread and biscuits for the Atlantic crews and for the West Indies trade.

Specialization increased with urbanization. As urban society became more sophisticated and as consumer tastes approached the quality of a metropolis rather than of a wilderness, few artisans of skill could remain engaged in general craft work. Carpentry, for example, was a general craft. By 1750, however, in most of the seaport cities carpenters had divided into joiners, housewrights, cabinetmakers, carvers, and chainmakers. It was evident that the relative handful of town builders in the rude log and frame houses had been replaced by a new generation of city dwellers more accustomed to comfortable domestic living. The demand for luxury craftsmen was another indication of increasing expectations in the colonial urban lifestyle. Silversmiths obtained a ready clientele in the port cities, while the cleaning and dyeing trades appeared to service urban fashion plates. The traditional do-it-yourself frontier tasks of candle- and soap-making were now performed by professional soap boilers and tallow chandlers. Finally, that symbol of eighteenth-century civilization, the wigmaker, became an indispensable part of the artisan population in colonial cities.

Diversity was a sign of prosperity, as evidenced by the success of many artisans. In Charleston, numerous artisans entered the planter class. As in the northern communities, where securing a country seat was the ideal of urban entrepreneurs, so in the southern seaports artisan-entrepreneurs looked to the land for investment opportunities. Slaveholding was also common among artisans in the coastal cities. Approximately one-half of Philadelphia's artisans, for example, owned slaves. Bakers, woodworkers, and metalworkers especially found slave labor helpful. For a young, ambitious artisan-entrepreneur, slaveholding was an important step in business expansion as well as a sign of newly gained affluence.

The desire to strive upward was a striking quality among artisans. The example of their neighbors, the merchants, added inspiration to the quest for financial success. As men of modest means but great ambition, they were naturally more affected by economic depression than were the merchants. The economic downturn following the Seven Years' War in 1763 engendered especially bitter times for the artisan, and renewed competition from English manufacturers, English restrictions on currency, and the additional annoyance of Parliamentary taxation produced widespread disaffection toward England among urban artisans. It was not surprising that, a decade later, these craftsmen who had hoped to pursue their crafts in a free-wheeling, free-enterprise economy stepped to the forefront of the Revolutionary movement.

Laborers presented an even more troubled urban work force as the Revolution approached. Living in squalid conditions on the outskirts of the coastal cities or huddled together in waterfront districts vacated by artisans and merchants, these individuals were at once the products and the victims of urbanization. Slaves performed a good portion of the unskilled labor in the coastal cities, accounting for nearly one-half the population of Charleston, one-fifth that of Newport, and one-sixth that of New York. For whites, the demand for skilled crafts meant that few would remain in the unskilled category for very long.

By 1750, however, urban expansion and manufacturing increased the demand for unskilled labor. In turn, the artisans were plagued by foreign competition and by domestic economic ills. Finally, the Atlantic trade had generated substantial wealth for a small portion of the merchants, and they utilized their profits in investment opportunities to generate more wealth. In short, the dream of the artisan-entrepreneur to enter the mercantile elite was becoming somewhat tarnished. These economic developments contributed to a relatively small, but nonetheless visible, permanent group of propertyless laborers. It was not until the nineteenth century that these urban occupational lines hardened, but the outlines of such a trend were already apparent in the colonial seaports by the time of the Revolution.

Notes

1. Quoted in Bayrd Still, ed., *Urban America: A History with Documents* (Boston: Little, Brown, 1974), p. 23.

2. Quoted in Arthur L. Jensen, *The Maritime Commerce of Colonial Philadelphia* (Madison, Wisc.: State Historical Society of Wisconsin, 1963), p. 2.

3. Quoted in Carl Bridenbaugh, *Cities in Revolt: Urban Life in America, 1743–1776* (New York: Capricorn, 1955), p. 24.

4. Quoted in Still, ed., *Urban America,* p. 14.

5. Quoted in *ibid.,* p. 30.

6. Quoted in Bridenbaugh, *Cities in Revolt,* p. 260.

7. Quoted in Jensen, *Maritime Commerce,* p. 3.

3.
All Sorts of Opinions:
Colonial Urban Society and Politics

The Puritans, for all their sense of special mission, were English to the core. In Puritan culture, "about ninety per cent of the intellectual life, scientific knowledge, morality, manners and customs, notions and prejudices, was that of all Englishmen."[1] The English influence was predominant in Boston and about as obvious in Newport, Philadelphia, Charleston, and the smaller Chesapeake towns.

But the English colonies were not settled entirely by Englishmen, nor were all colonists of one or even two or three faiths. Philadelphia, partly because of William Penn's tolerance for other religious groups and practices, contained Welsh, Swiss, and Germans, as well as Irish and Scotch-Irish. Charleston was settled mostly by English, many of whom came from Barbados with their slaves. But the growing southern city was also a haven for Huguenots (persecuted French Protestants) and a prison for black African slaves, who composed about one-half of Charleston's population by 1700. By that time, in fact, Africans made up almost one-quarter of New York's population and about one-sixth of Boston's.

Scotch-Irish and German immigration rose sharply in the early eighteenth century, spilling into the backcountry and adding to the populations of many towns, especially Philadelphia and those in the middle colonies. In the 1720s and after, the new waves of immigration overran the defenses of New England communities against "strangers," and brought new cultural elements to an increasingly cosmopolitan colonial urban scene.

America's most cosmopolitan city earned its reputation early. New Amsterdam, settled by the Dutch, fell into English hands in 1664. Though Englishmen made up only about a fifth of the city's population, they soon controlled most of the commercial activity. New York contained no fewer than five major ethnic and nationality groups: Dutch, English, French (mostly Huguenots), Africans, and Jews.

A series of European wars in the late sixteenth and early seventeenth centuries reverberated in the colonies, disrupting international trade and communications and bringing new residents to the cities. Sailors, refugees from the backcountry, runaways from the contending armies, and the usual human flotsam and jetsam cast up by troubled seas congregated in the towns, especially on the already bustling waterfronts, and tried the patience and peace-keeping devices of the authorities.

All in all, colonial towns experienced rising populations and increasing demands on city services throughout the period before the Revolution, and by 1776 their populations were on the whole more varied in terms of nationality, ethnic background, and religious preference than were those in rural areas. The influx of new nationality groups into the English colonial towns resulted in an early form of American nativism: Even Benjamin Franklin complained about the unfortunate influence of Germans in Philadelphia. In a nation of immigrants, however, such notions would not become deeply rooted and perverse until the nineteenth century. America was a collection of many different peoples, and this fact was especially and unavoidably apparent in virtually all major colonial cities.

Social Structure

Europeans came to this country from highly organized and socially stratified societies, societies in which each person had a place in the social scheme and more often than not social position was handed down from generation to generation. Some doubtless emigrated to escape oppression and persecution in their homelands, but an organized society was considered a prerequisite for civilized life. A disorganized social system without lines of order and authority was a frightening, rather than a liberating, experience for the average European. The emphasis was on *order*—whether in social life or town building. The purpose was not innovation or invention, but the establishment of traditional and comfortable customs and forms in a new environment.

Land was divided in New England towns on the basis of a clear social hierarchy: The wealthier citizens and the minister received the largest and best plots. In the beginning, every family could count on some land, but some families got more than others, depending on their position in the community. This arrangement was not merely accepted, but actively sought: Indeed the founders hoped that it would become fixed and final—setting forth a stable and persistent social structure. Forces beyond the control of colonial leaders—not the least of which was an abundance of available land—defeated many of these intentions. But the New England town, like hundreds of towns throughout the colonies, was molded initially in the image of the European peasant village, where social positions were clear and lasting. The goal was social harmony and order, not growth and change.

Along the frontier, a rough equality prevailed. This was less a product of ideology, however, than of limited economic development. The most pressing challenge was survival, not the acquisition of great wealth. In the towns and villages, a greater distinction existed between those at the top and those at the bottom of the social and economic scale. Where wealth was measured largely in land, most persons could claim some worth in a semiagricultural environment. But in colonial cities the distinctions were often acute, with large numbers of people holding very little wealth or none at all.

A major characteristic of colonial urban society was the presence of an elite wealthy class which controlled a disproportionate amount of the community's resources. Generally, the larger the urban place, the more disproportionate the concentration of wealth and the larger the numbers of citizens without real property.

At the top of urban society were professional people and more successful merchants. Physicians varied widely in their skills, social prestige, and earnings, but lawyers generally held the most wealth in towns and cities. The merchants who dominated the waterfronts and who imported goods at wholesale did very well indeed as a group. Classified in contemporary parlance as the "better sort," these people had the financial resources to expand their own economic interests, dominate the councils of municipal government, and indulge their tastes in books, art, music, and the finer things of life. The "middling sort," or middle-ranking groups, included shopkeepers, skilled artisans who had their own businesses, mechanics who benefited from the chronic shortage of skilled and semiskilled labor in colonial towns, and those professionals and merchants who could not be truly considered among the elite. Those who belonged to the middle group were usually able to acquire some property and lead relatively comfortable lives, though their fortunes were more likely to fluctuate depending on the shifts in the general economic pattern. At the bottom of the social and economic scale, among the "inferior sort," were unskilled laborers (many of whom were frequently without regular employment), indentured servants, and slaves. These people were likely to own no property, and their lives were often given over to the struggle for survival. There were exceptions to this general scheme, such as schoolteachers, who were miserably paid and thus relegated to the lower economic ranks despite their education and skills.

As cities grew and commerce became the dominant feature of urban economic life, the gap between rich and poor tended to widen. James Henretta's comparison of tax lists in colonial Boston reveals that in 1687 the top 15 percent of the city's property owners controlled 52 percent of the taxable assets of the town, while the top 5 percent held more than a quarter of the wealth. At the same time, around 14 percent of the adult males of Boston neither held property nor were dependent on parents or others for sustenance. These people, often young men seeking better opportunities in the urban setting, were dependent on wages, rather than upon property or investments, to make their way in the world. By 1771 Boston's taxable wealth was even more concentrated: 15 percent of the property owners accounted for almost 66 percent of the wealth, with the top 5 percent controlling more than 44 percent of the city's taxable wealth. And the nondependent, propertyless wage earners had increased from 14 percent of the adult male population in 1687 to 29 percent in 1771.[2] The trends toward a greater concentration of wealth at the top of the social and economic scale, an increase in the numbers of propertyless wage earners, and the relatively declining position of the middle-ranking economic groups (artisans, shopkeepers, and traders) over this 85-year period in Boston were reflected in virtually all the major colonial cities, despite the general prosperity of these groups.

In 1770 the top 10 percent of the population with taxable assets accounted for about half the wealth in Portsmouth, 40 percent in Newburyport, 44 percent in Albany, New York, 57 percent in Boston, and about 62 percent in Charleston. About a tenth of the households with taxable assets in Philadelphia controlled almost 90 percent of the taxable property, reflecting "a pyramid of wealth in which about 500 men guided the town's economic life."[3] The proportion of propertyless workers was considerably higher in the towns and cities than it was in the rural areas or small villages, reaching about 65 percent of the population in Charleston if black slaves are included in the figures.

There was nothing particularly unusual about this inequality in the distribution of wealth when it is compared with European patterns. But the possibility that New World opportunities would be limited to only a few disturbed a number of colonists and was perhaps one of the main reasons for the belief of Thomas Jefferson and others that only a rural society could foster and preserve a roughly equal balance of economic resources and political power among the general population.

In America, however, the concentrated wealth of the cities was not—as it was in Europe—confined largely to a permanent and closed aristocracy. A significant number, perhaps one-third to two-fifths, of the merchants in pre-Revolutionary New York City, according to Jackson Turner Main, were "self-made men" who rose to their positions from lower rungs on the social and economic ladder.[4] Room at the top did apparently exist for the lucky or especially enterprising, and people who could learn a trade stood a good chance of making a comfortable living. Whereas family status was the key in most of Europe, wealth opened virtually all doors in colonial America. It was possible, then, for artisans to become merchants, or even for modest farmers to become lawyers. The social hierarchy in America separated the rich from the poor, but the rungs of the ladder were not so far apart as they were in the Old World, and it was a ladder upon which people could move up or down.

Class distinctions in America grew more obvious in the later colonial years. As commerce, and later industry, played a larger and larger role in the urban and national economy, those persons and groups with the greatest financial resources were able to take advantage of new opportunities and thus consolidate their positions high in the social hierarchy.

Commercial success was often due to personal connections and access to financing and investment opportunities. Because of their favored position, those in the mercantile elite had an advantage to begin with, and it was one they exploited. And the members of the "better sort" also tended to dominate the policy-making process, especially in the larger cities. As Henretta observed of Boston, "All of the important offices of the town government . . . were lodged firmly in the hands of a broad elite, entry into which was conditioned by commercial achievement and family background."[5] In New York, too, where the highest tenth of the taxpayers in the early eighteenth century controlled 47 percent of the assessed wealth, political power was heavily concentrated, the rich holding office and the wealthiest individuals holding the most important positions.

As smaller towns grew into large cities, family association gave way to wealth as the bridge to success, and power and property became more concentrated in the hands of a relatively smaller percentage of the total urban population. These trends were first evidenced in the larger eastern ports, but they were repeated in the developing cities of the urban frontier and among the rising commercial towns of the interior, and were in fact dominant features in the North American urbanization process. The story of urban America was from an early date the story of the rich and the poor, the haves and the have-nots, seeking survival and opportunity in an ever more complex, demanding, and socially stratified society. The wealthy sometimes succeeded in winning the English merchant's goal of a country estate, and they also built stately town houses on the crowded residential streets of colonial towns. But the social distance between them and the rest of the population was widening, and their physical proximity to the middle and lower classes of the population would also vanish as new technologies permitted the growth of elite residential enclaves in the nineteenth century. What distinguished American society from that of Europe was not the lack of a class structure, but the greater prospect that those lower on the socioeconomic scale could rise.

Family, Church, and Tavern

The seventeenth and eighteenth century American city was a densely settled place, where people and institutions were located close together. The most important social institution was the family. Taken pretty much for granted, the family has only recently become the focus of serious historical study. This research has revealed that families in colonial America were basically *nuclear*. That is, they consisted of a married couple and their children, and perhaps a grandparent or other relative, very much like families of today. Kinship ties were very important and very strong, but extended kinship groups were rarely assembled under one roof in a single household.

The family was the basic unit of society throughout the colonies, but its importance was perhaps especially stressed in New England, where the preservation of the social order hinged on the lines of authority within families and between families and magistrates and the church. In New England, the family, not the isolated individual, was the chief constituent element of the town. Across the country, the family was a center for discipline and for the inculcation of social norms and religious values—and, in an age when residence and workplace were usually one and the same, it was also an institution for vocational training. While families were essentially nuclear, they also served a broad range of social purposes, from nurturing young apprentices who were learning a trade with a family member to housing and caring for indentured servants and keeping the elderly and indigent at public expense. In towns and rural areas, the family became a particularly important institution among black slaves, as they faced the harsh realities of a strange and cruel condition.

The large city doubtless placed great pressures on the family. Movement from place to place, economic dislocations, the early entry of children into the labor market, and eventually the separation of home and workplace were characteristically urban conditions that challenged family stability and authority. But the family was nevertheless fundamental to colonial urban society as it was in the countryside, and it was perhaps especially important for persons accustomed to a stable corporate society who found themselves in a new, and less stable, social environment.

The church was perhaps second only to the family as an important social institution, certainly in New England. Established churches had been for so long an accepted part of the institutional fabric of Europe—mainstays of the social order, allied closely with the monarchy—that the colonists naturally transported the institution, and the idea that religion is a handmaiden of government, to the New World. Various forms of Protestantism dominated colonial America. The Congregational church of New England was, indeed, an established church, supported by all taxpayers under law in parts of the region until the early nineteenth century. Presbyterianism in several forms was prevalent in the middle colonies. Also in the middle colonies were the Quakers, whose Pennsylvania colony welcomed an unusual diversity of religious persuasions. In the South, the Church of England was most influential—certainly in the port cities—though it was also active elsewhere by the eighteenth century. Roman Catholics (especially in Maryland and Louisiana), and Jews (who migrated to New York and other areas), Baptists, and religious dissenters like the followers of Roger Williams added considerably to the pattern of religious diversity.

The church's influence was apparent in the physical layout of the city. The meetinghouse was often the real and symbolic center of the New England town, a place where the congregation received the word of God and accomplished much town business as well. When new communities were formed, whether in a new territory or on the periphery of established towns, a minister and a congregation usually composed the core around which other settlers gathered. When a new church was erected in Boston to challenge the authority of the historic First Church, the very structure of the city seemed to shift along with the changes in religious sentiment and affiliation. And, of course, the Spanish towns were planned from the beginning to highlight the church's role in the community; the church building was either a centerpiece or a dominant architectural feature of the city structure. The spires of the colonial churches framed the skylines of most towns and cities, as the institutions themselves seemed to frame the lives of the inhabitants.

Anything resembling an established church was doomed to failure in America. The New England Congregationalists resisted the influx of Quakers, Baptists, Anglicans, and free-thinkers into their midst, but to no avail. New migrations of Scotch-Irish, Irish, and Germans brought new groups and beliefs to the colonies, and single denominations sometimes splintered into different sects and congregations. The religious impulse rose and fell from time to time and from place to place, and often existed apart from the established, institutionalized churches. The Great Awakening of the 1730s and 1740s swept over much of the country, from New England to the southern colonies. A number of itinerant ministers, like the English revivalist George Whitefield, who first arrived in America in 1739, offered salvation in exchange for repentance and fired an outpouring of religious enthusiasm across the colonies. Speaking in towns and cities as well as in rural hamlets, the preachers sometimes threatened the institutionalized church, casting doubt on unrepentant ministers and de-emphasizing the importance of denominational lines. Whitefield conducted a number of revival campaigns in North America, speaking in Savannah as well as in Boston. His oratory was powerful enough to sway even the cosmopolitan and urbane Benjamin Franklin to contribute a few coins to the cause: "And he finish'd so admirably," Franklin recalled, "that I empty'd my pockets wholly into the collector's dish, gold and all."[6]

Among other things, the Awakening brought new people into the Protestant fold, fragmented existing churches, prompted the founding of a variety of colleges and schools to serve the various sects, and offered perhaps the most significant shared experience in the colonies—encompassing alike rich and poor, rural and urban—prior to the Revolution. Urban society, for all its comparative sophistication and worldliness, was perennially susceptible to the call of "pure" religion, and the revivalists constantly frequented the cities for the very simple reason that they could reach the most people there.

Even the Great Awakening did not alter one important fact, however: The majority of colonists were not affiliated with any church. As New York's governor wrote in 1687, "of all sorts of opinions there are some and the most part of none at all."[7] Church membership was declining in New England by the last half of the seventeenth century, and many people in the middle colonies and the south had apparently never been touched with religious piety. The church remained a prominent, even essential, social institution, but it was not the only one. And for many urban colonists, certainly as the colonial era unfolded, the tavern became a much more central part of their lives than any organized church.

Taverns, inns, and coffee houses were usually places of great activity, where people gathered to exchange information, read and discuss the latest news from abroad, do business, find employment, hold auctions, celebrate special occasions, and generally enjoy social intercourse with their fellows. Taverns served a varied clientele, from rough sailors and vagabonds to ships' captains and leading merchants. Identified by the colorful names inscribed on shingles or plaques at the door, taverns were indisputably the major social institutions along the waterfront. The smells of rope, canvas, tar, pitch, a salt sea, and the grog and ale served in the taverns were characteristic of the wharf from Boston to Savannah. The arrival of a ship fresh from Liverpool with newspapers and mail aboard was a particularly significant event, bringing residents and newcomers alike into "The Wild Boar," the "Black Horse," or "The Green Dragon."

Some taverns and inns appealed especially to the colonial urban elite, offering sumptuous banquets and entertainment. Tavern shows of a less sophisticated sort—and the inevitable cock fights, ninepins, and billiards—attracted the rougher elements of the port cities, while coffee houses swarmed with assemblymen and politicians in Philadelphia, Williamsburg, and other government centers. New York boasted a fairly sophisticated social life even at this early date, and it revolved around the taverns. One New Yorker complained in 1734 of the "Luxury and Profuseness" characteristic of these places: "We strive who shall have the most Dishes of Meat at his Table, and in the best Order; who shall drink the richest Wine, who shall wear the most costly apparell."[8] Two Philadelphia establishments, the London Coffee House (opened in 1754) and the City Tavern (1773), were founded by merchants, and attendance at their customary midday gatherings evolved into a major habit of the entire commercial community. Some coffee houses developed quickly into taverns and inns, offering lodging as well as food and drink.

Inland towns had their taverns too, serving local residents and travelers who passed through by coach. Some cities, like Boston (where the first tavern was opened in 1634), took special pains to regulate these places and thus control or prohibit gambling, prostitution, brawls, and other vices and unseemly pursuits. But regulation was very difficult in the larger towns, and new taverns and inns kept appearing. They were not confined to towns, but they were characteristic urban institutions—places of communication, entertainment, social contact, bargaining, and variety. They existed by the scores and even hundreds in the largest cities, and their role remained an essential part of urban life.

Family, church, and tavern were the principal institutions in a developing colonial urban society that was rapidly distinguishing itself from the habits, customs, and social life in the countryside. And urban society already manifested certain common problems: poverty, crime and violence, moral transgression, and a fear of social disorder. The appearance of these problems was a sign of the maturation of urban society, as it was also a reflection of that society's fragility as America approached the era of political revolution.

Poverty and Social Disorder

America was a land of considerable opportunity, but for most people not a land of great riches. Subsistence farmers on the poor soils of the northern backcountry eked out a living, while unskilled laborers in the towns often went without work. One historian, Jackson Turner Main, estimates that around the time of the Revolution, about one-fifth of the total white population and some 40 percent of blacks could be classified as poor even by the standards prevailing at the time.[9] Most poor people lived in rural areas, but the towns and cities had their share. "In 1784," according to Raymond A. Mohl, "when New York City's population totaled about 12,000, one newspaper estimated that more than 1,000 families were supported by private and public charity."[10]

The English Poor Law of 1601 required that local communities support impoverished residents through taxation, and it was this legislation that set the context for colonial poor relief. In New England, most efforts went toward preventing poor people from settling down in the first place, thus alleviating any potential burden on the towns. Most towns actually restricted settlers to persons of some means, usually landowners. "Strangers" were watched closely and forced to move on lest they become a charge on the community. It was common practice in the northern colonies to require newcomers to post bond or otherwise prove their worth before they were allowed to establish residence. The great influx of people into Boston and other northern communities in the early eighteenth century made such measures impracticable, however, and most colonial cities were forced by that time to make some provision for the poverty stricken.

Poor people, especially the sick and elderly, were often kept in private homes at public expense. In other cases, outdoor relief—aid provided for the needy within their own homes—was provided. Assistance consisted of everything from cash grants to firewood, food, clothing, and medical care—such as it was. Poorhouses were erected in several cities to care for the indigent, and these were the first formal institutions established in this country to aid the poor. Taxes to support poor relief rose in virtually every city, but forms of charity differed from place to place. Boston was particularly notable for its efforts to care for paupers and other needy people. Charleston, on the other hand, had no public programs at all during the seventeenth century and continued to rely mostly on private—that is, largely church-oriented—benevolence well into the eighteenth. New York also fell behind most of the major towns in adequate provision for the indigent, though its tax rates increased significantly and most of the small municipal budget was devoted to poor relief. In 1736, a "Poor House, Work House, and House of Correction" was finally opened to meet a mounting need, and a new and larger facility was built in 1796.

Charity, in the colonial era as in later periods, carried a price for the beneficiaries as well as the benefactors. In New York recipients of relief were required to wear large colorful badges on their clothing as a condition of assistance. Colonists tended to attribute the condition of poverty to moral depravity or laziness, rather than simply to a lack of resources. Religious groups saw salvation as an ultimate solution to this worldly problem, and private and public agencies alike employed relief as a tool to instill proper habits and behavior among their charges. Then, as now, charity was criticized by some for destroying the incentive of people to make their own way in the world. As Raymond Mohl concludes in his studies of New York, "few proposals aimed at solving the social and economic problems of the urban environment; most programs concentrated on purging the poor of their supposed vices."[11] Nevertheless, virtually all colonial towns and cities had accepted a responsibility to provide for the indigent by the time of the Revolution—a responsibility that would grow as time progressed.

Those citizens who saw poverty as a reflection of the deterioration of social discipline and moral values had other ominous signs to worry them. Brawls became increasingly frequent, especially along the hectic waterfront, as the volume of trade rose and immigration swelled colonial urban populations. Drunkenness was also common and was made almost inevitable by the proliferation of taverns and grog shops and the rising number of sailors. Crimes ranging from theft to assault and even murder were on the increase as well, creating the necessity for some official action. Colonial cities had nothing resembling uniformed, professional police forces; a night watch and a few constables were the general rule. Charleston authorities were more attentive to the maintenance of social order because of the perceived threat of slave revolt, but even here law enforcement was informal and inefficient by twentieth-century standards. The problems of colonial cities were often less severe than those in the larger European ports and capitals, where an established "criminal element" flourished in fetid slums, but they were nevertheless troubling and growing more prevalent.

Certainly by Puritan standards, moral depravity was rampant by the eighteenth century. John Winthrop's dream of a Godly commonwealth was afflicted by reality from the beginning, but by 1750 the spirit of commerce and worldly pursuits prevailed in Boston. A hundred years later, Boston was only slightly less noted than New York for its bawdyhouses, and some women even solicited on the streets. Madams usually presided over their flocks near the swirling waterfront, catering to sailors, tradesmen, soldiers, and on occasion members of the gentry. Groups of angry citizens sometimes reacted violently against these blights on civic virtue—and the prospect of supporting illegitimate children with public funds—by burning the infamous houses or sending the prostitutes out of town. But it was a losing effort.

In the eighteenth century, especially, as the transient populations of colonial cities mounted, prostitution, gaming, drunkenness, and rowdy behavior became all too familiar.

American cities were born in the search for order as well as for opportunity, and it was only natural that colonists feared the threat of disorder and the breakdown of social norms. Stable communities remained a prerequisite for survival. Mob action was not uncommon, whether aimed at thieves, drunken rowdies, or prostitutes. As the Revolution approached, the colonial resentment against British troops grew much more explicit as well. But fears of disorder were starkly revealed in the harsh repression of blacks, both slave and free. A special system for controlling slaves developed fairly early in the colonies. In the South slave patrols, composed of hired or volunteer whites, kept a watch for runaways and prohibited gatherings of blacks. Elaborate slave codes were adopted to provide legal sanction for these measures.

When conspiracies among blacks were suspected, the reaction could be swift and brutal. A presumed "Negro conspiracy" in New York City led to harsh repression in 1741: Thirteen blacks were burned at the stake, eight were hanged, and seventy-one were sent from the colony. This degree of brutality was not frequent, but the fact that such incidents occurred at all indicated that the fear of black revolt pervaded both cities and rural areas—North and South—that contained substantial numbers of blacks.

The first century and a half of English settlement in North America produced a remarkably diverse and mature society very much on the European model. Urban social life was especially sophisticated, open to new ideas, and in touch with the rest of the world—certainly when compared with rural American social life. Colonial society was not constrained by entrenched monarchy or aristocracy, even though class distinctions did emerge very early, and thus America indeed offered more possibilities so far as average people were concerned. It was obvious by 1770 that the colonies were no longer mere appendages of the mother country but had developed a social life and political community of their own.

Political Community

The traditional role of town government in Europe was shaped by two major objectives: surviving economically and keeping things as they were. Virtually all sixteenth- and seventeenth-century towns were dependent on agriculture—an uncertain pursuit even in the best of times—and uncertainty led to caution in the conduct of public affairs. The survival of the community as a whole, rather than of particular individuals, and the maintenance of familiar and accepted patterns of farming and living were paramount concerns. Many Old World towns were governed by time-honored and unquestioned feudal traditions, and their lives were pervaded by the peasants' deep-rooted fatalism. The hope was for stability, continuity, and social order.

English towns were similar in many ways to those on the Continent. Under charter from the Crown, most towns had considerable authority and broad jurisdiction over their own affairs. Local governments focused especially on the regulation of trade, and such efforts ranged from establishing consistent weights and measures to licensing tradesmen and even to setting prices and wages. These regulations often benefited consumers, but the main goal was to protect local merchants from unfair competition. Indeed, landed gentry and commercial interests dominated local affairs. English towns were obviously not, in this period, centers for free-wheeling capitalism. Commerce, like other aspects of town life, was perceived in communal terms, and stability and continuity far outweighed economic growth as a motive for local policy.

As the eighteenth century opened, the great majority of English towns were governed by "closed" municipal corporations, small groups of relatively prominent and well-to-do people who generally served for life as leaders of the town and had the authority to choose their own successors. Because voting was limited to persons who were active in local commerce or paid taxes or fees to the town, participation of most citizens in local decisions was constricted. In effect, town government was closed to all except a select few—primarily those who were engaged in commercial activity.

Settlers in the New World did not set out to abolish these arrangements. In fact, they were careful to reinforce many of them at the first opportunity. Patterns of land division in New England were usually combinations of communal arrangements and limited private ownership (limited in the sense that property rights were dependent on "proper" use of the land and continued residence in the town). In the beginning, the elimination of conflict and disorder was at least as important as the just resolution of disputes. Also, town leaders were generally drawn from the ranks of the most prominent citizens. In short, the whole structure and process of colonial town government was initially designed to reinforce traditional patterns and goals.

There were important differences, however, in decision-making patterns and purposes between European towns and those in the colonies, and these differences became more pronounced with time. Some differences were products of conscious design, especially as conditions in the New World stabilized and settlers realized the opportunities for innovation, while others proceeded simply from the nature of things (the absence of an entrenched nobility, for example, or the ready availability of land). In general, political participation was much more open to the general populace in the New World than it was in England or on the Continent, and the notion of local self-government was greatly advanced in the colonies. The New England town experience was not entirely typical, but it reflects many of the initial purposes and political transformations that existed in the colonies as a whole.

The New England town differed from its counterparts in England and elsewhere in the New World in several important respects. For one thing, the overarching purpose of both local and provincial government in New England in the early seventeenth century was not merely to regulate trade or to manage the status quo but to carry out the will of God. In the Puritan theocracy, the magistrates were elected and were prohibited from serving also as ministers of the church, but they derived their authority ultimately from God. Theoretically, they could be removed (outside the electoral process) only if they endangered the souls of the citizenry. Though these arrangements were complex, magistrates and ministers did share a common cause, and the church—or, more properly, the individual autonomous congregations—lay at the heart of the community and determined much social and economic policy. Even though church members were a minority of the populations of many New England towns, most of the political leaders were drawn from their number, and general taxes were levied on the entire population to support the church (a practice that persisted into the early nineteenth century in Massachusetts and Connecticut).

New England authorities were thus primarily concerned with matters of public conduct, moral behavior, and public health and safety, rather than with economic regulation. In this, they also differed significantly from most towns in England and elsewhere in the colonies. In 1701, for example, less than a tenth of Boston's ordinances concerned trade regulation; most dealt with preserving the public welfare in a Christian context.

The Puritan community was *consensual;* that is, it was established on grounds that were agreed upon in advance by the inhabitants. The New England town's political legitimacy thus derived both from God and from the "consent" of the governed, and the town was considered, in a secular sense, to be the source of its own authority. The *covenant* was a contract binding town members to certain basic premises and procedures in the conduct of local affairs. It was a means of eliciting the allegiance of all individuals to the will of the group and to the procedures through which this will was determined and carried out. New inhabitants were often asked to enter into the town covenant before they could assume the status of citizens and participate in town affairs (to the extent, at least, that their station entitled them) or even hold land. The covenant was one way to achieve political and social stability and to control membership in the community.

The covenant played a less-important role in local government as time passed. The charter from colonial, and later from state, authorities was the real legal basis for municipal powers. But covenants of one form or another continued to play an important role in American political life, and aspects of the consensual political community were periodically manifested in perhaps the best-known example of local government in America—the New England town meeting.

The inhabitants of many New England towns gathered at least once a year for town meeting. Usually seated in the hard pews of the meetinghouse, the citizens elected their selectmen and a variety of lesser officials. They also discussed town policies, voiced complaints about particular problems, and debated issues ranging from the use of common lands to the annexation of surrounding territory. In the early seventeenth century, the substance of these meetings was not nearly as democratic and open as would be the case a century or so later. Deference to authority and the desire to avoid conflict were self-imposed restraints that ensured a good deal of stability and continuity. But the town meeting was, even in the beginning, a far different means of governing than had existed in the mother country.

The local political community in the American colonies, whether or not it was based on a covenant, was typically *unitary*. Executive, legislative, and judicial powers were all normally held by the city authorities. A variety of political constituencies vying for advantage had not yet appeared in most places, and the separation of powers did not emerge on the local scene until the eighteenth and nineteenth centuries. Politics, like the spatial form of most colonial towns, was compact and unified. As the towns grew larger, as new districts were added or created, as people developed attachments for particular areas or activities, and as religious commitments were less widely shared, political unity also began to evaporate. As communities grew more complex and less uniform in social composition and spatial arrangement, politics followed suit. In this case, too, New England provides a very good example.

Dedham, Massachusetts, was established, in the words of one historian, as a "Christian Utopian Closed Corporate Community," with a unitary and stable political structure based on a fear of disorder, deference to the wisdom of elected leaders, and a belief in the "one true way."[12] Within a generation, all of this began to change. By 1662 fully half of the adult males did not belong to the church, a trend that continued and undermined political unity and commitment to the original destiny of the town. By the end of the seventeenth century, the covenant was no longer enforced. And the settlement was no longer compact. The larger population, made up of new settlers and the children of the original inhabitants, began to group in various sections of the community and demanded some political authority based on these new subunits. As a result, precincts were established that remained part of Dedham but had their own identity. This spatial fragmentation reflected social and religious fractures, and the consensual nature of the community (and the unitary political system) was replaced by a more active and contentious brand of democratic politics, necessary to the resolution of differences among various groups and sections of the town. In addition, the amount of land became insufficient for the increased population, leading to growing numbers of nonpropertied persons and the emergence of a clear elite group.

These transitions were experienced, in one degree or another, throughout New England. Usually, the process was gradual; there was no sudden and dramatic collapse of organic unity into pluralistic conflict. In many communities, in fact, citizens went to great lengths to preserve the appearance—if not the reality—of stability and continuity. But changes occurred nevertheless. By the 1650s religion was becoming less important as a major governmental concern. In the early years of the decade, the town and provincial governments moved from Boston's meetinghouse to a new Town House, signifying an increasing separation of church and state that John Winthrop and the founders would have found most troubling.

As congregations split and proliferated and as the proportion of church members in the population declined, politics became at once more secular and more important as a unifying force in the community—or at least as the main arena for resolving disputes and carrying out the will and aspirations of the citizens. Political decisions touched the lives of everyone and could not in any event have been ignored. The church remained an important institution to be sure, but the underlying consensus of the Puritan fathers, shaped by religious piety and the notion of a single, unified community, began to wane as piety declined and as communities grew, new towns sprang up, and new immigrants with different religious persuasions arrived. Local governments were still concerned with noneconomic matters, with a broadly defined notion of the public welfare, but political action was concentrated less on the path to heaven than on the byways of this world.

Religion was never so important a driving force for settlement in those colonies outside New England, but a trend away from a unitary political community existed throughout America. However, towns differed considerably from section to section in their political arrangements. New England towns, as we have seen, were often established out of a perfectionist religious outlook, enjoyed a large measure of political autonomy, did not have formal charters of incorporation, and focused much of their policy on noneconomic matters, especially public welfare and behavior. In contrast, most other colonial towns and cities were founded out of a quite worldly desire for economic opportunity and a better life; their governments were much more concerned with economic than with social regulations; and while they defended their rights and prerogatives jealously, many had never been very free of outside influence and control.

The English model of municipal incorporation was especially prominent in the middle colonies. Of fourteen municipal corporations in America in 1750, for example, ten were located in Pennsylvania, New Jersey, and New York. There were two basic forms: the closed corporation and the open corporation. In the closed corporation the principal municipal officials—usually a mayor, a recorder, and aldermen—exercised a wide range of powers and could perpetuate themselves through long terms and through their right to appoint successors. Open corporations often possessed similar powers, but officials were periodically elected by "freemen" (property owners). New York City was governed by an open corporation, and annual elections were held for aldermen and councilmen. Philadelphia, on the other hand, maintained a closed corporate government, the members of which guarded their prerogatives closely and resisted movements toward popular election. The Pennsylvania assembly made several efforts to modify this often unresponsive and inefficient arrangement by establishing special-purpose boards whose members were elected and by creating additional elected positions (such as tax assessor and commissioner) outside of the corporation. By the time of the Revolution, although the Philadelphia corporation continued, many of its original powers were gone and its jurisdiction had been curtailed.

The British encouraged the exercise of broad powers by local governments. Presumably, localities would thus be in a better position to promote settlement and control trade. But local autonomy barely existed for some cities, and in any event it was difficult to maintain as provincial governments grew stronger. In Charleston, for example, the board of commissioners was appointed by the South Carolina legislature and was responsible to that body. As a result, one of the largest cities in the colonies was virtually without local authority or initiative for much of the colonial period. One of the results of this situation was a comparatively low level of municipal services in Charleston. Other cities, like New York, were underrepresented in colonial assemblies.

Perhaps the main difference in local politics between England and America was the wider political participation which prevailed in the colonies.

While only tradesmen and certain taxpayers voted in the English municipal corporation, the franchise was generally extended throughout the colonies—certainly by the late seventeenth century—to all freeholders. Since land was readily available in the New World (indeed, land ownership was sometimes required as a condition of residency in some New England towns), the majority of adult males could qualify to vote, even in closed-corporation cities like Philadelphia, Williamsburg, and Annapolis.

The majority of people in colonial towns, however, could not vote. The franchise was extended, at best, only to adult male property owners, who constituted perhaps a fifth of the total population. And exercise of the franchise was not automatically a solution for all ills or a guarantee of social or political change. In New York City, entrenched local officials encouraged a liberal use of the franchise to demonstrate their broad popular support, and thus retain their positions. As in our own day, voting was often a means of organizing political support and even of social control.

Political participation and leadership patterns differed by region and by period and also according to the size and type of town. Local political practices and situations were related to the size of the population and its economic roles and functions. In New England, frontier towns and villages often reflected very little concentration of economic and political power and a high degree of political participation. Medium-sized cities and secondary market towns were characterized by a greater concentration of wealth, a lower level of political participation, and the importance of family affiliation and economic position in office holding. In the largest cities like Boston, wealth and political power were highly concentrated, and it was here that the greatest number of provincial officials and decision makers could be found. On the other hand, the higher mobility rates in the larger centers meant that family affiliation was apparently less important than it was in many smaller places. In general, the larger the city, the smaller the proportion of the population to vote or hold public office, and the more likely that leadership positions would be occupied by persons of economic means and social prominence and that local citizens would be among the most influential provincial authorities.

Most of the Old World nation-states envisioned the re-creation in America of traditional European social and political forms, and to a large degree they were not disappointed at the beginning. Urban settlement was the most efficient way of organizing and exploiting the potential of the colonies—from the mercantilist perspective—and broad local authority was supposed to be used to carry out these purposes. Very tight controls over trade were especially needed in regions so far removed from the seats of monarchical authority. Inevitably, colonial towns and cities did exercise the authority they had, but increasingly for the purpose not of securing a new continent for the mother country, but rather of fulfilling their own best interests—interests that were, by the mid-eighteenth century, perceived in the context of the New World, not the Old.

The strict mercantile controls loosened with time, and communities developed their own identities and aspirations that were reflected, and indeed shaped, in their political activities and public policies. In the early and mid-eighteenth century most colonial governments recognized the crucial importance of solving a variety of problems attendant on growth, and responded in provisions for utilities, services, and protection of the public safety and welfare. This concern for local problems, this desire to maintain local authority and prerogatives, was eventually refashioned—not into a bulwark of British colonialism, but into a foundation for political revolution.

Notes

1. Perry Miller and Thomas H. Johnson, eds., "Introduction," *The Puritans: A Sourcebook of Their Writings*, 2 vols., rev. ed. (New York: Harper & Row, 1963), I, 7.

2. James A. Henretta, "Economic Development and Social Structure in Colonial Boston," *William and Mary Quarterly*, 22 (January 1965), 75–92.

3. Sam Bass Warner, Jr., *The Private City: Philadelphia in Three Periods of Its Growth* (Philadelphia: University of Pennsylvania Press, 1968), p. 9. Figures on Philadelphia are taken from this source, while those on the other cities are taken from Jackson Turner Main, *The Social Structure of Revolutionary America* (Princeton, N.J.: Princeton University Press, 1965), pp. 35–36.

4. See *The Social Structure of Revolutionary America*.

5. Henretta, "Economic Development and Social Structure," p. 84.

6. Benjamin Franklin, *Autobiography*, rev. ed. (New York: Macmillan, 1962), p. 102.

7. See Thomas J. Archdeacon, *New York City, 1664–1710: Conquest and Change* (Ithaca, N.Y.: Cornell University Press, 1976), p. 33.

8. Quoted in Carl Bridenbaugh, *Cities in the Wilderness: Urban Life in America, 1625-1724* (New York: Ronald Press, 1938), p. 427.

9. Main, *The Social Structure of Revolutionary America*, pp. 271–272.

10. Raymond A. Mohl, "Poverty in Early America, a Reappraisal: The Case of Eighteenth-Century New York City," *New York History*, 50 (January 1969), 5–27.

11. *Ibid.*, p. 6.

12. Information on Dedham is taken from Kenneth A. Lockridge, *A New England Town; the First Hundred Years: Dedham, Massachusetts, 1636–1736* (New York: W. W. Norton and Company, 1970), pp. 16–17.

4.
Maturing Cities

The Puritans reveled in their chance to create a more perfect community in a new land. Their mission was also, of course, a heavy duty. The stakes were high, and the struggle for survival was difficult. But as the first rude houses appeared along the rough streets that etched the fragile peninsula of Boston, the drama of New World settlement was revealed. A simple but important fact about American towns and cities was that they were very new, established in a virgin land.

For the first several generations, American urban places were quite primitive by European standards—in appearance as well as in their social and economic life. The disadvantages of newness were often obvious. But there were advantages too. The colonists had an opportunity to transplant the best features of an established civilization to a new environment and to experiment with untried ideas. Though it was a good time and place for utopian schemes, the colonists' first concern was to tame the wilderness and build civilized communities in the European mold. Thus, most early American towns and cities did not rise in a spirit of experimentation and invention. When lives and fortunes were at stake, the tried and true, the familiar and accepted, were always the first choice. But necessity was the mother of innovation in many instances, and even traditional forms and practices often assumed new guises in the different environment of the colonies.

In the process, colonial towns not only became larger, but they matured and developed economically, socially, culturally, and physically. Rude outposts were often transformed into miniature models of large English colonial cities, with museums, libraries, fancy shops and taverns, theaters, elaborate residences—and a host of urban problems, from fire and disease to housing shortages and waterfront brawls. These changes were important reflections of the evolution of clusters into market places, just as concentrations of capital and the rise of an urban working class signaled the ascendancy of commerce and presaged the industrial era yet to come.

Problems and Responses

Colonial and European cities had one major feature in common: They all experienced the problems endemic to urban places. Fire and disease were paramount problems, followed closely by crime and disorder, economic poverty, and inadequate streets and transportation. Unlike farms, cities could not easily exist in an organic balance with nature; adequate water and food supplies had to be imported in many instances from the surrounding region, and refuse had to be disposed of somehow. The denseness of the compact towns, so important to defense or spiritual regeneration, was also the cause of many problems. Colonial responses to these problems revealed a growing urban maturity in the New World and the extent to which American urban places were very much a part of the European heritage.

No danger was more frightening in colonial cities than fire. An errant spark from a lantern, a fireplace, or a spent match was all it took. The blaze could build instantly, growing out of control almost as it began, quickly consuming buildings and, if carried on a strong wind, whole blocks of buildings. The work of building new cities in the wilderness was, in this sense, a hostage of natural forces very difficult to contain.

Very severe fires struck Boston in 1676, 1679, and 1711, and the city experienced the worst conflagration of the entire colonial era in 1760. The very core of the town—some four hundred structures—was destroyed. The holocaust was so terrible that it seemed a judgment of God upon the town. The wooden buildings of Charleston were also ripe for disaster. Much of that city was devastated by fire in 1731, and again in 1740 when more than three hundred dwellings and a number of other buildings were consumed. Southern seacoast towns were also prey to other natural forces, like the hurricane of 1752, which severely damaged Charleston. But virtually no colonial town or city escaped the ravages of fire, which was as necessary to life as it was dangerous.

The sudden violence of fire was feared perhaps only slightly more than the convulsive and fatal effects of epidemic disease. Cities were especially susceptible to waves of illness because their high concentrations of population facilitated the easy spread of germs from one person to another. Larger seaports were also in the mainstream of international and intercolonial commerce, which carried, along with trading goods, dangerous organisms from far-off places. Smallpox, cholera, and yellow fever were especially deadly, striking quickly and claiming victims seemingly at random from among the population. All colonial settlements had bouts with fatal sicknesses of one kind or another, but towns in the semitropical climate of the South were particularly vulnerable. Almost every urban family was victimized at some time by the major scourges, in addition to the threat posed by the high incidence of other maladies such as tuberculosis, influenza, and dysentery. The mortality rate among infants and young children was high, and any infectious illness was extremely difficult to deal with in urban places.

Large numbers of people congregating in a small area made fire and disease especially dangerous and likely and also apparently increased the occurrence of crime, disorder, and violence. The Puritans provided for such possibilities through a demanding faith and through the notion of the consensual community: Those who refused to abide by town regulations and standards could go elsewhere. But as towns grew and new immigrants arrived and communities were clearly no longer consensual, these methods of social control became less effective.

Most of the disorder in colonial cities consisted of drunkenness, waterfront brawling, and the rough behavior of seamen and transient laborers in any urban setting. The rate of more serious crimes—theft, assault, and murder—did apparently rise during the colonial period, especially in the most heavily populated centers. But crime was not measured in epidemic proportions. Perhaps equally important was the widespread public *anxiety* about crime and disorder in the fragile social setting of new communities. Such fears focused particularly on blacks and Indians, who were considered, along with seamen, as the elements most potentially disruptive of the public order.

Problems of poverty, poor housing, and inadequate streets were also evident on every hand, but they were no more severe in the colonies than in the Old World. We have already discussed the extent of poverty and the various efforts at poor relief in colonial towns. A perennial housing shortage drove real-estate prices up and denied decent, solid dwellings to many Americans even at this early point in our history. Streets were perhaps the most important public utility, but their condition was rudimentary at best in most colonial towns in the seventeenth century. Roads and streets were typically unpaved, and rainstorms quickly reduced them to impassable quagmires. Even in good weather, narrow thoroughfares became congested with pedestrians, horses, coaches, carts, and wagons, creating one of America's oldest urban traditions—the traffic jam.

Colonial cities moved to deal with many of these problems. In some cases, their public-policy responses were adequate by the standards of the time. In others, they were virtually ineffective. And as time passed, the need for better local governance and services grew. In the case of fire, town leaders realized that they could do only so much once a blaze got out of control. Water was often in short supply, and local governments acted to dig new wells and even bring in water from nearby sources. Adequate urban water supplies were, in fact, demanded as much for fire control as for use in drinking and washing. Some of the larger cities had quite modern fire-fighting equipment, sometimes more advanced than that of major European cities. And the volunteer fire company was an American urban innovation, tracing its origins to the Union Fire Company of Philadelphia, organized by Benjamin Franklin in 1736.

The most effective measures were preventive in nature. Fire regulations in Boston were especially stringent. Laws passed in 1638 and 1646 by the Massachusetts Bay government prohibited smoking outdoors to reduce the fire hazard, and curfew laws were adopted for the same purpose. Night watches were established primarily to alert the townspeople in case of fire, though they were also supposed to serve a limited law-enforcement function. Defective and dirty chimneys were the major cause of fire, and some cities required periodic chimney cleaning. To the extent possible, localities encouraged construction in brick and stone rather than in wood, though the high cost of the alternative materials precluded their consistent use. Generally, fire-prevention regulations were widely violated and were enforced most strictly just after serious fires had occurred, as towns were periodically reminded of their importance.

European towns and cities were not known for their cleanliness, and this situation was generally true in colonial cities also. Household garbage was routinely dumped out of windows into the streets, where pigs and dogs consumed some of it. Human wastes were put directly into the ground, occasionally entering drinking-water sources. Boston, New York, and Philadelphia, among other cities, outlawed garbage disposal in the public streets by the beginning of the eighteenth century. And municipalities attempted to provide sufficient clear water for drinking and washing. Philadelphia's system of public wells distributed throughout the city was particularly notable, while New York's water was notoriously noxious.

These urban problems were not unique to colonial cities but were experienced by European cities as well. As problems typical of urban life developed in colonial cities, colonists attempted to find solutions. Colonial responses to urban problems varied greatly.

The greatest breakthrough in dealing with communicable diseases during the colonial era was the introduction of inoculation against smallpox in the Boston epidemic of 1721. While inoculation proponents did not fully understand how the process worked, and while many people were understandably afraid of the strange procedure and refused to be inoculated, it did show results. Inoculation grew more and more popular and became an accepted way of combating smallpox in the fifteen years before the Revolution.

Nothing resembling an organized police force appeared during the colonial period. New England towns typically had at least one constable, but law enforcement in the modern sense was not really a part of his role. When more-or-less organized night watches did appear, their primary job was, as we noted earlier, to provide early warning of fires and disturbances. Consistent with the idea of the consensual and compact community, citizens were expected to rely upon one another in maintaining public order. When towns became cities, however, and personal relationships were no longer the close ties among neighbors and coreligionists but those that exist among strangers and different social groups, this was not a sufficient remedy.

Municipal ordinances did ban certain kinds of activities—such as working on the Sabbath and public drunkenness—in addition to obvious criminal offenses. But rarely was a system established to deal with transgressors, other than a general reliance on public pressure. A major exception was Charleston, where the presence of a large number of black slaves induced whites to provide not only a strict slave code but also special patrols and enforcement measures. This system was frequently lax in its actual operation, but it existed in the event of emergency. Likewise, Boston passed a very strict code in 1724 curtailing the rights of blacks and Indians. Generally, though, towns and cities failed to develop effective and consistent means of dealing with crime and disorder. And as the Revolution approached, the deep-seated colonial resistance to established armies and uniformed police forces (symbols of "foreign" domination), postponed innovations in law enforcement until the nineteenth century.

Cities varied quite a bit in their responses to urban problems. Boston was generally advanced in its services to its citizens; this attitude stemmed in part from the Puritan attention from the beginning to matters of the public welfare. Charleston, at the other end of the spectrum, had a very poor, and often nonexistent, record of public services.

In some respects, colonial cities tried to escape from the problems so typical of cities in the mother country. The first answer to poverty in America was quite simply to prevent the poor from settling in the first place. But as solutions of this sort obviously failed, most towns and cities accepted their responsibilities, at least as they were perceived at the time in the light of English experience and tradition. For example, regulating trade, maintaining order, and dealing with natural disasters like fire and disease were established and accepted roles for municipal authority. Poverty had to be dealt with, though generally in a moralistic and condescending fashion. Building streets and providing adequate water supplies were perceived as both public and private responsibilities, with different cities emphasizing one approach or the other. Housing, however, was not considered a matter of public policy, except to the extent that poor housing might endanger other people's property.

The Changing Face of Colonial Cities

The sound of the hammer resounded in growing cities. As commercial uses crowded along the waterfront, many merchants and some artisans moved to higher, quieter ground. Though still close to waterfront activity, these residential areas were a beginning step in the separation of work and residence. While the arrangement of a shop in front, with living quarters located behind or above the shop, was characteristic of the coastal cities, residential neighborhoods appeared as outward manifestations of economic prosperity and urbanization.

The care, engineering, and expense usually associated with the building of public and religious structures were now applied to residential units. The use of more expensive and more permanent building materials affords a good example of the growing prosperity in the seacoast cities and also indicates the concerns over fire, health, and safety. Tile and slate began to replace wood roofing on Philadelphia residences at least by 1740, and a building boom in the decade before the Revolution inaugurated the city's first urban renewal effort by replacing wood tinder box homes with three-story brick structures—a less hazardous and more permanent statement of stability. New York City prohibited wood structures altogether after 1776 and required tile and slate on all roofs. But brick was expensive, and wood was the only realistic building material for most people. Circumvention of the law was thus common in New York. Even among the affluent of Charleston and Newport, brick was relatively uncommon.

While brick was an affordable indulgence for some urban merchants, merely finding a place to live was the greatest concern for the majority of urban dwellers in 1750. Population grew much faster than the housing stock. Construction laborers were in short supply, and since most people worked in and about the waterfront, proximity to that area was important. Carters and their wagons provided the only internal transportation system in the city, and these wagons were hardly mass transit vehicles. Thus, people's place of work had to be within reasonable walking distance of their place of residence.

Housing shortages and severe crowding were the inevitable results. In Philadelphia, William Penn's spacious blocks were subdivided to accommodate more housing. Small houses were even constructed in the once ample back yards of older homesites. A typical dwelling in that location was no more than 17 feet wide and 25 feet deep, with no more than 800 square feet of floor space and a story and a half of height. Space for housing was a premium commodity. English traveler Andrew Burnaby, touring Philadelphia in 1760, marveled that "Houses are so dear, that they will let for £100 currency per annum; and lots, not above thirty feet in breadth and a hundred in length, in advantageous situations, will sell for £1000 sterling."[1] When a family could not afford even the tiniest dwelling on a back lot, doubling and tripling up occurred. This lent an air of crowded squalor to the prosperous seaport.

Boston presented a similar aspect of spatial and human crowding. The tortuous streets of the North End near the waterfront included a jumble of people and houses. By 1750 a typical house in this area held nine or ten people, whereas a few decades earlier it was extremely rare to find more than seven persons in the same dwelling. Real estate had become an important urban product, and the ordering of space within the city was coming to play a crucial role in the quality of life.

Despite the unfortunate crowding and the high price of urban land, city residents spruced up their dwellings to make up in aesthetics what they lacked in privacy. Architectural styles of the facades lent a distinctive atmosphere to the dwellings of the seacoast cities, reflecting a variety of cultural influences and adaptations to changing demands of cost and space. Row houses—functional structures of 20-foot frontage and 75-foot depth—dominated in Philadelphia. They brought a measure of order and even interior spaciousness to the city's residential neighborhoods and seemed an appropriate solution in a community where crowding and congestion were commonplace. New York architectural styles were more varied because of the city's Dutch ancestry, and many homes had balconies to take advantage of the extensive harbor views. In Charleston, the stately elegance, impressive landscaping, and wide piazzas and balconies of the finer residences contrasted sharply with low, jerry-built wood structures in which blacks, laborers, and some artisans lived.

Inside these urban dwellings, owners displayed their penchant for function, comfort, ostentation, and just plain bad taste. If the exteriors had come out of stereotyped plan books, the householder could project his individuality with interior design. Wallpaper with Chinese-style decoration was the rage in tastefully decorated homes of the mid-eighteenth century. The furniture bore the mark of fine craftsmanship, and was carved in mahogany or walnut. Although the workmanship was local, the upholstery material probably had come from England.

While citizens were beginning to have both the leisure and the means to satisfy their domestic tastes, the city itself began to take on new raiment. Public buildings became more massive and imposing than ever, reflecting economic prosperity and confidence in the future. The classical style of architecture, which had dominated the reconstruction of London, began flowering in colonial cities in the eighteenth century. Columns and domes imparted a sense of authority and permanence to the public buildings they adorned. Peter Harrison, an English architect of considerable fame, left his substantial mark on the seacoast cities. The Sephardic Jewish synagogue in Newport and the Redwood Library, a miniature Doric temple, are two of the finest examples of Harrison's simple, yet impressive architectural style.

The concern over appearance was a physical sign of the urban triumph over the wilderness in a relatively short time. Soon, the interior settlements would turn to similar considerations. Amid the physical splendor, some spatial problems that would become serious obstacles to the urban quality of life in the nineteenth century were developing. Aside from Boston Common and the squares of newly settled Savannah, recreational space was generally absent from the colonial city. The pressure for housing had thrown the countryside back to the rural outskirts. The housing shortage helped to create other difficulties, as we have seen. While merchants and affluent artisans studied plan books, some of their neighbors were throwing together a few pieces of wood, packing in three people per room, and calling it home. It was not until the twentieth century that reformers began making some headway in solving the problem of housing for the poorer classes.

Cities pushed these problems of the back streets to the backs of their minds. Growth and prosperity and its physical manifestations were considered more appropriate thoughts and objectives. Each city prided itself on certain features of its physical environment. Philadelphia's distinctive row houses indicated at once the results of growth and the ingenuity of builders. Charleston's merchant planters promenaded along tree-lined streets while their costly urban mansions included facilities for balls and feasts. If Philadelphia was functional, Charleston was elegant. New York still retained a strong Dutch influence, and the Dutch word "stoop" had crept into English both linguistically and architecturally. Newport, with its neat frame houses, resembled an English fishing village. Finally, there was Boston. The venerable New England metropolis, whose merchants first searched the interior and the Atlantic, was no longer a Puritan village. In terms of size and affluence countinghouse now dominated meetinghouse. The North End with its narrow winding streets still retained its almost medieval character, though newer parts of the city took on the more common gridiron pattern. No one single physical characteristic was particularly outstanding. Taken as a whole, however, Boston's appearance was unique.

Despite these distinctions, all the cities shared one common physical feature: The waterfront was still the focal point of activity and attention because it was the hub of the city's economy. Beyond this crucial core American cities began to reflect in their arrangement some major urban characteristics that would persist into the twentieth century, notably the crammed and dismal districts of the poor and the resplendent homes of the wealthy. Permanent shopping areas, close to the waterfront—Hanover Square in New York, Market Street in Philadelphia, King Street in Boston, and the area along the Bay in Charleston—attested to the fact that a consumer-oriented economy had developed from the subsistence economy of the first years of settlement.

Urbanity

From the perspective of Europe, America was a strange and exciting place populated by wild animals and savages. One of the first missions of colonization was to transplant established European culture and institutions to the New World, to bring the wilderness fully into the ordered universe of the Old World. Thus, books were an important part of the cargoes landed in America from the earliest days of settlement, and theology often provided a purpose and boosted morale in difficult times. Later, when circumstances permitted, various fine arts made their appearance— literature, music, drama, and painting.

Towns and cities were central to the transmission of European culture and tradition to a new land. The greater population base in urban places provided support for schools, libraries, theaters, and museums as well as for major religious and political institutions. Urbanity and sophistication were not the properties solely of urban dwellers, but in a land of great distances and in a time of limited communication, these qualities generally had to be nurtured through contact with cultural sources—either the major centers of England and the Continent or the larger colonial cities.

Culture exists in many forms on many social and economic levels, but "civilization" in the eighteenth-century European sense meant a disciplined and orderly way of life under "proper" authority, organized according to accepted conventions of morality and fashion, with due attention to formal education and the arts. Culture and lifestyle were thus badges of class and social position and were not simply the result of choice. Indulgence in cultural activities was consequently not democratic or equalitarian in colonial America. It was often limited to the educated, the well-to-do, and the socially prominent. There was a "popular" culture too, of course—and it was in many ways more spontaneous, inventive, and relevant to the lives of the majority of people. But ideas and arts at whatever level thrived best where people congregated, where the currents of commerce brought new notions and styles, and where social elites could amass libraries, commission paintings, attend theaters, indulge their tastes in literature and fashion, and support artists, musicians, and actors.

In the beginning colonists were preoccupied with the demands of survival rather than with those of high cultural attainment. This remained true throughout the seventeenth century. Books from the mother country could be found in a number of private libraries, but the conscious pursuit and appreciation of various art forms was understandably neglected. And the art, music, and literature which did exist usually imitated European models or were imported directly from the Old World. If circumstances encouraged a concern with the practical, the spare religion of New England and the simple piety of Pennsylvania Quakers also cast suspicion on many Old World indulgences. Literature and art which did not serve God or His purposes were frowned upon, particularly if they inspired human pride, avarice, and the "lower" emotions. This was not a case of brutal repression, but the result of the creation of a cultural climate which discouraged worldly tastes and desires.

As cities grew and commerce developed, as the piety of earlier generations faded and new populations arrived, colonial culture took on a new and more varied aspect. Beginning in the early eighteenth century, newspapers appeared and then proliferated, the first books were published in America, nontheological writings became more abundant, and painting, music, theatrical presentations, and scientific investigations added a whole new dimension to colonial urban life.

The leading colonial cultural centers were, not surprisingly, the largest cities. Boston was pre-eminent in theology, literature, and higher learning—the result of generations of dedicated Puritan scholars and clergymen. New York boasted the most cosmopolitan social life among colonial cities, and the influence of various ethnic and religious groups stimulated a lively cultural life as well. Philadelphia was a hearty commercial town, with some of the best newspapers and a notable civic spirit, and it soon became the major publishing center. Charleston's very wealthy elite contained a number of educated people of refined tastes, but many of them spent a good part of the year in the upcountry. Whatever the cultural life of cities, however, it was invariably more advanced and active by European norms than anything to be found in rural areas.

Though the pursuits of high culture were usually confined to a leisured upper class, the literacy rate in the colonies was quite high by European standards. Because the Scriptures were so important to the Puritans, they placed great importance on the ability to read them directly. Instruction in at least the basics of reading and writing was thus especially stressed in New England, along with the training of clergymen to fill established pulpits and lead new flocks. Harvard College, the first institution of higher learning in the English colonies, was founded in 1636 at Cambridge, just outside Boston, to provide educated clergy, magistrates, and scholars. A modest effort at public education at the lower levels was also made in the Bay colony. The middle and southern colonies had a fair proportion of educated colonists, including a number of university-trained men. William and Mary College was founded in 1743 in Williamsburg, though most other instruction in the southern colonies was left to private academies and tutors who served generally well-to-do families.

Private libraries containing basic reference works as well as some of the latest literary and philosophical volumes from London bookshops were not uncommon among the colonial elite. John Harvard's three-hundred-volume collection, left to the College in 1638, constituted the first library for public use in America. Benjamin Franklin founded the first subscription library in 1732 in Philadelphia, which enabled members to draw upon a much larger number of books than they could possibly amass individually. The first library building appeared in Newport, Rhode Island, fifteen years later. The New York Society Library, dating from 1754, provided a significant resource for the cultural life of the city destined to be the largest in the country by the early nineteenth century.

Literature and book collections were not, of course, confined to cities; but the largest private collections, the first public libraries, and the printing and distribution of books were definitely urban features. Printing presses were brought to America quite early (Boston had a press a hundred years before Liverpool, for example), though large publishing projects—even those by colonial writers—were almost always done in London until the eighteenth century. By 1750 colonial publishing was much more prominent and active, and Philadelphia had emerged as the leading publishing center in North America, followed closely by Boston and New York.

The image of the city in colonial literature was, as in later periods, ambiguous and shifting. American writers were clearly preoccupied with agriculture, both because of its economic importance in a developing country and because the individual ownership of land and the discipline of American husbandry seemed so important to the evolving American character. Even the urbane Franklin insisted that agriculture was the basis of a good society, and Jefferson saw in the common yeoman a bastion against the concentrated and abused authority of European states and an answer to the struggling and dependent masses of Old World cities. "The mobs of great cities," he wrote in *Notes on the State of Virginia,* "add just so much to the support of pure government, as sores do to the strength of the human body."[2] The New England vision often looked to heaven rather than to earth. Anne Bradstreet's ideal city, for instance, was not of this world: "The City where I hope to dwell, / There's none on Earth can parallel. . . ."[3] Yet the young John Adams, after a visit to Boston in 1758, remarked on the city's elegance, learned conversation, and exciting activity as well as its tumult, noise, and dirt. Those inclined to favor industry and commerce were usually also in favor of cities and the higher degree of economic organization and opportunity they afforded.

Painting and music were prominent features of the European cultural scene. Not surprisingly, these arts were also far less advanced in America, though educated colonists were fairly successful in keeping up with the latest developments at a distance. Very few people could afford to collect great art, but prints, copies of great paintings, and maps were quite popular throughout the colonies and graced the walls of even modest houses.

The theater was also popular with the urban social elite, though theatrical productions did not appear until the eighteenth century. The Puritan suspicion of all public amusements inhibited theatrical development in Boston, but a number of plays were performed in Charleston in the 1730s and in most other large towns thereafter.

The refined arts of the upper classes became increasingly apparent as the Revolution approached, though they were perhaps not as vital in the colonial period as the ballads, songs, lively dances, and entertainments of popular culture. At taverns, wayside inns, and around waterfronts and city markets, a variety of sports and spirited performances flourished, especially as the pious restrictions of the seventeenth century wore off.

Achievements in the creative arts were difficult and infrequent in a society preoccupied with survival and growth. But science was quite a different matter. The mysteries of the New World inspired the curiosity of learned Europeans, and colonists were superbly located for launching geographical and naturalistic studies. The identification and classification of new flora and fauna began with settlement and continued throughout the colonial period. Colonists were also in the forefront of speculation about vast, and largely uncharted, areas of the continent west of the Alleghenies, and new discoveries often accompanied the waves of settlement and commercial ventures made by the coastal cities into virgin territory in the mid- and late eighteenth century. Colonial physicians produced some medical treatises on various subjects from inoculation to new drugs and potions that drew the attention of their English and European colleagues. Achievements in the various areas of science caused a good many colonists to be invited to membership in the prestigious Royal Society.

Newspapers and pamphlets were the principal means of circulating ideas in the eighteenth century—and they were usually fashioned in cities. The first regularly published newspaper in the colonies was the *Boston News-Letter,* which began publication in 1704. By mid-century newspapers existed in all the larger towns. Newspapers were crucial to all groups and classes in colonial cities, crossing the barriers between refined and popular culture. Commerce was highly dependent on information—about fluctuating prices on English markets, international conditions, commodity gluts and shortages, the latest finished goods available in London and Liverpool—and fresh news from abroad was rushed into print. Newspapers provided the source of many conversations in taverns and coffee houses, and as the Revolution approached they played a major role in disseminating political essays and diatribes against King and Parliament. Perhaps the most famous colonial newssheet was Philadelphia's *Pennsylvania Gazette,* purchased by Benjamin Franklin in 1730. Colonial printers also did a brisk business in pamphlets, handbills, and broadsides, some dealing with advertising and announcements and others with politics. These circulated through the fledgling mail system and were hawked in the streets and posted to walls, doors, and fences.

By the time of the Revolution most of the larger colonial cities contained libraries, theaters, concert halls, and at least several newspapers and printing establishments. Philadelphia, Boston, and New York led in the creative arts, while Charleston was perhaps foremost in the elegance of its elite social and cultural life. Colonial America had not developed a unique culture by any means; its arts and fashions were very much within the English and European pattern. But Americans were fashioning a sense of their own identity as a creative and maturing society removed from the Old World.

Revolution

The Seven Years' War between the British and the French ended with the Treaty of Paris in 1763. Almost immediately, a series of British actions stirred colonial opposition and paved the way for revolution in 1776.

The Proclamation of 1763 generally prohibited settlement west of the Alleghenies, blunting the designs many colonists had on these promising western lands. A year later the Sugar Act raised duties on non-British goods imported into the colonies (and prohibited some altogether); British customs laws and procedures for enforcement were substantially strengthened; and colonial issuance of paper money was banned. Taken together, these measures had a major impact on the colonial economy, which found itself weakened after the war in any case. The urban merchants, grown quite used to legal trading with nations other than Britain—and almost accustomed to smuggling—were faced with the prospect of disaster. Boston merchants took the lead, protesting these new British efforts to raise monies in the colonies and stifle commerce by agreeing not to import certain English luxury goods. The nonimportation movement spread to other colonies as dissatisfaction with British economic policies grew.

In 1765 Britain imposed the first direct tax on the colonies in an effort to offset the rising royal expenses in America. The Stamp Act placed taxes on legal documents, newspapers, broadsides, licenses, insurance policies, and other materials and documents, and almost immediately caused an uproar in America. The Stamp Act especially inflamed established, and influential, urban groups—printers, lawyers, merchants, ship owners, tavern keepers, and real estate speculators—at a time of general economic troubles. Resistance developed in most colonial towns and resulted in renewed efforts at nonimportation and, in most places, a refusal to use the stamps altogether. The Stamp Act was repealed a year later, though Parliament reaffirmed its authority to legislate for the colonies in all matters, including taxation.

In 1767 a new set of taxes, the Townshend Acts, stirred colonial protest and led to further nonimportation measures, and a year later British troops were sent to Boston to keep order and protect the King's customs officers. Eventually, in 1770, the Townshend duties were revised and limited only to tea. The nonimportation movement affected virtually all colonial towns and cities, especially Boston, New York, Philadelphia, and Baltimore, and was often marked by public gatherings to protest British policies. With the virtual repeal of the taxes, however, the movement quickly waned.

By 1772 and 1773 relations between Britain and the colonies again began to worsen. The Boston Tea Party in 1773, the dumping of 342 chests of tea into the harbor by organized groups of colonists, was a dramatic protest against the threat of an English monopoly over this single commodity and perhaps in a larger sense against trade restrictions on the colonies generally. The British retaliated in 1774 with a number of measures, including an act effectively closing the Port of Boston until Massachusetts Bay authorities were willing to pay for the destroyed tea. By 1775 the signs of potential armed conflict were clear.

The American Revolution was not declared by colonial towns and cities alone. But British economic and tax policies struck especially hard at the centers of commerce where merchants and artisans had managed to carve out for themselves a variety of markets upon which they had, indeed, come to depend. Largely town-based newspapers often fueled the flames of colonial dissent, and clearly reflected a rising sense of American identity and self-interest that was not by any means precisely the same as that of the mother country.

Merchants dominated political councils in the cities and were leaders both in the movement toward revolution and in the resistance to it. When the war came, some remained loyal to the Crown and continued their activities in British-occupied cities, some escaped to Canada or back to England, and others, of course, committed themselves and their resources to the Revolution.

The Revolutionary War brought economic turmoil to the colonies as well as armed conflict, though the consequences were not the same everywhere. The commerce of Philadelphia, which served as the center of the fledgling colonial government, and of Boston suffered extensively, while New York—captured by the British in September, 1776—spent much of the war under more-or-less normal conditions. Among other things, the continuation of New York's economy on a relatively stable footing as other towns struggled in uncertainty doubtless helped pave the way for the city's dramatic rise in the early nineteenth century, though the conflict was felt in the Empire City as well.

As the guns of the Revolution sounded, most of the major colonial cities were over a century old. They were no longer clusters of new settlers dedicated to survival and the maintenance of an organic community. They had become market places, with active mercantile elites, several interest groups, a variety of cultural, religious, and political institutions, dynamic commerce, and a new spirit of entrepreneurism and individualism. The emphasis of public policy had shifted from maintaining the good of the larger community to providing maximum opportunities for individuals and families. The voluntary associations formed to achieve various civic purposes were cooperative endeavors, to be sure, but they were nevertheless designed to fulfill the new spirit of private interests and individual fulfillment. More and more, the solutions to public problems were sought through private remedies, and the shape and life of American cities were determined by competition among individuals, families, and private interest groups.

As the Revolution ended in 1783 and the Constitution brought forth a new political era by 1789, the towns and cities of the new nation were prepared to play an even more significant role than they had before.

Notes

1. Quoted in Carl Bridenbaugh, *Cities in Revolt: Urban Life in America, 1743–1776* (New York: Capricorn, 1955), p. 15.

2. Quoted in Thomas Bender, *Toward an Urban Vision: Ideas and Institutions in Nineteenth-Century America* (Lexington, Ky.: University Press of Kentucky, 1975), p. 4.

3. From Bradstreet's poem "The Flesh and the Spirit." For further reading see Jeannine Hensley, ed., *The Works of Anne Bradstreet* (Cambridge, Mass.: Harvard University Press, 1967), p. 217.

II.
MARKET PLACE

 Faith and the merchant continued to direct the city-building activities of the young nation. The fertile river valleys beyond the Appalachians grew cities before they grew corn or cotton—a tribute to both faith and the entrepreneur. Once the entrepreneur's bold application of transportation technology had breached the mountains and connected the new cities of the West with the older cities of the East, a national market place evolved, generating prosperity both for the country and for the cities.

The local market place was also a feverish whirl of activity. Never before and never since has the American city experienced a rate of growth equal to that during the period from 1790 to 1870. Growth could have easily become chaos were it not for the guiding hands of business leaders who, through the economic and political institutions they controlled, ordered urban growth to ensure stability and prosperity. Local government especially became a significant force in directing the city's economic future.

The market place was both physical and philosophical focal point of nineteenth-century urban society. Considerations of education, social justice, and charity were generally secondary. The expansion of the urban economy also expanded urban poverty. Immigrants and blacks, lured to the city by the chance for increased opportunities, found life there difficult. Increasingly, urban space began to reflect the social stratification that was evident to travelers of the period. To be sure, all sorts of land uses continued to jostle for downtown space, and in the compact city the poor never lived very far from the rich. Toward the end of the period, however, distinct ethnic, racial, and social neighborhoods were developing, and residential uses were all but gone from downtown. By themselves, these spatial developments were not alarming, but as the city expanded geographically, they portended an increasing isolation and decreasing communication between the various groups within urban society. As the period ended, the faith of the city builders in limitless economic progress was intact, but heaven was a long way off.

5.
Re-creation:
The Planting of Cities

Urbanmania in the West

"This is the place where my people Israel shall pitch their tents." So spoke the Lord to Brigham Young as Young looked across the Great Basin of Utah toward the limitless horizon. On that hot July day in 1847 when Young and his ragged band of Mormons came upon this spectacular and forbidding landscape, a long journey had ended. It was a familiar American scenario— religious persecution, flight, the establishment of a new homeland. Brigham Young shared with John Winthrop an urban vision: the creation of a community drawn together by faith and operated under God's commandments. Jerusalem would be restored and the Lord would be triumphant.

A long journey may have ended, but a new struggle was beginning. Young, like Winthrop, was a city builder. With or without divine inspiration, Young's site selection reflected both common sense and religious purpose. The Mormons avoided the more fertile lands around Utah Lake so as to maintain friendly relations with the Ute Indians. Further, the Great Salt Lake was sufficiently isolated to ensure the new community's uninterrupted development and the freedom of members to pursue their religion without outside interference. The Mormons' earlier experience in Nauvoo, Illinois, which had ended with the murder of Joseph Smith, their leader, had convinced them that a thousand miles of wilderness was a needed buffer against Gentile intolerance.

Planning the new Jerusalem—Salt Lake City—was relatively simple. As in old Jerusalem, the temple would be the focal point for the new community. The plan itself adhered to the Philadelphia grid form, though Young and the Twelve Apostles (as members of the community's and the church's governing body were called) took care to preserve open spaces by providing for one-and-a-half-acre lots for aesthetic and agricultural purposes. Emphasizing the importance of the temple, the Mormon leaders chose the lots closest to the temple. The remaining lots were disposed of through lottery rather than sold. Land speculation was forbidden, a reflection of the financial and legal difficulties experienced by overzealous speculators at Nauvoo. By the end of 1848, Salt Lake City was on its feet and would soon become the new capital of Utah.

Brigham Young may have been the last Puritan. By 1847, faith was still the creed of city builders, but it was faith in growth and not in God that motivated their aspirations. Speculation was the very foundation of urban creation across the American continent. The temples men built from Pittsburgh to San Francisco were less to God than to men. The new cities aspired not to Zion, but to commerce. Indeed, commerce was "the goddess of Christianity."

The city builders of the post-Revolutionary period wore not the cloaks of clergy, but those of capital. City building was a financial enterprise. The capitalists of the East built the cities of the West and then developed technology to secure these fledgling metropolises to their economic bosoms. Urban centers blossomed in the West, helped to generate unprecedented growth and prosperity, and formed the crucial link in the urban chain that became the national economy by 1860.

"GAIN! GAIN! GAIN! is the beginning, the middle and the end, the alpha and omega of the founders of American towns."[1] The Revolution had opened half a continent to American enterprise, and eastern capitalists soon discovered that town building in the newly secured Ohio River Valley could be a profitable business. The American people seemed to be filled with wanderlust, as though they would not or could not rest until they had explored every blade of grass and every rivulet in the new territory. The people of the West required order, however. Hostile Indians, claims jumping, and inhospitable terrain awaited the eastern tourist in western lands. The new federal government in partnership with seaport entrepreneurs helped to order western space and facilitate safe settlement in exchange for a portion of the settlers' savings. In the process, fortunes and towns were made and lost, and the West was urbanized.

The process of town building as a speculative venture followed a general pattern, but with widely varied results. The speculator, typically an agent for an eastern-based real-estate company, purchased two hundred acres from the government. The next step was the survey and the division of the land into lots and streets in a gridiron pattern to facilitate sale. Stakes in the ground marked the subdivisions. Finally, the agent had a map prepared, showing not only the street and lot plan, but buildings as well. Often these structures existed more in the imagination of the town builder than in reality. Other times a few rude log buildings would suffice for civilization.

The map was merely the beginning of a strenuous and extravagant promotional campaign designed to lure easterners to the western promised land. Few if any of these prospective western urban residents would have the opportunity to make on-site inspections. For this reason, as well as because the competition for the real-estate dollar was intense, reality was irrelevant. Town building was strictly a matter of selling lots, and selling lots depended on promotion. With towns multiplying like rabbits across the western landscape, the promotional literature became the nation's greatest fictional resource.

A river location was deemed essential for success. The town of New Athens at the juncture of the Mississippi and Missouri rivers seemed certain of success, according to its promoters. It was, after all, "the most desirable spot in the known world." The speculators were evidently so touched by the geography that they expressed their rapture in verse:

Again shall Athens bid her columns rise,
Again her lofty turrets reach the skies,
Science again shall find a safe retreat,
And commerce here as in a centre meet.[2]

Unfortunately for those who purchased lots in New Athens and other paper cities, the grandiose futures predicted by sanguine promoters never materialized. Disappointed purchasers penned laments about scores of paper cities in the West. The account of one such unfortunate probably reflected the typical scene that confronted hundreds of prospective town dwellers:

There are no churches in the place, instead of four, as was represented to me. No respectable residences; no society; no women except a few woebegone, desolate-looking old creatures . . . no schools, no children; nothing but the total reverse of the picture which was presented to me. On the engraved romance (map) a "college" was imagined, of which no person here has even so much as heard the idea advanced.[3]

Such swindles reflected the enthusiasm which greeted the prospect of western urbanization. Americans seemed to be caught up in the mania of town building, as owning a town lot became a national fad. A trip down the Ohio or the Mississippi River in the 1820s offered a traveler a preview of what awaited him on dry land. According to one such voyager, all the passengers "were discussing the flattering prospects of the 'Great West'; . . . great cities and towns were named of whose existence I had no previous knowledge." It seemed to this traveler that along the river route there was a hopeful village "on either bank, every six or seven miles."[4]

The frenzy of town-lot speculation in the West continued unabated throughout the first half of the nineteenth century. When the urban veins in the Ohio and the Mississippi River Valley had been played out, the scene shifted to Kansas and later to Denver and San Francisco. The speculative mania gripped travelers to such an extent that rapid inflation fueled by easy credit inevitably followed in the wake of a successful promotional venture. The Panic of 1837 was probably the first major depression in the country where urbanization and its consequences played a significant role. In Chicago, where land values had inflated to an unrealistic $10 million, they plummeted to $1,250,000 almost overnight. The fact that town-lot speculation bore little relation to reality provided satirists with some excellent material. One newspaper in Augusta, Georgia, for example, apprised its readers of the "City of Skunksburgh," which lay hard by a "noble stream" that included "delicate minnows, a variety of terrapins, and . . . frogs which, in size, voice, and movement, are inferior to none." The elevation of the site was especially impressive to the writer. "A noble bluff of eighteen inches commands the harbor, and affords a most advantageous situation for military works." Awaiting the lucky visitor on arrival or shortly thereafter were an "Exchange and City Hall, a church, one Gymnastic and one Polytechnic foundation, one Olympic and two Dramatic theatres, an Equestrian circus, an observatory, two marine and two Foundling Hospitals, . . . seventeen banks, to each of which may be attached a lunatic hospital." This visionary scheme was signed by "Andrew Aircastle, Theory M' Vision, and L. Moonlight, Jr.& Co."[5]

Skunksburgh was only slightly more outrageous than some of the flagrant pieces of western urban promotion. The attraction of these fraudulent sites lay in the fact that the great cities of the Ohio and the Mississippi River Valley had also been promotional schemes at one time. The success of Chicago, Cincinnati, Louisville, Pittsburgh, St. Louis, and New Orleans—all river cities—kept hopes and gullibility alive. Each city had been the scene of speculative activity, but there ended the similarity with the paper cities. The mere fact of location on a body of water was no guarantee of urban success.

The growth of successful cities resulted from a break in the transportation of produce and manufactured goods. In 1778 George Rogers Clark had the foresight to establish Louisville as an interior military base. The new town offered the only major break in transportation between Pittsburgh and New

Orleans, a distance of two thousand miles by water. The falls of the Ohio River provided the fortunate break in transportation, and a sheltered harbor allowed Louisville to take advantage of the obstruction. Cincinnati's first settlers in 1788 were impressed by the fact that the mouth of the Licking River was just across the Ohio and it reached into the fertile bluegrass country of Kentucky. It was not difficult to conjure up the sight of Cincinnati "serving as the market center for this lush region."[6]

Not all of the new major urban centers enjoyed a felicitous river view. Some cities grew in spite of geography. Denver, founded in 1858, was strictly a gold rush community. Hard by the precipitous cliffs of the Rocky Mountains, Denver was 200 miles to the south, and 500 miles to the east and to the west, of the nearest urban settlements and possessed few redeeming geographic advantages other than its proximity to Pike's Peak. Brigham Young's Salt Lake City was another settlement where geography was not an advantage, except for the fact that the site was isolated from white civilization. Washington, D.C., was perhaps the most curious new community in post-Revolutionary America. Its location amid the swampy lowlands of the Potomac River was hardly a stroke of geographic genius. The location reflected more a Congressional compromise than a locational perspective.

Whether created by gold, God, or Congress, the instant cities, devoid of much geographic merit, eventually lent themselves to speculative enterprise as much as did geography's favorites. Both sets of cities sought to impart a sense of order and stability that would not only attract lot buyers but also serve as a foundation for future growth. The town plan became the vehicle for establishing order and reflected a good deal about the planners and their urban vision.

Eastern Cities in the West

Had William Penn been resurrected and been permitted to wander the urban West, he would have felt very much at home. And that was the point. Eastern cities were "home" to most of the western urban dwellers, and like the Puritans before them they sought to surround themselves with much that was familiar. Philadelphia, as one of the most populous and prosperous eastern metropolises, as well as one of the best planned and serviced cities, seemed a worthy model. As a result, William Penn's neat gridiron street pattern became the predominant urban form in the West. It was familiar, simple, and, above all, it facilitated the survey and sale of town lots.

Cincinnati, for example, reproduced Philadelphia's plan faithfully even to using the same street widths. The familiar plan, however, was superimposed on unfamiliar terrain. Topography had divided Cincinnati into two communities: the "bottom" only seven feet above the river and the "hill" which climbed quickly to form a mile-wide table. The tiered city as it appeared from the river "looked like a green and open theater carved out of the hills."[7] The symmetrical grid and the irregular terrain clashed, but the economy and orderliness of the grid won the day.

The legacy of Philadelphia went beyond the street layout to touch other aspects of the street system. In Cincinnati and even in St. Louis, which was modeled after New Orleans, the streets which ran parallel to the river were numbered as they were in Philadelphia. The names of the cross-streets, which bore the names of trees and plants like Sycamore, Vine, Cherry, Walnut, Chestnut, and Pine in the Quaker City, were transported en masse over the mountains. Most streets in Nashville and half the streets in Cincinnati bore Philadelphia names. Even more remarkable was the fact that the occasional alleys which broke the gridiron in Philadelphia as a result of rapid growth were reproduced in name, if not in space, in some western cities. When one western traveler observed that "no daughter is more like her mother than St. Louis is like Philadelphia," he might also have noted Louisville, Cincinnati, and Pittsburgh as legitimate offspring of the eastern metropolis.[8]

River cities were not the only practitioners of gridiron imitation. The gridiron invaded the prairie in northern Illinois as Chicago began to expand from its Lake Michigan shore. In the Far West, San Francisco offered the example of an inebriated gridiron staggering up colossal inclines and hurtling down precipitous declines. Either civil engineer Jasper O'Farrell was in a tremendous hurry when he laid out the town in 1847, or he had an unusual sense of humor. With Market Street (another good Philadelphia name) dividing the old Spanish city from the new American city, O'Farrell fastened a gridiron on the hilly American section, creating hardships for pedestrian and animal alike and forever confining the business district to the base of the hills around Market Street. (See Figure 5.1.) The redeeming factor in this plan, hurriedly implemented to accommodate the first wave of gold rushers, was that it provided the city with some instant order and a great many spectacular vistas, which make the city one of the most lovely and inspiring American cities today. To leave one's heart in San Francisco may refer either to the exhausting climbs up steep hills or to the breathtaking panoramas awaiting at the top—both, courtesy of the gridiron.

The grid did not effect such momentous results in other cities. Momentous it was not; monotonous it was. The grid provided endless vistas uninterrupted by squares or buildings. The pedestrian in the walking city had no relief from this monotony, nor from the chill winds that whipped down these corridors. A visitor to Cincinnati complained about "the dull monotony" of

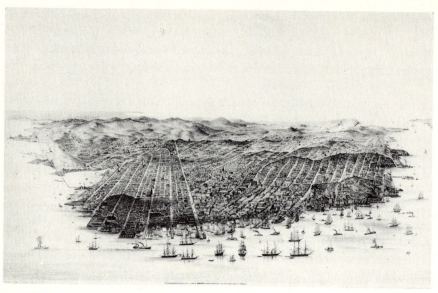

Figure 5.1   View of San Francisco, 1868
The gridiron conquering the hills. (Library of Congress)

the street system, while a disappointed visitor to St. Louis hoped for "a conflagration" that would "burn it [the city] to the ground" so that planners could start anew.[9]

In addition to visual poverty, the relentless grid seemed to foreclose variety in the urban landscape in terms of occasional parks, squares, and recreational spaces. Few promoters took advantage of their cities' river locations and plotted the grid right up to the waterfront. One critic regretted that Louisville had "turned its back upon the varied and interesting prospect presented by the Ohio and its Falls." Dwellings, warehouses, and stores grew where trees and grass should have. The grid marched across the West and conquered most of America by 1860. Cities and grids were so interconnected that one western resident could state flatly: "Curved lines, you know, symbolize the country, straight lines the city."[10]

Paris on the Potomac

One notable city resisted the grid, and, interestingly, of all the post-Revolutionary new towns, its plan represented one of the most imaginative and ultimately far-reaching conceptions of a city presented in America up to that time. Washington, D.C., a creature of Congress, mired in a bog, and avoided as much as possible, was the stage where French engineer Pierre L'Enfant played out a scene of immense grandeur and tragedy. To L'Enfant, urban space was a canvas on which to create an artistic masterpiece, not a piece of real estate.

Rejecting Thomas Jefferson's plan for a compact, gridiron city after the Philadelphia pattern as "tiresome and insipid," L'Enfant proposed an extensive city that would include the beauty of nature as well as the practicality necessitated by urban living. The two essential features of L'Enfant's plan, the Capitol and the "presidential palace," would lie at either end of a broad tree-lined avenue (Pennsylvania Avenue). Like Brigham Young's Salt Lake City and like the early New England communities, the federal city would have a focal point around which urban life and urban space could revolve. L'Enfant connected the focal points by a grassy mall. Along the north side of the mall a canal would run up to the Capitol and turn southward, cascading in front of the building. The canal would not only serve an esthetic function, but would also provide communication between the focal points and stimulate growth along its perimeters.

L'Enfant planned for fifteen squares (one for each state) adorned by statuary or obelisks. He hoped that settlement would grow around these nodes and that, ultimately, they would be connected. His plan also allotted space for religious and educational institutions. Leaving nothing to chance, this unique comprehensive plan also identified a business district along the canal complete with arcaded walkways.

The plan proposed a Baroque European city with broad diagonal boulevards radiating from the Capitol. L'Enfant's familiarity with the gardens of Versailles and the Champs Élysées influenced his ordering of space in Washington. He was not working for a king, however. City building in America had to be accomplished quickly and had to show a profit. L'Enfant's desire to complete the streets and public buildings before beginning the sale of town lots would inhibit growth and immediate cash flow. Both Jefferson and President Washington felt pressed "to show immediate results in the development" of the city.[11] L'Enfant was fired, lots were sold, and the grand plan was gradually whittled away, though it never died, as future events were to demonstrate. In the meantime, without plan or direction, the city floundered. Were it not for the presence of the government, it would have probably gone the way of the paper towns. Well into the nineteenth century, Washington remained isolated and mired. Thomas Moore, an Irish poet, captured the stagnant capital in a poem written in 1804, more than a decade after L'Enfant had first unveiled his grand plan:

This embryo capital, where fancy sees
Squares in the morasses, obelisks in trees;

Which second-sighted seers, ev'n now, adorn
With shrines unbuilt, and heroes yet unborn,
Though naught but woods and Jefferson they see,
Where streets should run and sages ought to be.[12]

Though Washington languished, it staved off the gridiron to some extent. Its very torpor made it relatively unattractive to speculators and prevented the grid from taking command. Elsewhere, the grid claimed new conquests. As the older cities of the East expanded, they abandoned the medieval cow paths that had served as streets and threw the grid across the newly settled areas of the city. Boston and New York both succumbed to the grid. In the latter city, the planners freely admitted the profitability of the grid over all other urban patterns. The legacy of the grid with its frequent intersections and shallow lots on a narrow island has been experienced by numerous motorists caught in Manhattan traffic. This was all in the future, though. In the past, the grid stood for order, profit, and urbanity. It linked diverse cities of the East and West together in the common bond of space. Soon, other even more important linkages would be formed as the new cities of the West and the older cities of the East drew together to form an urban nation.

Notes

1. Quoted in John W. Reps, *The Making of Urban America: A History of City Planning in the United States* (Princeton, N.J.: Princeton University Press, 1965), p. 349.

2. Quoted in Richard C. Wade, *The Urban Frontier; Pioneer Life in Early Pittsburgh, Cincinnati, Lexington, Louisville, and St. Louis* (Chicago: University of Chicago Press, 1964), p. 31.

3. Quoted in Reps, *Making of Urban America*, p. 371.

4. Quoted in Charles N. Glaab, ed., *The American City: A Documentary History* (Homewood, Ill.: Dorsey Press, 1963), p. 157.

5. Quoted in Wade, *Urban Frontier*, p. 33.

6. Quoted in *ibid.*, pp. 22–23.

7. *Ibid.*, p. 24.

8. Quoted in Bayrd Still, ed., *Urban America: A History with Documents* (Boston: Little, Brown, 1974), p. 101.

9. Quoted in Wade, *Urban Frontier*, p. 28.

10. Quoted in *ibid.*, p. 16, p. 28.

11. Quoted in Reps, *Making of Urban America*, p. 253.

12. Quoted in *ibid.*, p. 257.

6.
"The Goddess of Christianity":
The Economy of the Market Place

The Tortuous Journey of Trade

As the western cities gathered at the rivers, eastern entrepreneurs monitored their progress carefully. Their covetous eyes perceived that these urban newcomers were rapidly developing into important market centers by the 1820s. Pittsburgh, as the gateway to the West, built a flourishing commerce supplying travelers and merchants who funneled through the city. As early as 1794, 13,000 easterners passed through the city on their way to the West. By the early years of the nineteenth century, the city boasted twenty-three general stores. Once the easterners arrived at their western destinations, whether farmer or urban dweller, they depended on the urban merchant for supplies.

Western urban merchants were hard-pressed to keep up with the demand. The merchants' inventories of manufactured goods were short and expensive, sometimes 100 percent above the prices in eastern cities. The rivers which gave life to these western cities also restricted their growth. Both the Ohio and Mississippi flowed south. The rafts that plied the trade along these rivers during the first two decades of the nineteenth century—keelboats and flatboats—could not run against the current. The pattern of trade reflected this simple, yet awkward situation. Western urban merchants gathered up the agricultural produce in their immediate hinterland, floated it downriver to New Orleans, broke up the boat and sold it for lumber; then they shipped the crops to an eastern port and secured manufactured goods from eastern firms, which sent the goods on an arduous overland journey to the West.

The system frustrated everyone. The western farmer saw his profits eroded in transportation costs and in inflated prices for supplies and manufactured articles. Small profits inhibited agricultural expansion and thereby reduced the trade of the western urban merchant. The lengthy trade network victimized the western merchant by limiting the number of exchanges. The greater the volume of turnovers—buying and selling—the greater the profits. Eastern entrepreneurs were in like fashion vexed by the slow pace of commerce. In addition, they were unable to sell as many manufactured goods as they would have liked, since the exorbitant transportation costs reduced the attractiveness of these articles in the West. Even more alarming for eastern businessmen, cities like Cincinnati and Pittsburgh began to develop industries of their own. The mountains formed an effective trade barrier against eastern manufactures.

The potential of the West was great. Merchants in the eastern seaports paced the waterfront as they had done during colonial days. Their concerns, however, were beginning to turn away from the Atlantic world. European wars periodically ravaged the ocean trade. The West, on the other hand, offered an almost limitless field for commercial expansion. The Louisiana Purchase, the removal of the Indian threat, and above all, the growth of western cities encouraged eastern entrepreneurs. A hostile and unstable Europe clouded the fortunes of international trade. But the West, the West of golden harvests and golden cities, lay waiting to disgorge a mighty avalanche of commerce that would rain down upon eastern cities as if manna from heaven. Commerce would build cities, create wealth, and generate power. Commerce was, in the words of one eastern merchant, "the goddess of Christianity."

The goddess was elusive. The men of the waterfront, both East and West, began the task of changing nature. If rivers flowed south, their boats would steam north, and if mountains divided the regions, they would be thrust aside. A divinity could expect no less homage.

The Entrepreneurs:
Marketplace Engineers

The linking of the East and West through the bond of commerce is intimately connected with the development both of cities and of the nation. The result, an urban nation, was accomplished by a relatively small handful of energetic and farsighted people defying geography and often common sense. These urban leaders were the heart and the soul of their cities. The destiny of their communities was inseparable from the actions of these people.

Never before and never since has a group of people so dominated a nation's cities. Historians, fascinated with these powerful leaders, have combed the census, newspapers, and city directories in an effort to discover who they were. Although there were variations from city to city, the nature of the urban leadership was much the same throughout the country. The great characteristic of these people was their energy. They participated in almost every phase of urban life. They sat on the city council, on the board of trade, ran successful mercantile enterprises, invested in industrial and transportation enterprises, participated in philanthropic endeavors, and generally set the tone of life for their cities.

Their days were filled with an endless round of meetings and attention to their varied business affairs. In the evenings, reading the local press, catching up with correspondence from other cities and nations, and spending time with the family filled out a busy day. They cared about their cities. In the newer cities of the West, leaders were, of course, relative newcomers. In the older cities east of the mountains, they were generally well established. Whatever their tenure in the city, they soon became property owners and were involved in business and political activities. Although they were people of economic substance, they were not often among the wealthiest. The leadership of American cities, therefore, was drawn from the broad middle class, on the make, but not yet made; like their cities, growing, but not yet grown.

The responsibility which fell upon this leadership was enormous. The destiny of their city was, essentially, in their hands. A wrong decision, indecision, or lack of vision could result in a severe setback for a city. In the nineteenth century, one city's triumph was invariably another city's tragedy. The competition for commerce—the means to success—was fierce. All urban leaders understood that the resources of their hinterland and of the new West were finite. All cities could not share equally in the commercial bounty. There were no ties in the race for commercial empire, only victories and losses.

The key to commercial empire lay in forging links among cities in the East and West. The tortuous trade routes frustrated entrepreneurs in both sections. Most trade until the 1830s was intraregional. The road system and primitive technology were primarily responsible for the narrow scope of internal commerce. (See Figure 6.1.) In the early nineteenth century a road from Baltimore to Pittsburgh was the only interregional commercial high-

Figure 6.1   Conveyance of Tobacco to Market, Circa 1800

Small boats and rutty roads limited volume and raised costs of transporting crops to market. Most trade, therefore, was intraregional prior to 1830. (Library of Congress)

way in the country. Lackadaisical maintenance, the ravages of weather, and the difficult terrain made even local overland routes obstacles to the free flow of commerce. This is not to say that roads were unimportant commercial arteries. Baltimore flour merchants took road building very seriously in the early 1800s. A vigorous road construction program into western Maryland and Pennsylvania allowed the city to expand its wheat market significantly.

The ambition of Baltimore's merchants, however, went considerably further than their roads. The pattern of trade was still pretty much as it had existed before the Revolution. Seaport merchants established branch operations in the interior, and farmers opened trade relations with these branches, which in turn funneled the raw (wheat, for example) or finished (flour) product to coastal merchants. This trade should not be belittled since it was important to establish a local commercial base before looking to expand the commercial horizon. The point is that this base was limited. Since the cost, in the early nineteenth century, of transporting a ton of goods nine miles on inland roads equaled the cost of importing the same ton from Europe, the restrictiveness of overland trade can be appreciated.

But as America entered the 1820s and the dawn of the Age of Jackson, a new and confident spirit gripped urban leaders which mirrored the attitude of the rest of the nation. This was a confident and expansive time for America. The Louisiana Purchase and the acquisition of Florida had added significantly to the territory and prestige of the young nation. The recently completed war with Great Britain had not only brought a new surge of optimism, but it had also brought a genuine peace for the first time in over a generation. A heroic age was beginning, and the people in the nation's cities were in on its creation and fulfillment.

The Song of Steam:
Marketplace Technology

The first triumph was a triumph of technology. The steamboat revolutionized western trade as it ran both with and against the current of the western rivers. A colorful era began as steamboat whistles shattered the forested silence along the banks as the steamboat trade helped to found new cities and made old ones grow. Louisville to Cairo, Cairo to St. Louis, St. Louis to Memphis, Memphis to Natchez, and Natchez to New Orleans and back up again, the sidewheelers and sternwheelers churned up the muddy waters bringing produce and people to towns and cities along the shore. As the steamboat conquered space and time, it brought a piece of urban civilization wherever it went: A little bit of New Orleans, a little bit of Cincinnati, showboats, livestock boats, and passenger boats all steamed up and down the river accompanied by the song of steam.

The Mississippi River became the nation's major commercial highway. For a time during the 1830s, New Orleans surpassed New York City as the nation's leading export center. The steamboat stimulated growth in New Orleans and other river cities, while interior cities like Lexington, dependent on their status as crossroads communities, languished. Steam had made overland travel even more obsolete, and river communities hurriedly fixed up docks, wharves, harbors, and warehouses to accommodate the new Age of Steam and let their roads fall into disrepair.

Steamboats could not climb the mountains, and therein lay the cause of the continued isolation of East and West. The steamboat, however, provided several interesting lessons for observant urban leaders in both sections. First, technology could alter traditional patterns of trade heretofore dictated by geographic and topographic considerations. From the Hudson River to the Great Lakes to the Mississippi, the steamboat defied the current and facilitated reciprocal trade among communities. Second, those communities that through the bounds of their own geographic position were unable to take advantage of the steamboat retired from commercial competition and stagnated. The results of this failure to secure or to share in new technology implied a similar fate for other cities. Finally, the success of the steamboat uncovered a vast commercial potential in the West, a commerce in which eastern cities shared only with great difficulty.

The first technological breakthrough occurred in 1825 with the completion of the Erie Canal, which joined the Great Lakes and the Atlantic Ocean at New York City. With much pomp and ceremony, a crowd of notables which included Governor DeWitt Clinton of New York, who once resigned his seat in the United States Senate to run for mayor of New York City, and whom some people considered mentally unstable (for attempting to construct the canal, not for resigning from the Senate to run for mayor), dumped some Lake Erie water into the Atlantic. Clinton, whose urban vision included a majestic metropolis at New York City, almost single-handedly pursued and engineered the canal with great success.

The canal demonstrated urban man's preference for water travel and was heralded as the dawn of a new commercial era and as the making of New York City. Actually, as late as the mid-1830s little of the traffic on the canal came from beyond New York State. Also, the canal did not "make," but merely enhanced New York's commercial position. The city's aggressive merchants had already secured an international trade empire by 1825. The canal, however, much like the steamboat on the western waters, generated significant urban growth in upstate New York and helped to establish Buffalo, the canal terminus, as the fastest-growing city in the state.

Despite this scaled-down assessment of the canal's actual commercial impact, the completion of the canal reverberated throughout the urban nation and triggered a frantic search by cities for ways to the West. The merchants in these cities of course could not perceive the ultimately limited commercial impact of the canal. From their point of view, New York merchants, like the explorers of old, had constructed a northwest passage, and the fact that it was built by men and not by nature made the canal an even more inspiring example in this Age of the Common Man.

Leaders in both Philadelphia and Baltimore reacted to New York's coup in different ways. Both groups had been contemplating ways to reach the West since the turn of the century. Philadelphia's urban entrepreneurs, who had guided the city to first place by the time of the Revolution, had grown conservative after nearly a half-century of economic dominance. Their response was to imitate. They would construct a canal from Philadelphia to Pittsburgh, which would link up there with the Ohio River. The Philadelphia promoters soon discovered that the mountains running through the central portion of Pennsylvania formed an impenetrable barrier to a canal. Technology could conquer space, but water could not flow uphill. The alternative, to build a canal to the mountains and then a railroad to Pittsburgh, did not occur to Philadelphia leaders until 1831, by which time rival Baltimore was well on its way to breaching the West. It was not until the late 1840s after massive injections of state aid and near bankruptcy that Philadelphians completed a rail system to Pittsburgh.

Baltimore's merchants were more daring. They were, in effect, the new city on the block. Rising from complete obscurity to become the nation's third largest city in less than fifty years probably convinced the city's leaders that virtually anything was possible. In 1826 one of Baltimore's leading merchants, Evan Thomas, went to England on a business trip and observed first-hand a new British invention, the steam railroad. He reported back to his colleagues and on February 28, 1827, the railroad era in America began with the chartering of the Baltimore and Ohio Railroad. Using their own capital gained primarily from the wheat trade, Baltimore merchants began construction of what was still an untested technology in July 1828. Although the western terminus of the railroad—Wheeling—was not reached until 1853, the completion of sections long before that date provided conclusive evidence that the railroad was not only a profitable enterprise but possessed the potential for revolutionizing the patterns of trade. Unlike the steamboat, which used the natural waterways as its highway, the railroad was a completely artificial device realizing Jacksonian America's conquest of nature. The railroad could indeed climb tall mountains, leap yawning chasms, and ford raging rivers to deliver the bounty of the West to eastern shores.

The steam railroad became a legend in its own time. Railroads could attract population and promote "human enjoyment," and would "reorient society." Senator Charles Sumner of Massachusetts believed that "where railroads are not, civilization cannot be. . . . Under God, the railroad and the schoolmaster are the two chief agents of human improvement." A Presbyterian minister from New York went even further. He saw railroads as "the evolution of divine purposes, infinite, eternal—connecting social revolutions with the progress of Christianity and the coming reign of Christ."[1] Small wonder that communities enthusiastically embraced this Iron Messiah.

While the level-headed urban merchants absorbed these testimonials, they were more concerned with the immediate, practical benefits of the railroad, benefits to be obtained by transcending space and time to a greater extent than by either canal or steamboat travel. These practical benefits included expanded market territory and reduced freight rates. The railroad therefore increased the volume of traffic for urban merchants and correspondingly encouraged higher crop yields among farmers. Finally, railroads demonstrated the capability of diverting trade from the more established natural trade routes. Baltimore and other eastern cities were gambling that access to a railroad would induce Ohio River cities and their merchants to take their business from New Orleans to the eastern seaports.

The benefits of the railroad, both practical and alleged, generated a fierce competition among urban rivals. The dreams of cities both East and West were similar, and the story of the agony and ecstasy of railroad building followed the same scenario. In railroad building, urban leaders met their first major challenge of the marketplace era. The response very often determined greatness or also-ran.

In Chicago and St. Louis entrepreneurial decision making on the new technology sealed the future of both cities. While eastern cities eagerly stretched out iron arms to grasp the western trade, western leaders were hoping to make their community serve as the terminal market to the region and therefore as a focal point for eastern attention. Chicago's growth in the 1830s resulted to some extent from a transportation enterprise. A canal was projected from Chicago on Lake Michigan to the Illinois River and ultimately to the Mississippi River thus linking the Great Lakes with the "Father of Waters." Although the canal did not materialize until the following decade, the mere promise of one touched off a flurry of speculation in town lots and a resultant increase in population—an early indication of the attraction of a transportation system.

Chicago's business leaders, led by upstate New Yorker William B. Ogden, were more interested in the potential of the railroad, which they correctly viewed as the ultimate transportation weapon for their city. If they could attract eastern railroads and build railroads of their own across the broad prairie, the parade of commerce that now floated down the Mississippi River might be diverted eastward. In this scheme, Chicago's rival for western economic supremacy, St. Louis, was the main target.

St. Louis leaders recognized the threat from Chicago but placed their faith on the magnetic Mississippi to continue to attract produce as farmers and merchants shunned the new-fangled rattling hunk of metal from out East. It was a mistake. Just as Philadelphia merchants erred in opting for a canal, so St. Louis's entrepreneurs miscalculated in their reliance on the river. By 1870, Chicago was a major rail terminus, and its iron tentacles reached into the prairie to draw river trade away from St. Louis. During the 1860s, Chicago tripled its population while St. Louis failed to even double its.

In the South, New Orleans was the major beneficiary of Mississippi River commerce. The Crescent City knew no rival to its supremacy in the southern export trade, and as cotton production boomed in the 1830s, 1840s, and 1850s it seemed as though all New Orleans merchants had to do was to wait for this bounty to fall into their laps, for the Mississippi would always flow conveniently by their doors.

Some New Orleans leaders like banker James Robb realized that the penetration of the railroad into the West was an ominous portent for the future of the city's commerce. The New Orleans and Nashville Railroad was chartered in 1835 in response to the railroad efforts of other cities. Unfortunately, financial mismanagement and the lack of cooperation from cities along the proposed route doomed the railroad to failure. Not until the 1850s did interest in a railroad to the East revive. By then, however, it seemed as though every community in Louisiana had its own railroad project to promote for state funding. Since state resources were finite, New Orleans's Nashville enterprise waited in line and received only a token appropriation. Some leaders supported other routes, while other leaders remained unconvinced of the necessity of any railroad at all.

Indeed, the river continued to disgorge its commerce in the 1850s, but this activity obscured some very significant changes. The volume of produce received at the port of New Orleans continued to increase during the 1850s.

Western commerce, however, composed a declining percentage of the city's total volume of trade. Western produce accounted for 58 percent of the city's total receipts in 1820. Forty years later, western produce represented only 23 percent of total receipts. New Orleans's area of trade was being circumscribed. It was becoming limited to the cotton regions of the lower Mississippi River Valley. New Orleans, in short, was no longer a major interregional port, as railroads running West to East diverted trade from its "natural" path.

The case of New Orleans indicates an interesting feature of the decision-making process in antebellum cities. It was not enough merely to decide (or fail to decide) on a particular transportation system. Concert of action, appropriate financial support, and intelligent management were all parts of the transportation-planning process. Agreement among businessmen on one major transportation project was important, at least at the outset of a city's transportation program. Since energy, expertise, and financial resources were limited, to dissipate them among several projects was to benefit none.

Financing these internal improvements was a unique experience for American cities. Railroads required such large capital outlays that financing efforts typically involved individuals, local government, and the state legislature. The wide-ranging interests of the urban elite gave them inordinate influence in government at both levels. Though all state legislatures were dominated by rural representatives, railroads and their benefits transcended urban boundaries. State support of these projects was heavy in some states. Pennsylvania came close to insolvency for its financial efforts. In Virginia, three-fifths of the capitalization for railroads and canals came from the state treasury. This system of mixed enterprise was common throughout the country.

The financial initiatives, however, came through the urban leadership and their local governments. Between 1830 and 1860, Savannah invested $2.7 million in railroads. Business people in the city invested at least that much, since the private subscription for the Central Railroad alone was nearly $2 million. This financial support was repeated throughout the urban South. Funding for northern railroads was less localized. Chicago's network, for example, was constructed largely with eastern money. European investments also accounted for significant financial support for northern railroad projects. Railroads, therefore, provided one of the first major outlets for excess capital accumulated largely through commercial pursuits. The financial support given railroads in the urban South was an indication, further, that not all or even most excess capital went into land and slaves in that region.

Finally, railroads provided the urban elite with their first opportunity at corporate management. At times, the results were chastening. Mismanagement of funds, labor disputes, inadequate technical skill, and poor decisions about routes and timing plagued most railroads from time to time. Urban leaders often managed their railroads as weapons in commercial competition. The varying gauges of the tracks throughout the country attested to the desire of local entrepreneurs to maintain the break in transportation for their communities. Rate wars sometimes flared as rival railroads sought competitive advantages for passengers and freight. Eventually, management became more sophisticated and scaled their fares according to distance, with longer hauls receiving a lower per mile rate. The railroad was a convenient if sometimes rocky training ground for the urban leaders' future endeavors in corporate management.

Mastering the mysteries of corporate management while constructing and financing new transportation technologies demanded dexterity, intelligence, and wealth that only urban leaders could provide. If successful, their reward was economic growth and prosperity. Yet their efforts to secure commerce could not end with the railroad. It was only the beginning, an important one to be sure, of the implementation of a broad range of economic policy.

As the railroad stretched out to conquer space, its good results necessitated a number of economic decisions back home. Railroads whose existence was bound solely to agricultural freight were usually unsuccessful ventures. Crops had their particular seasons, but rolling stock, employees, and shareholders could not be laid off until harvest time. If the terminal city could provide its rural customers with manufactured articles and supplies, not only would the railroad operation be enhanced, but business for local merchants would also be increased. This point seemed obvious to urban leaders, but it was difficult to implement this idea. If they were content to play the middleman and merely transfer goods onto railroad cars, there was no problem. It was clearly preferable from a number of standpoints, however, for merchants to develop local industry themselves.

The establishment of processing industries, for one thing, would attract more raw materials—that is, produce—to the city. Processors in textile mills, flour mills, and tobacco factories could afford to pay farmers or their nearest market-town merchants high prices for their crops, since the processed product was worth considerably more than the commodity in its raw state. In addition, the existence of processing industries meant that capital would remain and recirculate in the community. Local merchants who had gone through the trials of constructing a canal or a railroad only to have to reship the produce they received to a processing center elsewhere, perhaps in a rival city, reaped only partial economic benefit from the transportation improvement. They could only sell their clients' produce as a raw material; marketing a finished product was, of course, much more remunerative. The merchant could, in turn, sell a portion of the finished produce—sweaters, trousers, dresses, cigars—back to his rural customers, thus providing the railroad with some reciprocal trade.

If the merchant could supply his rural clients (and urban ones as well) with farm machinery, household products, furniture, and even locomotives manufactured locally, this would increase urban self-sufficiency and provide more return freight for the railroad. Capital, once again, would be accumulated and would remain to enhance urban growth. Finally, farmers, city dwellers, and merchants outside of the city's immediate market area would be attracted by these diverse activities for investment or marketing purposes and eventually would establish relationships with local merchants that would serve to expand the city's commercial empire.

This scenario appealed to many merchants, and even before the railroad began to revolutionize trade patterns, they were forming groups designed to promote local industry. These groups, however, encountered numerous problems on the road to securing an industrial element for their cities in the early nineteenth century. Manufacturing required large injections of capital and labor, neither of which most cities possessed in sufficient reserves. Technology was another problem. Since water was the primary motive power, industry was limited to certain sites. Even after steam became tamed for industrial uses, its adaptation and the requisite machinery required skill in assembling, maintaining, and operating. Finally, there was a general antagonism in the country toward mixing industrialization and urbanization.

Although most people today automatically associate industry with the city, early-nineteenth-century Americans viewed the combination with distinct displeasure. The United States was still an overwhelmingly rural nation. Cities were viewed with enough suspicion. Unfavorable impressions of the besooted, overcrowded, and squalid manufacturing cities of England were common in the popular thought of the time. While some people recognized the necessity of industrial growth in order to achieve a measure of national self-sufficiency, they pictured industry in a rural setting. A writer for the American Society for the Encouragement of Domestic Manufacturers asserted in 1817,

Our factories will not require to be situated near mines of coal, to be worked by fire or steam, but rather on chosen sites, by the fall of waters and the running stream, the seats of health and cheerfulness, where good instruction will secure the morals of the young, and good regulations will promote in all, order, cleanliness, and the exercise of the civil duties.[2]

Francis Cabot Lowell, a frail Boston merchant, believed in this dream of factories nestled among the lovely New England hills and set forth his vision of industrial America at Waltham, Massachusetts, in 1813 at the falls of the Charles River. Lowell's financial backers, a group of merchants organized into the Boston Manufacturing Company, sank the considerable resources they had gained from commerce into erecting not only the textile mill but the workers' dormitories, churches, and schools. Using a power loom perfected by Lowell himself, the Waltham mill proved an immediate success and spawned another rural factory town—Lowell—four years later.

The towns themselves looked more like New England college campuses than like traditional mill towns. This was to the credit of the Boston Manufacturing Company. They constructed the factories to be indistinguishable from the buildings at Harvard University and included a belfry on each building and a grassy common nearby. The dormitories overlooked the rural countryside, and the very fact that they were called "dormitories" emphasized the connection between Waltham and Lowell and the college campus. Perhaps the most striking feature of these rural workshops was the labor supply. The grim and hopeless faces of European laborers were nowhere to be seen. Instead, the cheery, wholesome faces of New England schoolgirls peered out from behind the looms.

The New England farm girls were not the exploited proletariat feared by many Americans. They received relatively high wages, were given clean and decent accommodations, and attended school and church regularly. Working seventy hours a week, they yet found time, energy, and inclination to publish their own literary magazine. This was not a permanent laboring class, either. After two or three years the young women returned to their communities and, usually, married, bringing the savings of several years of factory work to grateful grooms.

The practice of employing these young farm girls who sang at their looms while composing poetry in their heads lasted for only a decade or two. Waltham and Lowell were victims of their own successes. With profits nearing 20 percent annually, the pastoral villages, especially Lowell, grew rapidly. Within twenty years, Lowell had developed from a small farm village of 200 persons to the fourteenth largest city in the United States with a population over 20,000. As one observer marveled: "The change seems more the work of enchantment than the regular process of human agency."[3] As if by enchantment, the rural landscape receded into the past. One young woman looked out from her dormitory window and saw her view of nature slowly but surely obliterated by another factory building as it rose story by story:

Then I began to measure . . . and to calculate how long I would retain this or that beauty. I hoped that the brow of the hill would remain when the structure was complete. But no! I had not calculated wisely. It began to recede from me . . . for the building rose still higher and higher. One hope after another is gone . . . one image after another, that has been beautiful to our eye, and dear to our heart has forever disappeared. How has the scene changed! How is our window darkened![4]

Soon, the young woman would also become a relic of the past.

Lowell's managers discovered that Irish immigrants worked cheaper and just as well, as newer technology no longer required the comparatively small, nimble hands of the farm girls. The once-comfortable dormitories filled to overflowing as a permanent work force settled in. Lowell had become a city with all of a city's attendant problems. The fiction of industry and countryside coexisting side by side was quietly laid to rest. Other, less pretentious industrial communities began to dot the New England landscape. For their founders, anxious to leave their rural past as far behind and as quickly as possible, urban growth was a major objective. The armory at Springfield, the textile mills at Holyoke, and Charles Goodyear's rubber factory at Naugatuck were merely a few examples of industrial and urban growth in New England. These gritty communities foreshadowed future urban industrial giants of the late nineteenth century. The glimpse into the future was not very pleasant.

The lessons of Lowell that impressed urban leaders to the greatest extent were the huge profits that could be extracted from industry. The capital accumulated from commercial ventures was dwarfed by the financial success enjoyed by industrialists. Then too, as urban populations increased, so did the demand for manufactured products. With the introduction of steam technology, industry was no longer tied to a specific location along a river, so cities could fill this growing demand. The railroad facilitated the transfer of industry from rural to urban locations by speeding the transit of raw materials ranging from crops to coal. The existing commercial services in the city further aided urban industry by helping with credit and legal arrangements. Finally, the city came to have an extensive labor pool as immigrants from Europe and from the rural countryside, who had been attracted to the city by its commercial opportunities, stayed because of the availability of industrial employment.

As a result of these developments, industry began to appear as an important element in the economic base of some cities. In the 1850s Cleveland leaders warned that the city of Cleveland would stagnate unless its industrial potential were realized. "No thinking man with capital will stop here," they warned, "when we have only commerce to sustain us. A manufacturing town gives a man full scope for his ambitions."[5] By the 1860s, Clevelanders must have taken heart, because their city was the manufacturing center of the Great Lakes and one of the fastest-growing cities in the region.

Southern cities embraced the new royalty as well. Their leaders were equally interested in diversifying their economies and expanding their trade networks. There was also the added incentive of securing a measure of economic independence from the North. A Mobile editor declared that domestic manufacturing was "the only safe and effectual remedy against Northern oppression."[6] Cities like Mobile, Augusta (Georgia), and Louisville developed manufacturing based on the cotton or tobacco grown in their respective hinterlands. Only Richmond, however, succeeded in approaching the ideal of industrial independence. Not only did Richmond have massive tobacco and flour milling operations, but it was also among the nation's leading iron producers by 1860, giving the city an industrial diversity that was unusual for most American cities.

While industry was a growing force on the urban economic scene, America's cities remained tied to a predominantly commercial economy. Specialized industrial centers like Lowell and Holyoke were the exception, as most communities utilized industry to enhance their commercial activities and prop up their heavy investments in railroads. The eagerness with which urban entrepreneurs embraced the new transportation and industrial technology portended a trend of the future, when technology would supersede social considerations and determine urban policy. Already railroads and industry were absorbing increasing amounts of capital, labor, expertise, and urban space. The sound of steam was the new urban music. Walt Whitman rejoiced at mid-century that the United States was a nation "of whom the steam engine is no bad symbol." Ralph Waldo Emerson, on the other hand, warned:[7]

Things are in the saddle,
And ride mankind.

There are two laws discrete,
Not reconciled,—
Law for man, and law for thing;
The last builds town and fleet,
But it runs wild,
and doth the man unking.

The Business Revolution:
Organizing the City for Profit

Urban leaders did not engage in this debate. They were people of action, not contemplation. Yet the new technology swirling around them and the commerce it delivered led them to appreciate the need for control. Railroads and industry had expanded their contacts beyond the local merchants and farmers to include merchants in other cities and regions. Business could no longer be conducted in the folksy, leisurely style of an earlier era. Merchants no longer had the time to watch for their ship to come across the ocean; they were immersed in a thousand details generated by the new internal commerce. Clearly some order and organization were required to facilitate the smooth flow of commerce and to maximize the profits and growth for the city.

If competing railroads from the same city resulted in loss to both, then competing merchants could expect similar difficulties. Competition was destructive and wasteful; order could not be achieved until rules were established and the effects of competition were minimized. The expanded contacts of local business people similarly required a new order. Merchants in Cincinnati might have dealings with bankers in New York, merchants in Pittsburgh, and country stores in the Ohio River Valley. The market they serviced was different in each case and fluctuated from day to day. It was necessary to keep apprised of these changes and conditions in order to conduct an efficient operation. Improved mail service and the introduction of the telegraph in the late 1840s reported these market alterations rapidly and accurately. The emphasis could no longer be on obtaining information much sooner than rivals, but must now be on the accuracy of decisions based on that information.

It was evident that these new relationships and technologies required something more than the merchants as individuals could provide. Before their commerce could become organized, they would have to organize. As the city outgrew the image of a tight-knit community clustered about the waterfront, individuals sought out each other and formed associations ranging from singing societies to charitable groups to ward off the anonymity of a growing city. Leaders were inveterate joiners. Part of their influence as leaders stemmed from the fact that they played dominant roles in civic organizations. It was only natural, therefore, that the leaders when confronted with commercial expansion that threatened to overwhelm them, decided to form organizations to make commerce rational.

In 1823, Cincinnati merchants banded together to set uniform commission and storage rates. This eliminated ruinous rate wars and regularized customer relationships by preventing or at least slowing the constant ebb and flow of clients to or from certain merchants depending on their rates. In short, uniform rates would allow merchants to plan ahead, select their inventory, and project their income.

Quality was another important concern. Some farmers, it was alleged, short-weighted their bushels or barrels. Others attempted to pass off tainted meat or milk products. If there were too many of these shenanigans, the city's reputation would suffer as these goods were exported. Individual merchants did not have the time or the equipment to establish effective inspection mechanisms. Together, however, Cincinnati's merchants required and instituted a centralized inspection system of goods that were destined for export.

Cincinnati's solutions were relatively simple adjustments in an era prior to the railroad. With the expansion of commercial space as a result of new transportation technologies, urban entrepreneurs had to consider their numerous rural clients, merchants and financiers in other cities, and their own self-interest before selecting an appropriate policy. In order to proceed intelligently, information on each of these actors in the commercial arena had to be current and accurate. The urban press was the major medium through which the business people organized information. Whether receiving or sending information through its columns, leaders soon learned that control of the local press was an essential feature of orderly commercial development.

By the 1830s merchants in New York and later elsewhere gradually captured control of the local press. Prior to this time, international and political news had dominated the pages of the press. Merchants were forced to uncover information about prices, crops, and market conditions from a variety of generally late and unreliable sources. The quickening pace of commerce in the era of steam required a quicker circulation of information. With the advent of daily newspapers in the 1830s—the so-called penny presses—this informational gap was closed to a great extent. Editors were usually leading merchants themselves and de-emphasized partisan politics.

The press furthered the city's business interests. First, the daily press published price current lists. Such information was essential for local merchants engaged in competition with colleagues in other cities. The list informed merchants of the prices of various commodities in other cities. If merchants in other cities were offering farmers $1.10 for a bushel of wheat while locally the price was $1, and if transportation costs were similar, local merchants would lose business to rivals. The price current list enabled merchants to keep abreast of these fluctuations and to adjust their own prices accordingly.

Equally important, the press functioned as the community bulletin board, apprising readers of events and services. Advertising was a major staple of income for editors, and business people patronized the columns with increasing frequency. For out-of-town customers, business people found advertising essential. Most urban presses circulated long distances from their home base. It was not unusual for commercial farmers and small-town merchants to subscribe to several urban dailies. The railroad conquered space not only for commerce, but for information as well.

The urban press was at its best as a local cheerleader. It coaxed, cajoled, remonstrated, and begged the city to take action, while also taking care to fire a few bombasts glorifying the urban future. Journals urged their urban readers to the offensive in pursuit of prosperity: "We hold it to be a self-evident truth," declared one urban editor in a familiar paraphrase, "that no community ever became great, that did not do something great themselves. Individuals may have greatness thrust upon them, communities never do."[8]

The religious fervor which editors imparted to the projects of the city leaders helped to organize not only commerce but the community as well. The press, according to one historian, was "the most important unifying element of urban culture" in the West.[9] It provided a sense of community for cities that were becoming increasingly fragmented by growth. The press's importance in both stimulating and rationalizing urban growth cannot be overstated. For example, the failure of the Leavenworth, Kansas, press to promote or at least to discuss the building of a bridge across the Missouri River was a major reason why Leavenworth lost in its commercial competition with Kansas City, where the press had played a more aggressive role. Finally, the press's importance is underscored by the fact that few towns were without a newspaper, and cities had several. Urban leaders throughout the nation could agree with Virginia's George Fitzhugh that "the meanest newspaper in the country is worth all the libraries in Christendom."[10]

The press informed and molded public opinion, but it could not regulate commerce. More formal organizations were required to take advantage of the information in the press and turn it into economic gain. The Board of Trade or Chamber of Commerce emerged as the major mercantile organization in the antebellum city. The board, along with the later creations, the commodity exchanges, provided a formal mechanism for the regulation and enhancement of trade. In addition, they served as convenient clearing-houses for information. Most boards initiated reading rooms or libraries where the latest issues of such commercial journals as *Hunt's Merchants' Magazine* and *DeBow's Review* were circulated. Newspapers from around the region were standard items as well.

The board functioned best as a formulator of plans for economic growth. It was here that merchants routed railroads and devised means for their financial support; that merchants drew up regulations for the conduct of trade; and that merchants developed plans for theaters, hotels, and warehouses to keep both their clients comfortable and their clients' produce safe. The board became the hub of the city's planning network.

This nerve center often became frazzled. Increased commerce meant increased contacts with individuals and groups representing a variety of interests. Conflict and adjustment were always present in the board rooms. Farmers, accustomed to bargaining with individual merchants, became alarmed at uniform price-and-standard regulations. They condemned "*coercive* measures entered into by a combination"[11] whenever and wherever merchants formed exchanges and regulated a particular commodity. Town and country agreed on transportation systems but were growing apart on other economic issues. While the commercial horizon of the farmer and the country merchant was usually limited to the nearest market towns, the urban merchant looked out upon a commercial world. Not only transportation technology, but financial arrangements and informational requirements bound cities to each other rather than to their respective hinterlands.

These urban relationships were not equal ones, however. Entrepreneurial decision making had been instrumental not only in transcending space but in reordering it. While merchants in some cities concerned themselves about the weight of corn, merchants in other cities were concerned about establishing timetables for their fleet of coastal steamers, about setting a time limit on credit payments, and about facilitating communications with dozens of their representatives in cities across the country. Both sets of decisions were important to doing business in each city, but both sets of decisions also spoke volumes for the type of economic influence each merchant exerted. One city had achieved local dominance and perhaps a measure of prominence in its region. Decisions in the other city had not only regional, but national ramifications. The scattered group of market centers that could hardly be called an urban network in the 1740s could be called by the 1840s a national urban system. The change, generated to a great extent by entrepreneurial decision making, exerted a significant influence on the cities in the nation and on the nation itself.

The National Market Place

The national urban system was centered at New York City. There, commerce, manufacturing, and capital gravitated in national tribute to a new economic power. The city's fine harbor and excellent geographic location were merely beginning points in the story of its rise to commercial supremacy. A series of far-sighted decisions and the willingness of the decision makers to take certain risks catapulted the city far ahead of its rivals. While other cities dreamed of a commercial empire, New York secured one.

The first commercial coup was recorded in the realm of foreign trade. During and after the American Revolution, New York merchants had assiduously courted English manufacturers. While other cities felt more protective toward their own industry and less receptive to British overtures, New Yorkers welcomed the trade unequivocally. When trade resumed following the War of 1812, the British dumped their manufactured surpluses with their New York merchants, and New York quickly became the national center for European manufactured goods. This meant that merchants from Boston to St. Louis shopped at New York to satisfy their customers' renewed demand for British manufactured articles.

Once the surpluses had been exhausted, it was possible that other cities could have established closer ties with British manufacturers and could have reaped similar benefits. New York merchants, however, headed off this possibility in 1818 by inaugurating the first regularly scheduled packet service to Liverpool. The Black Ball Line revolutionized the Atlantic trade. Now cotton farmers in Georgia, factors in Charleston, and merchants in Boston could plan the shipment and delivery of their goods with some precision. Produce no longer rotted on docks in America; manufactured goods no longer waited for ships on the other side of the ocean—these delays in the flow of commerce were no longer necessary. Time was money, as every businessman and farmer knew.

With their Atlantic trade in order, New York merchants turned their international advantages into domestic success. The Erie Canal was one of the early fruits of this policy. Less spectacular, but perhaps more important, New Yorkers inaugurated steamship services to coastal and Gulf ports to take advantage of the fact that New York, being right on the ocean, had readier access to these ports than did either Baltimore or Philadelphia, her two closest rivals. New York merchants, therefore, insinuated themselves into the commercial life of dozens of coastal cities. Vessels from New York not only engaged in coastwise commerce but brought resident agents to coastal cities to help local merchants market rural produce and arrange for the sale and distribution of domestic and foreign manufactured goods.

When the agents established relationships with local merchants, a quick ship and low-priced manufactured products in return were not the only inducements offered. The accumulative effects of aggressive decision making had made New York a financial center as well. The tremendous volume of business generated huge sums of capital which facilitated loans and other credit arrangements. Whether financing a Chicago railroad or extending credit to a Richmond tobacco manufacturer, New York money permeated local economies to a considerably greater extent than New York agents who arranged these deals.

New York's position as a trade center enhanced its reputation as an informational center. Merchants, manufacturers, and farmers did business in the Empire City with the knowledge that their transactions would receive the benefit of the latest and most sophisticated market information. The best lawyers, the wealthiest financiers, the sharpest accountants, and the best-informed merchants resided in New York and streamlined the methods of doing business. This "Business Revolution," as one historian has called it,[12] centralized trade in New York and in turn generated even more commerce. As one observer noted: "When once a city has acquired an established character as the great commercial emporium of a country, . . . the course of trade becomes settled by flowing regularly in the same channel." Scarcely any new commercial development occurred without New York merchants and financiers knowing about and, more important, taking advantage of it. "Every new mine opened, every town built up, comes into relations with New York; and every railroad, no matter how short, has one terminus here," noted one New Yorker in 1865 with cockiness, but with accuracy.[13]

The path of a nation's commerce indeed led to New York. The diversion of trade from its natural routes to artificial avenues altered the commercial geography of the country. The development of the "cotton triangle" provides a good example of the nature of these new patterns and their commercial impact. The cotton triangle exemplified how transportation innovations and the accumulation of business services in New York made the gravitation of the nation's most important trade to that city virtually inevitable.

New York merchants sent their agents into southern ports during the 1820s to purchase cotton from either the planter or his urban merchant. In addition, the agent extended credit to the local merchant, who, in turn, could then make credit arrangements with his rural customers. The agents then provided vessels to sail to New York where they would rendezvous with larger ocean-going ships for the trip to Liverpool. Thus New York merchants provided a market, shipping, and credit to southern merchants—an irresistible trio.

The triangle was institutionalized over the years through the working of several commercial developments. First, as the cotton culture spread throughout the South and as commercial services centered in the Northeast, regional economic specialization occurred. The southern economy both on the farms and in the cities revolved around the cultivation, marketing, and processing of a staple crop for its eventual delivery to a northern port like New York. Northeastern cities, especially New York, tailored their economies on the exchange and shipping of these commodities coastwise and overseas. By the 1840s this pattern had solidified.

Second, southern growth strengthened the pattern of trade. Southern cities which grew at impressive rates during the railroad era were serving as mere funnels to aggrandize northern ports. As one southern entrepreneur lamented: "We are mere way stations to Philadelphia, New York, and Boston."[14] When Savannah's railroad connections increased the city's commerce, for example, New York merchants promptly dispatched a fleet of vessels to inaugurate regular service between New York and the Georgia port. Southern cities traded relatively little with each other. Their economic existence depended, rather, on the interregional trade with the North. New York in extracting raw materials from the South also drained capital from the region. Fees for shipping, for commissions, and for interest on loans limited the profits from commerce, which in turn limited the capital available for investment in southern cities. Thus the slower growth rate of the South may have been due less to slavery than to the commercial supremacy of New York.

Finally, the growing railroad network re-enforced the pattern of northeastern economic supremacy. Southern railroad building extended primarily from the Atlantic coast cities like Norfolk, Richmond, Charleston, and Savannah westward. As northern railroad companies paralleled the Atlantic coast, they secured the bounty initially tapped by the southern railroads, which became for all intents and purposes feeder routes for northern lines. New Orleans was perhaps the greatest victim of this new economic geography (Tables I.2 and I.3 testify to its decline in the ranking of U.S. cities). The Mississippi River was no longer the great avenue of commerce it once had been as trade patterns took a west-to-east route, rather than a north-to-south one. In 1860 the Superintendent of the United States Census declared: "As an outlet to the ocean for the grain trade of the west, the Mississippi River has almost ceased to be depended upon by merchants."[15]

The South was not the only casualty in New York's march to commercial leadership. Other northeastern cities suffered by comparison. As the business and transportation revolutions centered in New York, European exporters took advantage of the city's connections and services by sending their wares to this port. By 1860 New York dominated the import trade with more than two-thirds of the nation's total value of imports coming into the port during that year. Boston, its nearest rival for imports, achieved only 11.3 percent of the trade. New York's dominance of the import trade helped to maintain the city's informational advantage and to attract immigrant labor.

This is not to say that New York alone stood out on the commercial horizon. In the regions of the South, the West, and even in the Empire City's backyard, the Northeast, cities grew and prospered and exercised considerable influence over their market areas. New Orleans, for all its troubles, continued to dominate the cotton trade of the lower South and drew such cities as Mobile, Memphis, and Natchez into its economic orbit. Cincinnati and Chicago, with effective rail connections and the development of the same services (though on a smaller scale) that made New York an attractive place in which to market, monopolized the wheat, corn, and livestock trade from the Great Lakes to the Ohio River and west to the Mississippi. Beyond the Mississippi, regional centers like Kansas City and Denver were securing rail connections tying them to the west-east pattern of trade. All of these cities were tied to others in their respective regions and ultimately to New York. By 1840, and certainly by 1870, it would be appropriate to speak of an urban network with regional and national linkages transmitting commerce, capital, people, and information over well-worn avenues of trade. (See Figure 6.2.)

The constant communication and economic interdependence of cities had important ramifications for the nation as it hurtled down the path of sectional disintegration during the 1850s. Leaders in American cities were, generally, moderating influences in the sectional conflict. To them, economic interest transcended sectional and ideological preferences. Commerce was the tie that bound. As Virginian George Fitzhugh put it: "Heretofore, domestic weakness and danger from foreign foe has combined the States in sustaining the Union. Hereafter, the great advantages of friendly and mutual intercourse, trade and exchanges, may continue to produce a like result."[16]

Prior to the American Revolution, America's fledgling cities were the focal points of radical sentiment and action. As the election of 1860 approached, leaders in the nation's cities spoke in moderate tones and counseled compromise instead of recrimination. At a large Union rally in New York City, Mayor Fernando Wood reminded the crowd that the issue of slavery was unimportant beside the crucial issue—"our continued commercial prosperity." Presidential candidate Stephen A. Douglas, another speaker, asserted that New York, the "great monetary heart of the American continent," required the maintenance of the Union. The four candidates—Abraham Lincoln from the relatively new Republican Party, an overwhelmingly northern group; Stephen A. Douglas and John C. Breckinridge, the northern and southern candidates, respectively, of the disintegrated Democratic Party; and John Bell, standard-bearer of a coalition of former Whigs and Democrats called the Constitutional Union Party—provided a splintered

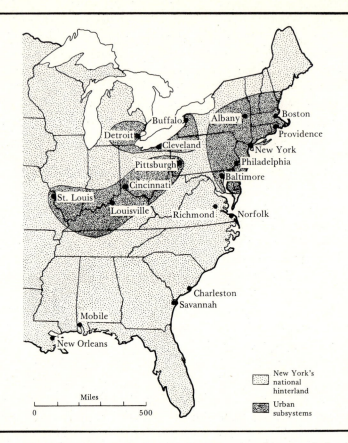

Figure 6.2   The National Urban System, 1840. (Reproduced by permission from the *Annals of the Association of American Geographers,* Volume 67, 1977, M. P. Conzen. The areas defining urban subsystems are after Allan R. Pred, *Urban Growth and the Circulation of Information: The United States System of Cities* [Cambridge, Mass.: Harvard University Press, 1973], p. 8.)

electorate with an unusual variety of presidential choices. City voters generally, however, narrowed their selections to Douglas or Bell, whom they perceived as the more moderate candidates. Voters in New York City turned in a two-thirds majority against Abraham Lincoln and John C. Breckinridge, while three out of four voters in Petersburg, Memphis, Louisville, New Orleans, and Mobile also voted against those candidates. Only in the Midwest, Lincoln's home territory, did the Republicans manage respectable showings. Even here, however, the Republican vote in the cities usually lagged far behind that in the countryside.[17]

It was easy to see why the merchant leaders spoke for sectional peace. Their prosperity and their city's growth depended on the maintenance of interregional commercial connections. The economic relations that they had carefully forged over several decades might not withstand the rigors of war. Equally important, during this time, they had built their community from a group of structures and activities clustered about the waterfront to a mature, expansive city with new institutions and a new ordering of space. As the urban leaders looked ahead with apprehension, they doubtless reminisced about earlier days when they were constructing their commercial empire and building their city. We can allow these merchants their wistful moments because they had helped to create a national economy laced together by an urban network. While this work was going on, they had engaged in another equally heroic activity: accommodating their city to the new economic order.

Notes

1. Quoted in David R. Goldfield, "Pursuing the American Urban Dream: Cities in the Old South," in Blaine A. Brownell and David R. Goldfield, eds., *The City in Southern History: The Growth of Urban Civilization in the South* (Port Washington, N.Y.: Kennikat Press, 1977), pp. 53–54.

2. Quoted in Thomas Bender, *Toward an Urban Vision: Ideas and Institutions in Nineteenth-Century America* (Lexington, Ky.: University Press of Kentucky, 1975), p. 29.

3. Quoted in *ibid.*, p. 40.

4. Quoted in *ibid.*, pp. 78–79.

5. Quoted in Bayrd Still, "Patterns of Mid-Nineteenth Century Urbanization in the Middle West," *Mississippi Valley Historical Review,* 28 (September 1941), 187–206.

6. Quoted in Goldfield, "Cities in the Old South," p. 57.

7. "Ode Inscribed to W. H. Channing," quoted in Leo Marx, *The Machine in the Garden: Technology and the Pastoral Ideal in America* (New York: Oxford University Press, 1964), p. 178.

8. Quoted in Goldfield, "Cities in the Old South," p. 60.

9. See Richard C. Wade, *The Urban Frontier; Pioneer Life in Early Pittsburgh, Cincinnati, Lexington, Louisville, and St. Louis* (Chicago: University of Chicago Press, 1964), p. 130.

10. Quoted in Goldfield, "Cities in the Old South," p. 60.

11. Quoted in *ibid.*, p. 63.

12. Thomas C. Cochran, "The Business Revolution," *American Historical Review,* 79 (December 1974), 1449–1466.

13. Quoted in Allan R. Pred, *Urban Growth and the Circulation of Information: The U.S. System of Cities* (Cambridge, Mass: Harvard University Press, 1973), p. 216.

14. Quoted in Goldfield, "Cities in the Old South," p. 86.

15. Quoted in *ibid.*, p. 87.

16. Quoted in *ibid.*

17. Figures and quotations are from Ollinger Crenshaw, "Urban and Rural Voting in the Election of 1860," in Eric F. Goldman, ed., *Historiography and Urbanization: Essays in American History in Honor of W. Stull Holt* (Baltimore: Johns Hopkins University Press, 1941), p. 50.

7.
Society in the Market Place:
A New Spatial Order

The Shape of Things to Come:
The New Market Place

The shape of the city confronting urban leaders by the 1840s was more complex than the relatively tight-knit cluster community of their forebears. The pursuit of economic growth was altering the spatial arrangements of structures, activities, and most important, of people. This was not a process that occurred suddenly, but one that took several decades to complete in most cities. The entrepreneurs charted these movements and reacted swiftly to take advantage of the new ordering of space, most of which occurred through economic forces beyond the merchants' control but which they nevertheless enhanced by their planning policy.

The emergence of a distinctive downtown area from an area containing clusters of economic and residential activities was one of the more momentous spatial developments of the period. Downtown was the economic heart of the city, and by virtue of that fact was the most important space in the city. Downtown came to include a variety of mercantile activities, financial institutions, warehouse facilities, cultural attractions, and, for a time, manufacturing establishments. These elements, while in close proximity to each other, were often set apart in groups of similar use. The larger the city, the more sharply defined was the location of downtown activities.

Downtown grew from the waterfront—that early focal point of American cities. The waterfront itself was no longer the economic center of the city, though its docks and warehouses were important components of downtown. The warehouses remained the city's storage facilities as water traffic and the new railroad termini along the waterfront brought produce from city and farm. Merchants maintained these structures because damp and infected storage areas were not conducive to good business. But these warehouses also came to have other uses in addition to holding produce. As the merchants learned to synchronize and schedule receipt and shipment of goods, warehouses were periodically empty. In such a choice location underutilization of space could not be tolerated. With restrictions on space, materials, and labor, some warehouses provided excellent locations for a city's nascent industry. Since most industry in this early period rarely employed more than fifty workers, the warehouses could comfortably house this labor force. These structures were especially suited to use by the garment industry and other handicraft industries, in that these industries used compact machinery, their labor requirements were relatively modest, and they required close proximity to wholesalers and retailers in order to have a market for their products. Thus, while many warehouses along the docks retained their function as storage facilities, some of these buildings began to form the city's first industrial district.

Not all industry nestled in the close quarters down by the docks. Other locations were more preferred in terms of proximity to customers or services and in terms of space requirements. New York City, which remained very much a commercial community, exhibited a varied pattern with regard to its industrial land use. Its industries were closely connected with its commerce, but only the printing and publishing industry continued to be housed in the old warehouse district. Shipbuilding moved away to the periphery, although it obviously remained on the waterfront. (See Figure 7.1.) The reason for the move was quite simple. Shipbuilding was an extensive user of space. Its sprawling presence along valuable downtown waterfront real estate would have involved a prohibitive expense. In short, shipbuilding was a loser in the competition for downtown space. It was forced out. The printing and publishing industry, on the other hand, required relatively little space to carry on its activities. Printers and publishers, therefore, were not bothered so much by high land prices because they required so little land. This, of course, placed them in a more competitive position, since they could afford to bid higher for downtown locations than could the shipbuilders. (See Figure 7.2.)

While industry established itself in varied locations, other economic activities were less footloose and were more bound to the formative downtown. This was particularly true of mercantile endeavors. The volume and complexities of trade required specialization. A merchant could no longer

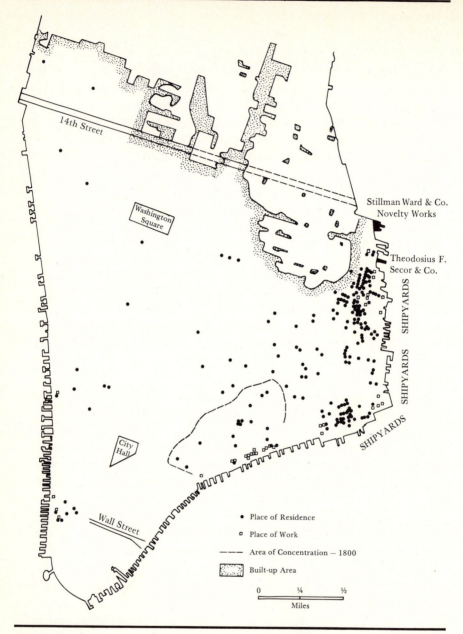

Figure 7.1   New York City's Shipwrights and Ship Carpenters: Places of Work and
Residence, 1800 and 1840

Note the expansion northward through 1840 of the shipbuilding industry from its
1800 location to the east of City Hall near downtown. Note also the continued
proximity of work place and residence, a major spatial characteristic of the marketplace era. (Reprinted from *The Spatial Dynamics of U.S. Urban-Industrial Growth,
1800–1914* by Allan R. Pred. © The MIT Press, Cambridge, Massachusetts.)

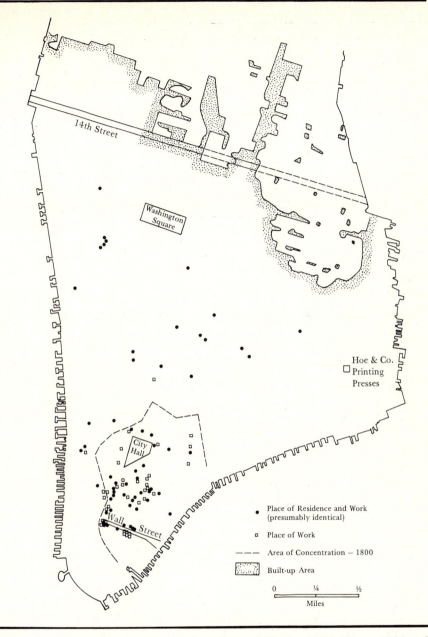

Figure 7.2 New York City's Engravers: Places of Work and Residence, 1800 and 1840

In contrast to the shipbuilding industry, the printing and publishing industry continued to be concentrated in or near downtown from 1800 to 1840. Like people in shipbuilding, printers and publishers tended to live near where they worked throughout this period. (Reprinted from *The Spatial Dynamics of U.S. Urban-Industrial Growth, 1800–1914* by Allan R. Pred. © The MIT Press, Cambridge, Massachusetts.)

wear several hats—wholesaler, retailer, and financier. The activities and requirements of each role were becoming well defined, and participation in more than one meant an inadequate mastery of both or of all three. In smaller market towns one merchant could conceivably perform all three tasks. In the larger cities urbanization and specialization went hand in hand.

Wholesalers generally occupied the waterfront sections of the new downtown. They usually owned the warehouses and even some of the docks. Their capital helped to establish industry in the warehouses. In addition to this new role, the wholesalers received European produce and retained the role of commission merchant, as they forwarded agricultural produce to other cities and abroad. The retailers, whose livelihood depended on close association and cooperation with the wholesalers, were nearby. Since their customers were usually individual citizens and occasional visitors, however, their location was not along the crowded, often filthy, and sometimes unsafe waterfront. They sought more comfortable accommodations where they could display their wares in relative spaciousness and cleanliness. It was much easier to attract and retain customers if the retailer showed his goods to advantage and made his shop distinctive. In the waterfront potpourri this was not possible.

By the 1830s the famous city markets, which had endured since the colonial period, were being upstaged by these merchant-showmen who had usurped many of the market's functions. Retail butchers, grocers, and fruiterers provided their customers with convenient, personal service. These establishments were generally in the better parts of town, while the old market houses were sometimes in crowded and unsanitary quarters. Finally, in the antimonopoly spirit that characterized Jacksonian America, it did not seem appropriate for one agency—the market house—to control the provisioning of the city. If free-enterprise entrepreneurs were to be trusted to build commercial empires, they certainly should be allowed to provide their neighbors with fresh food.

Besides the provisioners, an entire array of retailing activity began to appear in the expanding downtown. Dry-goods stores, ready-made clothing shops, and jewelry stores were some of the specialized establishments that grew away from the general store of an earlier era. For the shopper, the proliferation of these retail outlets must have been dizzying. No "one-stop shopping" here: It was in one store for an overcoat, in another for some cigars, in another for a harness, and finally to the shoe store or the tavern so the shopper could be fortified in one manner or another to continue the shopping trip. Increased consumer demand and affluence generated by the expansion of trade and the receding wilderness in the West encouraged retail specialization. By the same token, common sense indicated that the shopper, particularly in inclement weather, would be inconvenienced by these shopping rounds. It would be much more worthwhile, that is, profitable, if all the retail activities were brought under one roof. This idea did not necessarily result in a step backward to the general store, but rather in a giant stride into the future: The department store, replete with extensive inventories, items for every budget, sumptuous surroundings, and efficient, trained personnel to cater to the public's buying whims, was created.

By the 1850s consumers' appetites had been whetted sufficiently to create the demand for these emporiums, and merchants had accumulated sufficient capital in the larger cities to finance the undertaking. Boston's Jordan Marsh, Philadelphia's Wanamaker and Brown, New York's Lord and Taylor, and Chicago's Marshall Field were the marvels of their day as residents and tourists alike gaped at first sight of the latest innovation in retail establishments. Guidebooks and newspapers devoted considerable space to these commercial edifices, which, much like the cathedrals of medieval Europe, not only dominated the urban landscape but reflected the spirit of the age. The usually staid *New York Times* observed that Lord and Taylor, opened in 1859, was "more like an Italian palace than a place for the sale of broadcloth."

Writers, at least if they were from Philadelphia, reserved the most lavish praise for Philadelphia's department store, Wanamaker and Brown. During the 1860s it would be difficult to discover a building in the city that received more publicity than the Wanamaker and Brown building. A shopper entering the structure for the first time must have felt awed. Walking up Market Street several blocks removed from the waterfront, the shopper entered the store through a grand arch. The first floor included men's and boy's furnishings, with sufficient inventory to keep a modest retail operation in stock for quite a while. Although Wanamaker and Brown did not have escalators—escalators had not yet been invented—their substitute, a massive walnut staircase, seemed to meet with the approval of customers, who compared it with "the grand staircase at the Capitol at Washington." This evidently placed well-heeled shoppers in the proper frame of mind for spending money, as the Custom Department occupied the second floor. On the third floor the shopper could choose from a vast array of overcoats and dress coats. For the shopper who had not wearied or become insolvent, there were two more floors with assorted dry goods to wander through. If the shopper decided to purchase an article, the store was arranged like a mechanized factory to accommodate the purchase. One clerk wrote out a ticket, while another packed and delivered the article. If purchases were made on several different floors, speaking tubes and a dumb-waiter system coordinated these sales.[1]

These retail factories were part of the new downtown. The retail district which included these palaces became the mecca for tourists and residents alike. A visitor no longer went to the waterfront to take the pulse of urban life; he or she went to The Street—the block or group of blocks that included the city's retail trade. For here was an indication of urban prosperity: the type and extent of retail activities that the city's residents could support. Whether Canal Street in New Orleans, Market Street in Philadelphia, or King Street in Charleston, these thoroughfares became the showcases for downtown and for the city.

The showcase could not have shown so brilliantly, resplendent in white marble where today neon signs blink their messages, if it were not for capital. The entrepreneurs' single-minded objective of securing economic growth implied the accumulation of capital. Those cities that could accumulate the most at the fastest rate possessed more railroads, better credit, more industry, and more commerce, which in turn generated more capital, which in turn built more railroads, and so on. Growth, once in high gear, was self-generative, and capital was the grease that kept the urban machine rolling. The financial institutions which developed to lend, to invest, and to maintain capital came to occupy a specific place in downtown.

The urban financiers, the bankers, and the brokers typically began their careers as wholesale merchants. Before banks became commonplace, they would often lend a little money or sell insurance as a sideline. As banking laws were liberalized and as commerce expanded, these individuals discovered that trade in money was even more profitable than trade in produce. They converted their commission houses or the residences of merchants who had been pushed out of downtown because of high real-estate values into banks, brokerage firms, and insurance companies. With excellent access both to the old warehouse-manufacturing and wholesale districts and to the newer retail center, they provided credit information, insurance, investment capital, and investment opportunities to all sectors of downtown. Just as New York had become the nation's commercial center, it followed that it became a city of financial importance. "Wall Street" not only denoted a physical space at the lower end of Manhattan Island where the city's and the nation's financial institutions crowded the narrow street, but it also became a symbol of the city's economic power. Wall Street, atypical in its influence, was typical in its spatial configuration. Financial districts in cities elsewhere were concentrated in relatively compact areas adjacent to wholesale, retail, and industrial activities.

Downtown grew because the city had grown. It included in its relatively small space a variety of specialized activities that reflected the city's mature economy. Although downtown was not extensive by modern standards— four or five square blocks at most—its components had clearly defined spatial roles. Wholesalers remained by the waterfront, industries located in the warehouses, and retailers established themselves uptown in downtown. Financiers grouped together, carving out older sections of downtown and spreading to the new, as they linked the economic activities of the area with a chain of capital.

There was one important and familiar component missing from this downtown scene, however: people. True, downtown was crowded with people from early morning until late evening. But fewer people *lived* there. Though downtown grew in size and increased in density, peripheral areas were gaining population at a faster rate than downtown. In Philadelphia, for example, the areas along the Delaware River reached their population peak in 1830 and began to decline thereafter as outlying areas received a larger influx of residents.

Some residents left downtown for much the same reason that some industries established new quarters elsewhere. As the uses of downtown— wholesale, industrial, retail, and financial—increased, these uses required new space. Owners of private homes and town houses located in the path of economic development soon found themselves sitting on valuable real estate—too valuable not to be cashed in and perhaps too valuable for the owners to be able to afford to pay rising property taxes which were assessed on the value of the land. Every time a home changed hands or every time a newcomer sought housing downtown, the same story would repeat itself. Commercial, financial, and industrial users of spaces easily outbid the single-family homeowner for downtown property.

Then too, downtown was getting rather crowded, noisy, and, in some areas, unsafe. Entrepreneurs in the early city had sought out residences on or near the waterfront. Prestige, proximity to economic interests, and maintaining close ties with Europe made other choices unthinkable. But now the waterfront was more cluttered. It was the oldest section of the city, and even in the newer cities of the West, it did not age gracefully. It had always attracted those characters who lived on the margin of the law and of life, though now it seemed that increasing prosperity attracted more of these types. Finally, downtown was continually in a state of excitement. The pressure on local entrepreneurs experimenting with new policies, taking new risks with borrowed capital, and worrying about grasping urban rivals was sufficient to require a respite from this atmosphere. Remaining in downtown after business hours was no longer a convenience; for some, it was a burden.

The Residential City:
Preference and Technology

As merchants, clerks, artisans, and laborers were forced from downtown, a new spatial phenomenon evolved in the city: the residential neighborhood. As with downtown space, residential space came to be specialized. While all segments of urban society lived in close proximity to each other and even mixed together, there was beginning to be a clearly defined residential pattern based on economic status. Urban leaders and their colleagues who left the mélange of downtown settled in relatively homogeneous neighborhoods. Their residences were usually near enough to their downtown offices so that they could walk to and from work, for these were still very much pedestrian cities well into the 1830s. Downtown, after all, was the economic center of the city, it was the most prestigious area of the city, and now that personal preferences and economic forces had removed the residential component, by and large, from downtown, the next best thing was to live adjacent to it. An area in close proximity to the financial district was probably the most desirable residential location. The financial district exercised the greatest influence over the city's economy, it was relatively quiet, and leading financiers tended to reside near it, adding considerable status to the area.

By the 1860s the desire of the well-to-do to reside close to downtown was receding. Downtown itself was constantly expanding and shifting so that living near downtown one year might mean living in it the next. Also, migrants from the countryside and from abroad were crowding into the mile-and-a-half-square city. The compact city had become the congested city. This was especially so since land uses were not evenly dispersed throughout the small area, but rather were crowded in or near downtown. Congestion reached epic proportions in New York City, which was probably the most crowded city in the world with an average density of 135 persons per acre or 86,400 persons per square mile. With today's occupancy standards, a density this great is likely to be found in blocks of apartments of a minimum of twelve stories. In nineteenth-century New York, tenements ranged from two to five stories.

Advances in technology coincided with changing personal preference to relieve downtown congestion by enabling the residential city to be expanded beyond the borders of the market place. Although the significant technological innovations in intraurban transportation were not to appear until later in the century, several transportation systems developed that allowed the propertied to escape from close proximity to downtown. In doing so, these systems signaled the end of the pedestrian city.

The omnibus, an import from Paris, served as the basis of the first major transportation system to appear in American cities. It was in New York, not surprisingly, that omnibus service in the United States was inaugurated in the late 1820s. The omnibus, a covered vehicle drawn by two horses, carried about twelve passengers. It operated along fixed routes and made frequent stops to pick up and discharge passengers. The "city stages," as they were popularly called, proved immensely popular with business people and white-collar employees. By 1837 ridership in the city had increased to 25,000 per day. Few members of the working class were included in that group. One-way fares averaged 12½ cents. Unskilled laborers earned less than a dollar a day, while craftsmen rarely earned more than two dollars. Since it was the custom to go home for lunch, riding the omnibus would have eroded one-half to one-quarter of the worker's daily salary. By relieving residential pressure on the environs of downtown, the omnibus made feasible the relocation of a number of white-collar workers and their families. But for the urban worker, the fare structure and the price of housing precluded residence in "the upper part of the city."[2]

The omnibus helped to begin a modest movement to the suburbs. Traditionally, the urban periphery was the home of vagabonds and destitute immigrants. The crowding of urban space, though, and the reduction of commuting time brought about by the omnibus made the suburbs with their rural quietude potentially attractive residences. While in New York only a few omnibus lines ascended into suburbs like Harlem, in Boston the omnibus penetrated into suburban Dorchester and Roxbury with frequency. A new type, the suburban commuter, was born: "They reach their stores and offices in the morning and at night, sleep with their wives and children in the suburbs."[3]

The omnibus did not provide the ultimate transportation system, however. Its novelty caused citizens to overlook its more obvious defects for some time. The omnibus, according to Mark Twain, a very disgruntled passenger, "labors, and plunges, and struggles along at the rate of three miles in four hours and a half, always getting left behind by fast walkers, and always apparently hopelessly tangled up with vehicles that are trying to get to some place or other and can't."[4] The omnibus was too slow, it sometimes overturned, spilling its occupants onto the hard cobblestone or into the soft mud, and it was uncomfortable. By the 1850s the time had arrived for an improved system.

The horse-drawn railway was the basis for that improved system. It was heralded by urban residents as "the improvement of the age." The street railways, as they were also called, were simply railroad cars pulled by horses. Operating on tracks, the street railway generated less friction than the omnibus. A two-horse team, therefore, was capable of pulling a larger vehicle. The horse-cars usually accommodated forty riders in relative comfort without the jostle which accompanied a ride over the city streets on an omnibus. They were also not as accident-prone as the omnibus because they were confined to rails. Most important, while the omnibus rarely exceeded four miles per hour, the street railway whizzed along at six miles per hour.

The greater capacity of the horse-car and the relative speed at which one car could complete a run resulted in a lowering of public transit fares by one-half. Despite this reduction, the street railway was still beyond the means of most workers. Again, public transit failed to loosen the tightly packed tenement districts. By 1860 more than one-half of New York City's residents still crowded into dwellings below Fourteenth Street, an area one-tenth the size of the entire city. For these New Yorkers, the city was still very much a pedestrian place.

Other transportation systems had their urban debuts during the 1840s and 1850s, though they were even more exclusive than the popular omnibus or horse-car systems. The commuter railroad was effective in cities like Boston where suburbs were close, yet set apart by inlets and marshlands which made traditional overland communication difficult. The commuter railroad, which raced along at thirty miles per hour at top speed, made possible settlement far beyond the city line. Assuming that thirty minutes is the maximum time an individual would want to spend commuting and figuring an average speed of fifteen miles per hour, we see that the two-mile-square area of habitation could be at least tripled.

In extending into the rural countryside, the commuter lines performed another equally valuable service. They enabled city residents, for the first time, to receive fresh produce, especially milk, from the farms surrounding the city. Farmers in these areas began to specialize in highly perishable commodities which had found only a localized market before the railroad, since the wagon road was the only transportation link to the city. By the time milk and milk products, fruits, and vegetables would arrive at city markets, there would have been considerable spoilage, particularly on warm days. As the city expanded and pushed farms further out, deliveries became less frequent until the appearance of the commuter railroad. A New Yorker noted the marked improvement in the milk supply in 1850 over the "deleterious fluid" from "swill-fed cows, diseased through constant confinement and unnatural food," that passed for milk in the days before the railroad: "The railroads now bring fresh milk every morning from a distance of sixty miles in time for use, and consequently the proportion of healthy milk used has much increased, while the price at which it is afforded to citizens has been proportionally reduced."[5]

Although most Americans carried on a love affair with the railroad, some city residents disapproved of them. Commuter railroads never entered downtown. At best, the commuter would have a half-hour walk from the terminal to his office downtown or to adjacent areas. The noise, pollution, danger of fire from sparks, and the disruption of traffic led urban residents to ban the locomotive from the city. Some railroad companies merely detached the locomotive at the terminal and hitched up a team of horses in a version of the horse-car. The delay and inconvenience associated with this procedure kept suburbanization to a relatively low level.

For cities like New York and Boston where water hazards hindered the approach to the city, the steam ferry provided an additional system to serve suburban commuters. In the 1840s regular and reliable steam-ferry service was inaugurated from Long Island and New Jersey to New York. By 1860 twenty-six regular lines operated in New York waters. The most popular run, the Fulton Street ferry to Brooklyn, dispatched boats every five minutes. With a one-way fare of one cent, the ferry was within the means of everyone, though most workers rode the ferry for pleasure because the rapidly rising land values in Brooklyn precluded residence there. Some businessmen rode commuter railroads from rural Queens to the ferry slip. The rapid growth of suburban Brooklyn reflected the improved commuting facilities. From a sleepy suburb of 21,000 in 1820, it became a full-fledged city by 1860 with a population of 279,000.

The growing intraurban-transportation network played a significant role in the city's spatial expansion. Although its benefits touched a minority of urban residents, it relieved areas of potential tension and crowding. Development followed the omnibus and particularly the street-railway lines. The private transportation companies encouraged development by dealing in adjacent real estate as a lucrative sideline to their transit activities. The uneven distribution of built-up areas in some cities attests to transit's influence on space. In St. Louis, for example, horse-car lines stretched northwest from downtown. The northwest section of the city settled rapidly while for years the southwest remained sparsely populated.

Space and Class

Residential distinctions developed within these expanded urban boundaries. New York's Fifth Avenue, for example, was heralded as one of the most fashionable residential streets in the nation. Newer cities in the West also experienced a similar concentration of wealthy residences on a particular street beyond downtown. Even Chicago, among the newest of the western cities, carved out an attractive residential area. This location, known to Chicagoans as the "Garden City," provided an island of loveliness to residents fresh from the battles of downtown.

These streets and areas were not merely wealthy residential locations, they were extensions of the individuals who lived in them. The residences of the elite, like the retail palaces downtown, were the physical symbols of growth and prosperity. These physical expressions came in numerous forms—many of which were to remain staples of urban architecture to the present day: spacious brownstones, Greek Revival mansions, Italian villas, and French stucco town houses were merely some of the styles preferred by urban leaders. Although visitors could not wander through these homes in the way they toured department stores, if they could have done so, they would have undoubtedly been just as impressed. The villa constructed by Cleveland industrialist Amasa Stone, Jr., on Euclid Avenue during the 1850s typified both the beauty and the excess of European adaptations in the urban West. Stone's builders used over 700,000 bricks in the structure. The ceilings were recessed, with intricate cornice work making looking up just as much of a show as looking straight ahead. Mahogany, rosewood, and oak abounded on the stairs and floors. The home even boasted central heating and hot and cold running water—a luxury at that time—in nearly every room.

Prosperity generated affluence, but not, of course, for all. Other residential districts, less impressive but equally well defined, evolved in the city. The simple row house, that functional innovation of colonial times, housed the growing number of clerks, civil servants, and artisans. These middling groups could not afford sumptuous residences on Euclid Avenue but wanted the benefits of a single-family home. At the same time, they hoped to remain near downtown, where they worked and hoped to rise. The row houses, slapped together side by side, conserved space and, therefore, money. They could be built at the edge of downtown and still be affordable by the clerks and artisans. Philadelphia and Baltimore continued to be the

Figure 7.3   Philadelphia Row Houses, 1807

Substantial dwellings for the substantial middle class, spatially between the poor and the wealthy but looking always to the rich for inspiration. (Library of Congress)

major practitioners of row-house architecture. There were, however, several welcome improvements since the colonial period. The houses were usually larger—four to six rooms, instead of three—which allowed the family more living space and privacy, major deficiencies of the earlier structures. In addition, the front of the house, historically reserved for an office or shop, was now converted into a parlor as work and home became separated, thus giving the family even more space. Finally, the rising urban prosperity enabled these groups to spruce up their dwellings with carpeting, wallpaper, and furniture—many items of which had been luxuries during colonial days.

These row houses were generally located near the retail district of downtown. Few of the families living in them could afford the neighborhood adjacent to the financial district, yet they could afford to escape the increasingly undesirable areas along the waterfront. They were not far removed from the affluent, however. Often, the great residences of the wealthy were merely a block or two away. Occasionally, an expensive home interrupted the monotony of the row houses. These homes of the affluent, so near, yet so far, doubtless provided inspiration for some and perhaps frustration for others as symbols of what economic success could buy in an expanding commercial economy.

There were other groups in urban society with fewer dreams and still fewer residential options. Shut out of downtown and priced out of home ownership, lodging was a problem for these individuals. Part of the difficulty stemmed from a continuing housing shortage. Boarding houses and rental units converted from private homes attested to the shortage. These structures were either adjacent to the older wholesale section of downtown or were located in that district itself. Thus the anomaly arose of the city's poorest people living on the most expensive residential land in the city. Owners of these structures, in order to support them on the high-priced real estate, subdivided the buildings and charged inflated rents. These crowded one- or two-room apartments, often renting for as much as three dollars a week, placed a great strain on working-class families, few of whom earned more than one dollar a day. The sublandlord system made the housing situation even worse, not only by inflating rents but also by contributing to the deterioration of the building as well.

The sublandlord rented a group of houses in or near downtown from owners who had left for better residential neighborhoods. These leases were usually short-term, lasting only two or three years. During that time, the sublandlord desired to extract as much profit as possible from the dwellings. This meant high rents and few if any repairs. If the tenants complained, eviction or the threat of eviction was sufficient to mute most renters. A place to live was a valuable commodity in a city whose economy was expanding much faster than the housing supply. The irony of the situation was that the very commercial expansion which generated economic growth and wealth was daily removing structures from the housing stock, as houses were torn down to make way for warehouses and retail establishments or merely converted into these enterprises. Whether by destruction or conversion, some cities actually began to lose housing stock at the very time housing was an extremely scarce commodity.

The spread of the commercial area generated further deterioration and subsequent loss of housing stock by casting a pall over residential structures in the path of commercial advancement. Why improve a building that would, within a year or two, give way to a retail store or a bank? Invariably, this reasoning allowed some housing to stand unattended and ultimately uninhabited for decades. Finally, the expansion of downtown meant that there were many more jobs but that fewer people could live there. The result was extensive overcrowding of workers' quarters in adjacent areas, which, in turn, led to property deterioration and eventually to loss of housing stock.

The glittering retail emporiums and the stately banks contrasted sharply with the seamier side of downtown and its adjacent area. The competition for lodging in what was becoming a full-fledged tenement or slum district belied the conditions which existed inside these hovels. We have visited the commercial and residential palaces, as well as the more modest structures of the middle class. A visit to the other half of residential life brings with it awe and amazement as well, but of a different kind. In 1845 Dr. John Griscom, a New York physician, made the first comprehensive survey of slum housing in the city's history. His revelations shocked many, but it was not until several decades later that city officials undertook effective housing reform. The conditions he described were not peculiar to New York but were common to cities in all regions experiencing the growth pangs of economic expansion.

In a typical apartment that Griscom visited, he recorded that the walls and ceilings of the dwelling were "smeared with the blood of unmentionable insects and dirt of all indescribable colors." Since most sublandlords preferred short-term leases for their tenants, the apartments turned over every month or so, sometimes at highter rents, so few tenants bothered to clean the premises. The result was, according to Griscom, broken windows, chimneys "filled with soot, the whole premises populated thickly with vermin; the stairways, the common passage of several families, the receptacle for all things noxious, [and] whatever self-respect the family might have had . . . , crushed under the pressure of the degrading circumstances by which they are surrounded."[6]

There were some urban residents, especially newcomers from Europe and from the countryside, who could not afford even these wretched accommodations. They settled on the urban periphery, on semirural land that today we would call suburbia. There, the poor set up shanties just sufficient to keep out inclement weather. Since they were some distance from the nearest employment centers, they maintained a footloose life living off the land, drinking, and brawling, and meeting with premature death. These urban outskirts developed notorious reputations as districts of vice and corruption. Eventually, the expanding city would reach out and engulf these ring areas. The districts would maintain their degenerate character, though with significantly more crowding.

These were the darker sides of the residential city. The reflection from the broken pane was of a city becoming more spatially divided by economic status every day. Never was the prosperity of the city greater or the trappings of wealth more splendid or the burdens of poverty more miserable. These divisions were not the only divisions manifested in residential space. As the unity of the cluster city was shattered like the pane of glass, the emerging residential kaleidoscope included not only economic, but occupational, ethnic, and racial divisions as well. As the mercantile operations became specialized into retailing, wholesaling, and financing, occupations to service these distinct activities proliferated. Add to this a growing industrial component, and there was a further proliferation and specialization of occupational tasks. Each new group had distinct residential requirements and limitations. How they balanced their needs and their limits determined their lifestyles.

Spatial Reflections of Work and Ethnicity

The greatest victim of occupation specialization and, ultimately, of residential location was the artisan. While individual craftsmen continued to work in their own shops through the 1870s, industrial processes put many out of business or forced them into a factory routine. Social-mobility studies have indicated that industrialization forced roughly two out of every three artisans into the status of employee. The independent artisan was hardly that anymore. To make matters worse, the expansion of commercial ties brought the products of other cities and regions into competition with the craftsmen's productions. Competition from another source—cheap rural and immigrant labor—made factory goods less expensive. In the new consumer-oriented economy, what might have been lost in quality was more than made up for in price, variety, and quantity. While the artisan had dominated the urban labor force in the colonial period, by 1850 over half of the work force in the major cities was unskilled or semiskilled.

These unskilled and semiskilled workers were not merely employed in industry. Manufacturing was still a relatively minor part of most urban economies. The mercantile sector continued to employ the majority of workers, and their activities had increased significantly during the first half of the nineteenth century. Some examples of the new urban occupations include people to transfer goods from various railroad and steamboat termini across town or to wholesalers; construction workers to help build everything from a railroad to a house; clerks for the new retail operations; tanners, butchers, candle makers, bakers, and their employees to meet rising consumer demands; gardeners to tend the gardens of the wealthy; laundresses and seamstresses to take the burdens of household chores away from the wealthy; domestic servants to lighten the load even more; hucksters and peddlers to treat urban residents to exotic or inexpensive wares; and barbers and hairdressers because appearances counted in the business and social worlds.

The rapid increase of these "blue-collar" workers and the decline of the artisan solidified and widened the gap between employer and employee. If the American city was a city of shopkeepers in 1800, it was a city of working-class men and women by 1870, before the burgeoning of American industry. This division was reflected in the residential patterns. The stratification of economic wealth and its residential manifestations, discussed earlier, were underscored by the increasing occupational segregation. Once residence and work became separated—once merchants no longer resided above their countinghouses or stores and once artisans no longer utilized the front portion of their dwellings for work and display—a major criterion for residence was proximity to work. The shortage of housing and the high price of land in and near downtown were two major obstacles to the fulfillment of this objective. For the less affluent occupational groups, namely, most of them, the choice of residence involved some difficult decisions.

The incredible crowding and resultant residential decay which occurred in and especially adjacent to downtown was due to the fact that the majority of laborers worked in downtown. Since unskilled and semiskilled work was often short-term or seasonal, proximity to downtown meant easy access to other employment opportunities. Further, since working-class families frequently had several members of their family in the work force, residence farther away from downtown would add to their burdens as well. Finally, even after transportation developments had expanded urban space, most unskilled and semiskilled workers could not use transportation, since the fares were too high. They were still tied, therefore, to the pedestrian mode.

As the areas around downtown crowded with laborers, more affluent residents such as merchants and professionals left for more private residential neighborhoods. When transportation innovations negated the necessity of residing a pedestrian length away from downtown, the movement became an exodus. For example, in Philadelphia between 1829 and 1862, both the proportion of merchants who resided some distance away from their businesses and their average commuting length (measured in space rather than in time) doubled. A comparison of Figures 7.4 and 7.5 will illustrate this point. For lawyers working in New York City during a similar period (1835 to 1865) the average journey to work tripled. In other words, the residential areas about downtown were losing the economic and occupational mixture they had once possessed. The area was becoming increasingly a working-class neighborhood. Thus began the modern pattern of residential segregation so common in our cities today.

Although roughly three-quarters of a city's employment opportunities were in downtown, there was sufficient economic activity elsewhere to justify some residential concentration by occupation. Industries that moved to the urban periphery required a proximate work force. Factories were operated on a strict schedule. Workers could not afford long journeys on foot only to check in even a few minutes late. Yet, it was true that a number of factory operatives were drawn from the downtown area. A Massachusetts state official surveying housing in Boston during the 1860s told of a downtown resident who awoke before 5 A.M. and left home at 5:30 to make the 7 A.M. whistle at the peripheral factory. Explaining this seemingly inconvenient arrangement, the surveyor noted: "By living in town, chance work, when out of steady work, is more readily obtained. This is quite customary with workmen."[7] The lure of downtown as an employment center was greater than the convenience of residing close to outlying industry.

Figure 7.4   Journey to Work of Philadelphia Merchants, 1829

(From *The New Urban History: Quantitative Explorations by American Historians,* ed. by Leo F. Schnore. © 1975, Princeton University Press.)

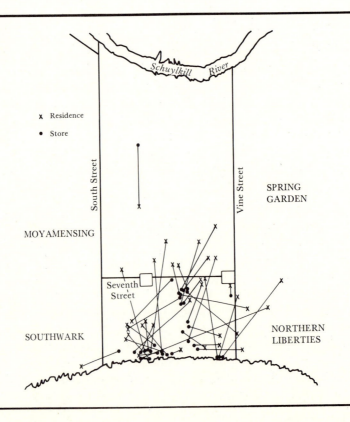

Residence by occupation was closely tied to the city's economic hierarchy. As immigrants began to comprise a more substantial element in the urban population, there was a tendency toward concentration, though this too conformed to the economic stratification. Prior to 1870, the great majority of immigrants were of German or Irish ancestry. By 1850, one-half of New York City's population was foreign born. At that same date, the Irish alone composed more than one-quarter of Boston's population. Cities in the West also received an important share of immigrants. More than one-half of the population of Milwaukee and Chicago was foreign born. Even in the South, which experienced relatively little immigration, the section's cities

Figure 7.5   Journey to Work of Philadelphia Merchants, 1862

Transportation technology, downtown crowding, and personal preference increasingly separated work place and residence for those who could afford to live in outlying residential districts (compare Figures 7.3 and 7.4). Workers generally remained near downtown. (From *The New Urban History: Quantitative Explorations by American Historians,* ed. by Leo F. Schnore. © 1975, Princeton University Press.)

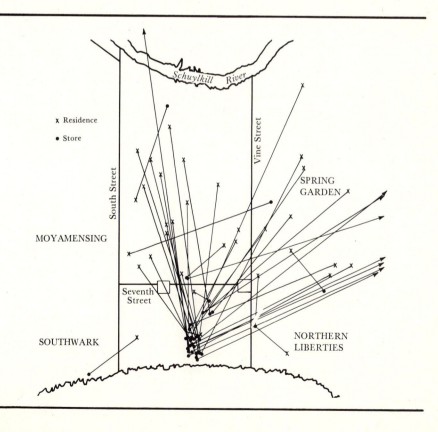

provided the vast majority of immigrant homes in the region. In the 1850s, Germans composed more than one-third of Louisville's residents. During the same decade, the foreign born accounted for more than a fourth of the white male householders in Richmond. Also in Richmond, immigrants composed 65 percent of the laborers and 47 percent of the craftsmen in the free labor force. Finally, the international flavor of New Orleans was well known, with 40 percent of its total population foreign born in 1860.

These antebellum immigrants were frequently scattered about the city. It was very rare, for example, to find the overwhelming majority of the Irish or Germans concentrated in one particular ward of the city. Yet wherever they landed, immigrants settled in groups rather than as individuals. The common bonds of culture, the forces of discrimination, the size of the immigrant group, and their economic and occupational status ensured that some concentration would occur.

Most immigrants, especially the Irish, joined the labor force at low occupational levels. These immigrants were most likely to find work in warehouse and terminal facilities down by the waterfront. Even skilled German and Jewish tailors and seamstresses worked in the warehouse district, where the early garment industry made its home. Proximity to the warehouses was an important concern, so the foreign born tended to re-enforce the pattern of downtown and its environs as a residential location of low economic status. Some German immigrants opened grocery stores, ice cream parlors, or small restaurants and were able to be more selective in their residential locations as their businesses usually bordered on the more fashionable retail district.

Thus while few German or Irish ghettos emerged during this period, immigrants, especially the Germans, experienced a concentration of residential settlement. In Milwaukee, for example, which possessed a relatively high percentage of foreign born, 83 percent of the German households lived in German neighborhoods in 1860, while only 47 percent of the Irish lived in Irish neighborhoods. This concentration was actually less than the residential concentration of the native born (53 percent). Factors of culture and occupation—the Irish were mostly unskilled and nomadic in terms of jobs and residences—accounted for this difference. In cities where the immigrant influx was proportionately less, there was less concentration.

The best evidence of residential clustering among Germans in many cities was the development of ethnic institutions which served both to solidify the German community and lend increasing importance to its residential space. To many native-born families their residential neighborhoods were merely places to live and sometimes, depending on the quality of housing stock, to despise. For immigrants, the neighborhood became an extension of their homeland and, regardless of the decay, it was a personal part of themselves. In Milwaukee, a German theater, German schools, newspaper, relief societies, fire companies, and even a baseball team developed alongside but separate from similar native institutions. The ethnic community that comprised not only residential but commercial, recreational, and religious structures as well foreshadowed the formation of the late-nineteenth-century ethnic ghettos that existed as separate entities in urban society.

Urban blacks were also drifting into more concentrated residential patterns by 1870, and in some cities these patterns were more evident than had been true of the immigrant population. It is more difficult to generalize about the black urban experience prior to 1870 because sectional and status differences complicated the picture. Wherever they were or whatever they were doing, urban blacks were invariably better off than their comrades in the countryside.

"Better off," of course, in relative terms. Some historians have used the word "caste" to describe the black experience in the urban North prior to 1870. In terms of civil rights, regardless of state constitutional provisions, they possessed few that could be exercised with unequivocal freedom. Black suffrage was maintained only in New England, and in New York state suffrage was granted only to blacks who possessed more than $250 in property. Should blacks attempt to seek redress through the judicial process, chances of relief were slim, given white judges and all-white juries. When Worcester, Massachusetts, broke tradition and allowed the town's blacks to serve on juries, an Indiana congressman predicted that this precedent

would allow a white man to be accused of crime by a negro; to be arrested on the affidavit of a negro, by a negro officer; to be prosecuted by a negro lawyer; testified against by a negro witness; tried before a negro judge, convicted before a negro jury; and executed by a negro executioner; and either one of these negroes might become the husband of his widow or his daughter![8]

White authorities in Cincinnati, evidently concerned by this potential progression of events, decided to rid the city of blacks in 1829. Cincinnati, on the Ohio River, was a haven for runaway slaves, and whites in the city feared their increasing presence. Local officials invoked a little-used state statute and gave their black citizens thirty days to leave town. Impatient for their removal, a white mob destroyed most of the black neighborhood in the city, prompting roughly half of the city's black population to leave for

Canada. After losing a good deal of their labor force, officials lifted the eviction decree. While Cincinnatians acted out their racial fantasies, numerous cities in the West and Northeast harbored similar fears and hatreds. There were, according to one foreign observer, "two nations—one white and another black—growing up together within the same political circle, but never mingling on a principle of equality."[9] More than a century later a federal commission investigating the riots of the 1960s would reach the same conclusion.

Despite the inferior social and political status of blacks in the urban North, there were opportunities for economic advancement. Like the immigrant, the black filled primarily menial occupational roles. In antebellum Detroit, for example, where the black experience was not particularly frightening, the small black work force (140) worked at twenty-six different occupations in 1850. This seeming occupational variety obscured the fact that every one of these jobs was in the unskilled and semiskilled category. Even more important, blacks remained locked into these occupations. Over the next two decades there was virtually no movement out of these low-paying and low-status positions despite the rapid expansion of Detroit's economy.

The situation of blacks in the urban South was in some ways better and in some ways worse than the position of blacks in the urban North. The presence of free blacks living side by side with slaves created some unusual racial patterns in southern cities. In northern cities, most blacks occupied the lowest rungs of the urban social ladder. In some southern cities, especially in the deep South—Mobile, Natchez, and New Orleans—the "free people of color," as they were called, enjoyed some wealth, freedom, and status. Free blacks filtered into skilled occupations and monopolized several. In Charleston, South Carolina, in 1860, three-quarters of the free black work force worked at skilled trades, especially barbering, carpentry, and catering. This was in marked contrast to the low occupational status of black workers in Detroit at the same time.

In a society where European immigration was relatively light until the 1850s and migration from the farm was slowed by general agricultural prosperity, the labor of black men and women was a valuable commodity. This probably accounts for the presence of free blacks in better positions in the urban South than in the urban North. Slaves, of course, were much more restricted in their options, but they too experienced upward mobility as southern cities pressed for economic growth. Urban slavery proved a flexible, profitable, and useful labor system. The flexibility resulted from the fact that the industrial and mercantile firms with sizeable work-force requirements hired slaves instead of purchasing them at a prohibitive collective cost. The slave-hiring system allowed the employer the flexibility of hiring for long- or short-term periods, depending on his needs, and it allowed slaves to earn bonus money, which a few used to purchase their freedom and others to buy extra food, clothing, or luxuries for themselves and their families. Some slaves actually hired their own time; that is, they contracted out to the employer who offered them the biggest bonuses and the best living conditions.

In terms of personal rights, slaves were constantly under surveillance, and free blacks experienced frequent harassment. The laws circumscribing the freedom of the free black were extensive in the urban South, but their enforcement was spotty. Laws requiring employers to ascertain whether their free black employees were in fact free were openly ignored as were laws requiring recently manumitted slaves to leave the state within a certain time period. As long as black labor performed an essential function in the urban South, there was a limited degree of choice and mobility for blacks, slave or free.

Therein lay the key to the decline in the situation of blacks in cities of both sections of the country. When their labor became expendable, they did too. As immigrants began to swell the urban population in some southern and in most northern cities, they entered into fierce and sometimes violent competition with blacks for the available unskilled and semi-skilled occupations. Invariably the blacks lost the battle and while cities and immigrants alike were caught in the whirl of progress, the black position in urban society deteriorated. In St. Louis by 1860, the large German and Irish populations had displaced free blacks in the latter's last occupational refuge, domestic service. In Baltimore, the same transformation occurred. The fact that skilled blacks could no longer find work in these cities was especially discouraging. The definition of "nigger work" had confined skilled blacks in such occupations as barbering, carpentering, black-smithing, and shoemaking. With immigration, the definition was constantly revised until it was abandoned altogether. For slaves a return to the plantation was the typical result of this sequence; for free blacks there were even fewer alternatives except to leave or to sink into abject poverty. In southern cities with less marked immigration, though, free blacks clung tenaciously to their skilled crafts. For cities in the North and West, the picture was bleak, even though blacks were already concentrated in lowly occupations. In Detroit, for example, the property holding of blacks and the relative status of blacks to whites actually declined between 1850 and 1870. To be black in the city meant to be poor and reviled.

The lowly, isolated social position of the urban blacks was reflected in their residential location: lowly and isolated. Blacks were the most residentially concentrated group in urban society. In Philadelphia, where both Irish and German immigrants were scattered throughout the city in small enclaves, blacks were concentrated near downtown. In Boston, blacks were confined to two areas: "New Guinea" along the wharves and the infamous "Nigger Hill" near downtown. More than one-half of the city's black population resided in the latter neighborhood, which one historian has described as a mixture of "combustible houses, bars, sailor dance halls, and low boarding houses," or, in the words of a contemporary, a "horrid sink of pollution."[10]

In southern cities there were rarely such concentrations of blacks. Blacks resided in every section of southern cities. If there was a tendency toward concentration, it was more along economic and occupational lines than by racial distinctions as was the case in northern cities. Blacks tended to live near their place of work. Since free blacks were employed in a greater variety of occupations than northern blacks, it was not surprising that they evidenced a wider variety of residential locations. The use of residential space by blacks in antebellum Charleston exemplifies this pattern. Though Charleston's blacks tended to be overrepresented in the poorer neighborhoods in and about downtown, they resided in all sections of the city. An all-black block did not exist. The degree of racial and ethnic segregation in the city was much less than segregation by status. In Charleston free blacks and poor whites were often neighbors, though this was becoming less true as the Civil War approached. Even so, the patterns of segregation conformed to economic rather than to racial divisions.

Blacks in the urban North took advantage of their residential segregation by developing institutions much like the immigrants. In the South, with its dispersed residential pattern, the divisions between slaves and freemen, the occupational distinctions, and above all the fear among whites of any associational activity among blacks reduced institutional formation. One great advantage possessed by their northern brethren living in a free society was the freedom not only to form social or religious groups, but also to develop organizations to further the civil rights of blacks. This means of agitation was closed to the southern urban black regardless of economic status.

In northern cities, as in the urban South, churches were the focal points of black associational activity. Churches extended their influence into mutual aid societies and into politics as well. During the 1840s throughout the urban North, there was a great deal of participation in the national Negro Convention Movement, which was designed to advance the civil rights of blacks in the region. Literary societies and black newspapers—rare in the urban South—shifted their efforts from more prosaic concerns to a strong advocacy of black rights. The black schools which flourished in northern cities were also helpful in apprising black children that their role in society need not be second class. Though most of these efforts were unavailing, it helped to prepare numerous blacks for leadership positions and imparted a sense of identity and pride to group members. In a segregated society, self-help was the only realistic alternative.

The Separate and Separating
Urban Societies

The development of downtown and the formation of neighborhoods throughout the city had a profound impact on the urban social order. The spatial reordering which began to occur in the early decades of the nineteenth century reflected new economic, occupational, ethnic, and racial realities. Downtown was the expanded focus of urban life; in some areas it was a glittering showcase, in others it was a grimy relic. Retail palaces and industrial warehouses occupied downtown space, and each contributed significantly to urban economic growth. Residential neighborhoods exhibited similar contrasts. The last vestiges of downtown housing were miserable dwellings with miserable people within. Only a few blocks away, financial barons sipped imported wine in spacious homes away from the din and offense of downtown. The urban leader became increasingly separated from his fellow citizens by occupation, ethnicity, and race. The growing corps of middle-echelon job holders could not provide the cement to keep urban society together spatially or socially. Their aspirations lay with the elite, even if their residences lay perilously close to the poor. Urban America was not becoming a society bound by a rigid class structure, but it was becoming a milieu where, more and more, class mattered.

Urban society had always maintained a three-tiered social structure with merchants and professionals composing the upper tier; the so-called respectable workingmen, including craftsmen, clerks, and shopkeepers, comprising the middle level; and unskilled and semiskilled laborers, the unemployed, and transients making up the lower tier. Wealth, along with residential location, was the primary measure of status by 1840. The major feature of this traditional hierarchy was the growing separation of the three tiers. As downtown expanded and as residential areas became differentiated, social classes in urban society were growing apart from each other.

The most serious social separation occurred between the elite and the rest of the urban society. Just as wealthy cities with extensive contacts continued to grow at an almost geometrical pace as growth proved self-generative, so too wealthy individuals almost naturally accumulated greater wealth and at rates considerably faster than their fellow citizens. As there was a hierarchy of cities, with New York pulling further away from the other cities with each passing decade, there was a hierarchy of people, with similar results.

The analogy with New York is especially appropriate since it was in that city that the greatest gap between social groups occurred. According to one popular New York newspaper, "the classes are so distinctly marked, that they exist, as it were, in different worlds. . . . No city in the world offers greater inducements to the rich than New York, or less to the poor."[11] In other large cities, similar though less-marked patterns were evident. Boston's leaders were accumulating wealth at such an impressive rate that between 1830 and 1860, their wealth quadrupled while the proportion of propertyless individuals in the city's population rose from 44.6 percent to 57.3 percent. Figures for western cities provided slightly less contrast and in southern cities the contrast was even less. It seemed that the largest and wealthiest cities evidenced the greatest social inequality.

Statistics are merely general representations of the growing social chasm. In day-to-day urban life the disparities in the social structure were manifested in several different ways. The associational activity of the various social groups tended to draw them further apart. Fraternal organizations, literary societies, and churches tended to divide along class lines. Urban society, in fact, seemed in danger of becoming overorganized. As early as 1815, Cincinnati, barely removed from the frontier, seemed to be undergoing the associational mania: "Twenty sermons a week—Sunday evening Discourses on Theology—Private assemblies—State Cotillion Parties—Saturday Night Clubs, and chemical lectures . . . like the ague, return every day with distressing regularity."[12] On the more serious side, the proliferation of associations tended to decrease communication across class lines. Individuals moved in tighter and tighter social circles.

The lifestyle of the wealthy, through their associations, became increasingly removed from the rest of urban life. A glimpse of this lifestyle underscores the inbred and exclusive nature of the elite. New York again represented the ultimate in high life. A mansion on Fifth Avenue, carriages and horses for transportation, a pony for the younger children, a saddle horse for the older ones, and a yacht were prerequisites to enjoying the good life.

Then there is the opera and the theatre, unless, as one New York millionaire has chosen to do, he chooses to build a theatre of his own. There are balls, costumes, and otherwise . . . and last, though not least, there is shopping at . . . Lord & Taylor's and such other economical places, where really a lady could not expect to get anything to wear short of a morning's bill of two or three thousand dollars. Ah! money may be the root of all evil, but it is a mighty pleasant esculent for the New York market.[13]

This is not to say that the rest of urban society went without recreation. For working-class people fatigue precluded such activity during the week. Awakening at dawn and returning home after dark after putting in eleven or twelve hours a day, six days a week, at work left little time or energy for recreation. The most common working-class recreational activity was drinking. The tavern was the race course, the ballroom, the salon, and the resort combined. In frontier cities where a good many adventurers from the lower echelons of eastern urban society had drifted, drinking was a constant activity. San Francisco, for example, had over 2,000 saloons, or one tavern for every 117 residents. Since most bars offered free lunches, drinking usually began in the early afternoon. Unfortunately, alcoholism became a severe problem in cities and added to the burdens of the working class.

Religion was another activity that tended to widen the disparity between classes as it accentuated the economic cleavages. Religion was an important force in cities at this time. Religious institutions launched charity drives, operated schools, provided recreational space, and imparted important values in a changing society. Like cities, however, religious denominations engaged in rivalries of their own. In an era when large church membership signified success, the number of members in a given church became increasingly important. Many denominations guarded their domains protectively while seeking converts at the same time. Through it all, however, the Episcopal, Congregational, and Presbyterian churches tended to remain the repository of the elite, while those who were not members of the urban leadership tended to practice the more evangelical Protestant faiths, Catholicism, and Judaism. You could almost tell an individual's position in society by the church he or she belonged to.

The associational activity and the social and religious lifestyles of urban residents confirmed the growing inequality in urban society. The elite were a well-defined and relatively homogeneous group. As one historian has asserted, they were "bound together by economic interest, fortified by constant social contacts, and set apart by wealth and education."[14] Their isolation was even greater than it might appear at first because entry into this group from the lower rungs was difficult. Historians conducting social-mobility studies of a variety of city types and sizes generally agree that the rags-to-riches stories were few. For the most part, the elite tended to be a self-perpetuating group. They intermarried and rarely conducted business or social affairs with anyone outside of their class. They also attended the "right" schools, preferably Harvard or a comparable university. Under these circumstances it is not surprising that there were few breakthroughs. In addition, by 1870, social mobility between the tiers was generally less than it had been a generation earlier. As the contacts of the elite were contracting, so were opportunities to enter the privileged class.

This does not mean that decade after decade, individuals and families below the leadership group did not enhance their position. They did, and frequently too. If success is measured by the accumulation of property, during any given decade roughly one-third to one-half of the members of the second and third social tiers were successful. A purchase of a store, a horse, some new furniture, and the ultimate in urban advancement, a home, were within reach of numerous urban workers. While there was, therefore, movement within a tier, movement between classes was unusual. Chances were that this modest mobility was achieved without a change in job status or residential location.

Mobility, of course, varied from city to city. In older cities like New York and Boston, the social structure was more stable. In newer cities like Cincinnati and Chicago, where economic growth was more rapid and where an entrenched leadership did not exist, movement up and down the social ladder was easier. In these western cities, however, economic growth and maturity resulted in decreased social mobility.

The decline in mobility solidified certain roles in urban society, as had already been evidenced by spatial patterns. The various groups in the city began to identify themselves as permanent members of their social strata. Though many members of the working class hoped for and attained improvement in their economic condition, few realistically pursued the objective of entering the entrepreneurial ranks. Business leaders, for their part, more than likely grew up in the sheltered confines of an elite family and had virtually no contact and little in common with the working-class life-style.

The social and religious associations of these urban groups reflected this separation. With the formation of exclusive economic organizations came the official recognition of the permanency of the social order. Businessmen formed boards of trade and exchanges because they shared the same objectives and assumptions about economic growth. Workers also organized into economic associations through which they expressed their common economic interests. Though most of these associations were short-lived, while they existed, they provided workers, collectively, with their first formal opportunities to express the new facts about working-class life.

These workers' associations were common in the larger cities where class divisions were sharpest. The old, almost filial, relations between masters, journeymen, and apprentices had broken down earliest in these cities. Cut adrift in a society where associations were becoming the major vehicles of advancement, workers sought out each other. The earliest groups were divided into masters, journeymen, and apprentices, reflecting the growing estrangement of these craftsworkers. With the decline of the artisan class as a whole, broader organizations emerged to protect their eroding status. In 1828, Philadelphia's craftsmen formed the Working Men's Party. The group espoused a number of wide-ranging reforms designed to overhaul society: free universal public education, abolition of compulsory militia training and of imprisonment for debt, and close regulations on the sale of liquor. Although the artisans continued their decline, the Pennsylvania legislature passed all of these reform measures during the next two decades.

Of more immediate use to artisans was the growing union movement, which organized artisans and unskilled workers together, thus demonstrating the artisans' new identification with the employed, rather than with the employer. Between the spring of 1835 and the fall of 1836, six thousand craftsworkers and unskilled union members won the ten-hour day and higher wages in a succession of strikes. It would be almost a century before trade unionism would compile such a glittering record.

The division of urban society into separate and at times hostile groups accompanied and followed naturally from the segregation of space. The geographical expansion of the city had altered both residential and commercial space not only with economic, but also with social consequences. Downtown stood as a monument to business acumen, but parts of it were reminders of the inequality that had risen with it. Urban expansion, whatever the social costs, was not a process that could be reversed. The more the size of the city grew spatially, the greater the spatial segregation. The development of downtown and the formation of separate residential neighborhoods were merely the beginning of a series of spatial events, continued to the present, which liberated some groups and trapped others.

America's cities grew up in the first half of the nineteenth century. Pressures applied by economic prosperity and population growth generated the early phases of expansion, and transportation systems extended the city line to an even greater extent. One city, San Francisco, hemmed in by water and hills, even expanded out into the bay. Another, Philadelphia, gathered up its suburban neighborhoods one day in 1854 and increased in size from two square miles to one hundred and twenty square miles. Though the expansion of few cities duplicated that of San Francisco or Philadelphia, urban space fanned outward from downtown in rapid fashion. Citizens were acting upon their desires for more space, quiet, and beauty—visions that would continue to expand urban settlement. There were some growing pains. The working class remained trapped in the city center, burdened by lack of mobility and a deteriorating housing situation. Public transit and the availability of new residential space did not relieve their burdens. They were not the only group to feel the pangs of growth, however. Residents clamored for streets, protection from disease and crime, and a general improvement in the quality of life. As urban leaders had reached out to organize the hinterland and streamline the processes of trade, so they now looked inward to make their city worthy enough to be the repository of their new commercial empire.

Notes

1. Quotations and other details of this description of the arrival of the department store are from Bayrd Still, ed., *Urban America: A History with Documents* (Boston: Little, Brown, 1974), pp. 148–149.

2. Quoted in *ibid.,* p. 86.

3. Quoted in Elizabeth Dougherty, "Nineteenth Century Transportation Modes and Their Influence on Urban Spatial Forms," unpublished paper, Virginia Polytechnic Institute and State University, March 1976.

4. Quoted in Still, ed., *Urban America,* p. 197.

5. Quoted in *ibid.,* p. 86.

6. Quoted in Charles N. Glaab, ed., *The American City: A Documentary History* (Homewood, Ill.: Dorsey Press, 1963), pp. 121–122.

7. Quoted in Still, ed., *Urban America,* p. 121.

8. Quoted in Leon F. Litwack, *North of Slavery: The Negro in the Free States, 1790–1860* (Chicago: University of Chicago Press, 1961), p. 93.

9. Quoted in *ibid.*, p. 102.

10. Quoted in Oscar Handlin, *Boston's Immigrants: A Study in Acculturation* (Cambridge, Mass.: Harvard University Press, 1941), p. 96.

11. Quoted in Still, ed., *Urban America*, p. 155.

12. Quoted in Richard C. Wade, *The Urban Frontier; Pioneer Life in Early Pittsburgh, Cincinnati, Lexington, Louisville, and St. Louis* (Chicago: University of Chicago Press, 1964), p. 157.

13. Quoted in Still, ed., *Urban America*, p. 155.

14. Wade, *Urban Frontier*, p. 209.

8.
The Business of Government and Services

Urban leaders looked over their expanded domain and set out to control its physical growth so that it would enhance, not interfere with its economic growth. Controlling growth did not mean limiting it, for any growth was good and was to be nurtured, not stunted. Rather, control meant order to ensure that the city's rapid spatial and population expansion would not induce chaos and therefore retard economic development. The leadership approached this task as they approached the problem of directing economic development. They took command of and worked through local organizations, especially local government, to formulate and implement their plans for action. In devising their policies, they assumed that their interests for economic growth were synonymous with the community's interests. They therefore measured their policies for ordering growth by the standard of benefit to the business community, for what benefited business benefited all. Under this banner, the trappings of urban maturity were achieved by American cities, disorder in urban society was reduced, and the spatial and hence the social inequalities that had come to characterize urbanization were perpetuated.

Advancing Political Technology

Local government was to be the primary engine to accomplish the task of ordering the city. In the process of doing so, local government grew from an unnoticed, ineffectual institution to an important and influential force in urban life. City officials in the late eighteenth century had held largely honorary positions and had exercised very little impact on public policy. Charters granted by the state prohibited them from raising revenues; nor could they spend beyond what little money they received from licenses and fees, as there were stringent debt ceilings imposed by the city charter. In 1821 Cleveland's revenue, for example, amounted to the princely sum of $80.02, a modest amount even for a city of 600 residents.

As both the population and the size of the city grew, urban government began to assert itself. In response to the changes in the urban environment, leaders prompted government to act. Officials responded, but in a limited way. In Jacksonian America the individual, not the government, bore the primary responsibility for solving problems. Only when the individual or his or her private organization had failed to overcome the difficulty, then and only then would government respond. Governmental response, moreover, would not exclude the individual, but would occur in partnership with the citizens. It was a mixed-enterprise approach to establishing order. There were two major reasons for the caution of public officials. First, government intervention implied an interference with private property and the regulation of living habits, two areas in which Americans insisted on privacy. Second, active intervention meant fiscal support. Once state-granted charters were amended to approve revenue-raising powers, the burden of supporting new programs fell upon the leaders themselves, since the property tax was the greatest source of revenue. Local government which consisted primarily of the community's business leaders implemented plans only when the benefits to the city's economic growth outweighed the costs to the propertyholders. This simple cost-benefit ratio ruled the provision for urban services designed to order urban growth.

The structure of local government was another factor in restricting government's intervention into community life. The city council, composed either of two bodies or of one, was the dominant urban political institution. In the early nineteenth century, this body legislated for the city, executed its laws, and served as the lower court system of the city. As long as local government was a caretaker, this combination of legislative, executive, and judicial functions went unchallenged. But, as government came to play a large role in urban life, such concentration of power was viewed as alien to American traditions and some of the council's powers were transferred to the mayor.

Until the 1820s the urban mayor was primarily a ceremonial figure with duties restricted to minor judicial matters. As the city grew and divided into wards to facilitate administration, the mayors came to be the only major officials with a city-wide constituency. Instead of being chosen by the council, they were now chosen by the city. This change increased their independence and ultimately their power. As city government grew, so did the mayor's patronage powers. Several local officials were directly responsible to the mayor. In addition, in some cities the mayor possessed veto power over the council's acts.

The mayor's advances over the council were not difficult to achieve. Government by committee was not a very expedient and decisive method of governance. The trend toward bicameral councils usually meant that it took twice as long to push legislation through the council, which decreased its stature even further. Under the ward system each member of the council represented only a portion of the city. This seemed to frustrate action as well. Only large projects that benefited all wards or projects that benefited the business district enjoyed a relatively smooth passage through the council. On other types of proposals, it was difficult to reach a consensus. On one thing, however, all council members, as business leaders, agreed. They all subscribed to the "psychology of scarcity." The doctrine, in the words of historian Michael Frisch, "elevated thrift, minimal consumption, and avoidance of debt to moral imperatives."[1] In other words, the council saw to it that local government played a limited but constructive role in community life.

Local government became another business institution designed to order growth. Government promoted rather than regulated business. Laws regulating markets, weights and measures, and prices—common during the colonial era—were quietly repealed by the 1820s. Government allowed private organizations like the board of trade to set the standards that governed commerce. More important than what the political institutions did not do was what they did to promote economic growth.

"The interests of commerce," declared one Philadelphian, "as connected with politics, are so striking, that it is difficult to separate one from the other."[2] Indeed, it was hard to tell where the private sector ended and the public sector began. The participants in both business and public life were the same. When it came to supporting the plans for economic growth, local government officials abandoned their lethargy and pledged huge sums to support railroads, harbor improvements, and canals. Their frugality in providing urban services contrasted sharply with their generosity, even extravagance, in supporting projects to promote economic growth. That was the key: The simple cost-benefit analysis worked here, too, because these projects were absolutely essential to economic development. As new charter provisions gave communities greater freedom in raising revenues and greater discretion in compiling debt, the business community discovered a willing ally with greater resources and credit than they could muster individually or in their private groups.

Local government was the strong, silent partner in building a commercial empire. The cities of Philadelphia, New York, and Baltimore were heavy investors in railroad and canal lines. In the South, where local capital was the predominant method of financing internal improvements, city governments subscribed enthusiastically to railroad stock.

Local government was at its partisan best not only in spending money, but also in saving it, particularly as far as the merchants were concerned. As noted earlier, the property tax was the major revenue source for most cities. The expanded role of local government obviously required increased revenues. City councils went through some interesting contortions in attempting to squeeze revenue out of new sources while stabilizing the property tax. In 1841 Savannah officials attempted to close the gap between revenue and expenditures by imposing an income tax on residents, which some viewed as a method to get the working classes to pay the equivalent of property taxes without owning property. The expected public outcry forced the council to repeal this tax.

Such public protest about local government policies was rare in American cities. One reason local government was able to reflect business views so vigorously was that there was so little input from other segments of the city. Though universal white male suffrage was common in cities by the 1830s in the midst of Jacksonian Democracy, interest and participation in municipal elections and in government remained low among a majority of people. Very little of what government did, except for determining the tax structure, affected most urban residents; hence, the occasional protests usually were in objection to increased taxes. Local officials governed for one particular group in urban society and neglected the others. Only when neglect became callous disregard did public protest arise and then quickly subside. In this atmosphere it was not surprising that business leaders believed their interests to be synonymous with the community's interests, and so the government was theirs. If, as historian Edward Pessen has suggested, "influence and power are manifested, above all, in the actions of government,"[3] it is instructive to look at government as it ordered urban society through the implementation of urban services. In that way, we not only can see how American cities matured, but we also can confirm the total dominance of economic objectives not only in the use of space, but in the determination of public policy as well.

Urban Services: Policy Reflections
of Economic Objectives

Streets were the major concern of local government, at least in terms of the time councilmen spent deliberating various subjects. This was not surprising. Streets, after all, like railroads and canals, were also arteries of commerce. They facilitated communication among people engaged in business and between merchants and their customers. It was not unusual for cities to devote one-fourth of their budgets to street cleaning and paving. In the cost-benefit formula, good streets were obviously essential to economic development.

A good street, though, was hard to find. Muddy when it rained, dusty when it did not, and easily passable only occasionally, urban streets resembled steeplechase courses rather than pedestrian and wheeled-vehicle thoroughfares. A popular story of the era told of a citizen who rushed into the street to help a man buried up to his neck in mud. "No need to worry," the entombed victim replied, "I have a horse underneath me."[4]

The need for improving the condition of the streets, and especially for paving them was there, to be sure. Few urban streets were paved, however, despite the time and money expended by the city for this purpose. City funds were applied only toward paving the major thoroughfares—the business arteries of the city. This made good sense in terms of impressing visitors like customers, tourists, and potential investors. As an Alexandria paper noted: "There are few things which operate against a city more than bad streets, and especially when they are the principal ones."[5]

The method of financing these paving projects provides a good example of the mixed-enterprise approach to local government. It also demonstrates why most streets in the city remained sunk in mud and ruts. Requests for street paving did not originate in council, but with the property owners on a particular street. When two-thirds of the property owners on a street requested paving, it was considered a valid request. The city typically approved the petition and set about paving the street, assessing abutting owners a portion or all of the total cost. In reality, most property owners refused to pay the assessment. Since a number of these propertied individuals sat on the city council, the dilemma facing the council may be appreciated. Does the council allow a major business thoroughfare to go unpaved because of a few miserly property owners? No indeed! Surely, such a major undertaking with economic ramifications for the *entire* city could legitimately be borne by the public treasury. And so it was. This line of reasoning was an indication not of cynicism on the part of urban leaders, but rather of their genuine belief that what benefited business benefited all and that government, as representative of all, should and could finance the project.

Street cleaning followed a similar pattern, though here the problem was more complicated. City streets, in addition to being generally unpaved, were usually extremely filthy. New York by all accounts possessed the dirtiest streets in urban America. "With the exception of a very few thoroughfares, all the streets are one mass of reeking, disgusting filth, which in some places is piled to such a height as to render them almost impassable by vehicles." But New York had a great deal of company: Places "too foul to serve as the sties for the hogs" and "filthy in the extreme," streets where a pedestrian might "literally go entangled in pigs' tails and jaw bones" and "me[e]t with the putrefying carcass of a dead dog," were some of the descriptions of filth in the streets of various American cities.[6] Evidently, the gentleman up to his neck in the mud in the story cited earlier was encased in a more exotic concoction than he probably realized.

The problem of street cleaning seemed insoluble. Horses alone dropped tons of manure and gallons of urine daily. But this was the age of rationalism, when it was believed that all problems had a solution; it was also the era of transcendentalism, when it was assumed that people could accomplish almost anything they set their minds to; it was, finally, the age of business. And dirty streets implied a disorderly community and possibly an unhealthy one. Both implications were bad for business. "It is of vast importance to the trade and prosperity of Norfolk," an editor warned, "to say nothing of the lives of the people, that the standing pools in our streets should be removed by the . . . councils instantly."[7]

Local government mobilized into action on several fronts. Evidently believing that street cleaning was a beastly business, several cities assigned to animals the bulk of the street-cleaning chores. Pigs were the most popular, scavenging streets in New York, St. Louis, and Cincinnati. By the 1860s, a new sense of public dignity and an overpopulation of greedy porkers led to a discontinuation of the use of pigs as street scavengers.

For cities that were serious about their street-cleaning efforts, this zoo parade could only be a temporary expedient because the cure often became worse than the disease. City councils, therefore, contracted with private companies or with individuals to clean, or scavenge as it was called, city streets. Unfortunately, these contracts were often political rewards rather than genuine performance agreements. In New York, it was said, the only way to have the streets cleaned was to bribe the city councilmen.

This is not to say that local government expended little effort and money on street cleaning. As the Norfolk editor stated, there were good business and health reasons to be concerned about clean streets—but only certain streets. The major business streets were generally clean, regardless of the condition of the rest of the city's streets. Predictably, it was the streets that were most neglected—those in the poorest sections of the city—that were most dirty and most likely to foster the spread of disease. They were also the least visible streets, and business leaders, always keen to present a good image at the least cost, felt justified in directing local government's street-cleaning efforts, meager as they were, toward the few main business streets. The inequity of the situation did not go unnoticed, and some leaders themselves pointed this out to their colleagues: "It has been too much the practice to cause the large thoroughfares to be scrupulously cleaned," New York's Mayor Ambrose Kingsland warned some councilmen "while scarcely any attention is paid to the smaller and less frequented, but most densely populated streets in the city."[8]

The limited role of government, exercised again in favor of a particular segment of the community, should not obscure one innovation in sanitary planning that had occurred in several cities by the mid-nineteenth century. The introduction of modern sewers in the 1850s in some cities was a marked improvement in public-sanitation efforts. Prior to that time, sewer systems had merely consisted of drains that prevented the flooding of roads and cellars and had had little to do with waste removal. Soon, the drains became clogged with garbage and animal carcasses and ceased to serve even as drainage facilities as the solid waste matter festered. In 1842 Edwin Chadwick, an English sanitary reformer, perfected a sewer that was periodically flushed with water, which would dislodge solid waste. During the 1850s this design was used with positive results in a number of American cities. Once again, however, the application of this innovation was limited. The city installed these water-carriage sewers only on the petition of property owners. If this situation sounds like that of street paving revisited, it is. New York constructed sewers for one-fourth of its streets during the 1850s, almost none in the working-class districts. It was not until the late nineteenth century that sewer systems were installed throughout the city.

One of the major arguments for clean streets and proper waste removal was that filth contributed to the possibility of epidemic disease. Few events struck more terror into the hearts of city dwellers than an epidemic. Once an epidemic began, its course seemed relentless. Prior to the discovery of the germ theory of disease, physicians were powerless to deal with epidemics. The only proven remedy was flight. For those who remained behind, the chances of contracting the disease were great, as the shockingly high death tolls reveal. A yellow fever epidemic in Philadelphia in 1793 took the lives of 5,000 people, nearly one out of every ten people residing in the city; in an 1849 cholera epidemic St. Louis lost one-tenth of its population; in 1853 yellow fever ravaged New Orleans, killing 11,000 people; and in 1855, Norfolk was decimated by a yellow fever epidemic that carried off nearly one-sixth of its population.

Physicians attempted futile remedies in the face of this onslaught. Calomel, a white mercury compound, was a popular prescription for cholera. Large doses induced mercury poisoning, if the patient had not died from cholera first. A common remedy for disease was bleeding, which weakened the patients and probably hastened their death. To check diarrhea, a prevalent symptom of cholera, the president of the New York State Medical Society suggested plugging the rectum with beeswax. Strychnine, electric shocks, and tobacco-smoke enemas were also popular cures. Little wonder that one survivor quipped: "Cholera kills, and doctors slay, and every foe will have its way!"[9]

As cities grew, the frequency of these destructive epidemics increased. Business leaders took a special interest in disease prevention. Disease was bad for business. No farmer wanted to trade his crops for yellow fever, and no investor wished to see his capital sunk into a sickly city. Epidemics were expensive: Commerce stopped, prominent leaders were carried off, and urban reputations were damaged. One physician estimated that New Orleans lost $45,000,000 in commerce during its yellow fever epidemics of the late 1840s. In addition, rival cities' newspaper editors were quick in attempting to dissuade farmers, tourists, and investors from traveling to a competing city by publishing reports of that city's inherent unhealthfulness. It took some communities years to recover from the shock of a severe epidemic.

Given this depressing litany, it would seem obvious that local government would offer its treasury to preventing disease. This was not the case, however. There was general agreement that cleanliness and quarantine were the two most effective policies against disease. The urban record on maintaining cleanliness has already been exposed as a haphazard and somewhat inefficient process. Quarantine was similarly spotty. Quarantine involved the detention of vessels, crew, and cargo that had originated from a port where epidemic disease was raging. The period of detention usually lasted for twelve days, after which time, if no case of the disease had appeared on board, the ship was free to proceed to the dock and unload its cargo. Quarantine, of course, slowed the flow of commerce; it created delays and threw off schedules. Most merchants viewed quarantine as a restraint of trade. In addition, in the medical opinion of the time, epidemic diseases were not communicable and quarantine was therefore irrelevant.

The ineffectuality of local government institutions in the area of public health was purposeful. Cronies at the port and on the board of health would assure that business interests were faithfully protected. In other words, quarantine would not be invoked, and physicians would not carp about the city's poor health—a situation which urban rivals were certain to pick up. Also, the news of an epidemic would not be divulged until the very last moment to protect the city's image. When an independent group of physicians broke the silence about a cholera epidemic in New York, a prominent banker asked whether the "eager physicians had any idea of the disaster which such an announcement would bring to the city's business."[10] Well could one disgusted Cincinnatian remark: "Every consideration of health . . . yields to the views of mercantile convenience."[11]

To the business leaders, their poor performance on health matters was the result of another simple and justifiable cost-benefit analysis. The benefits to be gained by comprehensive public-health planning did not offset the costs to the taxpayers. While this may appear to be a mechanistic and even tragic way of looking at something as vital as the city's health, from the perspective of the leaders and given their knowledge of the course of disease, it may be construed as a reasonable position. First, it was not clear that maintaining a clean city did prevent disease. Epidemics visited cities that were considered clean by the standards of the time. Savannah expended $200,000 to drain the lands around the city and place them under dry cultivation. Epidemic disease was just as frequent a visitor to Savannah as to other cities. Second, since physicians were virtually unanimous in avowing the noncontagion of the epidemic diseases, it seemed useless to expend funds on implementing a quarantine policy.

The particular view of disease held by urban leaders was perhaps most important in influencing their decisions to provide only a minimum of health services. While by the 1840s few believed disease to be a divine judgment against individual sinfulness, there was a widespread belief that disease and immorality were strongly related. In the views of the time, intemperance, lack of religion, and vice, shortcomings associated with the poorer classes, ensured a predisposition toward disease. The statistics seemed to support this view, as plagues attacked primarily the poor and working classes. In the 1832 cholera epidemic in New York, most of the victims were buried either in Potter's Field or in St. Patrick's cemetery, attesting to the poor and Irish composition of the dead. Since poverty was considered a moral affliction of sorts, there was no need to reward immorality with public expenditures for health.

Yet, as epidemics became more frequent and began to spread from the squalid residential districts to the more fashionable areas of the city, attitudes began to change. New opinions, both lay and medical, but primarily new medical ideas, which were based on extensive empirical research rather than on haphazard guesswork, laid the foundation for health reform. New York's John C. Griscom prepared the first systematic study of a city's health problems. Packed with statistics and clinical observations on a wide variety of health-related subjects (including housing, as mentioned earlier), the report set the standard for future studies of public health. Griscom viewed sanitary reform as the cure for all of the city's social ills. He advocated a vigorous education program in addition to a comprehensive cleanliness campaign.

Though Griscom's work did not lead directly to public action, it stimulated a number of private citizens to work for reform. In 1847 the American Medical Association was formed. Impressed with Dr. Griscom's work, the members formed a committee to promote and secure similar sanitary surveys from committees throughout the country. In Boston at the same time, a middle-aged bookseller and amateur statistician, Lemuel Shattuck, issued a census for the city, which included some shocking figures on infant and maternal mortality and on the prevalence of disease. In 1850 he published a more comprehensive report on health throughout the state, which contained equally pessimistic figures. Shattuck strongly recommended the professionalization of health reform by the establishment of independent state and local boards of health composed of physicians and free of political influence.

Shattuck's report convinced physicians and a few other concerned citizens that relegating the task of carrying out sanitary reform to the business leadership was not the appropriate strategy for implementing public-health policies. A group called the Citizens Association, formed in New York in 1864, provided the final impetus toward the realization of physicians' recommendations, based on their research over the previous two decades. The Association divided the city into twenty-nine districts and assigned a physician to survey each district. The resultant report included a recommendation for a professional independent metropolitan board of health, which the state legislature imposed on the city in 1866. New York, thus, became one of the first cities in the nation to have such a body responsible for the city's health. The cholera epidemic of that year provided the new board with sufficient public support. From a moral failing to an eradicable specific disease, the public view on disease had progressed significantly in two decades. Now, "there could be no public virtue without public health."[12]

The quality of drinking water was closely related to the state of public health. A popular water source in New York during the late eighteenth century was used also as a common sewer in which some people did their daily wash and others flung dead dogs and cats. Wealthy New Yorkers generally imported casks of pure water from the countryside, while the poor were left with using what amounted to a sewer for their water supply. As the city expanded and land use in certain sectors became overcrowded, the quality of the water supply declined even further. The high water table in some cities like Lexington, Kentucky, resulted in frequent mixture of water with cesspools in the more densely populated districts. For those who relied on river rather than on well supplies, growth also caused problems. St. Louis residents slaked their thirst from the Mississippi River, though they were advised to allow the water to stand in jars so the dirt could settle.

The city of Philadelphia was the first to respond to the problem of creating a pure water supply, which is so conducive to health. Employing the new technology of steam, engines pumped water from the Schuylkill River into a reservoir, whence a network of pipes carried one million gallons of water into the city each day. Unlike most other urban services, local government played a significant role by establishing the administrative machinery to run the system and by financing the project entirely through the city treasury. Financial difficulties plagued the waterworks from its opening in 1801. Ultimately, demand outstripped supply, and the Schuylkill became polluted, thus reducing the quality of the water. Nevertheless, the city provided a large portion of the population with relatively pure water for the first time. Inspired by the Philadelphia example, other cities invested in municipal waterworks.

The provision of a pure water supply was one urban service that affected a relatively broad spectrum of the population. The willingness of cities to undertake a waterworks reflected not only a penchant for modernity, as exemplified by steam-engine technology, water-tight masonry, and tunnels, but also an awareness that water was closely related to two growing problems in the city: disease and fire. The accumulated evidence of systematic sanitary reports pointed to the close connection between polluted water and disease. Fire prevention became more difficult as density increased. Water pumped with steam power offered more reliable pressure and quantity for fighting fires.

The nature of the water supply was not the only problem involved in fire prevention. The haphazard methods and institutions of fire fighting were probably equally important. As public health moved toward independence, professionalism, and consequently, effectiveness, local government began to see the virtues of a professional, public fire-fighting force. The switch from bucket brigades to hydrants in the early nineteenth century was a major improvement, but the continued prevalence of volunteer companies was not. Depending on their size, cities possessed anywhere from a half-dozen to thirty volunteer fire companies. These companies were clubs of men who met periodically for social purposes and occasionally to fight fires. They were essentially fraternal organizations whose hobby was fire fighting. There was fierce competition between the companies, which often erupted at the scene of the fire into a full-fledged melee. It was not uncommon for members of fire companies, who habitually fortified themselves with alcohol to generate sufficient bravery to fight conflagrations, to turn their hoses on each other while the fire burned merrily away.

Local officials watched these goings-on with increasing apprehension. In some cases it was their property that was under siege. In addition, the city more than likely donated some equipment to the various companies. To see the city's investment abused in this manner was disconcerting. As a result, urban government gradually brought order to the chaos of fire fighting by first bringing all volunteer companies under the supervision of one appointed public official, screening membership, and, beginning with Cincinnati in 1829, paying a modest salary. These regulations evolved to produce professional, independent fire departments in most cities by the 1860s. Fire fighting, like disease prevention, required a systematic and professional solution.

While the city was organizing to fight fires, it was also developing the means to fight crime. It was not safe to walk the streets of most cities after dark. As the urban population increased and grew more diverse, and as divisions in society sharpened, the crime rate rose. Most violent crime then, as now, occurred in the poorer districts of the city with both victim and perpetrator being members of the lower tier of society. There was also, however, an annoying rise in crimes against property, such as burglary and arson. Wealth was more apparent but less attainable than ever before. Even more aggravating to the situation was the fact that local authorities were impotent when dealing with criminal activity.

Though most cities possessed a group of individuals called a night watch, this "force" was inadequate and, for the most part, ineffective. The members of the night watch often held jobs during the day and used this tour of duty to catch up on their sleep. Some watch members were more of a menace than the criminals they reputedly sought. When they were not perpetrating crimes themselves, they usually were found at the local tavern. The New Orleans and New York night watch vied for the title of the most corrupt and disorderly watch in the nation during the first half of the nineteenth century. In order to improve urban defenses, some cities hired a day patrol to complement the night watch. The day constables were not much of an improvement, primarily because there were so few of them.

St. Louis was typical, employing fifty constables to protect a citizenry of 100,000 in the 1850s.

It was not surprising, therefore, that most American cities were unsafe at night. In the newer cities of the West, in particular, violent crime was commonplace. Periodic shootings and drunken brawls occurred during the formative years of western cities like Houston, Denver, and San Francisco. In the older cities, such disorderly behavior was less frequent, though the form it took threatened the fabric of urban society much more. Mob violence or riots increased in eastern cities after the 1830s. Philadelphia, the staid city of brotherly love, averaged one major riot a year between 1834 and 1842, a frequency that would be scandalous today. Cities like Boston, Baltimore, Louisville, New York, and Washington, D.C., were also victimized by mob outbursts, though with less frequency.

The origins, nature, and participants in the urban riots reflected both the growing divisions in urban society and the inadequacy of law enforcement. The animosity between Catholics and Protestants accounted for a good portion of the mob violence in the nineteenth-century cities. Substantial Irish immigration during the 1830s brought the situation to a boiling point in some cities. The competition for employment and the fact that the Irish always seemed willing to work for lower wages fueled Protestant prejudices. Equally important, there existed a deep distrust of the Catholic religion. The separate schools, the hierarchical organization of the church, and the anti-Protestant traditions among Catholics roused fears in American cities. A riot erupted in Philadelphia in the spring of 1844 stemming from a controversy over the use of the King James version of the Bible in public schools, to which Catholics had objected. A group of Protestants foolishly held an anti-Catholic rally in an Irish neighborhood, and in the inevitable battle that occurred, a Protestant teenager was shot and killed. The incident touched off three days of uncontrolled rioting which left six people dead, a score injured, and $250,000 worth of property damaged, including two Catholic churches, which were destroyed. The local police were totally ineffective, and the militia, almost all of whom were Protestant, made only half-hearted attempts at controlling the mobs.

Catholics were not the only victims of the sharpening divisions in urban society. Blacks and their white abolitionist associates were frequent targets of mobs. In addition to the Cincinnati outbreak described earlier, there were collective disturbances in Detroit, Philadelphia, and Boston. On three separate occasions between 1834 and 1844, blacks and abolitionists were victimized by mob violence in Philadelphia. The most serious riot in 1838 involved the destruction of a meeting hall used by abolitionists. In 1835, a bumper year for riots—thirty-seven occurred throughout urban

America—racial conflict descended on Washington, D.C. A drunken mob of whites, provoked by the discovery of a huge stockpile of abolitionist literature, went on a two-night rampage in the black community, burning several buildings but fortunately killing no one.

Two interesting factors emerge from an examination of the riots between 1830 and 1860. First, the participants in these violent outbursts represented a broader spectrum of urban society than one would suspect. Second, the uninhibited manner in which the mobs proceeded about their objectives reflected the inadequacy of the meager police forces of the affected cities.

American mobs were undefinable. While some of urban society's less fortunate individuals constituted a portion of these lawless gatherings, artisans, clerks, and even some leaders participated in the urban riots of the period. The mob that destroyed the abolitionist meeting hall in Philadelphia, for example, included mostly "well-dressed gentlemen." Generally, "groups from every part of the social spectrum used violence at one time or another in their dealings with other groups."[13]

Violence was an accepted means of settling disputes in American cities because it was deemed desirable to use force to achieve great social ends. The antiabolitionist mob in Philadelphia believed they were preserving order by striking at a group that openly acknowledged its position above the law. The poor Protestant working people believed they were saving the city and perhaps the nation from what they considered to be the insidious doctrines of the Roman Catholic church. The spirit of the times encouraged these beliefs. Andrew Jackson, the national hero of the period, was himself a man of action and, at times, of violence—but always for the cause of good. To riot, therefore, was to be "a kind of apotheosis for democratic man," to be John Wayne "en masse."[14]

Despite the romance of collective violence and its deep roots in American urban tradition, civic leaders began to have second thoughts about these mass expressions of ill will toward the city's social outcasts. A number of the employees of the business leaders had participated in the affairs, and there existed a deep-seated fear that violence against social outcasts, such as blacks and the Irish, would lose its edge after a while, and the hunters would seek bigger game. After all, the issue of employment was a major one in a number of the urban riots. Entrepreneurs were also fearful that the increasing violence would injure the city's reputation. A lawless community was not an especially safe place for investment. A St. Louis editor summarized the feelings of the business leaders of his city when he advised that "the prosperity of our city, its increase in business, the enhancement in the value of its property . . . depend upon the preservation of order. . . ."[15]

While civic leaders realized that public demonstrations of unhappiness could not and should not be curtailed, the control of such groups before they reached the violent stage was the objective of local officials. A visible, substantial, and professional police force was obviously necessary to achieve the goal of an orderly city. During the 1840s and 1850s, the cities most affected by mass violence—Philadelphia, Boston, and New York— consolidated their separate day and night police into one, uniformed force supervised by an appointed, salaried official. Though politics would continue to predominate in the choice of personnel for several decades, the "cop on the beat" soon became a familiar sight in cities across the country.

The police service was a further indication of the growing divisions— both spatial and economic—within urban society. Police protection continued to be inadequate in the crowded working-class districts of the city. Since visitors rarely ventured there and since space separated the retail district and the residential districts of the more affluent from the working-class districts, violence in this quarter could be tolerated. Some crime, vice in particular, was not only tolerated but actually protected. Criminal activity thus took on a spatial character too. The necessity of a uniformed, professional police force also demonstrated the depth of division that had grown up in the American city: Protestant versus Catholic; white worker versus black worker; antiabolitionists versus abolitionists; and employee versus employer. The consensual social order that had been sufficient to control the colonial city was no longer present.[16] The policeman was now the buffer between urban society's hostile groups.

Urban leaders were sensitive to the divisions in urban society. Their single-minded objective of generating economic growth did not rob them of compassion toward the poor. In an orderly society, poverty could have no place. In the process of systematizing health- and property-protective mechanisms, local officials launched an array of social services that fit their business-oriented conceptions of what charity ought to be. Officials' views of poverty underwent a familiar sequence of changes—from the idea that poverty was a moral affliction to the view that it was a condition remediable through a professional application of scientific policies.

The Caring City:
The Provision of Social Services

Poverty occupied a peculiar position in urban thought. Amid the rhetoric and reality of urban plenty, poverty cut a curious and wide figure in urban society. It was easy to explain poverty away in the nineteenth century because it seemed so incongruous. Drunkenness was believed to be the major cause of poverty. As a New York editor stated succinctly: "If there was no rum there would be no poor houses."[17] Drink not only ruined the will to work, but also wasted the precious little money accumulated by families. The temperance movement was probably the most extensive of all antebellum reform movements, and temperance plays and literature graphically depicted the horrors of drink. Lonely orphans, pining widows, and, above all, abysmal poverty, were portrayed as the inevitable legacies of drink.

Fortunately for the poor, these attitudes did not represent society's unanimous judgment on their condition. Others were careful to make the distinction between the "deserving" and "undeserving" poor. To be sure, the "undeserving" poor were thought to suffer from the same strains of immorality as were projected by the hardliners. There were also those poor, however, who, through being disabled, widowed, or orphaned, slipped into poverty as a result of forces beyond their control. The working poor was another group that was worthy of consideration. It was this latter segment of the poor that was most difficult to explain away. These were sober, religious, hard-working men and women. By society's definition of poverty, they should not be poor. Yet thousands of these individuals hovered on the brink of economic ruin.

The working poor of Philadelphia were probably no different from their colleagues in other cities. They spent the major portion of their lives employed at several jobs simultaneously "to maintain their families." Should illness or disability occur, it fell upon them "as a scourge most severe."[18] Their annual income averaged about $200, or $3.85 a week. The minimum budget for a family of five in the 1850s was $10.57 per week, which included food, clothing, fuel, and rent, and left 37 cents for any incidental expenses from newspapers to furniture. Even skilled crafts workers rarely earned more than $9.00 per week. Since rent was fixed in advance, the flexibility in the budget had to come from food, clothing, and fuel.[19]

The city and its more fortunate residents were increasingly concerned about these "deserving poor." The humanitarian strain of the early nineteenth century, which had spawned such movements as those for abolition of slavery, public education, and women's rights, also contributed to the organization of charity associations. These private groups sought to systematize relief work. Given the widespread belief that charity itself contributed to poverty, members felt that the application of relief had to be carefully and closely monitored. In the early decades of the nineteenth century, societies for the prevention of pauperism appeared in several cities. Urban leaders formed the membership for these groups, which rarely lasted more than five or six years. The return of prosperity in the 1820s and the members' own limited and conservative views of charity were the reasons behind the short-lived nature of these organizations. Nevertheless, in their meticulous, if biased, reports and in the hospitals and orphanages they maintained, the societies left an important legacy to future relief activists.

In the meantime, local government took an increasing interest in public charity. Members of the city council, after all, were likely to be directors of the new private relief efforts, and in the typical blurring and blending of their activities in the public and the private sector, they began to employ government machinery to attempt to solve the growing problem of poverty. The need for a public effort was clearly evident by 1820. In New York, nearly one-tenth of the city's residents received relief during the winter months. Other large cities possessed similar numbers of potential welfare recipients—numbers too extensive for the conservative private organizations to service.

Local government devised two responses to the problem of urban poverty, both of which reflected the economic and social attitudes of the business leadership. The first type of relief was seasonal. During the winter months, the city council budgeted a small amount for wood, clothing, and some food for distribution to the poor. There was little systematic screening of supplicants, with the result that an indeterminate number of paupers never received the city's relief. Cities rarely appropriated more than 2 percent of their annual expenditures for relief efforts, of which the outdoor charity program was but a small part. The second form of charitable activity was the heart of government's contribution toward relieving the condition of the poor. Since the seasonal ministrations merely provided stopgap measures to arrest poverty, it was obvious that more elaborate mechanisms were required to deal with this increasingly troublesome problem. Local leaders relied on institutions to mitigate urban poverty. The almshouse, or poorhouse, was the major local government relief effort. The idea was to isolate the poor from their immoral environment outside, provide religious instruction in certain instances, and above all, inculcate a belief in the benefits of hard work.

Generally, only the elderly and the immigrant patronized the poorhouse. These were people who were overwhelmed by society, and their entrance into a public-charity facility was an admission of their failure to cope with city life. Poor people usually fared better by begging in the streets than by submitting themselves to what amounted to voluntary incarceration. As a last resort the public almshouse did little to relieve poverty, but it did provide a shelter for the most desperate poor.

Just as the inadequacy of public-health policy stimulated the development of professional groups and plans among private individuals, so the unsuccessful public-charity efforts generated reaction among the growing body of social service experts. The reform sentiment of the 1830s, the lengthy depression which followed the Panic of 1837, and the belief that all problems were soluble also helped individuals to coalesce into effective organizations for the eradication of poverty. The Norfolk Association for the Improvement of the Condition of the Poor, organized in the 1840s by young entrepreneurs, typified the new systematic private-charity efforts. The founders of the Association viewed poor relief in much the same manner as they approached marketing procedures. Organized aid to the poverty stricken was another means of coping with urban growth. Members praised the advent of "a systematic plan for the judicious distribution of alms to the poor of the city."[20]

The group divided the city into districts, and its members made visitations to the homes of the poor. These visitors were the forerunners of the modern social workers. Although they were not professionals, their methods served as guideposts for professionals during the late nineteenth century. The task of these visitors was narrow. They were to root out "artful mendicants" and "give to none who will not exhibit evidence of improvement from the aid afforded." This was the familiar distinction of "undeserving" versus "deserving" poor of an earlier era, though practiced more scientifically.[21]

If poor relief contained an element of social control among the good intentions, the support of public education exhibited a similar pattern. Since the late eighteenth century, public education had been synonymous with charity education. The stigma of pauperism ensured that schools would be ill-attended and curricula would be heavily laced with moralism. Like reformers in other fields, nineteenth-century educators sought to remove the association between public education and poverty from the public mind. Local government, armed with new taxing powers, provided financial support for the goal of truly universal public education. Social and economic realities, however, were to thwart that goal at least until the latter part of the century.

As industry became part of the city's economic base, the attraction and the necessity of employment reduced education's ecumenical objectives. This tendency can be clearly seen in an industrial community like Lowell, Massachusetts. There, local leaders established free public schools in 1835 with the hope that the increasing Irish population would avail themselves of the opportunity to become assimilated into American society and achieve some upward social mobility. To make the system more attractive to Irish parents, who were naturally suspicious of a Protestant-run school system, leaders hired Catholic teachers and used textbooks that "contained no statement of facts not admitted by that faith, nor any remarks that reflected injuriously upon their system of belief." Lowell High School, the apex of the system, was to be a "place where the rich and the poor may meet together." Education in Lowell failed to achieve its prescribed goal. The Irish attended public schools for a while, but there was no noticeable advancement in their status. They remained destined for mill work, and, in fact, many Irish youngsters and their parents avoided the school system as a luxury that did not put bread on the table. Finally, the attitudes of the educators themselves were hardly egalitarian, even if their objectives were. "Their assumptions," as one historian has asserted, "were elitist. . . . They were largely concerned with the problem of social order in the city. . . . [C]ivic leaders acted on the belief that institutions could be devised to inculcate into the poor, especially the children of poverty, qualities that would enable them to raise themselves to middle-class respectability."[22] To inculcate these qualities without providing the opportunity for upward social mobility was to do a great disservice to these people. This remains a problem with which educators today are grappling.

The growing public concern over poverty and education indicated that the economic framework in which urban leadership operated was indeed a broad umbrella that could provide shelter for some of the hopeless as well as for the hopeful. The broader view of urban society implied in the provision of social services was also evident in the perceptions of the city's diminishing esthetic environment by local government officials. Urban leaders had grown up in a time when rural virtues went unquestioned. In addition to creating social problems and the need for urban services, spatial expansion and urbanization caused environmental problems as well. The receding rural environment became a governmental concern, as economic and esthetic objectives coincided to produce an urban environmental policy.

The Esthetic City:
The Provision of Environmental Services

With the rapid spatial expansion of American cities, open spaces had been gobbled up at a voracious rate. The city's physical appearance, its dense residential quarters, its gleaming, almost antiseptic edifices, and its denuded landscape represented a distinct and sometimes painful contrast to the more attractive countryside. The premium on urban space gave residential, commercial, and industrial land uses preference over open spaces. Since most urban real estate was in private hands, few property-holders could be expected to leave valuable space as open land. Following the initial stages of growth, however, the business community became alarmed at the rate at which the countryside was receding and the resulting loss in their city's quality of life. Long before ecology became a watchword for environmental concern, urban residents expressed and acted upon their needs for open spaces.

The first efforts at preserving and creating the natural environment were modest. Tree-planting programs became a civic responsibility by the 1820s. Charleston became famous for the beautiful palmettos and magnolias that lined its streets and passed an ordinance protecting them. Baltimore, Albany, and New York passed similar ordinances. Southern cities tended to be more conscientious in their tree-planting efforts than their northern counterparts. Blistering summer heat and the overwhelmingly rural nature of the region probably accounted for the urban South's leafy vigilance.

City officials were not merely concerned with providing shade and beauty for their residents. They hoped to impress visitors: "Strangers and visitors to our town notice the improved appearance of many of our streets in consequence of the beautiful shade trees that have, in recent years, been planted along the sidewalks." Trees could therefore be justified in the cost-benefit balance so important to community leaders. As an image improver and a comfort to customers, a tree was, in words of an Alexandria editor, "worth double the cost of planting and rearing [it]."[23]

From a belief in the efficacy of planting trees, the city's environmental consciousness expanded and soon promenades and public squares were built. While these amenities had obvious benefits, they were too small to be common recreational areas for the entire city. In an increasingly congested city, the countryside could not be injected in bits and pieces here and there. The movement for public parks in the 1840s underscored the insufficiency of public space in cities. Urban residents were so starved for recreational space that the pastoral cemeteries on the outskirts of cities had become a major recreational attraction by this time.

Although this penchant for cemeteries as recreational areas on the part of the living seems a little macabre, it was logical in view of the absence of other alternatives for city dwellers seeking rural relaxation a short distance from their homes. Rural cemeteries, as they were called, in fact came to be planned as recreational space. Jacob Bigelow of Boston planned Mt. Auburn, the first rural cemetery, in nearby Cambridge in 1831. The cemetery was a striking contrast to the congestion and encroaching gridiron of an expanding Boston. At least one visitor fell in love with the place on first sight:

The avenues are winding in their course and exceedingly beautiful in their gentle circuits, adapted picturesquely to the inequalities of the surface of the ground, and producing charming landscape effects from this natural arrangement, such as could never be had from straightness or regularity. Various small lakes, or ponds of different size and shape embellish the grounds; and some of these have been so cleansed, deepened, and banked, as to present a pleasant feature in this widespread extent of forest loveliness. . . . The gates of the enclosure are opened at sunrise and closed at sunset, and thither crowds go up to meditate, and to wander in a field of peace.[24]

The cemetery, in short, was everything the city was not: Its pathways contoured gracefully with the natural topography, as shown in Figure 8.1, in contrast to the relentless gridiron of the city; it was natural, where the city was artificial; and it was a place of rest—for the dead, of course, but for the living too—while the city was a place of care and toil. Little wonder that these cemeteries, carved out of rural space on the urban periphery, soon became popular attractions. Between April and December, 1848, nearly 30,000 people visited Philadelphia's lovely Laurel Hill Cemetery, with "most of the visitors . . . simply out for a good time."[25] Soon these spots of rural quietude became landmarks and main attractions in a visitor's itinerary. Guidebooks boasted of the rural cemeteries like Greenwood Cemetery in New Orleans and Cave Hill Cemetery in Louisville.

The rural cemeteries, however, became too popular. Rowdy behavior, litter strewn from Sunday picnics, and the frequent juxtaposition of mourners with people "out for a good time" stressed the need for a more exclusive use of open land—both for the living and for the dead. At the height of the popularity of rural cemeteries as places of recreation, the urban parks movement was born. *New York Post* editor William Cullen Bryant launched a campaign to bring a general recreation area to that long-deprived metropolis. The result of his efforts was Central Park, the first major urban park in the country. The designers, Calvert Vaux and Frederick Law Olmsted, created a planning gem that became the prototype for parks everywhere. The park included five different and separate road systems, ample recreational space, a maintenance of topographic features, and such innovative design features as depressed roadways to keep vehicular traffic both separated from and out of the view of pedestrian traffic. Vaux and Olmsted provided for a music hall, a flower garden, an arboretum, several fountains, and, with consummate foresight, a police station. Although the park stretched through largely uninhabited territory from its southern boundary at Fifty-ninth Street to the northern periphery on One hundred tenth Street, where it was difficult to discern where the park ended and the countryside began, Vaux and Olmsted justified their decision to destroy as little of the rugged terrain as possible, with remarkable vision:

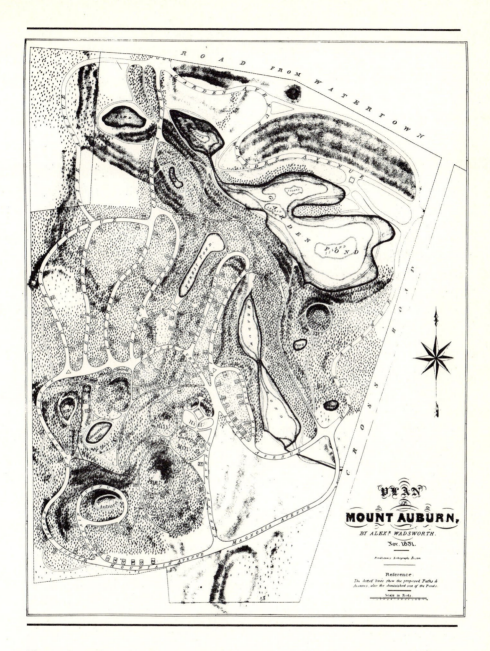

Figure 8.1   Plan of Mount Auburn Cemetery, Cambridge, Massachusetts, 1831
Winding pathways and naturalistic landscaping contrasted with the relentless and unimaginative gridiron. (From *The Making of Urban America* by John W. Reps. © 1965, Princeton University Press.)

The time will come when New York will be built up, when all the grading and filling will be done, and the picturesquely-varied rocky formation of the Island will have been converted into formations for rows of monotonous straight streets, and piles of erect buildings. There will be no suggestion left of its present varied surface, with the single exception of the few acres contained in the Park. Then the priceless value of the present picturesque outlines of the ground will be more distinctly perceived, and its adaptability for its purpose more fully recognized.[26]

Frederick Law Olmsted, a Connecticut Yankee who before the Central Park assignment had never succeeded at anything including a stint at farming on New York's Staten Island, set about to bring the country to the city in the form of parks. Throughout the nation, from Baltimore to Berkeley, Olmsted designed parks and playgrounds for urban residents. Equally important, he inspired park movements in other cities. Eventually, it became unfashionable and regressive for a city not to design a park. Parks were as important as street lights, paved thoroughfares, and department stores. They were emblems of modernity and progress, two qualities the business leadership could not fail to appreciate.

In Herman Melville's novel *Pierre,* published in 1852, a young country girl asks Pierre as they enter New York, "Think'st thou, Pierre, the time will ever come when all the earth shall be paved?" At the time the novel was published, the answer was a cautious "no" for most cities. Civic leaders had begun to preserve open space and to create pastoral elements in an urban setting.

As they mended their growing and changing society, civic leaders introduced some order into their own procedures. The trained professional, whether planning a sewer system, distributing charity, or designing a curriculum or a park, was becoming an important part of urban life, a partner with local government, though the latter often lagged behind. The mixed-enterprise relationship was sometimes stormy, especially in the field of public health, but eventually the partners reached an agreement to order urban society so that it could be made more efficient. Though professionals often couched their rhetoric in egalitarian and reformist terms, and though the actions and inactions of public leaders confirmed their belief in the city as a market place, the results of their policies complemented each other. Business leaders and business space retained their primary roles and grew more prosperous, while the condition of the rest of urban society showed only slight improvement. Both professionals and officials came from similar backgrounds and espoused similar philosophies. The strong support given to public schools by local merchants reflected not only their willingness to assume a civic responsibility, but also their belief that the classroom was an effective environment in which to purvey their economic and social values.

Regardless of the motives of the public leaders, the city of 1870 at least looked and felt better than had the city of 1800. Some streets were paved, gas lighting adorned the thoroughfares, sewer systems flushed many city streets, water tasted more like a drink than like a liquid menace, the poor need not starve or remain in perpetual ignorance, and all citizens could enjoy a stroll in the park on a Sunday afternoon. Clearly, there were many things right about the American city in 1870, and some of the things that were wrong were being attended to by well-meaning individuals through public and private organizations.

A unique environment had developed, resplendent with modern technology, yet encrusted with grinding poverty; supporting a society with a penchant for order, yet with disorder tugging at its sleeve; influenced by a leadership concerned about the welfare of all, yet framing that concern within the narrow scope of economic growth. What kind of place was this? Americans both inside and outside the city sought an answer to this question as they became alternately alarmed, enchanted, enraged, and ecstatic over the prospect of urban life.

The City as a Way of Life:
Reflections from the Market Place

The nineteenth-century city, the ambivalent creation of civic leaders, evoked ambivalent emotions from the American people. Though most Americans did not live in cities at mid-century, they were fascinated by them. The city was exotic: its different peoples, its gleaming department stores, its base and profligate poor, and its size rendered the city made-to-order for popular novelists of the time, and an eager public hung on every word of the "mysteries and miseries" of the city.

Popular novelists such as New York's George G. Foster told of liberated men and women enjoying the day and night life of bustling and bawdy New York. The new urban woman was a particular delight to Foster and his readers. Lize, a recurring character in his stories, is one such woman who "never feels herself at home but at the theater or the dance. . . . She is perfectly willing to work for a living, works hard and cheerfully, as any day laborer or journeyman mechanic of the other sex." Foster assures his readers that Lize is not a housewife, but an independent working woman:

"She rises before the sun . . . swallows her frugal breakfast in a hurry, puts a still more frugal dinner in her little tin kettle . . . , and starts off to her daily labor. . . . From six to six o'clock she works steadily, with little gossip and no interruption save the hour from twelve to one, devoted to dinner." However, Foster informs us, this rigorous schedule does not dull Lize's demeanor or disposition. "Her very walk has a swing of mischief and defiance in it, and the tones of her voice are loud, hearty, and free. Her dress is 'high' and its various ingredients are gotten together in utter defiance of those conventional laws of harmony and taste."[27]

In many respects Lize exemplified what Americans found intriguing about the city. She enjoyed life, she played hard, she was independent, and she flouted traditional stereotypes about women. She was different, as the city was different and diverse. To readers in rural America, these were the intriguing aspects of urban life. They realized, as one magazine editor did, that "the great things in history have not been done in the country.... If [a person] has talent and ambition, he will surely burst away from the relentless tedium of potatoes and corn, and earn more money in an hour by writing a paragraph exhorting people to go and hoe corn and potatoes, than he would by hoeing them for a day."[28] Some rural readers took this to heart and decided to join Lize and her friends in the city.

The city was a sensual show. Its excitement enticed readers, prospective residents, and writers. They were not interested so much in the city as a field for scientific study, as they were in glorying in the city's spectacular achievements. While the nation's early writers—James Fenimore Cooper and Washington Irving—had regaled their audience with tales of rural and frontier life, a new generation of writers celebrated the city. Few expressed the song of the city better than New Yorker Walt Whitman. One can almost see and touch the city and its treasures cataloged by Whitman:

The splendor, picturesqueness, and oceanic amplitude and rush of these great cities, the . . . lofty new buildings, facades of marble and iron, of original grandeur and elegance of design, with the masses of gay color, the preponderance of white and blue, the flags flying, the endless ships, the tumultuous streets, Broadway, the heavy, low, musical roar, hardly ever intermitted, even at night; . . . the assemblages of the citizens in their groups, conversations, trades, evening amusements . . . , these, I say, and the like of these, completely satisfy my senses of power, fullness, motion, etc., and give me, through such senses . . . a continued exaltation and absolute fulfillment.[29]

If the city brought Whitman "absolute fulfillment," to others the increasing urbanization of America generated deep concern, alarm, and disgust. It would be incorrect to divide America's attitudes toward the nineteenth-century city into prourban or antiurban sentiment. Some of the most vigorous critics of urban life were the urban reformers, who frequently acknowledged that their own ideas and happiness could never be attained in any environment other than a city's. Nevertheless, these individuals expressed their misgivings about the rapid growth in size and population of the cities and the impact of this growth upon city residents and ultimately upon the nation itself.

America had always been an agricultural nation. It had been the place where, in Emerson's words, "the embattled farmers stood, / And fired the shot heard 'round the world"; it had been the place where brave yeomen tamed a wilderness and turned it into productive farms; and it had been a place where the virtues of rural life were the subject of everyday homilies to most people. The city was an intruder into this pastoral country. The city was a European concoction that stripped liberty and dignity from the common people. In a nation of common people, the importation of the city was not welcomed. It was un-American. "I view great cities," wrote Thomas Jefferson to a Philadelphia correspondent, "as pestilential to the morals, the health, and the liberties of man."[30]

In a nation where democracy was still an experiment, the city represented an alarming specter. In the late eighteenth and early nineteenth centuries, as cities began to intrude into the national consciousness, national leaders sounded warnings. Historian David Ramsey predicted in 1793: "Your towns will probably e're long be engulphed in luxury and effeminacy. If your liberties and future prospects depended on them, your career of liberty would be short." George Washington in his usual succinct manner warned that "the tumultuous populace of large cities are ever to be dreaded."[31] And Jefferson, as we have seen, believed that the "mobs" of large cities are inimical to sound democratic government. As cities grew and became the homes for diverse populations and ideas (the same features that had attracted the other writers), the perceived threat to liberty remained severe. "In the formation of a nation's education," wrote one woman at mid-century, "as of a national character, the country more than the city must control. The city becomes cosmopolitan; its people, blending all nationalities, lose distinctive national characteristics, and . . . love of country as well."[32]

It was but a small step from viewing the city as un-American to depicting it as ungodly. As religious fervor swept the country during the first half of the nineteenth century, new sects, reform movements, and a missionary concern for the unredeemed permeated both city and countryside. A certain amount of self-righteousness crept into these religious movements, and critics mixed genuine concern for the souls of unfortunate city dwellers with a bit of condescension and revulsion. Certainly there was sin. By the time of the Civil War, New York, a city from which critics constantly drew their most horrible examples, contained more than two hundred houses of prostitution, for example. The remedy seemed simple to a Brooklyn divine: "We must preach Him IN THE CITIES; for nowhere else is the need of this greater, and nowhere else are the opportunities for doing it more numerous and inviting."[33]

In addition to the usual catalog of sensual sins, there was an equal concern as to whose God really reigned in the cities. Was it the God of Abraham or the God of Mammon? As medieval urban dwellers had built cathedrals as an expression of their faith, nineteenth-century city dwellers constructed department stores and brokerage houses as the palaces of their faith. Brigham Young was far away and John Winthrop was long dead. There seemed to be no one left to prick the urban conscience into attending to something more immortal than a marble facade. To critics, everyone seemed engrossed in the "eternal hunger and thirst after money, to the exclusion of almost every other pursuit." The pursuit began at an early age. "As soon as a boy can read, write, and cast up a bill, he is withdrawn from school and placed at a desk, there to be initiated into the mysteries of buying and selling."[34]

The headlong rush of city dwellers toward economic gain lent an air of impersonality to the city, as critics perceived it. The only relationship that seemed to count was the one between man and money. Personal interaction was typically a means to that end, rather than an end in itself.

Existence in the lonely crowd of the cities was an unnatural human condition, but it had become a natural condition of urban life. Mark Twain, whose keen perceptions of western life would earn him a national reputation, visited New York early in his career and referred to it as "a splendid desert—a domed and steepled solitude, where a stranger is lonely in the midst of a million of his race."[35] A mechanistic order seemed to characterize city living as the routine of business and factory dominated the life cycle. Those individuals who were not able to relate to their money interacted with their machines. In the words of Henry David Thoreau, a writer who witnessed the grim realities of New England industrial life first hand, "men have become the tools of their tools."[36]

Civic leaders were distressed about these allegations against their environment. They were aware of the city's shortcomings, and they worked hard to improve the situation. The inauguration of social and environmental services were examples of this awareness of the need to seek a remedy for urban problems. It was also unfair, they believed, to generalize from a few unfortunate urban experiences to all of the cities in the nation. Moreover, it was naive to throw garlands and praise over rural America. One urban champion found country life "instead of a bed of roses to be one of thorns."[37] As to charges that cities are the natural repositories of sin, a Richmond resident agreed that "there is a great amount of vice in cities," but only, he argued, "because there is a great amount of humanity. The country is not without vice. There is probably more scandal and gossiping in a small town in twenty-four hours than there has been in London or New York for the last one-hundred years."[38]

The city and the country were indeed divergent paths of the American experience. To perceptive and even not-so-perceptive observers, each city presented a distinct character of its own, which distinguished it from the other cities. One well-traveled gentleman summarized these distinctions as follows: "New York is the most bustling; Philadelphia the most symmetrical; Baltimore the most picturesque; and Washington the most bewildering."[39] Visitors remarked about the distinctive French influence in New Orleans, the homes of Natchez, perpetually shrouded in Spanish moss, and the frantic pace of San Francisco, which led one resident to boast: "We are a fast people here. There is no stopping or halting—no time to breathe a full breath—not time to eat or sleep—and scarcely time to drink or gamble. You have heard of our fires. They throw light on our character; we burn down our city in a night and build it in a day."[40]

So while cities borrowed each other's innovations with impunity, they maintained their own unique characters. A visitor could indeed tell whether he or she was in Chicago or Mobile, though both had gridiron streets, new urban parks, and a dozen other characteristics in common. This uniqueness was all the more remarkable considering that city leaders generally strove for the same goals and set similar priorities in building their communities. For those who charged that the city fostered impersonality and anonymity, the distinct identity of each city indicated that at least some individuality flourished. It was also a demonstration that only a city could support such a variety of architecture, peoples, shops, gardens, or whatever it was that lent a special character to that particular city.

It was probably only fitting that such variety should elicit such a confusing stream of support and detraction for the city. Someone like Walt Whitman found his romantic yearning tugging in two directions at the same time, as he trumpeted the city in one breath and implied in his *Leaves of*

Grass that democracy and the pastoral life are synonymous. Such contradictions were common, even within the same individual. Anyone who has ever lived in a city for any length of time knows that it is an environment that can be wonderfully exciting, yet extremely frustrating. This is the urban condition. Civic leaders helped to build ugly warehouse districts and allowed working-class housing to fester, while they built expensive parks and squandered millions on railroads. Though the contradictions in such behavior were apparent from the outside, to the leaders such practices were merely good business and were in keeping with their own sense of the general welfare, two ideas that were difficult for them to separate.

The city represented the best in American society and, at times, the worst. Pursuit of profit permeated urban life, determining space, social structure, and government policy. Yet there was room for humanitarian concern. During this period when the market place dominated urban activity, providing for charity, public health and safety, pure water, and a better natural environment became important elements of public policy. Though these humanitarian movements were carried out within the framework of economic growth, they nonetheless improved urban life. That the great reform movements of the period bore urban origins is not coincidental. The city was the environment where it was all possible.

If cities offered marked contrasts within their borders and elicited diverse reactions from both within and without, few doubted their growing influence. A national economy had developed with cities at the focal points; the nation's literary and artistic talents found the city to be a receptive environment for their creative efforts, regardless of their criticism of that environment; and the major technological achievements of the day occurred in the city, from developing water-supply systems and sewers to gas lighting. Civilization, in short, resided in the city, even if it was a bit rough around the edges.

By 1870, the city was grudgingly accepted as an integral part of American life in contrast to the stepchild status of a half-century earlier. Certainly, good public relations and the conscious effort at environmental planning had something to do with this acceptance, but it was the city's inescapable influence that led to its becoming a part of the American consciousness. This is not to say that Americans now loved the city; far from it. For at least a half-century, though, the city had been the subject of magazine articles, newspaper features, books, sermons, conversations, and thought. The American city was no longer a mere curiosity; it was an established fact of American life. The city had not only expanded spatially into rural land and tied the farms inextricably to the city, but it had also expanded into the rural mind, for better or for worse. The next decades would be exciting. As the national spotlight shone on the city, it would expose serious ailments that would spur great activity to heal the urban sores and again give to the nation the best, and in failure, the worst of American life. Few would disagree with Frederick Law Olmsted's view of the urban and national futures in 1868: "Our country has entered upon a stage of progress in which its welfare is to depend on the convenience, safety, order and economy of life in its great cities. It cannot prosper independently of them; cannot gain in virtue, wisdom, comfort, except as they also advance."[41] That is the kind of place the American city had become.

Notes

1. Michael H. Frisch, *Town Into City: Springfield, Massachusetts, and the Meaning of Community, 1840–1880* (Cambridge, Mass.: Harvard University Press, 1972), p. 44.

2. Quoted in Edward Pessen, "Who Governed the Nation's Cities in the 'Era of the Common Man,'" *Political Science Quarterly,* 87 (December 1972), p. 610.

3. *Ibid.,* p. 595.

4. Quoted in Charles N. Glaab, ed., *The American City: A Documentary History* (Homewood, Ill.: Dorsey Press, 1963), p. 115.

5. Quoted in David R. Goldfield, "Pursuing the American Urban Dream: Cities in the Old South," in Blaine A. Brownell and David R. Goldfield, eds., *The City in Southern History: The Growth of Urban Civilization in the South* (Port Washington, N.Y.: Kennikat Press, 1977), p. 75.

6. Quoted in Lawrence H. Larsen, "Nineteenth-Century Street Sanitation: A Study of Filth and Frustration," *Wisconsin Magazine of History,* Spring 1969, pp. 239, 240.

7. Quoted in Goldfield, "Cities in the Old South," p. 70.

8. Quoted in Bayrd Still, ed., *Urban America: A History with Documents* (Boston: Little, Brown, 1974), p. 176.

9. Quoted in Charles E. Rosenberg, *The Cholera Years: The United States in 1832, 1849, and 1866* (Chicago: University of Chicago Press, 1968), p. 68.

10. Quoted in Rosenberg, *The Cholera Years,* p. 27.

11. Henry A. Ford, *A History of Cincinnati, Ohio* (Cleveland: L. A. Williams & Co., 1881), p. 74.

12. Rosenberg, *The Cholera Years,* p. 5.

13. Michael Feldberg, *The Philadelphia Riots of 1844: A Study in Ethnic Conflict* (Westport, Ct.: Greenwood Press, 1975), p. 182.

14. David Grimsted, "Rioting in its Jacksonian Setting," *American Historical Review,* 77 (April 1972), p. 393.

15. Quoted in Theodore M.Hammett, "Two Mobs of Jacksonian Boston: Ideology and Interest," *Journal of American History,* 62 (March 1976), p. 860.

16. John C. Schneider, "Community and Order in Philadelphia, 1834–1844," *Maryland Historian,* 5 (Spring 1974), p. 22.

17. Quoted in Benhamin J. Klebaner, "Poverty and its Relief in American Thought, 1815–61," *Social Science Review,* 38 (1964), p. 383.

18. Quoted in David Montgomery, "The Working Classes of the Pre-Industrial American City, 1780–1830," *Labor History,* 9 (Winter 1968), p. 13.

19. Sidney Lens, *Poverty: America's Enduring Paradox* (New York: Crowell, 1969), p. 88.

20. Quoted in Goldfield, "Cities in the Old South," p. 79.

21. Quoted in *ibid.*

22. This and the preceding quotations about the school system in Lowell are from Thomas Bender, *Toward an Urban Vision: Ideas and Institutions in Nineteenth-Century America* (Lexington, Ky.: University Press of Kentucky, 1975), p. 127.

23. Quoted in David R. Goldfield, *Urban Growth in the Age of Sectionalism: Virginia, 1847–1861* (Baton Rouge: Louisiana State University Press, 1977), p. 197.

24. Quoted in John W. Reps, *The Making of Urban America; A History of City Planning in the United States* (Princeton, N.J.: Princeton University Press, 1965), p. 326.

25. *Ibid.*

26. Quoted in *ibid.,* p. 336.

27. Quoted in Still, ed., *Urban America,* p. 141–142.

28. Quoted in *ibid.*, 196–197.

29. Quoted in Still, ed., *Urban America,* p. 198.

30. Quoted in Glaab, ed., *The American City,* p. 52.

31. Quoted in Bender, *Toward an Urban Vision,* pp. 3, 4.

32. Quoted in Glaab, ed., *The American City,* p. 62.

33. Quoted in Bender, *Toward an Urban Vision,* p. 11.

34. Quoted in Glaab, ed., *The American City,* p. 50.

35. Quoted in Still, ed., *Urban America,* p. 198.

36. Quoted in Leo Marx, *The Machine in the Garden: Technology and the Pastoral Ideal in America* (New York: Oxford University Press, 1964), p. 247.

37. Quoted in Glaab, ed., *The American City,* p. 56.

38. Goldfield, *Urban Growth in the Age of Sectionalism,* p. 251.

39. Quoted in Raphael Semmes, *Baltimore as Seen by Visitors, 1783–1860* (Baltimore: Maryland Historical Society, 1973), p. 116.

40. Richard E. Amacher and George W. Polhemus, eds., *The Flush Times of California by Joseph Glover Baldwin* (Athens, Ga.: University of Georgia Press, 1966), p. 13.

41. Quoted in Bender, *Toward an Urban Vision,* p. 13.

III.
RADIAL CENTER

You could almost feel the beat of the late-nineteenth-century city. It possessed a dynamism and a rhythm that seemed to drive it and its residents at a furious pace. The factory whistles, the trolley bells, the rushing of a thousand feet on pavements, the wails of babies in packed tenements, the endless clanking of coins, and the voices of a dozen different dialects: this was the new urban symphony. The rising crescendo of activities foretold new wealth, new technology, new peoples, new triumphs, and new miseries. Its music echoed down man-made stone canyons, and out to brand-new suburbs. Chicago was one of the greatest arenas for this energy and expansion. Devastated by a disastrous fire, the city rose from its ashes to become an even greater metropolis than its early boosters had ever dreamed possible. Theodore Dreiser, a young, impoverished novelist from Terre Haute, Indiana, walked its new streets in the 1880s and recorded his impressions in *Sister Carrie:*

Chicago was . . . a giant magnet, drawing to itself, from all quarters, the hopeful and the hopeless. . . . It was a city of over 500,000, with the ambition, the daring, the activity of a metropolis of a million. Its streets and houses were already scattered over an area of seventy-five square miles. . . . The entire metropolitan centre possessed a high and mighty air calculated to overawe and abash the common applicant and to make the gulf between poverty and success both wide and deep.[1]

Indeed it seemed as though many cities were "giant magnets" attracting a numerous and diverse population. "Urbanization," as pioneer urban historian Arthur M. Schlesinger, Sr., observed concerning the 1880s, "for the first time became a controlling factor in national life."[2] Between the Civil War and World War I the number of urban residents increased from 6,200,000 to 42,000,000. (Tables I.3 and I.4 show the specifics of this increase.) Even more impressive than sheer numbers, however, was the significant geographic expansion that accompanied and sometimes, as Dreiser intimated with Chicago, overtook population growth. By 1920 it was appropriate to talk about metropolitan areas, even regions, whereas such concepts were rarely mentioned or even thought of in 1870. In the Northeast, a confluence of blacks, immigrants, and rural natives swelled urban populations. By the end of World War I, the populations of Massachusetts and Rhode Island were more than 90 percent urban, with 80 percent of the residents in nearby New York and New Jersey residing in cities. In the upper Midwest and on the Pacific coast, more than half of the people lived in cities.

The metropolitan areas within these regions registered spectacular gains. The New York City area included a staggering 8 million people; Philadelphia, 2,500,000; and the metropolitan areas of Boston, Detroit, and Pittsburgh exceeded 1 million people. Individual cities, which gobbled up suburbs and villages faster than they could fill them, similarly experienced rapid growth, though geographic expansion inflated the figures to some degree. Between 1910 and 1920, New York added nearly 1 million people; Detroit, already a large city by 1910, grew by 113 percent during the decade, Los Angeles by 80 percent, and Cleveland by 40 percent.

The pattern of urban growth was as significant as the population figures. Relatively few new cities contributed to this growth. The cities that had dominated or had begun to dominate their regions in the 1870s and 1880s—New York, Chicago, Atlanta, Houston, San Francisco—increased their magnetism by 1920. The growth of these cities as well as of similar giants during this period made the era "not only the age of cities, but the age of great cities."[3]

The spatial organization of these great cities foretold an era of vibrancy for both the center and the periphery. For the first, and perhaps the last time, a precarious equilibrium was established in the new metropolitan regions. The dazzling display of downtown, with its financial and commercial wealth, was complemented by the brand-new suburbs—representing the culmination of an urban dream that was now within the reach of thousands who looked outward for comfort and inward to downtown for work and play. The era of the radial center had begun.

Notes

1. Theodore Dreiser, *Sister Carrie,* rev. ed. (New York: W. W. Norton, 1970) p. 11.

2. Quoted in Charles N. Glaab, ed., *The American City: A Documentary History* (Homewood, Ill.: Dorsey Press, 1963), p. 173.

3. Quoted in Bayrd Still, ed., *Urban America: A History with Documents* (Boston: Little, Brown, 1974), p. 207.

9.
The Economy of the Radial Center

Radiant Centers and Radial Suburbs

The rhythm of the late-nineteenth-century city, while often frantic, had a definite pattern, a pattern that consisted of a constant ebb and flow between the percussion and brass of downtown and the more subtle sounds emanating from the periphery. The urban economic elite, in their familiar roles, were conductors of this symphony, orchestrating the exciting rhythms of downtown and the quieter andante of the suburbs. The concert was all the more spectacular as it took place on a vastly expanded stage. The accumulation of wealth by a larger portion of society and the growth of a middle white-collar class broadened the audience as well. The tastes of the newly prosperous were not well refined, however. For a while, it seemed as if the expanding stage would distract these untrained listeners from the music itself.

The expansion or decentralization of the urban population that commanded this attention accelerated during the late nineteenth century. Though some historians have attributed this process to advances in transportation technology, especially during the 1890s, the patterns of decentralization had already been well established by that time. Without discounting the impact of the electric trolley, there were several other factors involved in the radial movement to the urban periphery. First, as commercial and institutional uses crowded into an expanding downtown, the movement outward for residential uses was inevitable. Since the newest homes with the most land were available on the periphery, these locations became popular, especially as businesses moved out toward the periphery as well. Second, as blacks and immigrants spilled over into residential districts near downtown, the central part of the city became a much less desirable area in which to live. Third, the growing power of government, the increase in the size of financial and insurance institutions, and the growing professionalization in fields like education and social work produced a substantial new middle class with modest affluence. The movement outward, heretofore made up of executives, now was swelled by civil servants, teachers, and insurance agents. The prestige associated with living beyond the center of the city could now be theirs as well. Finally, the peaceful, verdant periphery offered a sharp contrast to the congestion and pollution of the city.

The development of the suburb was the most common result of the movement outward, and the attractions the suburbs presented in contrast to the city proved irresistible. Suburban enthusiasts, many of whom were real-estate speculators, promoted the suburb as earlier boosters had promoted new towns on the urban frontier. They billed the suburb, not necessarily as an escape from the city, but as a world like the one the city used to be—uncluttered, yet exciting. As one writer declared, "the suburb unites the advantages of city and country. . . . The country's natural surroundings, the city's social surroundings." Still, it was the rural quietude that was most attractive about suburban living. One suburbanite summarized his lifestyle to city friends and advised, "if you want to bring up a family, to prolong your days, to cultivate the neighborly feeling, . . . leave your city block and become like me. It may be a little more difficult for us to attend the opera, but the robin in my elm tree struck a higher note and a sweeter one yesterday than any prima donna ever reached."[1]

The rapid population growth of suburbs attested to their popularity. As early as 1873, Chicago boasted nearly one hundred suburbs with a combined population of more than 50,000. Boston's suburbs registered prodigious gains in the thirty-year period from 1870 to 1900. During that time the number of suburban dwellers increased from 60,000 to 227,000. Not only the larger cities, but smaller ones as well experienced the suburban phenomenon. Cleveland, Richmond, Memphis, Omaha, and San Francisco sprouted large populations in their suburbs.

The suburbs were a real-estate bonanza. With land in the city either occupied or very expensive, land ownership in the city was confined to the people with a large amount of capital. In the suburbs, however, land was abundant, undeveloped, and relatively cheap. Thus, instead of supporting a few wealthy speculators, the development of the suburbs enabled literally thousands of urbanites to become involved in real-estate transactions. The land in the Boston suburbs of Roxbury and Dorchester, for example, was owned by 9,000 different people in 1900.

Surprisingly, despite multiple ownership, the land-use patterns of suburbia were predictable, almost dull. Although Frederick Law Olmsted planned innovative suburbs for the wealthy, most suburbs did not have the benefit of creative master plans. For the most part, suburbs reflected the spatial shortcomings of their cities. The faithful gridiron dominated the suburb as it had the city. It made subdivision much easier. Since the typical suburban lot owner was middle class, he could not afford to lavish money on the preparation of his lot, especially since he had to bear the cost of running utilities to the lot. It was cheapest to reduce the footage of curbs, pipes, and paving. A subdivision, therefore, was likely to contain the maximum number of lots fronting on the street, which meant that the more cross streets there were in the subdivision, the more frontage lots it would contain, and the lower the lot-preparation costs would be. Esthetically, it was monotonous, if not ugly. The proliferation of streets inherent in this situation led one historian to remark that "there was nothing in the process of late nineteenth-century suburbanization that built . . . neighborhoods: it built streets."[2]

Sam Bass Warner, Jr.'s, study of Boston's suburbs demonstrated that the uninspiring spatial patterns extended to the lifestyle of suburban residents as well. Suburbs were the logical spatial extensions of the events that were occurring in the city. Homogeneity met the eye at every turn in a walk through one of Boston's suburbs. With 9,000 decision makers this seems to be an unlikely turn of events, but in what probably was their first experience with real estate, conformity was safety, while difference was risk.

Housing styles in Boston suburbs were unimaginative and were directly related to the cost of land rather than to the owner's esthetic sense. On the most expensive lots in the inner suburbs, multiple dwellings on small lots were common. The three-decker, a narrow, three-story detached wooden structure with one apartment on each floor, was a popular residential choice for those who sought suburbia but were able to afford only an apartment on a narrow lot with little of the pastoral beauty synonymous with the suburban ideal. Lot owners sought to protect their investments by building what was already being built in an area, so one or two architectural styles predominated.

For those who could afford larger lots and bigger homes, as well as the expense of high transportation costs, living in the less dense, more distant suburbs approached the suburban ideal to a greater extent. Here, the more prosperous members of the middle class built "shingle style" houses—

large, rambling houses on relatively small lots—that imitated, in style at least, the grander city mansions of the urban elite. Exterior and interior finishing work was variable, thus imparting a greater individuality to these suburban residential streets, though the decision to build a large house, rather than to spend the money on a larger lot reflected more of a city than a rural ideal.

By looking at the prevalent residential architecture in a suburb, it was easy to tell the economic status of the residents. City residents, moving out to the suburbs, found income-level compatibility to be more important than ethnic or religious homogeneity. Several suburban communities adopted covenants ensuring the similarity of structures and land use, but not of ethnicity or religion. The sameness also ensured a degree of stability in a period of rapid change. To an outside observer, a particular suburb may have been monotonous to look at, but to residents there were psychological benefits in similitude. There was comfort in knowing that your neighbors were neither better nor worse than you were. So a pattern of suburbaniza-tion evolved in which communities were distinct and segregated from each other, but in which each community shared the common characteristic of homogeneity. As geographer Peter Goheen has noted, "suburbs comprised many social worlds within each of which status was equal and between which great distinctions could be made."[3]

The suburban movement sorted out and segregated migrating urban residents, but it was also an amazingly democratic movement. The suburbs were open to virtually half of the urban population, regardless of ethnic or religious background. The movement outward was the culmination of a dream, especially for immigrants. The inner suburbs were referred to as "zones of emergence," and rightfully so, as immigrants "began to take their place in the general life of the American middle class."[4]

Transportation technology played a significant role in the evolution of these "zones of emergence," since frequent, relatively inexpensive, and reliable service directly to downtown was a prerequisite before immigrants could move out to the suburbs. Although the late nineteenth century was a fertile period for transportation innovations such as the cable car and the subway, the electric trolley had the greatest impact on urban and suburban space and lifestyle. The trolley was similar to a horse-drawn railway, except it had no horse. However, the application of electricity to such a transporta-tion mode was a great deal more complicated than its description.

The electric trolley or streetcar was perfected by Frank Sprague, a young electrical engineer, who employed a four-wheeled device pulled along an overhead wire to transmit the electricity to the car. He called the device a *troller;* hence the derivation of the popular name, *trolley.* Sprague tried out his experiment on the streets of Richmond, Virginia, in 1888. By 1900, only 2 percent of the nation's cities had not converted their horse railway lines to electricity.

The trolley accelerated various spatial developments in the city. (See Figure 9.1.) The attractions of the trolley, which was cleaner, faster, and cheaper than the horse railway, made location near its tracks an asset for businesses. As the trolley tracks radiated outward from downtown, commercial land uses radiated outward with it. Since property values along the streetcar routes increased considerably, residential use declined, but it sometimes combined with commercial uses to form a combination store and residence, with the business located below and the residence above. This pattern extended out into the suburbs.

The appearance of commercial land uses far away from downtown was part of a larger movement encouraged by the trolley: the decentralization of business. As people moved outward, businesses moved also to service the peripheral residents. Commercial districts typically developed along the streetcar line at the intersection of a major avenue. Outlying residents usually relied on neighborhood stores for their daily needs, while still traveling to the downtown area for clothes, entertainment, and the good bargains at department stores. And downtown was only a quick and inexpensive trolley ride away.

The streetcar companies were privately owned, often by converted horsecar entrepreneurs, who exhibited the same proclivity to speculate in real estate that they had previously shown. The rapidly growing suburbs presented lucrative opportunities, and companies extended their tracks virtually into the countryside to take advantage of the land uses that developed along trolley routes. Occasionally, some trolley companies would overextend their lines in the suburbs, hoping for rapid development that did not materialize. In Pittsburgh, rampant real-estate speculation and inattention to improving service in already settled areas brought companies into serious financial difficulties.

Although no trolley operator would admit it publicly, his major concern was with real-estate profits, rather than with providing an efficient mass-transportation system. Reformers, however, greeted the advent of the streetcar with great enthusiasm and hailed it as the first truly *mass-transportation* system the city had ever had. Federal investigator Carroll Wright developed an entire spatial scenario, in which the streetcar would enable skilled workers to move to the urban periphery, thereby relieving congestion in the central city, reducing the demand for housing, and thus lowering rents to improve the standard of living of the poor.

It never happened. Adna F. Weber, who wrote perceptively on urban

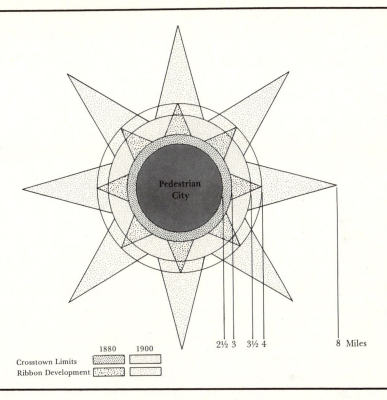

Figure 9.1 Spatial Expansion Along Radial Transportation Routes. (From *Cities and Immigrants: A Geography of Change in Nineteenth-Century America* by David Ward. Copyright © 1971 by Oxford University Press, Inc. Reprinted by permission.)

social and population trends around 1900, explained why: "Even to the highly-paid skilled workman the five-cent fare is unduly burdensome, especially if he has a large family; to the lowly-paid day laborer or sweat-shop worker the prevailing rates are actually oppressive."[5] The streetcar was the transportation system of the middle class. Its use resulted in middle-class residential development out into the suburbs, but the residential districts of the inner city remained as congested and as poor as ever. The trolley's services to the growing middle class were reflected in record patronage of mass transit. In Pittsburgh, for example, ridership increased from 46,299,227 passengers in 1890 (prior to electrification) to 168,632,339 in 1902, despite only a 50 percent increase in the city's population. For the inner-city resident, however, a ride on the trolley was a luxury and was reserved only for an occasional weekend excursion out into the country where the new amusement park offered respite from life in the slums.

Although the streetcar was irrelevant for central-city residents, it was an essential component of central-city business life. The radiation of the trolley lines from the downtown area attested to the continued importance of that urban space. In the early 1900s, Rich's Department Store in Atlanta boasted that no fewer than five trolley lines terminated at or near its doors. It made good economic sense for the trolley entrepreneurs to pay this homage to downtown. While the city was expanding outward, exciting things were occurring in the interior of the city.

The entrepreneurial spirit that had played a crucial role in the process of urbanization since colonial times continued to direct urban affairs as the city expanded and developed an industrial economic base. Since the industrialists usually had built their fortunes from commerce, urban leadership maintained a continuity throughout the period. Downtown remained the focus of the city's major institutions and retained its importance as a local, if not a regional, showcase. The motto of the day remained "men and not natural advantages made great and prosperous cities."[6]

By the 1890s, however, most of the competitive economic battles matching transportation technology against natural advantages had been fought. The urban leaders and their boards of trade now sought advantage in appearance and innovation in their own community. The days of flinging railroads across the hinterland were behind them. Downtown became a renewed focal point for booster activity. This did not mean, however, that the days of town creation and fierce urban rivalry were gone. On the western urban frontier, scenes similar to those that had taken place during the competition for growth a generation earlier were being played out. These city-building activities merit some mention, because it is important to reiterate that the process of urbanization was constantly being renewed. The only aspect that differed was the geography.

The catalog of new winners and losers ran westward from Kansas and Oklahoma. In Kansas during the 1870s and 1880s, boosters in towns like Abilene, Dodge City, and Ellsworth sent agents to Texas, provided a range of services, from women to credit, for cattle owners, and enticed railroads in order to get a share of the Texas cattle trade in much the same way as easterners had coveted the western wheat fields. In 1889 the greatest town-promotion scheme, the Oklahoma land rush, began with visions of Chicago and New York dancing in the heads of prospective boosters. Rushing to make up for lost time, towns on the Oklahoma prairie sprouted waterworks, electricity, and even mass transportation within months of being rescued from prairie grass.

Farther west, the railroad excited promoters as it had once tantalized eastern boosters. The extension of railroads to southern California touched off a frenzy of town promotion. Frauds abounded, as usual, with one promoter successfully marketing 4,000 lots in the Mojave Desert. The area became so crowded with towns that in Los Angeles County there was an average of one town for each mile and a half of railroad track. Los Angeles, the terminus of two major railroads, became the location of the most vigorous town-promotion activities. Among the items churned out by boosters in the early years of the twentieth century were "several crimson and gold booklets . . . , twenty newspapers, three volumes of scenery, two city guide books, a 200-page volume having to do with climate, twenty-seven letters from real estate firms, six motor-car catalogs, two volumes of California verse, a song book and a photograph of a citron-tree."[7]

The railroads, which had given easterners accessibility to Los Angeles and to its promoters, figured prominently in other promotion schemes for western towns. Railroad corporations that had traditionally been involved in real-estate enterprises became involved in town-promotion enterprises. Railroad entrepreneur George Francis Train (his real name) dreamed of creating, as he put it, "a chain of great towns across the continent, connecting Boston with San Francisco by a magnificent highway of cities."[8] He promoted Tacoma, Washington, terminus of his Union Pacific Railroad, as the first great metropolis in this chain. Train's grandiose scheme never materialized, of course, and Tacoma became indistinguishable from hundreds of other towns that owed their existence to the railroad.

The development of Colorado Springs, Colorado, by General William J. Palmer of the Denver and Rio Grande Railroad was the only innovative creation in the era of railroad-inspired communities. Palmer envisioned a great resort distinguished by a unique plan that took advantage of the magnificent backdrop provided by Pike's Peak. A landscape architect was hired to ensure that the major spatial elements of the town—the resort hotel and, of course, the railroad depot—fit in gracefully with the natural environment. Colorado Springs proved to be not only esthetically pleasing but profitable as well.

While the West brimmed with the town-promotion fever that had at one time afflicted older regions, urban leaders in established cities were thinking less of selling town lots than of maintaining an attractive climate for business investment. In this regard, the spatial and esthetic evolution of the downtown area became a primary concern of the boosters. Downtown proclaimed its importance in a riotous display of light. New York's Broadway—"the Great White Way"—glistened with electric lights so powerful that it seemed modern technology had accomplished the impossible by turning night into day. The hearts of other cities similarly brightened with the coming of electricity. In 1880 Wabash, Indiana, became the first city in the country to be entirely lighted by electricity. Downtown businesses especially profited from the introduction of electricity, as show windows presented brilliant displays to prospective shoppers in the evening.

The rapid expansion of the urban consumer market as well as the mass production of consumer goods required new marketing procedures. With the aid of electricity and a good dose of the booster spirit, mass outdoor advertising on the tops, sides, and fronts of downtown buildings, as well as on billboards radiating from the central business district, reminded potential customers about a wide variety of products. The pitches were remarkably familiar: "Is your wife pale?" a billboard inquired. "Is she discouraged, does she drag herself about the house and find fault with everything? Why do you not tell her to try Dr. Lanahan's Life Preservers?" Another advertisement exclaimed, "Don't be a chump! Go and get the Goliath Bunion Cure."[9]

The introduction of electricity and popular advertising revealed part of a changing profile of downtown. The central business district was continuing a process of differentiating space within its own area that had begun in the antebellum period (Figure 9.2). As the city itself was expanding, so was downtown, pushing residential uses farther out toward the periphery. The financial district—banks and insurance companies in particular—experienced rapid spatial growth during this period, reflecting its importance to the urban economy. For regional financial centers, the clustering of financial institutions became an impressive sight in the downtown. In Atlanta, for example, the prime downtown location, called Five Points, included no fewer than thirteen banks and insurance companies.

The retail district was another distinct spatial entity within the expanding downtown. By 1900 department stores were dominating retail activity; and when urban residents talked about going "downtown," this is the area to which they were usually referring. The department stores typically occupied strategic locations along the trolley tracks. Specialty shops, which displayed luxury goods, were generally a separate cluster, located within the retail district but definitely separate from the department stores and their mass clientele. New York's Fifth Avenue was probably the most prominent specialty district in the country.

The entertainment district was a growing and increasingly important part of downtown and often tended to be its leading edge. Thus, as the theater district in New York moved northward toward Times Square and beyond, retail activities began moving northward too. In the 1890s New York's principal hotels, restaurants, and theaters were clustered on Broad-

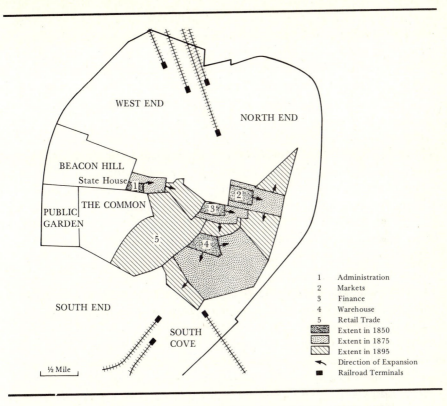

Figure 9.2   Expansion of Boston's Central Business District, 1850–1900

Note especially the recent and extensive growth of retail land use and the expansion of the warehouse district, which reflects the city's importance as a wholesale center. (From *Cities and Immigrants: A Geography of Change in Nineteenth-Century America* by David Ward. Copyright © 1971 by Oxford University Press, Inc. Reprinted by permission.)

way between Fourteenth Street and Thirty-fourth Street. As residential land uses moved northward on the narrow island, downtown followed, led by the entertainment district. By 1900 a new theater district had emerged at Forty-second Street, and new hotels and restaurants rallied around the opulent Plaza Hotel far up on Fifty-ninth Street, which had been rural countryside just a half-century earlier.

While downtown was segregated into specific uses, and those uses, in turn, were separated into even more differentiated uses, a new physical force was making its presence felt: the skyscraper. Skyscrapers were both a practical response to the spatial exigencies of downtown and a social comment on the nature of urban life. By the 1890s the office building had emerged as a major type of land use in downtown. Corporate administration required huge staffs to keep track of regional and national operations, and downtown, as the communications and prestige center, was the logical location for corporate offices. As downtown gained in importance, however, real-estate prices rose. In most central business districts, space was measured by the number of feet fronting the street, so precious had a downtown location become. The average front-foot value in downtown Chicago, for example, rose from $500 in 1877 to $4,000 in 1891, an increase of 700 percent. With downtown real estate so expensive, it was not surprising that industries seeking to expand left the area altogether. The only alternative was to build up; this was impractical for a factory, but ideal for an office building, provided that the appropriate technology was available to accomplish it.

The major technological breakthrough occurred when Chicagoan William L. Jenney, inspired by a bird cage, erected a steel skeleton to support a building's roof and walls instead of using heavy masonry, which had limited building heights to ten to twelve stories. Jenney's building, the Home Insurance Company, erected in Chicago in 1885, became the prototype for skyscrapers constructed in downtowns between 1890 and 1920. By eliminating the supporting masonry walls, Jenney reduced the weight of the building, drastically increased its height, and permitted greater admission of light as well as the expansion of interior space, now free of the ponderous masonry walls. At just about the same time, electric elevators were perfected, and the skyscraper became convenient as well as practical.

The skyscraper reflected the changing economy of the city. The merchants had given way to the corporation men, and to an economy that floated on mergers and capital transfers much more than on ships sailing the world's oceans. As the corporation and the factory dwarfed individual activity, so the skyscraper dwarfed both people and other structures. A New Yorker looking down a heretofore quiet residential Park Avenue in 1920 saw "a strange thing—an enormous office building against the back of which outlines itself the spire of a church. A big office and a little church; what a change since the Middle Ages!"[10] And, he might have added, the structures reflected a significant change in values as well.

Above all, the skyscraper was practical. It incorporated all of the latest technologies and materials, while saving corporations staggering land costs. Its lithe but sturdy frame provided abundant quantities of air, light, and space. The skyscraper was a cultivation of "the service to Mammon . . . with an effort to attain . . . higher artistic ideals." Practicality was the guiding principle of the Chicago School of architecture, a group of Chicago-based architects of skyscrapers and smaller office buildings. As one member of the school lectured, "Be as artistic as you can, but do not for a moment forget that you are not pictorial artists, but architects, and that your art is of little value unless you are practical."[11]

It was inevitable, however, that the architectural expression of urban values was eventually taken out of the hands of the architects by the people who really counted, the entrepreneurs. If their downtown was to be distinctive, architecture would make that distinction. Ornamentation and lavishness replaced utility, with classical and Gothic facades eclipsing the simplicity of earlier skyscraper forms. The fifty-two-story Woolworth Building, built in 1913, was probably the ultimate in the new entrepreneurial, attention-grabbing style. Louis J. Horowitz, the architect of the structure, attempted to dissuade Frank Woolworth from erecting the building claiming it would be an economic fiasco because the expense of preparing the facade alone would never be recouped by office rents. Woolworth was unimpressed by the argument, and although he acknowledged that his building would never pay its own way, he correctly believed that the building would be a giant advertisement for his five-and-ten-cent stores.

The concern with showmanship revealed itself in the residential architecture of the downtown entrepreneurs. As their wealthy predecessors had erected urban mansions as physical symbols of their success, so turn-of-the-century entrepreneurs also indulged in extravagant display. This time, however, they viewed a fine home as a matter of civic duty rather than simply as an expression of achievement. A Springfield, Massachusetts, journalist put the matter as a public imperative: "The rich man has no moral right to deny the community that graceful expression of his prosperity which a beautiful home conveys. . . . An ugly or mean house becomes a crime against the public."[12] Unfortunately, some leaders took their public responsibilities too seriously and constructed mansions large enough to house a good portion of the public and styled with such a potpourri of architecture that any citizen could locate his or her favorite style somewhere on or in the house. The homes constructed by railroad and silver-mining tycoons in western cities reflected the desire to demonstrate that the wealth of the West could enable its possessors to outdo some of the most outrageous structures of the East. This would affirm the region's urbanity, despite its recent removal from the sagebrush. Charles Crocker of the Central Pacific Railroad ensconced himself on San Francisco's fashionable Nob Hill with, according to one critic, a "four-story, $1.25 million monstrosity, a delirium of the wood carver." Crocker's mansion rivaled the garishness of Mark Hopkins's New York estate, which was, in the words of another skeptical observer, a "maze of towers, turrets, and gables" covering half a city block.[13]

It seemed evident that physical display had been elevated (or lowered) to public art form to further the reputation not only of the individual entrepreneur, but of the city itself. It was but a small step from viewing a downtown skyscraper or a sprawling residence as an important physical attribute for the city to envisioning an entire downtown, and even a city, festooned in the latest and most arresting styles as essential to the city's prestige. The radiant-center mystique became the guiding plan for a new vision of the city itself, befitting its economic grandeur. This vision, embodied as the City Beautiful movement, received its ultimate inspiration from the Chicago World's Fair of 1893.

The City Beautiful

The Columbian Exposition, as it was formally known, was called to celebrate the four hundredth anniversary of America's discovery. The idea presented itself too late for its backers to make the appropriate 1892 opening, but the timing of the event was the only aspect that was wrong. In contrast to the sprawling, ugly industrial cities that were becoming common at that time, the classical buildings rising from blue lagoons, with their white plaster-of-Paris facades gleaming in the sun, seemed to be a vision of a lost utopia. Observers called it the White City, and it epitomized cleanliness, grandeur, beauty, and order. The lush green lawns and the frequent display of statuary combined with the architecture to impart a classical flavor to the entire exposition. A writer for *Harper's New Monthly Magazine* could scarcely conceal his ecstasy: "The fair! The fair! Never had the name such significance before. Fairest of all the World's present sights it is. A city of palaces set in spaces of emerald, reflected in shining lengths of water which stretch in undulating lines under flat arches of marble bridges and along banks planted with consummate skill."[14] (See Figure 9.3.)

The fair was remembered long after its physical manifestation was gone. Its greatest impact lay in the new perspective it gave urban leaders of the city's potential for physical beauty and the effect of that beauty on the public consciousness. Chicago architect Daniel H. Burnham, who played a leading role in implementing the physical ideals represented by the fair, recalled the fair's legacy nearly two decades later: "The beauty of its arrangement and of its building made a profound impression not merely upon the highly educated part of the community, but still more perhaps upon the masses, and this impression has been a lasting one."[15] The city no longer need be perceived as an ugly, ungainly giant, but rather as a beautiful, graceful physical creation of human beings. The entire city could be downtown.

Figure 9.3   The World's Columbian Exposition at Chicago, 1893: The Grand Basin Viewed from the Peristyle

As the suburban cemetery presented a sharp contrast with the dull city surrounding it (see Figure 8.1), so the "White City" differed greatly from the dirt and inefficiency of Chicago. (National Archives)

The municipal art movement was one of the earliest manifestations of the City Beautiful movement. The fair had demonstrated the beauty of sculptural and pictorial decorations for public buildings and parks. The Municipal Art Society of New York, a leader in the field, espoused even broader programs. Europe was as much an inspiration for their plans as was the fair. They admired the broad boulevards, plazas, and monuments of European cities, but could do little to impose such drastic alterations of space on New York. They fought pollution with a similar lack of success. It became apparent that beauty was worthwhile only until it became disruptive or expensive.

The growth of local improvement societies was a more successful attempt at beautification. It was most popular in smaller cities. Originating in Springfield, Ohio, in 1899, improvement societies became so numerous that the National League of Improvement Associations was formed a year later with a pledge to preach "the gospel of Beauty and the cult of the god sanitation."[16]

While these organizations stimulated numerous beautification projects, the culmination of the City Beautiful movement occurred with the development of two grandiose urban redevelopment plans designed to enshrine "the gospel of Beauty" on a citywide scale. The first plan began modestly enough as a proposal to improve the park system of Washington, D.C., in commemoration of its centennial as the nation's capital in 1900. With the help of local architects, politicians, and national figures like Daniel H. Burnham and landscape architect Frederick Law Olmsted, Jr., the modest proposal blossomed into a full-fledged plan to redevelop the city along the lines originally suggested by Pierre L'Enfant in 1790.

Employing the major principles of the City Beautiful movement, the architects developed the mall as a formal open space terminating near the Capitol in front of a plaza containing equestrian statues of three Civil War generals. The mall would accentuate three major physical focal points: the Capitol, the White House, and the Washington Monument. Directly west of the monument was the Lincoln Memorial, and continuing west across the Potomac, the Custis-Lee Mansion in Arlington National Cemetery. Borrowing ideas from both the palace at Versailles and the White City, the planners projected a long reflecting pool with a formal park on either side connecting the memorial and the monument. With support and funding from Senator James McMillan and his Senate Park Commission, the city of Washington today faithfully reflects the City Beautiful ideals of the 1901 plan (shown in Figure 9.4).

Daniel H. Burnham, a leading participant in the Washington redevelopment plan, devised an equally grand scheme for Chicago in 1909. The Commercial Club, a prestigious group of prominent business leaders, commissioned Burnham to develop a plan for Chicago. It seemed only appropriate that the site of the White City should be recast in its image. With both the White City and Paris again serving as models, Burnham hoped to direct the attention of Chicago towards its lakefront heritage. He planned for a system of beaches and harbors along the lake, dominated by a huge civic center. As in Paris and in Washington, broad boulevards would radiate from this new focal point. In order to relieve congestion and liberate traffic circulation in the downtown area, Burnham included a beltway around the central business district. Burnham demonstrated that a beautiful city could be an efficient city as well, since efficient "transportation for persons and goods," especially in downtown, was a major objective of his plan.[17] The Chicago plan was too bold, however, and although some of its suggestions on lakefront land use were followed, most of its traffic-circulation system remained on the drawing board.

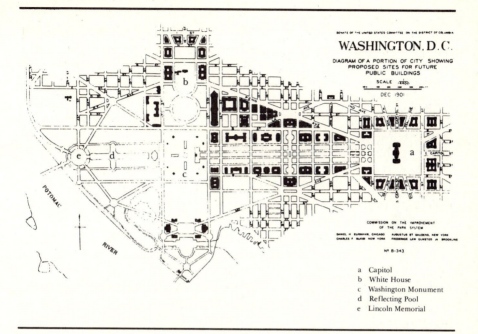

Figure 9.4   Plan of Washington, D.C., 1901
A resurrection of L'Enfant's plan in modern City Beautiful style. (From *The Making of Urban America* by John W. Reps. © 1965, Princeton University Press.)

The Chicago plan represented an important transition in the ordering of urban space. It was more than a city beautification plan in that it included provisions for subdivision regulations on the urban periphery, requirements for railroad terminal relocation, and farsighted statements discussing the regional impact of the reordering of urban space. In sophistication, scope, and philosophy, it was different from the beautification plans that had preceded it. The plan ushered in a new era in the ordering of urban space. It was the herald of the city-planning movement.

The City Efficient

Business leaders, of course, had been planning for generations. Their organizations had typically encouraged efficiency in economic affairs, the corporation being the latest invention of business technology. Efficiency plans were common in the new giant industries and were applied to corporate management and work force alike. It was but a small step from orchestrating the urban economy to ordering urban space, the physical extension of that economy. The City Beautiful campaigns had proved that civic leaders could alter urban space for the good. But much remained to be accomplished. The late-nineteenth-century city was radiating outward toward suburbs that were filling up almost as soon as land was subdivided. Some of this rapid growth had not been orderly. Street systems, in the words of one critic, "follow the individual judgment and advantage of the land owner, giving no heed to the advantage of the best interests of the community." The critic also deplored the rapid advance of sprawl: "Residences go up in the remote parts of the city . . . in order to escape the erratic tendency of shops . . . to fasten themselves upon a colony of houses . . . only, however, to draw other small shops." The result of this leapfrogging "is a large sprawling combination of city and village. A sharp division of localities, or even streets, according to use does not exist." The basic problem with this situation was that it created uncertainty, which, in turn, "is a direct hindrance to improvements."[18] Ultimately, property values would decline.

The expanding city required land-use controls, and the City Beautiful movement was too narrow and its connections with enhancing economic development too tenuous to have significant impact on the ordering of urban space. By 1909 the City Efficient was replacing the City Beautiful as the guiding philosophy for those who wished to improve the urban environment through spatial policies. John Nolen, a Massachusetts landscape architect, was a leading figure in the City Efficient movement. As one historian has noted of Nolen, "the absence of beauty troubled him less than the faulty street arrangement, the condition of the waterfronts, the uncoordinated transportation, and the unsanitary and demoralizing influences of slums." In short, "urban growth . . . was too important to continue unplanned and uncoordinated, the product of countless shortsighted and selfish private decisions."[19]

The control and ordering of urban land use was a major goal of the City Efficient movement. There were few precedents for the implementation of such a program in American cities. European cities, once again, provided models for American cities groping to maintain an orderly process of growth. Since the last quarter of the nineteenth century, German cities had divided their land area into specific use districts: residential, industrial, commercial, institutional, and mixed. In the 1880s, Modesto, California, had experimented with a similar land-classification or zoning scheme, dividing the city into two districts: one district prohibiting Chinese laundries, and the other district permitting them. It was a thinly veiled attempt to confine the Chinese population to a certain area of the city and actually had little to do with the broader purposes inherent in the German plan. For the next two decades, cities such as Baltimore, Boston, and Indianapolis passed laws limiting tall buildings to certain streets, but these too were narrower than the German classification system.

New York became the first city to enact a comprehensive zoning ordinance comparable to the German plan. The concern for orderly growth and maintenance of property values so essential to the City Efficient philosophy played a major role in developing a land-use classification for the city. The specific problem related to the rapid growth of the garment industry, which had expanded out of its cramped Lower East Side location northward to other residential and commercial districts. The expansion was coming perilously close to Fifth Avenue, where the city's luxury shopping district was located. The Fifth Avenue Association, composed of the Avenue's shop owners, demanded that the city prevent the incursion of the garment industry, with its tall buildings, Jewish immigrant workers, and the inevitable refuse left by industry. Since the city leaders had heard similar complaints about the potential conflict in land uses in other parts of the city, they decided that the time was appropriate for a comprehensive solution to the problem. Under the leadership of Edward M. Bassett, a Brooklyn lawyer, the city drafted a comprehensive zoning ordinance that became the prototype for similar plans in 591 cities throughout the country during the next decade.

As with most reforms of the period, zoning was, essentially, a conservative land-use tool that aimed to protect property values by projecting present land use into the future. Zoning reinforced and made more rigid the highly segregated spatial patterns then emerging in American cities. Not only by segregating different classifications of land use like commercial from residential, but also by differentiating types of residential structures such as single-family and apartment dwellings, zoning determined who was going to live where. As one historian has noted, "just as zoning had given wealthy retailers of Fifth Avenue a means of defense against the encroaching garment factories, so subsequent zoning gave suburbanites a defense against 'undesirable' activities and people."[20]

Zoning, at the heart of the City Efficient movement, was not any more successful than the City Beautiful programs at solving basic urban problems. By 1917, when John Nolen and his fellow land-use reformers founded the American City Planning Institute, the forerunner of the American Institute of Planners, planning had come to be synonymous with spatial controls, order, and the maintenance of property values. A genuine opportunity had been missed. "Zoning could not clean slums, nor provide adequate housing for those elements of the population whom the commercial builder could not profitably accommodate, nor establish criteria for satisfactory residential environments."[21]

Some planners believed that given the political and especially the economic realities of urban life, significant manipulation of space to provide a better environment was impossible. The creation of entire new communities where planners could apply their theories from "scratch" was an attractive alternative to tinkering with an urban environment where spatial and social problems were so complex. This was not necessarily an abandonment of the city as the site for spatial experimentation, but rather a more indirect method of relieving some of the city's problems. The new communities could serve both as testing models for methods that might be used on a larger scale in cities and as receptacles for the relief of urban congestion, which planners viewed as a serious social problem.

The Garden City

An English social reformer, Ebenezer Howard, drew up the basic outline for these communities. Howard believed that there were natural limits to the spatial and population growth of communities and that by 1900 most of the major cities had exceeded those limits. Howard's planned "garden city," as he called it, would include the essential features of urban life, such as business, industry, and education, and some of the attributes of the country, such as public parks and private gardens. By maintaining a balance between city and country, density could be controlled.

While this description sounds suspiciously like an idealized suburb, the garden city differed from a suburb in at least one major respect. Howard's community would be self-contained. Unlike the situation in a suburb, in the garden community there would be a minimum of dependence on the city. Residents would work in the community, go to school there, play there, and patronize its entertainment facilities. This self-containment would relieve the burdens placed on the city, not only by decreasing traffic congestion, but also by loosening the crowded living conditions in working-class districts. These garden cities would be constructed specifically to attract workers and their families. In this manner the large cities would be aired and life there would improve. Howard hoped, in short, that "the success of the new garden city would give back to the overpopulated center the fresh air, sunlight, and beauty that its own inordinate growth had largely robbed it of."[22] Thus, the garden city was as much a scheme to save the large city as it was to create a new, attractive "middle landscape" environment. In 1904 Howard and several colleagues began construction of Letchworth, outside of London, as the prototype garden city. Though it was not as self-contained as Howard had hoped, Letchworth was an imaginative, attractive, and successful working-class community that today still reflects its original plan.

The idea of the garden city struck a responsive chord among some American urban reformers who relished the opportunity to create miniature White Cities and also save the old ones. Further, it was, in a sense, an opportunity to renew the faith in city building—that great optimism that had spurred men and women to cross the ocean or the desert in search of the perfect urban environment. The first garden city constructed along Howard's outline in this country was Forest Hills Gardens, in Queens, New York, sponsored by the Russell Sage Foundation in 1909.

Forest Hills was a successful example of the benefits derived from comprehensive planning. The community was an orderly, attractive environment that included neat Tudor-style homes on spacious lots; winding roads that represented a fortunate escape from the thralldom of the gridiron; a shopping center, rather than the commercial strip that was characteristic of many suburbs; public schools; and small parks scattered throughout the development so that families could have easy access to open spaces. Unfortunately, the planners allocated little space for industry and other employment opportunities to encourage self-containment—a major attribute of the garden city. More important, despite the rhetoric of the planners, few workers could afford the homes and lots devised for the community. As a means of decongesting New York City, Forest Hills was useless. As historian Roy Lubove summarized the experience, Forest Hills "proved nothing except the obvious—that attractive suburban communities could be created for those able to afford them."[23]

Despite continued interest in the concept of the garden city, it would be almost two decades before another serious effort was launched to create one. It did not seem feasible to construct garden cities with all their amenities and expect workers to afford to live there. In America, the emphasis was on the garden portion of the garden city, and Howard's more subtle social objectives did not receive sufficient attention.

The radiant centers, radial suburbs, cities beautiful, efficient, and garden were the more overt manifestations of the urban economy. The audience doubtless enjoyed the show, which featured the virtuoso conductor, the urban entrepreneur. As with any performance, however, the preparation was long and arduous. The economy showcased by downtown, resplendent in the suburbs, and framed by spatial protectors was only the visible tip of the urban economic iceberg. Let us go backstage to the dim rehearsal hall, beyond the cheers and the physical order and beauty of the performance.

Twilight's First Gleaming:
Steel-Driving Cities

If you had lived in the 1880s and had approached Pittsburgh at nightfall, you could hardly have failed to be awed by the surrealistic grandeur of the city's industrial might. At the city's edge, the outlines of the steel mills hulked like specters against the darkening sky. As a contemporary observer saw it, "Fiery lights stream forth, looking angrily and fiercely up toward the heavens."[24] This observer was looking at the industrial bowels of the country. The battleships at sea, the skyscrapers of great cities, and the locomotives steaming across the plains began here. Yet Pittsburgh was only part of the national industrial realm. Since the Civil War, dozens of cities had longed for and achieved the joys of twilight's first gleaming: that fiery reminder that wealth and growth lay in the smoky sky.

Chicago and Cleveland with their excellent rail connections facilitating the movement of important industrial raw materials, especially coal and iron, built their own steel mills. But these are familiar names in urban industry.

Figure 9.5   Pittsburgh at Night. (Library of Congress)

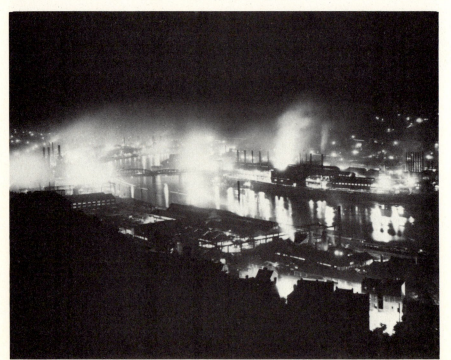

Milwaukee, noted for its breweries, also opened its city to iron and steel plants following the Civil War. The city developed related industries, such as machinery and motor production, until, by 1910, only Buffalo and Detroit had a higher percentage of workers engaged in manufacturing pursuits.

In the South, Birmingham was the region's major industrial phenomenon. As late as 1869 the city did not exist. A combination of railroad connections and coal, limestone, and iron deposits transformed the north Alabama woods into a thriving industrial community. In thirty years there were five hundred manufacturing establishments, most related to iron and steel production. Between 1880 and 1910 the city's population had increased from 3,800 to 130,000, and the city was producing more than $12 million worth of manufactured products.

The Birmingham story indicated, if it was not apparent already, that the city and industry formed a profitable partnership, especially if the city was close to natural resources. The connection was enhanced by the concentration of labor, the accumulation of capital, large consumer demand, and the presence of supporting facilities from railroad depots to retail stores that were found in the city. Also, the technological advances of the late nineteenth century were most effective when applied to large-scale enterprises, which, in turn, required vast inputs of capital and labor: elements which only a city could provide.

In the steel industry, large-scale production was impossible until the costs of mixing wrought iron and carbon could be reduced. In 1859 Englishman Henry Bessemer developed a process which significantly reduced the amount of coal necessary to make steel. Several years later, German-born William Siemens invented the open-hearth process, which produced a higher quality of steel essential for building construction and machinery manufacturing. As demand increased and production costs declined, sprawling operations became feasible, and cities became the logical repositories for such plants.

The steel industry was not the only activity to benefit from innovation and an urban location. The clothing industry achieved similar advantages. Prior to the Civil War, most clothing was custom-made. The tailor and perhaps several helpers were the major clothing manufacturers. The demand for Civil War uniforms, the influx of cheap immigrant labor, and above all, the introduction of the electric sewing machine generated a vast ready-made clothing industry, organized along mass-production lines, with dozens of sewing machine operators working under one roof. Home industries declined, and in warehouses and converted tenements a new industry churned out apparel for retail outlets. New York with its large immigrant work force and burgeoning local demand became the national garment center, though cities like Baltimore and Boston turned clothing manufacturing into major industrial enterprises.

If bigness was becoming commonplace in manufacturing, it was also becoming evident in the administration and distribution of the products, and for the same reason: reduced costs. Free-enterprise competition could be expensive, at least for the industrial corporation. Corporate consolidation seemed to be the most efficient method of reducing competition. Though some of the tactics employed by one corporation in gobbling up another were unsavory, if not illegal, by 1910 a few large producers controlled the steel, farm machinery, rubber, oil, and meat industries, respectively.

Merger enabled the new larger corporations to take even greater advantage of modern technology and expand their manufacturing operations. Plants became tightly organized fiefdoms, occupying extensive portions of urban real estate and employing thousands of people. The stockyards in Chicago, the center of the meat trust, typified the sprawling, comprehensive industrial operations common by 1900. (See Figure 9.6.) Upton Sinclair, in his 1906 novel *The Jungle*, exposed the working conditions in the meat-

Figure 9.6   Union Stock Yards, Chicago, Circa 1878—A City in Itself. (Library of Congress)

packing plants. Although the plants revolted him, his minute descriptions of the activities within the slaughterhouses indicate a fascination, if not admiration, for the application of the technology of mass production in the meat industry.

The meat plants employed 30,000 people, and at least 100,000 more depended on their salaries. This constituted not only a city, but a large city at that. This mechanized community, which caused Sinclair to marvel at "the wonderful efficiency of it all," elevated butchering almost to an art form. Hogs, for example, were sent down chutes hoisted up on their hind legs and sent along an assembly line, where one man slit their throats. The half-dead hogs were then summarily dispatched into a churning cauldron of boiling water from which they passed "through a wonderful machine" which removed their bristles. The hogs, by now quite dead, were strung up by the machinery again and passed between two lines of workers, each with a specific task to perform on the carcasses from severing the head to removing the entrails. Sinclair vividly depicted this procession of men and carcasses: "Looking down this room, one saw, creeping slowly, a line of dangling hogs a hundred yards in length; and for every yard there was a man, working as if a demon were after him."[25]

After the carcass spent twenty-four hours in the chilling room, a new process was begun on another floor: cutting up the carcass, with each man responsible for a different part of the anatomy. Finally, the bottom floor housed the pickling and packing rooms, where the various meats were prepared for shipment. Not one part of the hog was wasted in this process, as products from fertilizer to food were disgorged from the factory. Reflecting on what he had seen, Sinclair observed: "It was all so very businesslike that one watched it fascinated. It was pork-making by machinery, pork-making by applied mathematics."[26]

The immense presence of such industrial operations obviously had a considerable impact on the city and upon the process of urbanization itself. Industry had generally outgrown its close association with the central business district by 1900. The demand for space, both vertical and horizontal, drove industrial uses outward. The clothing industry in Baltimore, for example, was centralized in warehouses next to downtown. The introduction of sewing machines and the consequent expansion in operations made incursions by the industry into tenement districts away from the central business area necessary. Moreover, since these districts housed the work force (primarily immigrant labor), such a location was convenient to both employer and employee.

Some industries could not find such beneficial accommodations within the city and moved to the suburbs. Heavy industries like steel, for example, reduced their noxious influence on the environment by locating on the urban periphery. There, where land was cheap, manufacturing could go on with sufficient room for future expansion. As communities in themselves (like the stockyards), the manufacturing plants had little need for close proximity to downtown. The workers were spared lengthy commuting trips, as some employers constructed workers' housing adjacent to the factory site.

Some industrialists attempted to create new communities beyond the metropolitan area. George H. Pullman, proprietor of the famous sleeping-car manufactory in Chicago, constructed an elaborate town south of the city complete with brick homes for the workers, a street system that emphasized residential privacy, a hotel, schools, churches, and libraries. A plan of Pullman, as the satellite city was called, is shown in Figure 9.7. Pullman disintegrated in 1894 during a violent strike that resulted from the proprietor's overbearing involvement not only with his employees' working lives, but with their lives away from work as well.

A little more than a decade later, Elbert Gary, Chairman of the Board of a new conglomerate, the United States Steel Corporation, bought a vast tract of land east of Chicago on Lake Michigan and called the place, not surprisingly, Gary. The new industrial town was almost as comprehensive as

Figure 9.7   Plan of Pullman, Illinois, 1885

A town planned down to the last detail, including the lives of the workers. (From *The Making of Urban America* by John W. Reps. © 1965, Princeton University Press.)

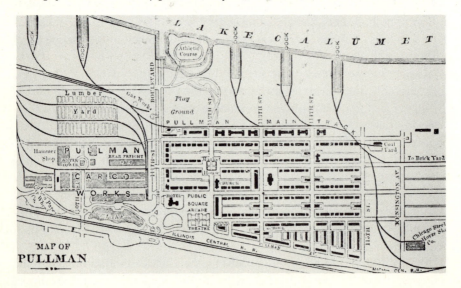

Pullman, with the exception that the proprietor, remembering no doubt his colleague's difficulties, exercised less control over community life. Labor relations were not any smoother in Gary, however, than in Pullman—there was a bloody strike in 1919—and for all of its planning, the city was indistinguishable from the grimy metropolises that hugged the Great Lakes. Another opportunity for creating a positive industrial environment for both management and labor through the resources of private enterprise had been lost. More successful, though on a considerably smaller scale, was another United States Steel development, this one outside of Birmingham, Alabama, which included neat homes for employees and attempted to introduce some esthetic influence into the smoky environment through professional landscaping.

Few industrialists, however, were willing to sink the large amounts of capital and time required to build a community from the ground up. Most contented themselves with finding appropriate locations within or near a city, depending on their spatial and labor requirements. A portion of the garment industry, for example, still hovered near downtown, especially where tenements were close by. Others, like shipping, required close connections with a natural resource, in this case, water. While the dockside location remained, shipbuilders moved farther up- or downriver to better suit their industry. Finally, steel, rubber, and glass factories located on the urban periphery. Thus, there existed three industrial rings reflecting the different land use and technology requirements of each industry.

The diffusion of industrial land use inevitably meant the diffusion of residences, particularly for the large work force required by the new technology and organization. In the preindustrial era, it was common for workers to reside adjacent to the central business district because this area encompassed the city's major employment basin. Industrialization brought the growth of residential nodes adjacent to plants. The so-called "back of the yards" neighborhood on Chicago's periphery housed the work force for the meat plants. Birmingham's steel workers similarly clustered around the mills east of the city. Even in Greensboro, North Carolina, which hardly rivaled Chicago, industrialization meant residential dispersal. In fact, residence was so tied to the factory in Greensboro that the community failed to develop a thriving downtown, as commercial uses built up around the industrial nodes.

The residential proximity of workers to their factories was solidified by the fact that workers still could not afford the daily trolley fares despite major technological advances in mass transit. With more than one member of the family working in an industrial economy and with women and children receiving meager wages, trolley or cable car rides were reserved for special occasions rather than used for daily commuting. It was industrial development then, rather than transportation innovations, that led, initially at least, to the city's physical expansion.

Living within a ten-minute walk to the factory, many of these workers knew with great intimacy that the impact of industry upon the city went beyond spatial change. The natural environment of the city, never particularly chaste, began to deteriorate rapidly. Steel-driving cities might generate imposing twilights, but the stench and smoke permeated the atmosphere seven days a week. A visitor to Pittsburgh in 1884 left a vivid account of the perpetual twilight that covered the city. Of the buildings he wrote: "whatever their original material and color, [they] are smoked to a uniform, dirty drab." Of the atmosphere during the day he observed that "a drab twilight hangs over the town, and the gas-lights which are left burning at mid-day, shine out of the murkiness with a dull, reddish glare." The sun, when it could be seen, looked "coppery through the sooty haze."

The hilly vistas that the visitor once knew were now not only obscured, but obliterated as well, victims to the steel mills' insatiable demands for coal. The hills, he wrote with much feeling, "have been leveled down, cut into, sliced off, and ruthlessly marred and mutilated until not a trace of their original outlines remain." Even the peaceful and pastoral Allegheny River fell victim to the industrial onslaught. An oil barge occasionally sank "and its freight, liberated, refuses to sink with it, and spreads itself out on the surface of the stream."[27]

Indeed, the urban rivers in the industrial cities were becoming garbage dumps for industrial waste. The water around Baltimore in the 1880s smelled "like a billion polecats" according to one observer, while the Cuyahoga River in Cleveland was "an open sewer through the center of the city."[28]

The environmental costs of urban industrial development were great. The human costs were equally significant. Industry rearranged the city and the air and water as well, but the impact on the urban majority—the workers and their families—went considerably beyond residential location and esthetics.

Working Is Not a Living:
Labor in the Industrial City

Workers shared very little of the wealth generated by urban industrialization. By 1900 notoriously low wages, even in the efficient conglomerate industries, had created a large urban subsistence class. A family with small children "has a small chance of living properly" off the wages of a factory worker, the Massachusetts Bureau of the Statistics of Labor concluded in 1882.[29] Confirming this diagnosis were the wages of common laborers, over 14,000 of them, at the Carnegie Steel Works in Pittsburgh. Most earned less than $12.50 a week, while conservative state government estimates calculated that $15 a week was necessary to support a family of four. A group of Illinois investigators reported that even skilled workers—the former artisan class—"fail to make a living" in Chicago's factories.[30]

Wages fluctuated from industry to industry and from skill to skill. In Philadelphia, for example, some skilled workers in the largest plants received nearly $2.50 a day for a six-day week, while skilled personnel in tiny garment industry sweatshops earned only $1.65 a day, less than some unskilled workers in a nearby shoe factory. Despite these distinctions, however, it is worthy of note that only the skilled worker in a large-scale industrial operation met the minimum subsistence requirements for heads of families.

Working hours were scarcely better than the wages. Typical factory operatives worked ten hours a day in the 1880s, six days a week. Hours, like wages, however, tended to vary widely. Canners, for example, worked a staggering total of seventy-seven hours a week, while some workers in the construction industry had achieved the eight-hour day. In the steel industry, workers put in a twelve-hour day. Since the mills remained operative twenty-four hours a day, once every two weeks when the workers changed shifts, one work group stayed on the job for twenty-four hours.

The impact of these lengthy working days on the workers' lives was significant. Toward the end of the work day, they were obviously very tired and apt to be careless. Employers took few precautions for their employees' safety. Between 1907 and 1910, for example, nearly 25 percent of the recent immigrants employed at one of the Carnegie steel mills in Pittsburgh were injured or killed each year. In Chicago's meat plants injuries were part of the daily routine, most caused by carelessness brought on by fatigue or long-term exposure to the intense heat or cold of working conditions. Meat cutters working rapidly with sharp knives would contract a numbness in their fingers by the end of the day, leaving them prone to slicing off part of a digit. As Sinclair wrote, "it was to be counted as a wonder that there were not more men slaughtered than cattle."[31]

Away from the factory, the impact of long hours was equally numbing. Sunday was a day most working people looked forward to. They were usually so exhausted from the work week that sitting or lying in the house was the extent of their recreational activity. During the week, of course, any activity other than eating or sleeping was out of the question. As one machinist testified with considerable poignancy before a United States Senate investigative committee in 1883:

They are pretty well played out when they come home, and the first thing they think of is having something to eat and sitting down, and resting, and then of striking a bed. Of course when a man is dragged out in that way he is naturally cranky, and he makes all around him cranky; . . . and staring starvation in the face makes him feel sad, and the head of the house being sad, of course the whole family are the same, so the house looks like a dull prison.[32]

The adverse impact of industrialization on family life was becoming apparent by the 1880s, though it took a generation to alter wages and hours in the factory so that the worker could enjoy a life outside the factory. Meanwhile, reformers could only raise public awareness. The questions asked by Pittsburgh civic leader Paul U. Kellogg in 1908 could have only one reply: "How much citizenship does Pittsburgh get out of a man who works twelve hours a day, seven days a week? How much of a father can a man be who may never see his babies except when they are asleep; or who never gets a chance to go off into the country for a rolick with his boys?"[33]

Workers attempted to deal with the problems of long hours by living as close to the factory as possible. The environmental conditions were apt to make even this convenience detrimental in the long run, however. Once the worker was inside the factory, options were further reduced because of the rigorous discipline imposed. International Harvester, a midwestern agricultural machinery manufacturer, presented each employee at its Milwaukee plant with a lesson book composed of thirty lessons, the first one of which was a primer on factory discipline:

I hear the whistle. I must hurry.
I hear the five minute whistle.
It is time to go into the shop. . . .
I change my clothes and get ready to work.
The starting whistle blows.
I eat my lunch.
It is forbidden to eat until then.
The whistle blows at five minutes of starting time.
I get ready to go to work.
I work until the whistle blows to quit.
I leave my place nice and clean.
I put all my clothes in my locker.
I go home.[34]

This exercise was particularly effective with European immigrants and rural Americans. The shock of factory regimen on all workers was likely to be great and lasting. The routine was tedious, boring, and repetitive. Such work was so dehumanizing that, as the machinist alleged, the worker "becomes almost a part of the machinery."[35] In Chicago, Jewish glovemakers fought the subdivision of labor in their industry despite the prospect of higher wages. Though making gloves nine hours a day was an onerous task regardless of the method of production, the workers at least achieved some satisfaction with their finished product: "You cling to the variety, the mental luxury of first, finger-sides, and then, five separate leather pieces, for relaxation, to play with! Here is a luxury worth fighting for!"[36]

When not constrained by factory discipline, workers were oppressed by the conditions around them. The garment industry sweatshops were exactly what their name implied. The succinct words of a Chicago investigator provide some insight into the conditions of the workers: "The father, mother, two daughters, and a cousin work together making trousers at seventy-five cents a dozen pairs. . . . They work seven days a week. . . . Their destitution is very great." The entire family of eight lived and worked in a three-room tenement.[37] The reorganization of the garment industry meant that manufacturers subcontracted the sewing and finishing of garments to contractors. The contractors were charged with gathering the labor and supplying accommodations, materials, and machines, thus relieving the manufacturers of these expenses. In order to maximize their profits, the contractors squeezed workers into attics, lofts, and dwellings. Barely adequate for living, these dark, damp, and ill-ventilated quarters were abominable for working.

Low wages, long hours, dulling work, and loathsome working conditions were onerous enough for grown men. The prevailing wage structure, however, made it unlikely for a family to subsist on the wages of one member. Children and women were forced into the factories too, and the consequences to them were even uglier than the impact upon the men. By 1900, it was against the law in many states for children to work before they were sixteen years of age. Since children usually received a third of the pay of an adult, and since many factory positions were relatively mindless, children often found it easier to find employment than their parents; hence they were valuable as a necessary income source. Some textile mill owners in the South, in fact, employed only women and children well into the 1930s. Child labor, serving both the interests of the parents and the employer, resulted in widespread violations of these laws until the fourth decade of the twentieth century.

The results of child labor were predictable: physical and mental debility. Social workers told of children in Chicago who refused candy at Christmas. They later discovered that the youngsters worked six days a week in a candy factory and hated the sight of candy. Then there was the seven-year-old girl, a four-year veteran of the garment industry, whose long hours of toil "day after day with little legs crossed, pulling out bastings from garments," resulted in paralyzed and contorted legs from lack of use.[38] Finally, the story that came to epitomize the miseries of child labor appeared in urban reformer Jacob A. Riis's writings in the 1890s and again in Upton Sinclair's *The Jungle* a decade later. In both versions the story told of a small boy, perhaps eight or nine years old, who was employed by a local factory to carry beer from a nearby saloon (though the law specifically forbade such sale to minors) back to the plant. Occasionally, the boy would himself imbibe, until one day he had too much to drink and fell asleep in a cellar where rats gnawed him to death.

These accounts represent the most severe consequences of child labor. Most working children did not die, nor were they irreparably damaged, physically or mentally. They all, however, lost their childhood. A generation, perhaps two, of working-class children shared the adult burden of factory work, the adult recreation of the saloon, and the adult feelings of fatigue and purposelessness long before they attained chronological adulthood. Ultimately, they shared the premature death of their fellow workers.

A Woman's Work . . .

For working women, the situation was scarcely better, though motherhood offered an occasional respite from the factory routine. Young working-class women, whether married or single, had few options in the urban industrial society. More precisely, they had two. They could go to work in a factory or they could, in the words of one Chicago writer, "tread the cinder path of sin."[39] Maggie Johnson's brother in Stephen Crane's 1892 novel *Maggie: A Girl of the Streets* described the choice more succinctly: "Mag, I'll tell yeh dis! See? Yeh've eeder got t' go on d' toif er go t' work." Maggie went to work.[40]

Theoretically, a young working-class woman could look forward to marriage. It was unlikely that she could marry a prosperous man, since such a match was frowned upon in late Victorian society and, more important, the opportunity for meeting young men of a higher social class was rare in the segregated spatial and lifestyle arrangements of the industrial city. Marriage to a working man offered no release from factory work, given the prevalent wage structure. While childbirth resulted in temporary "vacations," the absence of appropriate medical care and the presence of unsanitary conditions made the process of childbearing a dangerous procedure for both mother and infant.

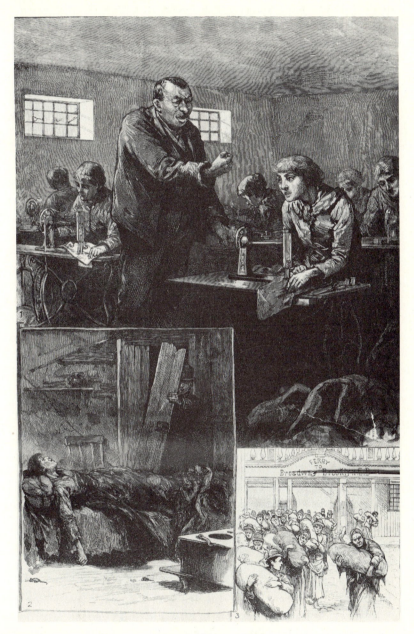

Figure 9.8   Life and Death in the Sweatshop, 1888

The caption of this figure, which appeared in *Frank Leslie's Illustrated Newspaper* in 1888, read: "The Female Slaves of New York—'Sweaters' and Their Victims: (1) Scene in a 'Sweater's' factory, (2) the end, (3) scene at the Grand Street ferry." An exhausting and unrewarding life is portrayed here, and yet the sweatshop was one of only a few options open to working-class women. (Library of Congress)

Living close to factories, as many workers' families did, complicated household chores for the housewife. If she was fortunate enough to have city water, the great water demands of the factory often curtailed the flow to a trickle from dawn to dusk. The alternative was to haul water or arise at five in the morning to fill up tubs and buckets. The technological advances that revolutionized housekeeping in the late nineteenth century—washing machines, central heating, toilets, iceboxes, gas, and electricity—were generally too expensive for working-class families. Even ice, at 42 cents per week for a very small block, was a luxury, so food shopping was a daily routine. Since the housewife purchased items in small quantities, she purchased in the most uneconomical fashion. Quality was another problem, since working-class districts received the poorest foodstuffs, including milk doctored with formaldehyde. Planning and preparing meals, given these constraints, were arduous chores.

The factory was worse. Six dollars a week was a typical salary. On these wages, a married working woman often pulled her family up to a subsistence level. For a single woman attempting to fend for herself in the city, such wages allowed her to eat, in short story writer O. Henry's words, little that was more nourishing "than marshmallows and tea." Lodging rarely meant more than one room, and recreation was affordable once or twice a year. Dulcie, the factory girl O. Henry wrote about, had twice been to Coney Island, a popular resort in Brooklyn. " 'Tis a weary thing," he wrote, "to count your pleasures by summers instead of years."[41]

The factory stole not only recreation but also youth from the working woman. Francie Nolan, the young turn-of-the-century working-class heroine of Betty Smith's novel *A Tree Grows in Brooklyn*, captured the futility of the working woman with these observations:

You work eight hours a day covering wires to earn money to buy food and to pay for a place to sleep so that you can keep living to come back to cover more wires. Some people are born and kept living just to come to this. Of course, some of the girls will marry; marry men who have the same kind of life. What will they gain? They'll gain someone to hold conversations within the few hours at night between work and sleep.[42]

The temptation to break from this deadening scenario must have been great. For married women, comfort in husband and children was the only diversion possible, if fatigue allowed them that. Cheap amusements were attractions for single working girls, if they could afford to squander precious pennies on the cheapest forms of entertainment. There were few other recreational alternatives. As reformer Jane Addams noted: "Apparently the modern city sees in these girls only two possibilities, both of them commercial: first, a chance to utilize by day their labor power in its factories and shops, and then another chance in the evening to extract from them their petty wages by pandering to their love of pleasure."[43]

It was not surprising that many working-class women entered the world of prostitution. There were different types of prostitution, though all forms generally resulted in a rising standard of living. Frequently, white-slavery merchants enticed young and bored factory girls into the business. Sometimes, in return for rent, food, and clothing, a resourceful woman would attach herself to a well-to-do man. She might join one of the many brothels that flourished in all cities. The life of a lone streetwalker was the last resort for desperate women. There was never any shortage of working girls in prostitution. "So is it any wonder," asked the Chicago Vice Commission, "that a tempted girl who receives only six dollars per week working with her hands sells her body for twenty-five dollars per week when she learns there is a demand for it and men are willing to pay the price?"[44]

Certainly the routine of the brothel was a sharp change from factory life. English writer William T. Stead commented on the daily regimen of one Chicago house of prostitution in 1894. The girls rose just before noon and were served cocktails. They dressed and "took another refresher. At breakfast they had wine. Then the day's work began." At fifteen-minute intervals, the girls would sit in couples at the windows and beckon at each passing man. Police were of little concern since most houses operated under police protection. "At five they dined, and then the evening's business began, with more drinking at intervals, all night through, to the accompaniment of piano-playing with occasional dancing and adjournments."[45]

In at least one sense, however, prostitution was more difficult than factory work. The prostitute was a total social outcast. In Victorian America, prevailing attitudes concerning women's sexual behavior took little account of the realities of urban life. Indeed, even the most trivial moral transgression earned social ostracism. Kate Chopin, a St. Louis novelist of the 1890s, caused a tremendous uproar with her books describing adultery, female alcoholism, and divorce. Theodore Dreiser found himself the target of a boycott because his novel *Sister Carrie* did not condemn the conduct of the title character who lived with a succession of men, including a married man. Dreiser's heartfelt explanation at the end of what he knew would be a controversial novel placed Carrie's conduct in its appropriate urban industrial context, but it fell upon largely unsympathetic eyes:

If honest labour be unremunerative and difficult to endure; if it be the long, long road which never reaches beauty, but wearies the feet and the heart; if the drag to follow beauty be such that one abandons the admired way, taking rather the despised path leading to her dream quickly, who shall cast the first stone? Not evil, but longing for that which is better, more often directs the steps of the erring.[46]

The working woman's dreams were eventually extinguished by the factory or the brothel. The industrial city rose in condemnation against sexual immorality but was generally silent on the immorality of the economic order. O. Henry, whose stories were generally apolitical, could not contain his rage in his story about Dulcie. Instead of ending the story with one of his characteristic surprise endings, he related the following dream:

I dreamed that I was standing near a crowd of prosperous-looking angels, and a policeman took me by the wing and asked if I belonged with them.
"Who are they?" I asked.
"Why," said he, "they are the men who hire working girls, and paid 'em five or six dollars a week to live on. Are you one of the bunch?"
"Not on your immortality," said I. "I'm only a fellow that set fire to an orphan asylum, and murdered a blind man for his pennies.[47]

The city was not yet a place where a working-class woman could find opportunity and caring. As Betty Smith told of Francie Nolan's grandmother and her feelings when her daughters, in turn, gave birth to daughters: "She wept when they gave birth to daughters, knowing that to be born a woman meant a life of humble hardship."[48]

The Workers' Response

The obvious question we are tempted to ask when we look at the lives of "humble hardship" that were endured by both working men and women is why they did not organize, protest, and strike to change the conditions. Workers did all of these things, as we will see, but certainly not in proportion to the ills which afflicted them. There were several reasons for the relative passivity of the urban industrial labor force. First and most important, the supply of labor constantly outstripped the demand. Although large-scale industrial enterprises required immense work forces, the urban population, swelled by migrants from rural areas, Europe, and Asia, easily filled all the available jobs and left a sufficient excess to keep wages low and labor fairly docile. Unemployment and underemployment were common aspects of industrializing cities, especially for newcomers. Although unemployment figures for the period are scarce, one machinist estimated that approximately 20 percent of that skilled craft were unemployed in New York City. With competition for positions so severe, an employer had significant leverage on a protesting employee. In some industries blacklists were created that excluded "troublemakers" from work in other factories. As the machinist informed Senate investigators: "If they know that we open our mouths on the labor question . . . we are quietly told that 'business is slack' and we have got to go. Many of my trade have been on the 'black list,' and have had to leave town to find work."[49] Since many workers' families lived on the borderline between subsistence and starvation, the loss of one family member's wages could have tragic consequences.

In plants that employed a large number of immigrants, some of the workers viewed their factory careers as short-term. They hoped to save enough money and then return to Europe. Also, since immigrants had little in the Old World experience with which to compare it, factory life probably did not seem as burdensome initially as it did to natives or second-generation immigrants. Finally, some employers hired different nationalities for different tasks, precluding any factorywide organization because of language and cultural distinctions.

The relative spatial separation of the workers' places of residence was another factor that inhibited concerted action. The presence of one or two distinct working-class districts, as there are in many European cities, was rare in America, as workers clustered around specific industries wherever they were located: on the periphery, downtown, and in between.

Despite these obstacles, some workers organized and disruptions, sometimes violent ones, occurred. The Knights of Labor, formed following the Civil War, attempted to attract a variety of laborers and professionals into its fold. Its membership grew from 9,000 in 1879 to over 700,000 by 1886. This rapid growth resulted more from the desperation of laborers than from the organizing abilities of the leadership. Terence V. Powderly, who assumed the presidency of the organization from its founder Uriah Stephens, maintained Stephens's antistrike philosophy, thereby neutralizing the major weapon labor had at its command. The nationwide strike in 1886, which the Knights had futilely attempted to prevent, and the strike's subsequent collapse led to widespread disillusionment with the union leadership. In December of that year, a group of disaffected members formed the American Federation of Labor with Samuel Gompers, a cigar maker, as its president. It disavowed the Knights' antistrike stand and adopted a more militant stance with regard to wages, hours, and working conditions—issues that the leadership of the Knights had barely addressed.

The AF of L was much less comprehensive in membership and considerably more structured than the Knights of Labor. The new union was organized along craft lines and generally included only skilled workers. Using to advantage the vernacular of the time ("business unionism," he called his approach) Gompers pushed his program for a better life for workers. For forty years he toiled at this task. By the time Gompers died, the eight-hour day and sanitary and safe factory conditions had been established in many industries.

The groping of workers to find some vehicle through which to express their concerns was frustrating because national organizations, by their very nature, functioned slowly, if at all, and local groups, hoping for widespread membership, lacked focus and often deteriorated into social clubs. Despite many obstacles, such as differences in crafts, skill levels, language, and aspirations, and despite spatial separation, the desire for dignity and a decent living sometimes overcame these barriers and erupted onto city streets. Between 1877 and 1894 there were a series of strikes that were remarkable for their ferocity. Included were the great railroad strike of 1877, which paralyzed most of the nation's railroads; the Homestead steel strike of 1892 in Pittsburgh, which culminated in a violent shoot-out between workers and hired detectives; and the Pullman strike of 1894, which shut down the railroads again.

The national rail strike of 1877 brought the desperation of workers to a national forum. Beginning as a localized disturbance in Martinsville, West Virginia, in response to a wage cut (after more than a year of wage cuts), the walkout soon spread to Baltimore and Pittsburgh. In the former city, workers surrounded the armory, trapping the state militia inside. The soldiers opened fire and killed ten persons. In Pittsburgh, strikers destroyed a considerable amount of railroad property including 2,000 freight cars. In a matter of days, the strike had spread to Chicago, Indianapolis, and Buffalo.

In Chicago, railroad workers were joined by factory employees in a general strike. Without any formal organization, work came to a halt in Chicago and workers demanded wage-and-hour reforms. Workers and their families massed in the streets of the city's working-class neighborhoods. In the lumber district in the western part of the city, observers estimated that 25,000 people, or virtually the entire district, were out in the streets. Pitched battles with police followed, with the workers eventually routing the police. Reinforced by federal troops, the police charged into the district the following day only to discover that the lumber workers had been joined by stockyard workers wielding butcher knives. The superior fire power of the police and the United States Army, however, succeeded in dispersing the workers, who regrouped in small bands to carry on guerrilla warfare until exhaustion overtook both sides after four days and nights of disturbances.

The violence in Chicago in 1877 verged on class warfare, and newspaper accounts of the strike compared the scene with some of the worst upheavals in European cities. It was, as one historian has observed, "the first expression of a national working class—as an expression of collective anger over the transformation of working people's lives. . . ."[50] As middle-class Chicagoans armed themselves and as journalists and officials ignored the legitimacy of the workers' grievances to dwell on the "mob mania," it seemed indeed that the social divisions of urban industrial Europe were at last taking root in American cities.

In the years that followed, working conditions remained unrelieved and, in some industries, worsened. Not surprisingly the violence continued. In the spring of 1886, for example, another rail strike mobilized 190,000 men primarily in Chicago, Cincinnati, and New York. In addition to railroad workers, meat packers and skilled factory hands joined the walkout. The worst violence occurred, once again, in Chicago where police shot a worker, triggering a series of events that climaxed with a bomb explosion at a Haymarket Square workers' rally that killed seven policemen and touched off a riot.

The collective expression of anger that erupted periodically and violently during these decades moved many employers to greater intransigence. Some employers acknowledged the miseries of their employees but attributed their condition to the workers' own failings. One employer, in public testimony, expressed a widespread feeling among his colleagues that "the chief cause of the impecunious condition of millions of the wage classes of this country is due to their own improvidence and misdirected efforts."[51] Other employers made less pretense about searching for the causes of their workers' discontent. Said one: "I regard my workpeople as I regard my machinery. So long as they can do my work for what I choose to pay them, I keep them, getting out of them all I can."[52]

Some employers, of course, did not subscribe to these hostile views. A few employers launched programs to improve factory conditions and the lot of the workers. Though motives for welfare capitalism, as it was called, varied widely, it marked the first major recognition of the legitimacy of workers' complaints. In Milwaukee, for example, at the opening of a new plant, an agricultural machinery company threw a ball for its workers, and once a year thereafter treated workers to a picnic. The same company, E. P. Allis, also contributed to an employee benevolent association to care for injured workers.

More comprehensive was the program launched by International Harvester in Chicago in 1902. The company hired stenographer Gertrude Beeks as a "social secretary" to implement a welfare program. Beeks inaugurated women's dressing rooms, a new ventilation system, a lunch room, rest rooms, lockers, and a dancing platform. She also installed individual baths and improved the company's medical services. Finally, vocational education classes were established.

Some of these programs seem suspiciously beside the point. The important issues of wages and hours were not addressed. Some historians have suggested that these programs contained an element of social control. That is, they were attempts to ensure peace and divert attention away from more substantive concerns. It is true that some industrialists, like the McCormick family of International Harvester, were probably genuine in their concern about their employees. They did pay their workers relatively high wages, though they also vigorously quashed any union activity in their plants.

Other than conscience or fear, there was little motivation for an employer to expend time and capital on extensive welfare programs. As class divisions widened, employers found little common ground between themselves and their employees. Aiding the industrialists' reluctance for reform were the ethnic, cultural, and occupational differences among the workers. Further, during the 1880s and for a generation afterward, new population elements began to surge into the city. The renewed supply of labor maintained the intensity of labor competition and convinced few employers to initiate reforms.

The new urban residents, however, were more than factory fodder. Their presence altered, and in some instances, came to dominate the city. Their cultures and complexions added diversity and often conflict to urban society. Finally, their spatial arrangements added new dimensions to the urban geography. The city neither absorbed nor rejected these newcomers, but both the newcomers and the city were forever changed by the contact.

Notes

1. Quoted in Bayrd Still, ed., *Urban America: A History with Documents* (Boston: Little, Brown, 1974), p. 259.

2. Sam Bass Warner, Jr., *Streetcar Suburbs: The Process of Growth in Boston, 1870–1900,* rev. ed. (New York: Atheneum, 1974), p. 158.

3. Peter G. Goheen, "Interpreting the American City; Some Historical Perspectives," *The Geographical Review,* 64 (July 1974), p. 372.

4. Warner, *Streetcar Suburbs,* p. 66.

5. Quoted in Still, ed., *Urban America,* p. 256.

6. Quoted in Carol E. Hoffecker, *Wilmington, Delaware: Portrait of an Industrial City, 1830–1910* (Charlottesville, Va.: University Press of Virginia, 1974), p. 39.

7. Quoted in Still, ed., *Urban America,* p. 227.

8. Quoted in John W. Reps, *The Making of Urban America: A History of City Planning in the United States* (Princeton, N.J.: Princeton University Press, 1965), p. 402.

9. Upton Sinclair, *The Jungle,* rev. ed. (New York: Signet, 1960), p. 58.

10. Quoted in Still, ed., *Urban America,* p. 253.

11. Quoted in Frank A. Randall, *A History of the Development of Building Construction in Chicago* (Urbana, Ill.: University of Illinois Press, 1949), pp. 12–13.

12. Quoted in Michael H. Frisch, *Town Into City: Springfield, Massachusetts, and the Meaning of Community, 1840–1880* (Cambridge, Mass.: Harvard University Press, 1972), p. 154.

13. Quoted in John A. Garraty, *The New Commonwealth, 1877–1890* (New York: Harper & Row, 1968), p. 15.

14. Quoted in Reps, *Making of Urban America,* p. 501.

15. Quoted in *ibid.,* p. 497.

16. Quoted in Jon A. Peterson, "The City Beautiful Movement: Forgotten Origins and Lost Meaning," *Journal of Urban History,* 2 (August 1976), p. 425.

17. Quoted in Joseph L. Arnold, "City Planning in America," in Raymond A. Mohl and James R. Richardson, eds., *The Urban Experience: Themes in American History* (Belmont, Cal.: Wadsworth, 1973), p. 25.

18. Quoted in Charles N. Glaab, ed., *The American City: A Documentary History* (Homewood, Ill.: Dorsey Press, 1963), p. 261.

19. Roy Lubove, *The Progressives and the Slums: Tenement House Reform in New York City, 1890–1917* (Pittsburgh: University of Pittsburgh Press, 1962), p. 220.

20. Sam Bass Warner, Jr., *The Urban Wilderness: A History of the American City* (New York: Harper & Row, 1972), p. 31.

21. Lubove, *The Progressives and the Slums,* p. 245.

22. Lewis Mumford, *The City in History* (New York: Harcourt, Brace & World, 1961), p. 517.

23. Lubove, *The Progressives and the Slums,* p. 227.

24. Quoted in Glaab, ed., *American City,* p. 235.

25. Sinclair, *The Jungle,* p. 41.

26. *Ibid.*

27. Quoted in Glaab, ed., *American City,* pp. 236–237.

28. Quoted in Garraty, *The New Commonwealth,* p. 192.

29. *Ibid.,* p. 129.

30. *Ibid.,* p. 137.

31. Sinclair, *The Jungle,* p. 84.

32. Quoted in Henry Nash Smith, ed., *Popular Culture and Industrialism, 1865–1890* (New York: Anchor, 1967), p. 279.

33. Quoted in Glaab, ed., *American City,* p. 432.

34. Quoted in Gerd Korman, *Industrialization, Immigrants, and Americanizers: The View from Milwaukee, 1866–1921* (Madison: State Historical Society of Wisconsin, 1967), pp. 144–145.

35. Quoted in Smith, ed., *Popular Culture and Industrialism,* p. 274.

36. Quoted in Herbert G. Gutman, "Work, Culture, and Society in Industrializing America, 1815–1919," *American Historical Review,* 78 (June 1973), p. 546.

37. Quoted in Garraty, *The New Commonwealth,* p. 137.

38. Quoted in Lubove, *The Progressives and the Slums,* p. 210.

39. Quoted in Glaab, ed., *American City,* p. 315.

40. Stephen Crane, *Maggie: A Girl of the Streets,* rev. ed. (Greenwich, Ct.: Fawcett, 1960), p. 29.

41. O. Henry, "An Unfinished Story," in Abe C. Ravitz, ed., *The American Disinherited: A Profile in Fiction* (Belmont, Calif.: Dickenson, 1970), p. 34.

42. Betty Smith, *A Tree Grows in Brooklyn* (New York: Harper & Row, 1943), p. 319.

43. Quoted in Glaab, ed., *American City,* p. 354.

44. Quoted in Allen F. Davis, *Spearheads for Reform: The Social Settlements and the Progressive Movement, 1890–1914* (New York: Oxford University Press, 1967), p. 137.

45. Quoted in Glaab, ed., *American City,* pp. 309–310.

46. Theodore Dreiser, *Sister Carrie,* rev. ed. (New York: W. W. Norton, 1970), p. 368.

47. O. Henry, "Unfinished Story," in Ravitz, ed., *American Disinherited,* p. 36.

48. Smith, *A Tree Grows,* p. 57.

49. Quoted in Smith, ed., *Popular Culture and Industrialism,* pp. 279–280.

50. Kenneth Kann, "The Big City Riot in 1877: Chicago." Paper presented at American Historical Association Convention, Washington, D.C., 1976.

51. Quoted in Garraty, *The New Commonwealth,* p. 144.

52. Quoted in Robert H. Bremner, "The Discovery of Poverty," in Allen M. Wakstein, ed., *The Urbanization of America: An Historical Anthology* (Boston: Houghton Mifflin, 1970), p. 243.

10.
Yearning to Breathe Free:
Urban Society and the Great Migrations

The Foreigners

From the 1880s to 1920 American cities were rejuvenated with a new faith. The vision of a John Winthrop or a Brigham Young had been the vision of unusual men for the fulfillment of an unreachable dream: a city of heaven on earth. This type of aspiration returned again as many unusual men and women broke with their homelands to pursue their hope for a better life in the cities of the New World. These new urban pioneers, unlike Winthrop or Young, foresaw no new Zion in the form of American cities. To be sure, many were devoutly religious, but it was not a re-creation of heaven they were seeking. Though some came from Europe to escape religious or political persecution, most immigrants simply wanted an opportunity to improve their condition, earn a decent income, and, as one Lithuanian immigrant in Sinclair's *The Jungle* boasts, count themselves as good as any other man.[1]

The American city, in the midst of industrial expansion, seemed to offer that opportunity, and the "new" immigrants, as they were called to distinguish them from their northern European predecessors who had come before the Civil War, settled overwhelmingly in the cities. During the 1880s, when the migrations from southern and eastern Europe first assumed significant proportions, more than 5 million immigrants came to America, or twice as many as had come in any previous decade. Two-thirds of these newcomers were job-seeking males.

But this was merely the beginning of a series of great migrations. Between 1900 and 1910 a record number of immigrants—8¾ million—entered the United States. In the next decade, 5¾ million arrived; this figure is remarkable considering that Europe was at war and travel was virtually impossible for four of those years. Though roughly one-third of these immigrants eventually returned to their native countries, the net migration figure is still significant.

Given their objectives, it is not surprising that immigrants tended to settle in, or more accurately, to overwhelm the cities. In 1890 roughly one-third of the nation's population lived in cities, while nearly two-thirds of the foreign born resided in urban areas. By 1920 an impressive three-fourths of the foreign born lived in cities. Individual city statistics were even more indicative of the close link between urbanization and immigration. This was especially true of medium-sized industrial cities. As early as 1900, three-quarters of the population of Buffalo was either foreign born or native born of foreign parents. By 1890 nearly nine out of ten Milwaukee residents fit this description. (See Table 10.1.) The "new" immigration even made inroads into the Deep South. In industrial Birmingham, one-quarter of the white factory workers were either first- or second-generation immigrants.

Europeans not only brought themselves in great numbers, but they brought their distinctive cultures as well. The shock of uprooting themselves from their ancestral homes and resettling in a strange country was significant, but it was not sufficient to dislodge traditions that had accumulated over centuries. Although American soil might at first seem inhospitable to such cultural graftings, the American city, in many ways, proved an extension of the European environment. The immigrants' daily lives during their first years, even their first decades, were guided as much by the Old World as by the New.

Although the immigrants from southern and eastern Europe may be lumped together under the heading of "new" immigrants, the timing of their arrival in this country is one of the few things they had in common. Cultural differences extended not only between various national groups but within national groups as well. In discussing the immigrant experience in urban America, it is misleading, therefore, to generalize about the "Italian" experience or the "Jewish" experience, let alone about the "new-immigrant" experience. In order to account for these distinct experiences, we must return to the Old World because there lay the roots of the immigrant in urban America.

It would be impossible, of course, to review the distinctions among the hundreds of different immigrant groups that came to American cities be-

Table 10.1   Constituents of the Population of the Great Cities, 1890

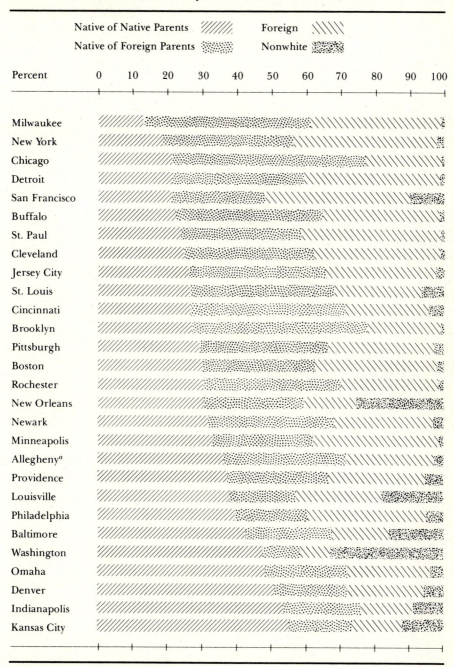

*a*Once an independent city, Allegheny is now part of Pittsburgh.

Source: U.S. Bureau of the Census, *Eleventh Census, 1890* (Washington, D.C., 1895), I, pt. 1: plate B, p. xcii.

tween 1880 and 1920. An example from the largest national group to emigrate—the Italians—will suffice to demonstrate the richness and diversity of immigrant life in urban America.

Since Italy was not a unified country until 1870, it was not to be expected that the people who migrated from the new country would think of themselves as Italians; and they did not. Loyalty centered around the province. Thus, in Chicago by 1920 there was not one "little Italy" but rather seventeen separate colonies located throughout the city. In some cities, like New York, there were divisions not according to province, but according to town. Thus, on one street were immigrants from Cinisi; on another street perhaps a mile away, former residents of Palermo; and several miles uptown, migrants from Avigliano—all communities in Sicily, yet each with distinct traditions.

Provincial loyalties were not a phenomenon of the new immigration, but were common to all immigrant groups. Germans who had migrated as early as the 1830s still thought of themselves as Bavarians, Prussians, or Saxons as late as 1900. Within those provincial divisions there were religious and political distinctions as well. These differences accounted for the variance in their response to American urban life among the different groups of Germans.

The relationship between provincial background and New World urban experience was placed in sharp relief in a study of Chicago Italians from the Mezzogiorno (southern Italy and Sicily).[2] The study also demonstrated the danger of generalizing about the culture and experience of a national group. The *contadini* (peasants) came from towns, not farms. The stereotype of rural immigrants overwhelmed by American cities and by the consequent problems of adjustment to city life did not apply here, if in fact it was an accurate description of the experience of any national group. The family was the basic institution in the Mezzogiorno. In fact, family ties, nuclear and extended, were so strong that voluntary associations in the towns were rare. This is probably the reason for the great difficulty experienced by the *contadini* in developing national mutual aid societies in American cities. Beyond the family, everyone was a stranger.

The Mezzogiorno was a land of violence. Violations of family pride or honor, especially of a sexual nature, were dealt with harshly by the offended family. Southern Italy possessed the highest homicide rate in Europe. Family revenge prevailed in American cities as did another southern Italian custom, extortion under threat of death. The extortionists, known collectively in Sicily as the Mafia, made their way across the Atlantic and became a vicious presence in neighborhoods of southern Italians.

Thus, crime and violence in Italian districts, which some historians have attributed to the frustrations and disorganization of American urban life, were cultural legacies from the Old World.

Other Mezzogiorno folk customs not only survived the Atlantic crossing but also thrived in American cities. Southern Italians were Catholics but had little use for the church or the clergy, associating the hierarchy with exploitation and oppression. Accordingly, they transferred their devotion to saints. This practice gave their religion a folksy, almost pagan aspect. "Magic, not religion, pervaded their everyday existence." The *contadini* went to church "to be christened, married, or buried and that is about all."[3] These traditions persisted in Chicago, where feast days honoring the saints became the major neighborhood events.

The study of the *contadini*'s roots in Italy underscores the importance of looking to Europe for an explanation of immigrant life in American cities. Galician Poles, for example, placed significant value on steady work and close family ties. The concept of upward mobility, so fascinating to American historians, was irrelevant to the Poles and was not part of their aspirational framework. When they came to a city like Pittsburgh, success was achieved by steady, if dulling, factory work and a rich family life. Thus, premigration attitudes influenced the type of work and hence the lifestyle of Pittsburgh's Poles.

Other more specific traditions also persisted and sometimes created strange scenes in American cities. Jewish immigrants especially held fiercely to Old World ways, perhaps because, more than any other group, their sufferings had accumulated over centuries. The Jews also had no national ties; they were literally without a country. Their loyalties were concentrated on their religion and on the customs which emanated from it. Sabbath observances, dietary customs, and dialects were assiduously maintained and reinforced through the synagogue, Sunday schools, Yiddish theater, and the press. This was particularly so of the Russian Jews, who were part of the new immigration. Their isolation and strict adherence to tradition were strengthened by the hostility between them and their German Jewish brethren who had migrated a generation earlier and were practicing a more Americanized brand of Judaism. The kosher meat wars of the early 1900s were an indication of the vigorous survival of an ancient custom. The "wars" were periodic outbursts of violence by Russian Jewish housewives retaliating against price hikes made by kosher butchers. These altercations were common in Russia and prevailed at least through the first two decades of the twentieth century in America. The 1902 kosher meat war turned into a regional boycott affecting kosher butchers in several

Figure 10.1   The Lower East Side, New York City, 1902

This crowded neighborhood housed several ethnic groups. Shown in this photo are Italian immigrants. (Documentary Photo Aids)

major northeastern cities. As in the Old World, the women vandalized the butcher shops, but did not steal any meat. The custom was to punish, not to steal.

These remnants of Old World culture, which translated into distinct urban American lifestyles, led contemporary observers to report that the new immigrants were distinct from the rest of urban society. Social workers talked of walking into neighborhoods and finding a European community delivered intact on American soil. New York City's Lower East Side, where

Figure 10.2   Fifth Avenue, New York City, 1902

Several miles removed spatially and light years away socially from the Lower East Side, these fashionable New Yorkers parade along Fifth Avenue on Easter Sunday in 1902. (Documentary Photo Aids)

150,000 Jewish immigrants crowded together in one of the world's most densely populated areas, was a favorite subject for investigators eager to describe the immigrants' unique lifestyle to their curious readers. Journalist Edward Steiner in 1902 captured the special flavor of the district where "street signs are written in Hebrew letters, and the passerby is invited . . . to purchase a prayer-mantle or 'kosher' meat, to enter a beer-saloon or a synagogue. . . . Everything is for sale on the street, from pickled cucumbers to feather beds."[4] Philadelphia social worker Emily Dinwiddie's account of an Italian neighborhood in that city similarly illuminated the foreign atmosphere of the district. It described "black-eyed children, rolling and tumbling together, the gaily colored dresses of the women and the crowds of street vendors, that give the neighborhood a wholly foreign appearance."[5]

Ethnic Space: The Neighborhood

Accounts like these gave contemporary readers the impression that most immigrants resided in homogeneous communities isolated from the rest of society. *Ghettos,* as these neighborhoods were called, were believed to be the major spatial element in urban immigrant settlement. Recent studies have demonstrated, however, that few immigrant districts were homogeneous.

As it is difficult to generalize about immigrant lifestyles, so it is difficult to generalize about ethnic residential habits. Where an immigrant lived depended on many factors besides ethnicity. The size and ethnic mix of a city may have had something to do with residential decision making, but it is not certain which combinations promoted ghettos (neighborhoods where 50 percent or more of a particular ethnic group resided) and which favored smaller residential clusters within neighborhoods. The rate of urban growth may have been related to ghetto formation in that the absence of new housing would lock immigrants into specific neighborhoods for longer periods of time, while a vigorous housing market would increase geographic mobility. Different stages in the immigrants' life cycle, too, may have affected residence patterns, with older people tending to be less likely to move. Finally, as we noted earlier, employment opportunities rather than ethnic camaraderie may have determined residential patterns. Workers of various ethnic backgrounds clustered around a factory, and even if one provincial or national group dominated several streets, the neighborhood as a whole was ethnically mixed. Also, the employment opportunities of downtown led a variety of ethnic groups to cluster together there. The Lower East Side of Manhattan, for example, which scholars have repeatedly pointed to as the Jewish ghetto par excellence, was actually closer to an ethnic potpourri than an ethnically pure downtown neighborhood.

The relationship of city size, ethnic mix, urban growth, and employment to ethnic residential patterns can be seen by examining residential patterns in both Detroit and Omaha. Polish immigrants were Detroit's most visible ethnic group from 1890 to 1920. In their residential patterns, they tended to dominate neighborhoods numerically, though employment opportunity vied with ethnicity as the major reason for their doing so. The Poles came to Detroit as unskilled laborers in the 1890s and entered the construction trades located on the city's west side. They eventually dominated the west side of Detroit, but only for a short time. By 1910 Poles were leaving their old neighborhood for the urban periphery, where the new auto industry was developing. They established dominance in that district, too. The sheer size of the Polish community and the tendency of community members to be attracted to the same type of work helped to create a ghetto neighborhood.

In Omaha, a smaller city, where one-third of the population was foreign born, most foreigners were scattered fairly evenly throughout the city in 1880. In 1900, the effects of the "new" immigration began to register in terms of spatial location. Some Russian Jews clustered in neighborhoods near downtown, but most of this immigrant group lived elsewhere. Other groups such as Italians and Czechs also exhibited some clustering, but the pattern of domination common to Polish immigrants in Detroit did not develop in Omaha, at least through 1920.

Omaha's immigrants enjoyed a high degree of residential mobility that inhibited the formation of ghetto neighborhoods. This mobility in all directions toward the urban periphery tended to decrease residential clustering by 1920, though small Jewish and Italian clusters remained, more as reference points for the majority of those groups, than as expanding residential neighborhoods.

It is difficult to pinpoint one particular reason for the relatively diffuse residential pattern exhibited by Omaha's immigrants. About all that can be done is to contrast the situation in Omaha with the conditions in Detroit. Omaha was not dominated by large-scale heavy industry with massive labor requirements that could, in turn, create distinct ethnic neighborhoods. Equally important was the fact that Omaha had a fluid housing market that was constantly expanding in all directions to meet the population requirements. Finally, there were some intangibles, like Omaha's smaller size and its relative newness, that inhibited the growth of distinct, isolated communities. The examination of the tendency of the same immigrant group to develop very different residential patterns in different cities is an area of historical inquiry that is relatively new and needs further exploration before we can isolate the crucial factors that determine the residential preferences of immigrant groups.

Whether a particular immigrant group dominated a neighborhood or not, they attempted to put some psychological, if not physical, distance between themselves and the rest of the urban population. Immigrant institutions were valuable in establishing the distinction and in enhancing the identity and solidarity of the ethnic group. While the residential patterns of a particular group changed from city to city, the types of institutions upon which the immigrants relied usually did not.

If, in some cities, it was difficult to discern specific ethnic neighborhoods, it was usually possible to locate a spatial clustering of institutions that immigrants scattered about the city referred to from time to time. As such, the institutions, more than the number or relative strength of a particular ethnic group, defined an immigrant community. The family, mutual aid societies, and larger charity organizations, encompassing an entire national group on occasion, were among the earliest immigrant institutions because the need for these institutions was greatest in terms of basic survival.

The charitable organizations were frequently connected with religious institutions. Religion had occupied an important position in the immigrants' Old World existence, and did so in their new urban homes as well. The church or synagogue was a physical focal point in the community, even to the relatively aloof Italians, because the church or synagogue was much more than a place of worship. It was a school where Old World values and language, as well as religious training, were transmitted. It was a recreational facility where immigrant children could come as an alternative to the streets. At times, community leaders would gather there to discuss important matters and perhaps to seek some divine guidance. Finally, it functioned as an auxiliary institution for charitable purposes.

The numerous functions performed by the church or synagogue made it imperative that the local community control it. Polish parishioners wanted Polish priests, and Russian Jewish communities wanted Russian rabbis. At times the nationality of the minister became such a heated topic that some Catholic national groups threatened to secede from the church. During the 1890s the nationalism of various Catholic groups became so intense that a movement for administering the Catholic church in America by nationalities rather than by dioceses went all the way to Rome before it was squelched.

Religion was important to the immigrant community because it was a traditional link with the Old World past. Some institutions had only tenuous ties to the European background, but conditions in American cities required them. New arrivals were often prey for unscrupulous rooming-house proprietors or bogus employment agents, who promised to secure the immigrant a job for a fee paid in advance. Some charitable organizations devoted a portion of their funds and personnel to meeting the boats or trains carrying newly arrived immigrants. They would help to find lodging for the newcomers and even place the new arrival in contact with a prospective employer.

The Italians developed a unique system of initiating newcomers into urban life. The strength of kinship ties inhibited the formation of the kinds of large-scale charitable organizations that other groups had established. The Italian newcomer instead turned to the padrone, a townsman who had achieved some status in America and who was familiar with urban American customs. The padrone performed most of the functions that institutions executed for other immigrant groups. He extended credit, bought groceries, and found lodging and, most important, employment for the new arrival. For each of the functions performed for the immigrant, the padrone received a commission, usually from the immigrant. Frequently, this arrangement began in Italy with the padrone paying for the steamship ticket to America. Most historians recognize that the padrone performed necessary functions given the suspicion of southern Italian immigrants toward strangers, but they also believe that the prices exacted for these services were in many cases excessive. The padrone system flourished until families and, later, labor unions were strong enough to assume the padrone's functions.

Making It

Once the newcomers were settled, the dull routine of work dominated their lives. It is not an exaggeration to state that a generation sacrificed itself so that the future generations would enjoy a better life. The immigrants' dreams focused, in many instances, on their children. The formula for success soon came to be hard work for the parents and education for the children. For immigrants, education had been a temporary and sometimes inaccessible luxury in the Old World. The value of education was recognized, and education was highly prized, especially in Jewish villages in Russia. But even there, religious institutions performed the educational function, since few Jews entered the secular Russian educational system. Education in Europe was a class phenomenon, a privilege of social standing. The popular immigrant view of America was that it was a relatively classless society. If there was an aristocracy, it was an aristocracy of learning, not of blood. Education was the road to that aristocracy and the way out of a lifetime of toil and poverty. For these reasons, immigrants nurtured and supported educational institutions with an almost religious fervor.

To Francie Nolan, the heroine of Betty Smith's *A Tree Grows in Brooklyn,* education was indeed a religious experience. As Francie entered the little dilapidated library in her neighborhood, "the feeling she had about it was as good as the feeling she had about church." Later on, Francie's mother

Katie, despondent over the future, suddenly had an inspiration of the way out for her children: "An answer came to Katie. It was so simple that a flash of astonishment that felt like pain shot through her head. Education! That was it! It was education that made the difference! Education would pull them out of the grime and dirt."[6]

It was not, of course, that simple. First, respect for the value of education varied widely among immigrant groups. German and Jewish immigrants placed much faith in the powers of education. On the other hand, Polish immigrants, with their emphasis on family and work, were relatively indifferent to education, some even seeing it as an interference with work. Another problem was the sometimes conflicting educational objectives espoused by immigrants. Katie Nolan's revelation related to the objective of upward economic mobility to be gained by education. Some immigrants saw education as a means of perpetuating Old World traditions, values, and language. Urban public school systems were rarely the appropriate educational institutions for fulfilling that objective.

In fact, public schools were generally horrible institutions in turn-of-the-century cities. The flood of immigrants caused serious overcrowding, and both administration and curriculum were in a state of chaos. The worst physical facilities were inevitably located in immigrant districts. With sometimes as many as one hundred children packed into a dimly lit and poorly ventilated classroom, it was not far-fetched to look upon the school as an educational extension of the factory. "Brutalizing is the only adjective for the public schools," Betty Smith wrote.[7]

The teaching was generally as inadequate as the physical facilities. Teacher salaries were low, and most teachers viewed the profession merely as an alternative to factory work. Married women were prohibited from teaching. Betty Smith observed that, as a result, "most of the teachers were women made neurotic by starved love instincts. These barren women spent their fury on other women's children in a twisted authoritative manner."[8] Although Smith's analysis undoubtedly exaggerated the situation, at least some teachers must have resembled her profile. The atmosphere of the school was one of rigid discipline and conformity, down to the uniforms worn by the children. Smith recognized, however, that this strict regime had some value for immigrant children, who frequently came from homes where instability and insecurity were common. She wrote: "So Francie felt a certain safety and security in school. Although it was a cruel and ugly routine, it had a purpose and a progression."[9]

The sense of security notwithstanding, it was not surprising that some immigrant parents had little respect for the city's public schools. Even when reformers tried to tinker with the system by installing vocational courses, there was a feeling that this merely fed the public stereotype of an immigrant as fit for nothing better than common labor. Some Catholic immigrant groups developed their own system of parochial schools. Yet even here, loyalty to these private educational institutions varied. If the local public schools included such ethnic-oriented courses as language and history, Catholic immigrant parents would not hesitate to send their children to these schools. The parochial schools, especially in Polish and Italian neighborhoods, were established more for cultural than for religious purposes. Expense was also a problem, though some dioceses arranged liberal scholarships for Catholic immigrant children. Local control was another factor in school choice. Where immigrant parents could dominate local public school policy and curricula, public school enrollment was high. Correspondingly, if clergy of a different nationality controlled the local parochial school, there would be little incentive for immigrant parents to send their children there.

Jewish parents were, on the whole, most supportive of public educational institutions. In their Old World villages imposed segregation had forced them to establish their own schools. Thus, they viewed free public education as both a luxury and a freedom. Adherence to the parochial schools in the American city would merely perpetuate, they felt, the segregation they had experienced in Europe for centuries. Yet they realized that to retain their identity as Jews, their children had to be grounded in religion, Hebrew, and history. Accordingly, the parents established Sunday schools and after-school educational centers to supplement public school education. For the deeply religious or Orthodox Jews, yeshivas replaced the public school system as the primary educator of the young. Only a minority of a city's Jewish children attended this parochial school, however.

Education in Jewish districts was not solely for the young. Adult educational institutions developed with less emphasis upon Jewish traditions and more upon English reading and writing skills. The importance assigned to this function was indicated by the fact that the most prominent structure in New York's Lower East Side Jewish community was the Educational Alliance. Its popularity among adult Jews is evident from the comments of one observer who visited the Alliance on a hot Sunday in July 1902: "This gigantic building, covering a block and containing forty-three classrooms, is entirely inadequate to meet the demand. The main entrance is always in a state of siege, and two policemen are stationed there to maintain order and keep the crowding people in line."[10]

The eagerness for the services of the Educational Alliance was part of a larger desire for success in the American city. There was, however, a price for success: casting off some Old World traditions and exchanging them for the American way of doing things. This tension always existed in the immigrant neighborhoods. The conflict between Europe and America was sometimes a generational battle. Yet even among the older traditionalists, perceptible changes were occurring, as they inevitably would in the dynamic urban environment. Immigrant institutions like the press and the theater would preach the rewards of adherence to tradition and the penalties of denouncing one's ethnic heritage. At the same time, the press emphasized the value of English, and English words began to creep into ethnic theater. In the Yiddish theater, which served the Jewish communities, one could hear strange English-Yiddish concoctions such as "gemovet" and "gejumpt" mingled with "pananas" from South America.

The traditionalists fought a losing battle. Life in the city militated against a wholesale transplanting of European village life. First, many immigrants had come from areas with stagnant or declining economies. Economic opportunity, in fact, was one of the major reasons for migration. The American city, on the other hand, presented numerous economic possibilities, and the greater the opportunities the more rapid the process of assimilation.

Striving for success became a major objective of life, and if traditions were obstacles, they would be discarded. Religious traditions were the first casualties for David Levinsky, journalist Abraham Cahan's semiautobiographical Russian immigrant in New York: "The striking thing was that it was not a world of piety. . . . Very few of the women who passed my push-cart wore wigs, and men who did not shave were an exception. Also, I knew that many people with whom I came in daily contact openly patronized Gentile restaurants and would not hesitate even to eat pork."[11] Few immigrant neighborhoods were so isolated or self-contained as to avoid contact with the larger urban society. The young immigrant "on the make" would come to know the appropriate standards of urban behavior necessary for advancement, and conformity was one of those standards.

Conformity sometimes forced abandonment of traditions. Sabbath observances, wedding ceremonies, and saints' festivals that did not conform to the unbending discipline of the factory were modified. Orthodox Jews from eastern Europe, for example, held a festival on the eighth day following the birth of a son. Since Sunday was the only day off from the factory, the parents had to plan the event for that day, regardless of whether it was the right day or not. "The host and his guests," one historian noted, "know it is not the right day and they fall to mourning over the conditions that will not permit them to observe the old custom." The day becomes "one for secret sadness rather than rejoicing."[12]

Perhaps it was small consolation for some, but conformity sped the process of residential and economic mobility. David Levinsky's adoption of the urban lifestyle paid very well: "I was born and reared in the lowest depths of poverty and I arrived in America—in 1885—with four cents in my pocket. I am now worth more than two million dollars and recognized as one of the two or three leading men in the cloak-and-suit trade in the United States."[13] Few immigrants, of course, followed Levinsky's rags-to-riches path. In their own view, however, many immigrants were successful. Adhering to a philosophy of what historian Stephan Thernstrom has termed "ruthless underconsumption,"[14] some immigrants saved enough to move from their initial cramped residences to houses on the urban periphery. Owning a home and property around it, however small, was the definition of success for many immigrants. Sam Bass Warner, Jr., in his study of Boston's late-nineteenth-century suburbs[15] contended that within a generation portions of Boston's ethnic communities were suburbanized. After a generation in Philadelphia, by the 1870s some Irish had attained what historian Dennis Clark has called "the cult of residential contentment" north of the city where they were "flying the lace-curtain flags of domestic satisfaction."[16]

While residential mobility was a possibility within a generation, occupational mobility was considerably more difficult. The relative absence of occupational mobility may have resulted from the immigrants' own expectations of improvement. It is quite possible that an ethnic group's definition of success did not include a change from blue-collar to white-collar occupations. Polish immigrants in Pittsburgh, for example, defined success as passing down blue-collar positions from father to son as well as gaining a steady income, and home ownership. Though historians have typically employed occupational mobility as one measure of success, it is clear that some immigrants did not. It is also evident that some groups, Jews and Italians, for example, hoped for a change from manual to nonmanual labor in the next generation. This is why education received such a high priority, especially among Jewish immigrants. Although figures on the subject are unavailable, it seems obvious that a much lower percentage of Jews and Italians than Poles achieved success according to their own definition, albeit the Poles' definition was more limited. In terms of happiness and frustration levels, therefore, more Poles may have been contented with urban life than members of some other ethnic groups.

Occupational mobility also varied from city to city depending in some part on the rate of economic expansion in a particular city. An expanding economy created more white-collar positions and hence more opportunities for urban residents—many of whom were first- and second-generation immigrants. New York's Jews and Italians, for example, probably fared better than compatriots in other cities because of New York's rapidly growing economy after 1890.

Material success could bring its own disappointments, including a loss of ethnic identity and accompanying guilt. David Levinsky successfully pursued his dream of wealth. Yet Cahan ends the book with a moral, a reminder that Levinsky's old values of family and God held greater value in the end than the pursuit of profit. As the book ends Levinsky confesses: "My sense of triumph is coupled with a brooding sense of emptiness and insignificance, of my lack of anything like a great, deep interest. I am lonely. Amid the pandemonium of my six hundred sewing machines and the jingle of gold which they pour into my lap I feel the deadly silence of solitude."[17]

Wealth did not necessarily mean the loss of tradition any more than a home in the suburbs signified a severance of ties to the old neighborhood downtown or by the factory. Compromises obviously had to be made, but then the process of assimilation was a series of compromises. Abandonment of ethnic culture was rare, which is the reason the old immigrant district retained a special psychological importance long after a group's initial dominance or even cluster in the area had dissipated. Institutions, friends, relatives, and food products continued to draw later generations and, more recently, people of all ethnic backgrounds.

There were, of course, the "left behinds"—those immigrants who remained rooted where they had landed and were irrevocably tied to their Old World ways. Tradition was security and the city could be terribly insecure. We do not know much about the "left behinds," except that at least in the first generation they were the majority of the immigrant population. They are there, as are the factories, to remind us that mobility in urban America had its obstacles for the immigrant. Indeed, the accomplishments of the ethnic minorities, especially in the second generation, seem all the more significant in view of urban society's prevailing attitudes toward them.

The antagonism toward the immigrant cannot be passed off as the attitude of an occasional bigot. Leading molders of public opinion doubtless expressed not only their own, but prevailing beliefs about immigrants. No group remained unscathed. Americans "pretty well agreed," claimed the *New York Times,* that the Italian and Russian immigrant was "of a kind which we are better without."[18] A Jersey City newspaper referred to striking Irish laborers as "a mongrel mass of ignorance and crime and superstition, as utterly unfit for its duties, as they are for the common courtesies and decencies of civilized life." In 1884 the prestigious *Chicago Times* suggested a solution to what the editor felt was an alarming invasion of Slavic immigrants into Chicago: "Let us whip these slavic wolves back to the European dens from which they issue, or in some way exterminate them."[19]

Discrimination in housing and employment were concrete expressions of these attitudes. It took at least a generation for these views to change or at least not be broadcast publicly. It was rare to find such inflammatory statements toward immigrants after 1920. Not coincidentally, it usually took one generation for the immigrants to achieve some residential and occupational mobility, if they achieved it at all. The immigrants, regimented by factory work, concerned about their internal conflicts between tradition and conformity to American urban life, buffeted by adverse public opinion and occasionally by overt actions, and beset by the usual anxieties and doubts newcomers would face in a strange environment, ultimately came to call the city home and to possess a sometimes fond and sometimes melancholy attachment to their neighborhoods. If the present were onerous, the future, in the city at least, could be brighter. This was the hope of the American city—the hope of tomorrow. The immigrants would understand what the Detroit rabbi meant when he declared that the Jew was no longer a man without a country. "He has found his Canaan in America."[20]

John Winthrop, Brigham Young, and now the millions from Europe had grasped the special meaning of urban life. Another group of migrants believed in the city as their predecessors had believed. Their dreams reflected a past filled with denials—of their ability, their intellect, and even of their humanity. Like the Europeans, they came to the city to have their dreams fulfilled. Unlike the Europeans, they remain in the city and their dreams, if they still dream, are unfulfilled. They were the urban pioneers who remained in the wilderness.

The Blacks

At the turn of the century 90 percent of American blacks were located in the South, and only 17 percent of southern blacks lived in cities. By 1960 almost 40 percent were found outside the South, and nearly three-quarters of all blacks were urban. In the course of six decades, the nation's blacks had redistributed themselves across the land, comprising almost a fifth of the populations in the Northeast and Midwest. From the most rural of America's major minority groups, they became one of the most urban. (For details, see Table 10.2.)

Southern blacks drifted northward throughout the late nineteenth century, numbering about 19,000 a year between 1890 and 1910. Black migration to southern cities rose during the first decade of the century, presaging

Table 10.2   Number and Percentage of Blacks in Selected Central Cities, 1900, 1920, 1950, 1970

	1900 No.	1900 %	1920 No.	1920 %	1950 No.	1950 %	1970 No.	1970 %
New England								
Boston	11,591	2.1	16,350	2.2	40,057	5.0	104,707	16.3
Providence	4,817	2.7	5,655	2.4	8,304	3.3	15,875	8.9
New Haven	2,887	2.7	4,573	2.8	9,605	5.8	36,158	26.3
Middle Atlantic								
New York	60,666	1.8	152,467	2.7	747,610	9.5	1,688,115	21.1
Buffalo	1,698	9.5	4,511	9.9	36,645	6.3	94,329	20.4
Newark	6,694	2.7	16,997	4.1	74,965	17.1	207,458	54.2
Philadelphia	62,613	4.8	134,229	7.4	376,041	18.2	653,791	33.6
Pittsburgh	20,355	4.5	37,725	6.4	82,453	12.2	104,904	20.2
South Atlantic								
Baltimore	79,258	15.6	108,322	14.8	225,099	23.7	420,210	46.4
Washington	86,702	31.1	109,966	25.1	280,803	35.0	537,712	71.1
Richmond	32,230	37.9	54,041	31.5	72,996	31.7	104,766	42.0
Charlotte	7,151	39.5	14,641	31.6	37,481	28.0	72,972	30.3
Charleston	31,522	56.5	32,326	47.6	30,854	44.0	30,251	45.2
Savannah	28,090	51.8	39,179	47.1	48,282	40.4	53,111	44.9
Atlanta	35,727	39.8	62,796	31.3	121,285	36.6	255,051	51.3
North Central								
Cincinnati	14,482	4.4	30,079	7.5	78,196	15.5	125,000	27.6
Cleveland	5,988	1.6	34,451	4.3	147,847	16.1	287,841	38.3
Detroit	4,111	1.4	40,838	4.1	300,506	16.2	660,428	43.7
Milwaukee	862	0.3	2,229	0.5	21,772	3.4	105,088	14.7
Chicago	30,150	1.8	109,458	4.1	492,265	13.6	1,102,620	32.7
Indianapolis	15,931	9.4	34,677	11.0	63,867	15.0	134,320	18.0
Gary	—	—	5,299	9.6	39,253	29.3	29,695	52.8
St. Louis	35,516	6.2	69,854	9.0	153,766	17.9	254,191	40.9
Kansas City, Mo.	17,567	10.7	30,719	9.5	55,682	12.2	112,005	22.1
Minneapolis	1,548	0.8	3,927	1.0	6,807	1.3	19,005	4.4
South Central								
Birmingham	16,575	43.1	70,230	39.3	130,025	39.9	126,388	42.0
New Orleans	77,714	27.1	100,930	26.1	181,775	31.9	267,308	45.0
Memphis	49,910	48.8	61,181	37.7	147,141	37.2	242,513	38.9
Nashville	30,044	37.2	35,633	30.1	54,696	31.4	87,877	19.6
Louisville	39,139	19.1	40,087	17.1	57,657	15.6	86,040	23.8
Houston	14,608	32.7	33,960	24.6	124,766	20.9	316,551	25.7
Dallas	9,035	21.2	24,023	15.1	56,958	13.1	210,238	24.9
Mountain								
Denver	3,923	2.9	6,075	2.4	15,059	3.6	47,011	9.1
Salt Lake City	278	0.5	718	0.6	1,127	0.6	2,135	1.2
Pacific								
Los Angeles	2,131	2.1	15,579	2.7	171,209	8.7	503,606	17.9
Oakland	1,026	1.5	5,489	2.5	47,562	12.4	124,710	34.5
San Francisco	1,654	0.5	2,414	0.5	43,502	5.6	96,078	13.4
Portland	757	0.9	1,556	0.6	9,529	2.5	21,572	5.6
Seattle	406	0.5	2,894	0.9	15,666	3.3	37,868	7.1

Source: Condensed from Table 4.3, pp. 406–407, in Bayrd Still, *Urban America: A History with Documents.* Copyright © 1974 by Little, Brown and Company (Inc.). Reprinted by permission.

a much larger movement northward during the next ten years. Half a million southern blacks left the region, primarily for the Northeast and Midwest, between 1910 and 1920.

A combination of factors caused blacks to head northward and cityward. An agricultural malaise, created in large part by the infamous boll weevil that decimated southern cotton fields, drove a number of black and white tenants and sharecroppers off the land, or at least made their continued existence there supremely difficult. Without a major cash crop, farming came down to a question of simple survival. Further, the southern racial climate was harsh and restrictive, and it was especially severe in rural areas. Blacks were disfranchised in the 1890s and were systematically excluded and segregated. And periodic lynchings in the late nineteenth and early twentieth centuries were particularly brutal reminders of second-class citizenship. The North may not have seemed as much the promised land of freedom as it had appeared to escaping slaves on the underground railroad, but its cities held out the promise for a better life. The Chicago *Defender,* one of the leading black newspapers in the nation, attained wide circulation among blacks in the South and urged their brethren on: "To die from the bite of frost is far more glorious than at the hands of a mob. I beg you, my brother, to leave the benighted land."[21] The biblical imagery, tightly woven into slave lore, reappeared in the northern migrations when the migrants compared their exodus to the "Flight out of Egypt" and "Going to Canaan." Indeed, a group of migrants speeding north on a train from Mississippi to Chicago stopped their watches, fell on their knees, and sang the hymn "I Done Come Out of the Land of Egypt With the Good News" as they crossed the Ohio River.[22]

It was not only the racial situation in the South that created this religious fervor, it was the economic conditions in northern cities as well. Southern blacks were deeply tied to the soil—as were many southerners—and available evidence indicates that lynchings did not significantly increase the numbers of local blacks who left. The attractions of the urban North were probably most important, especially the opportunities for jobs, higher wages, and a better life. These were, after all, the major attractions for millions of European and Oriental immigrants. Significantly, as economic opportunities increased, so did black migration, especially to industrial cities like Chicago, Cleveland, Detroit, and Pittsburgh.

Chicago, as the terminus of the Illinois Central Railroad, was a particularly favorite destination among blacks from Mississippi, Louisiana, and Arkansas. During World War I, when foreign immigration stopped, industries in Chicago and in other northern cities developed labor shortages. For a period of eighteen months beginning in January 1916, more than 50,000 blacks entered Chicago, most on free tickets supplied by local industries. The *Defender* took this opportunity to flood its southern readers with job listings, success stories, and editorial entreaties. The newspaper's efforts were so successful that white authorities in the labor-depleted South confiscated the paper in many areas. However, the word continued to get through as labor recruiters, friends, and relatives passed the message of high wages, plentiful jobs, and city excitement. As one contemporary wrote of Chicago: "this city is really the land overflowing with milk and honey."[23]

True enough, blacks found work in the city as they migrated in record numbers after 1890. The World War I employment bonanza was a temporary divergence from the depressingly typical pattern of black employment during the migration years, however. The range of occupational opportunities open to blacks was severely limited by discrimination and by increasing competition from the other urban migrants, the foreign immigrants. In most northern cities at the turn of the century, the typical black was employed as a common laborer or a servant. Even more discouraging was the absence of any occupational mobility for decades. Low-paying unskilled jobs were not merely the first step toward better things for blacks, as they were for immigrants. A rigid job ceiling prevailed, limiting blacks to menial and manual tasks. In Cleveland between 1890 and 1910, the occupational status of blacks remained stationary, while immigrants registered impressive gains during the same period.

Since the skill levels of both the southern and foreign migrants were roughly similar, they sought the same employment. In almost every case until World War I, the immigrant won the competition. Although the blacks' occupational status was always low, there were certain positions that were recognized as their preserve in northern cities. With large-scale immigration after the 1870s, such monopolies crumbled, especially in barbering and in service occupations. Fannie Barrier Williams, a turn-of-the-century black activist in Chicago, complained that between 1895 and 1905, "the colored people of Chicago have lost . . . nearly every occupation of which they once had almost a monopoly."[24]

The situation was equally dismal in Detroit in the late nineteenth century with Italians taking over the barbering profession and the Poles working on the docks, where once only blacks had worked. As more and more blacks found themselves unemployed, underemployed, or forced into backbreaking common labor, frustration naturally grew. Blacks, after all, had established bases in northern cities since the antebellum period, while many of their foreign competitors were recent arrivals. A black whitewasher in Detroit summarized the disillusionment of his race in 1891: "First it was de Irish, den it was de Dutch, and now it's de Polacks as grinds us down. I s'pose when dey [the Poles] gets like de Irish and stands up for a fair price, some idder strangers'll come over de sea 'nd jine de family and cut us down again."[25]

Blacks began to participate in urban industry in appreciable numbers only during World War I. Industrial employment did not change their low occupational status, however. Moreover, they faced the same problems adjusting to the factory regimen as foreigners encountered. Finally, the growing unions that promised some improvement in workers' conditions usually bypassed blacks. Unions were generally organized around skilled crafts, and few blacks were involved in those occupations. Blacks also had earned reputations as strikebreakers. Employers, during the periodic and sometimes violent labor struggles, would import trainloads of blacks to replace striking workers. Though only a few blacks knew vaguely the issues involved in these disputes, their role did not endear them to union organizers.

The lack of options confronting blacks in the search for employment matched similar frustrations in their quest for a place to live. The word "ghetto" was more appropriate in describing residential locations for blacks than for any foreign immigrant group. More important, even if some foreign groups dominated a residential area, that dominance was only temporary; for blacks it was, and has continued to be, a permanent condition, paralleling their lack of occupational mobility. One historian has described the black residential experience as "the enduring ghetto."[26]

Racial Space: The Ghetto

The black ghetto has persisted since the antebellum decades when such spatial concentrations were rare. In New York, for example, there were several black enclaves dispersed throughout the city. Each enclave, however, was a homogeneous community of blacks, emphasizing their spatial isolation from the rest of the city. In Detroit in 1860, although they represented a fraction of the population, four out of every five blacks in the city lived at the convergence of three wards, a concentration unique in the city at that time. Following the Civil War, as blacks completed the first stage of their migration process, southern and border cities developed patterns of spatial segregation as well. In Washington, D.C., as early as 1880, a twenty-block area in the southwest quadrant of the city was more than three-quarters black. In Atlanta in the 1890s, blacks dominated an area east of the downtown, known as "Sweet Auburn" after the avenue that cuts through the ghetto. Finally, boomtown Birmingham was barely two decades old before blacks there lived in almost total isolation from whites.

As black migration to northern cities advanced rapidly after 1900, the pattern of residential isolation became more pronounced. Between 1910 and 1920, as ethnic concentrations began to dissolve, black ghettos expanded in size. The expansion in most cities generated a great deal of white hostility. Blacks were confined to the least desirable and most dilapidated housing, usually situated adjacent to the central business district. The rapid influx from the South strained the already overcrowded dwellings. Unable to expand into commercial land-use areas, blacks sought nearby residential districts that invariably contained white residents.

The whites usually formed protective associations pledging not to sell to blacks and occasionally resorted to violence to oust a black family or two that happened to move into the area undetected. Although these tactics were successful for a while, the availability, for whites, of homes on the urban periphery and the fear of the black population usually resulted in the expansion of the black ghetto into the previously white district. While the neighborhood might remain integrated for a time, within a decade it was indistinguishable from the rest of the ghetto.

There were a few exceptions to this pattern, but they all resulted in an "enduring ghetto," regardless of the differences in origin. In Cleveland and in some smaller cities farther west, blacks clustered in but did not dominate certain residential neighborhoods in the late nineteenth century. The reasons for the relative absence of ethnic concentrations in Omaha, as discussed earlier, apply to blacks in these cities as well: the newness of the cities and the favorable housing market. By 1920, however, the word *ghetto* was appropriate for the black residential experience in these cities.

Harlem was unusual among black communities. Unlike most ghettos, Harlem was not the least desirable residence area in the city. In 1890 the community on the northern edge of Manhattan Island was predominantly white and middle class with a hint of the countryside on its fringes. By 1920 it was a teeming black ghetto on the way to becoming one of the nation's most notorious slums.

The transformation began in the wake of a mad carnival of land speculation touched off by the extension of the subway in the late 1890s. As so often happened with speculative enterprises on the urban periphery, the area became overbuilt. As the boom collapsed, black realtors, especially Philip A. Payton, Jr.'s Afro-American Realty Company, moved in to take advantage of the bargain prices in the area. Payton leased apartment houses from hard-pressed white owners and rented units to blacks at high rental rates. Although Payton eventually overextended himself, the opening of Harlem to blacks after 1905 was the first wave of a black rush into the community. The attractions of moving "uptown" to a middle-class neighborhood must have been great for blacks who were denied access to decent residential districts in the city. Unfortunately, many blacks who moved to Harlem could not afford the rents, so doubling- and tripling-up occurred. The stately brownstones built to house one family now sheltered four or five. Overcrowding led to deterioration and a serious decline in the quality of life. By 1920 Harlem was a ghetto.

The blacks' occupational status and their residential isolation were distinct badges of second-class citizenship. As blacks moved about the city, there were numerous other reminders of their lowly position. Segregation was a fact of black life. In addition to occupational and residential segregation, blacks encountered discrimination in public facilities, in education, and in the legal system. Beginning in the 1870s and accelerating after 1900, segregation dominated race relations in American cities despite the presence of federal and state civil rights legislation, and the absence of local regulations enforcing segregation. Restaurants, hotels, and theaters threw up the color line, though most of these facilities were too expensive for the average black in any case. Prohibitions against intermarriage between blacks and whites were common. Blacks were systematically barred from recreational facilities and usually forced to maintain separate educational facilities. Where an integrated school system existed as in Detroit, separate desks for white and black children were common.

In southern cities after the Civil War, segregation was an improvement over the antebellum policy of excluding blacks from public and educational facilities altogether. The Republicans who ran southern cities during the Reconstruction era had no intention of integrating southern urban society, but they did hope to provide equal facilities for the segregated blacks. The separate-but-equal policy died with the end of Reconstruction, and blacks were relegated to inferior educational facilities and public accommodations.

The unanimity of cities in segregating blacks and in restricting their choices revealed, of course, deep-seated prejudice against them. The popular culture of the era depicted blacks in the most uncomplimentary manner. Vaudeville and minstrel shows, popular urban entertainment at the turn of the century, included such black characters in their repertoire as "Useless Peabody" and "Moses Abraham Highbrow." Songs of the period denigrating blacks such as "All Coons Look Alike to Me" and "I Wish My Color Would Fade" were common numbers at performances. The black image received little rehabilitation with the advent of a new urban mass entertainment, the motion picture. In fact, the rather innocuous, stupid,

good-timing black of the earlier shows was replaced by a more evil carica-
ture following David W. Griffith's pioneering 1915 film *Birth of a Nation,*
which set box office records. Griffith's film was so powerful and so negative in its depiction of blacks that it touched off riots in several cities,
triggered a series of NAACP lawsuits, and inspired the resurrection of the
Ku Klux Klan.

As historian Gilbert Osofsky has observed, the black stereotype common
in the nation's cities at the time ran counter to virtually every American
ideal. "The Negro was conceived of as lazy in an ambitious culture; im-
provident and sensuous in a moralistic society; . . . childlike in a country of
men." In Osofsky's words, the black "seemed more fit to be a servant, a 'half
man,' than anything else."[27]

Immigrants quickly adopted these stereotypes. Prejudice against blacks
seemed to be the American thing to do. A black New York school principal
stated the situation more graphically: "Pat O'Flannagan does not have the
least thing in the world against Jim from Dixie, but it didn't take Pat long
after passing the Statue of Liberty to learn that it is popular to give Jim a
whack."[28] The problem was that these popular prejudices were periodically
extended into a good many "whacks" against blacks.

Violent clashes between blacks and whites were inevitable given the prevailing white attitudes. The great migration after 1900 seemed more like
an invasion to white residents of adjacent neighborhoods and to those
white laborers already concerned about the oversupply of labor. The year
1919 witnessed widespread and bloody racial violence. Race riots occurred
in twenty-six American cities. The timing of the riots was not surprising
when we consider that by this time blacks had achieved some success in
breaking into industrial employment and therefore were more threatening. Also, with the cessation of European immigration, the continuing
black migration became even more evident, especially to the immigrants.
Serious violence occurred in Chicago, where a record number of blacks
had migrated during the two previous years. A good portion of these new
migrants secured employment in the meat-packing houses on the city's
South Side, already the site of Chicago's black ghetto. Expansion into contiguous white neighborhoods became inevitable and tensions built along the
slowly shifting boundary lines separating black from white residential
areas. After months of unprovoked attacks on blacks by white youths, a
full-scale riot erupted during the summer of 1919 when several blacks
attempted to test the segregation of a neighborhood beach. Thirty-eight
people lost their lives, making the confrontation one of the bloodiest racial
outbursts prior to 1965.

The Chicago riot demonstrated to whites that blacks must learn their place in urban society. Blacks, though, had learned this lesson long before the summer of 1919. In their own communities they sought to establish a separate society, a much more self-contained and isolated one than the immigrants had formed to preserve their foreign heritages. Unlike the foreigners, the blacks had no other options.

Although segregation provided blacks with the opportunity to create their own institutions, there were several obstacles to overcome before the ghetto could be called a community. First, there were divisions within the black ghetto as numerous as the differences among immigrant groups, but the differences among blacks were not as neatly defined spatially and culturally by provincial groups as they were for the immigrants. The ghetto included West Indian blacks (primarily in New York), southern rural blacks, southern urban blacks, and northern urban blacks. There were poor blacks, well-to-do blacks, and blacks of all degrees of poverty and wealth in between. The division between oldtimers and newcomers was most serious of all. The rapid influx of blacks from the South after 1900 resulted in deteriorating race relations and the imposition of harsher restrictions on black life in the city. Further, the majority of migrants were both illiterate and ignorant of urban ways of life, thus confirming some of the prevailing white stereotypes. This annoyed the oldtimers, as they had worked assiduously for decades to earn the respect of the white community. They called the newcomers "lazy," "overdemonstrative," "uncouth," and "undesirable."[29]

Since the oldtimers held leadership positions in the ghetto, their coolness toward the migrants presented another obstacle to ghetto unity. The oldtimers cherished their ties to the white community and viewed the creation of black institutions as a threat to the integrated society they still hoped for—a hope that was becoming increasingly unlikely of fulfillment for them and impossible for the vast majority of blacks. Even when the oldtimers had created institutions prior to the great migration, such as the black church and black social clubs, these had tended to divide rather than to unite the black community. The religious affiliations of the newcomers, primarily Baptist or Pentecostal, added to these divisions.

As the migration from the South overwhelmed the oldtimers, their ideals eventually became engulfed as well. The integrationist philosophy was replaced by the philosophy of racial solidarity and self-help propounded by the urban followers of Booker T. Washington. The old elite, dominated by professionals and a few business people with connections to the white community, gave way to a new leadership of middle-class business people who viewed the ghetto in terms of economic opportunity for themselves and their fellow residents. The large and growing concentration of blacks ensured a local market.

The new middle-class leadership was most interested in developing black capitalist enterprise. Black business began to blossom in the ghetto after 1900. Although service enterprises predominated, there were several successful examples in other fields such as real estate and cosmetics. Robert Abbott's Chicago *Defender* became, by 1920, the largest black-owned business in the country. The newspaper was sensational and flamboyant, and sometimes concocted stories to capture reader interest. But it also played a significant role in the great migration during World War I. Ignored by the white urban press, blacks enthusiastically supported the *Defender*. White discrimination also helped to launch black-owned amusements, such as dance halls, amusement parks, and a professional baseball league. Crime and vice were other forms of black business that also flourished in the ghetto.

The life spans of most black businesses were very short. Reliance on a black-only clientele was risky because of the limited resources possessed by ghetto blacks. The value of black businesses to the ghetto was also questionable. Black realtors tended to perpetuate spatial segregation. Most black businesses were so small that they employed only one or two ghetto residents. The overwhelming majority of black workers not only depended on white employers for their wages, but also worked outside the ghetto. Finally, black landlords were hardly more virtuous than their white counterparts in exacting high rents and in demanding prompt payment of those rents.

More lasting and ultimately more helpful to the ghetto were the institutions founded to improve the quality of life more directly. One of the major reasons why these institutions were both lasting and helpful was the presence of white financial, managerial, and moral support. In Chicago in 1891, black physician Daniel Hale Williams established Provident Hospital, the nation's first interracial hospital. Leading white Chicagoans such as industrialist Philip Armour and Florence Pullman provided the major financial support. The hospital was successful, but not as an interracial experiment. By 1915 most of the staff and physicians were black. The black doctors and nurses who came through the hospital's internship program could not find positions at white hospitals.

The organization of black branches of the Young Men's and Young Women's Christian Association was a beneficial addition to ghetto life, providing living accommodations, social facilities, and employment information for young blacks. White financial angels funded the "Y" projects. In

Chicago, Julius Rosenwald of Sears, Roebuck, was the white financial inspiration behind the black YMCA in that city. By 1910 black settlement houses modeled after white versions had appeared in several cities, though participation of neighborhood blacks in their educational and nutritional programs was low.

Two institutions with less immediate roots in the ghetto, the National Urban League and the National Association for the Advancement of Colored People, complete the list of major black self-help institutions. White sociologist Robert Park presided over the creation of the Chicago chapter of the Urban League during World War I. The League coordinated black welfare efforts, lectured in churches, and helped to organize block clubs and improvement societies. The League also operated a manual-training school. Much of the League's efforts were aimed, admittedly, at counteracting white stereotypes of blacks as dirty and lazy. Further, by emphasizing improvement of the ghetto and vocational education, the League was perpetuating black spatial and occupational patterns. Given the nature of white society at the time, however, it is difficult to see how other alternatives would have served blacks better or sustained white financial support.

The NAACP was, like the Urban League, a national institution with branches in most of the major cities where black ghettos existed. Mary White Ovington, who was instrumental in the formation of the NAACP, was a wealthy heiress who dabbled in Socialist Party politics. Responding to a speech given by black leader Booker T. Washington and to an article written by reformer William English Walling in 1909 on "The Race War in the North," Ovington decided that blacks' acceptance of their caste status must be changed in order for the caste itself to be broken. Calling a meeting of like-minded friends in New York, including Walling and Henry Moskowitz, a settlement-house leader, Ovington spearheaded the formation of the NAACP in 1909. The three principals in the Association's establishment were white.

The Association's early activities included attempts to broaden and enforce state civil rights legislation and a protracted and probably ill-advised legal battle to ban Griffith's film *Birth of a Nation* from theaters in major cities. With its emphasis on action, combined with the growing frustrations of black urban life, it would seem that the NAACP would have attracted a wide following in its first decade. The absence of qualified black local leadership, however, hurt the organization. For blacks who had learned the necessity, if not the virtue, of self-help, it was difficult to rally around white leaders. The black middle class that provided much of the ghetto leadership by World War I were more concerned with developing black businesses and in advancing local institutions and political organizations. In their view, the challenge to the segregated city was apt to be a long and bitter struggle, so why not conserve energy and cultivate the resources of the black ghetto?

The average black, which meant the poor black, could not yet afford the luxury of concern over civil rights. For him, and countless other black migrants, jobs, food, and decent housing were needs the ghetto institutions could not fulfill. Yet, there was one ghetto institution, a venerable one at that, that maintained the ties to southern roots and fostered hope of another kind: the black church. Since the antebellum era, it had espoused the self-help philosophy. With black leadership and with mostly black financial support, it was one of the few ghetto institutions that could truly call itself "black." Following the trend of white churches, black congregations offered social services to less fortunate parishioners and provided blacks with an opportunity for expression and for leadership not available to them in the white-dominated city. By giving them an opportunity to come together periodically under one roof, the churches gave ghetto residents some sense of common destiny, a necessary counterbalance to the strong strain of individualism current in the black ghetto.

The spatial manifestation of the black's misery, the ghetto, expanded and hardened its boundaries between 1890 and 1920. The institutions that evolved during that time came into existence as a result of blacks' exclusion from the white urban world. Immigrant institutions, most of which had roots overseas, were organizations voluntarily formed both to ease the transition to urban America and to retain the traditions of the past. This was not true of black institutions, except for the church, which probably accounted for its overwhelming support. By 1920 most immigrants were beginning to make their way in the urban world in terms of occupations and residential areas. The blacks remained where they were and if they dared to challenge the status quo, frustration and physical injury would be the only certain results. Was this what southern blacks had left their homes for?

In 1908, black leader W. E. B. Du Bois wrote that the "country was peculiarly the seat of slavery, and its blight still rests . . . heavily on the land, but in the cities . . . the Negro has had his chance."[30] Although the chance was remote for blacks, the city still held out possibilities. It was possible to open a business and perhaps have some success. There was, after all, the example of Lillian Harris, who had been born in poverty in the Mississippi delta. She migrated to New York City in 1901. With five dollars she purchased a baby carriage, a boiler, and pigs' feet. With her gastronomic stock she wheeled her carriage throughout Harlem, expanding her restaurant on wheels and saving her profits carefully. By World War I, "Pig Foot Mary," as she was known, was a wealthy landlord. She eventually retired to southern

California where she died in 1929. To be sure, Lillian Harris, like David
Levinsky, was unusual in her environment. The point is that it is difficult to
imagine such upward mobility occurring in the Mississippi delta. The city
represented this opportunity, even though few blacks were able or, more
accurately, were allowed to participate. The potential to advance remained,
and, given the relative hopelessness of rural life for blacks, it is no coincidence that the blacks are the most heavily urbanized group in American
society today.

For the time being, however, the city was a trial for most blacks. If
immigrants were beginning to achieve success according to their own definitions, many blacks were not. For workers of any background, the factory
robbed them of dignity, family life, and the joys of childhood. The city was a
place of great misery at the turn of the century, but equally important, it was
a place where people cared. Perhaps some cared for the wrong reasons, but
the unhappiness which gathered around them demanded some ameliora-
tion.

Helping the Other Half:
Poverty and Its Relief

By the 1890s an uneasy feeling was developing that two widely disparate and
separate societies were emerging in America's cities. Urban reformer Jacob
Riis in his exposure of poverty in New York, *How the Other Half Lives* (1890),
wrote that "the half that is on top cares little for the struggles, and less for the
fate of those who are underneath so long as it is able to hold them there and
keep its own seat."[31] That the evidence uncovered by Riis to support his
conclusion seemed new and startling indicates how isolated and fragmented
urban society had become. Knowledge of this division was a necessary first
step toward attacking the city's most dangerous and pervasive problem:
poverty.

The urban poor constituted a large segment of the urban population. The
group included workers as well as the unemployed, aged, widowed, and
disabled. The poor encountered staggering obstacles due to the very fact
that they were poor. In what became a perverse cycle, these obstacles, in
turn, served to perpetuate their poverty. The simple matter of purchasing
consumer goods illustrated the principle well. Coal kept urban residents
warm during the winter. Like most other commodities, the unit price was
cheaper if the quantity purchased was larger. The poor, however, were
unable to afford coal in large quantities. They purchased the fuel by the
basket, paying almost double what they would have paid if they had been
able to afford to buy by the bin.

Figure 10.3   Rich and Poor, 1873

A widening gap between rich and poor characterized late-nineteenth-century urban America. (*Harper's Weekly,* January 11, 1873)

In the purchase of food products the poor encountered the same economic realities. In addition, the quality of food sold was usually lower in the poorer districts. The poor not only had few alternatives, but their ignorance made them prey to adulterated products. Upton Sinclair cataloged the typical grocery list that confronted poor "back-of-the-yards" residents in Chicago: "pale-blue milk . . . watered and doctored with formaldehyde; . . . tea and coffee, sugar and flour had been doctored; . . . canned peas had been colored with copper salts, and their fruit jams with aniline dyes." But suppose they had known better? Sinclair replied: "What good would it have done them, since there was no place within miles of them where any other sort was to be had?"[32] The new spatial organization in industrial cities, with manufacturing plants located toward the periphery and workers living near them, left residents far away from more reliable and less expensive downtown establishments. The poor faced similar problems in the purchase of clothing and housing—paying more for less.

Being poor was not only expensive, it was stressful. Jacob Riis related how one day he came upon an Irish laborer with a hatchet in his pocket. As a result of a disability caused by his job, he was unemployed with seven children and a wife to provide for. So that the city would not take away his children, he planned to murder them. Fortunately, he was arrested before he could carry out his mad plan. Riis also told of a "hardworking family of man and wife . . . who took poison together . . . because they were 'tired.' "[33] It was not surprising that suicide rates were highest in the poorest districts.

The stress on family life was great, even if there was a wage earner in residence, as we noted earlier. Industrial accidents and higher mortality rates generally increased the likelihood of single-parent households and the accompanying hardships associated with the loss of a wage earner. Poverty had its greatest impact, though, on the children. Infant mortality among the poor usually exceeded the citywide norm by one and a half to two times. For the children who lived, poverty and its attendant evils hardened them very early in life. Violence and death were common accompaniments of poverty. Children learned early that alcohol was one of the few means of escape from the strains of being poor. The prevalence of prostitutes inaugurated both boys and girls into sex. One former slum resident reminisced about his childhood years that it took "years to learn that sex can be good as well as evil; more than the thing truck drivers bought for fifty cents on my street."[34] Finally, given this type of environment it was not surprising that children sought refuge in street gangs as a source of protection, excitement, and identity.

Even the forms of entertainment sought by the poor distressed reformers who believed that the sensual and raucous pleasures in which they engaged not only threatened their moral and physical well-being, but also maintained them in their impoverished state. The saloon, of course, was an oft-mentioned institution in reformers' reports, which ignored its social functions and concentrated on its role in fostering alcoholism and thriftlessness. The so-called dives, however, were more obnoxious to reformers than the saloons. Dives, in the words of one investigator, were "dance-halls where abandoned women congregate to try their charms on easily tempted men." Often, these bistros were basement rooms that sold doctored liquor and were havens for criminals and prostitutes. The women "patrons," the investigator discovered, had typically "given up their positions in the shops and factories to earn their living in the dance-hall."[35] Since the poor had precious little money to spend even on necessities, these dives, though providing temporary and perhaps necessary diversion, merely ensnared them deeper in the web of poverty.

As distressing as the manner in which the poor lived was the type of housing in which they lived. Housing was the indelible and most obvious badge of poverty because it was the most visible. The term *slum*, which described the housing of the poor, was a mid-nineteenth-century creation. The timing coincided with the spatial isolation of the poor in distinct residential districts. With the exception of workers' residences coalescing around the grimy factories on the urban periphery, the slums were located in the city's oldest housing on the edge of the central business district. Slum housing was invariably filthy, overcrowded, and overpriced.

In his writing Jacob Riis introduced many Americans to the central-city slum by taking them on a tour of housing in lower New York's Mulberry Bend neighborhood. A typical apartment there consisted of a parlor, which included the kitchen, and "two pitch-dark coops called bedrooms." There were a total of three beds "if the old boxes and heaps of foul straw can be called by that name." Riis related that "the closeness and smell are appalling." In July when the temperature reached 90 degrees outside, it was at least 115 degrees inside the apartment, which housed six people.[36] At this point, Riis's tour turned to melodrama, a favorite device he used to rouse his readers' sympathy and anger: "Here is a door. Listen! That short hacking cough, that tiny, helpless wail—what do they mean? Another child dying. With half a chance it might have lived but it had none. That dark bedroom killed it."[37] Unfortunately, Riis's melodramatic statement was probably accurate.

It was not necessary to sensationalize the miseries of slum life to appreciate them. The dry statistics of density told an appalling story. In New York's tenement district, the density of 986.4 persons per acre in 1894 was the highest in the world. (Today, by comparison, the densest areas of our cities rarely have more than 400 people per acre.) Laws prohibiting overcrowding were simply not enforced. It was difficult to pay the rent without overcrowding. Further, the effect of enforcement would be to turn people out into the streets, creating further hardships for tenants. In the extremely short housing supply, an apartment, no matter how vile, was a desirable commodity. Riis related how the tenants he interviewed insisted on retaining their anonymity for fear of arousing the landlord's wrath and facing consequent eviction. In this situation, tenants would rarely force landlords to make necessary repairs on the dwellings. Overcrowding and deterioration would continue.

The tenement was a structure which facilitated overcrowding in poor neighborhoods. Since the land in these districts was close to the central business district, it was expensive. A builder, in order to get the most out of the lot, had to cover virtually all of it with the structure. To make the building a profitable enterprise, as many apartments as possible were packed within the five or six stories allowed by law. By the 1870s it was clear that the builder's quest for profits had to be balanced by the poor's right to decent housing. Accordingly, in 1878 a trade journal, the *Plumber and Sanitary Engineer,* announced a competition for a tenement design on a 25 × 100−foot lot, the size of a typical lot on which builders constructed their tenements. The winning design would have to show the attributes of providing safety and comfort for the tenant and profit for the builder.

Architect James E. Ware won the competition with a design that came to be called the *dumbbell* tenement. The building was five or six stories high and contained fourteen rooms on a floor, seven running in a straight line on each side. There were four families to a floor. A stairwell dominated the center of the building; light came from windows overlooking an air shaft. City authorities were so impressed with the design that they required every tenement bedroom to include a window for ventilation. The dumbbell, with apartment bedrooms overlooking the air shaft, was thus codified.

The dumbbell tenement proved to be a very dumb idea. The coveted windows overlooked an air shaft twenty-eight inches wide and enclosed on all sides. (See Figure 10.4.) It did not provide any ventilation, but rather was a health and safety hazard. The shaft was a convenient duct for flames to leap from one story to the next and a garbage dump that reeked with foul odors, especially in the hot summer months. The shaft also proved to be an excellent echo chamber for noise. So much for the windows. The building itself occupied nearly 90 percent of its lot, so landscaping and recreation areas were impossible. Finally, the bedrooms, despite the "amenity" of the

Figure 10.4   Air Shaft of a Dumbbell Tenement in New York City, Circa 1900

The air shaft, the most attractive feature of the award-winning dumbbell design, extended five stories and "lit" forty-five windows. (National Archives)

window, were tiny alcoves measuring at most 7 × 8½ feet in size. It was apparent that future attempts to house the poor would have to take less account of builder's profits.

The housing-reform movement really began when the failure of the dumbbell tenement became evident in the 1880s. Housing held a particular fascination for reformers because they believed that many of the evils of poverty stemmed from the environment created by poor housing. The concern over housing was part of a larger trend toward viewing poverty from an environmental perspective. The early-nineteenth-century view of poverty as an inherent moral failing that was virtually insoluble had been replaced by a more professional attitude that stressed causes beyond the control of the poor. Since people could alter their environment, poverty could be solved through environmental reform. With this view in mind, an army of college-educated men and women began to probe the environment of the poor, collect data, and urge legislation based on their findings. The spatial isolation of the poor in separate residential districts was evidence in itself of the impact of environment. Housing, as the most visible aspect of that spatial isolation, naturally received the greatest attention of the new professional reformer.

A chorus of reformers agreed that the environment in general, and housing in particular, was the major cause of urban poverty. Federal investigator Carroll Wright summarized his tour of slums in a dozen cities during the 1890s by concluding that "bad housing is a terribly expensive thing to any community. . . . It explains much that is mysterious in relation to drunkenness, poverty, crime, and all forms of social decline."[38] Novelist Stephen Crane explained that his novel *Maggie: A Girl of the Streets* (1893), about a young girl who grows up in the slums and eventually becomes a prostitute, was written "to show that environment is a tremendous thing in this world, and often shapes lives regardlessly."[39] Crane was especially concerned about the impact of the tenement on children. Urban reformer Felix Adler probably summarized the relationship between housing and human behavior most succinctly and pointedly: "Squalid houses make squalid people."[40]

The course of action seemed clear: Improve the housing of the poor, and the poor will improve. Some attempts, though well-meaning, were unsuccessful. Since private enterprise built the tenements, any housing-improvement scheme would have to ensure a margin of profit for builders. The so-called model-tenement movement was an example of good intentions and meager results. In 1877 Brooklyn realtor Alfred T. White completed a series of model tenements. The tenements were built around courtyards that served as recreation space. Reading rooms and baths were some of the development's attractions. The buildings were safe, clean, and well constructed. Unfortunately, although rents were modest and White sought only a 5 percent yearly profit from his development, the rents were beyond the reach of the poor. Most of the tenants were, at the least, skilled workers and nearly all were white and native born. Finally, while White indeed made his 5 percent return, his colleagues constructing regular tenements reaped profits of at least 10 percent. There was little incentive, except philanthropy, to construct model tenements and, in any case, few of the poor could afford to live in them.

Reformers turned instead to controlling regular tenements through legislation. New York City became the leader in the housing-reform movement. The city not only had the worst housing conditions in the country but would come to have the nation's most humane housing laws. Lawrence Veiller, a product of New York's City College, was the architect and moving force behind much of this legislation. Veiller was deeply committed to restrictive legislation as the method of providing decent housing for the poor. His philosophy was codified in the New York Tenement House Law of 1901. The triumph of that legislation was the prohibition of the notorious dumbbell tenement. The law also limited tenements to five stories, required a bathroom for each apartment, and included strict fire-protection measures. Veiller had little patience with those reformers who recommended broader, more indirect solutions to the city's housing problems such as improved transit facilities to disperse the poor, new communities beyond the urban periphery, construction of model tenements, and tax reforms to redistribute wealth. As Veiller argued:

We must get rid of our slums before we establish garden cities. We must stop people living in cellars before we concern ourselves with changes in methods of taxation. We must make it impossible for builders to build dark rooms in new houses before we urge the government to subsidize the building of houses. We must abolish privy vaults before we build model tenements.[41]

Veiller's philosophy of restrictive legislation as the major element of housing reform reached beyond New York to influence other cities. Actually, the five-story tenement was not the typical slum housing in cities across the country. In Philadelphia, for example, there existed what housing investigator Emily Dinwiddie called "horizontal tenements." Very little of Philadelphia's housing stock was built for the express purpose of housing the poor. Instead, the poor lived in small alley and row houses (Figure 10.5). The living conditions, however, were similar to those in the worst accommodations in New York. In one three-story row house, for example, thirty-three people lived in seventeen rooms, only one-third of which were bedrooms. The alley houses were smaller and equally as bad. Dinwiddie recalled that the houses "had cellars flooded with sewage . . . the foul water standing about a foot deep in all but one of the buildings. Often the walls were overgrown with mould from the moisture, as well as tapestried with cobwebs and thick with dust and dirt."[42]

In Chicago, one- or two-story houses were common dwellings for the poor, as they were in Buffalo. Conditions were the same regardless of architectural variation. Thus, other cities were able to apply Veiller's princi-

Figure 10.5   Philadelphia Slum Houses, 1896

Not all slums were built according to the dumbbell design, as these three-story row houses demonstrate. Compare with Figure 7.3, an earlier generation of Philadelphia row houses. (National Archives)

ples on the importance of regulating conditions and hazards *within* buildings. In order to promote the passage of uniform building codes throughout the nation, Veiller founded the National Housing Association in 1910.

Many reformers, however, believed that the emphasis on building codes was too narrow a focus. Environmentalists wondered whether—since legislation changed only the interior of buildings while the slum neighborhood itself remained the same—the poor would ever be released from poverty; they could be released from bad housing, perhaps, but not necessarily from poverty. The young men and women who formulated and implemented a wide range of urban reforms from politics to poor relief were convinced that the roots of urban poverty were many and that they lay deep within urban society.

The basic premise guiding these reformers—men and women of mainly middle-class, native-born parentage, who believed that as their country had a mission to bring democracy to the dark corners of the earth, so they had the duty to bring a decent life to the benighted sections of the city—was that the spatial isolation of the poor had created an environment, which, in turn, had produced a multitude of deviant effects, including poverty. Indeed, the descriptions of slum dwellers rampant through the literature of the period depict an almost subhuman race inhabiting the slums. Edward Bellamy's account of such a neighborhood in Boston in his reform novel, *Looking Backward,* was typical:

As I passed I had glimpses within of pale babies gasping out their lives amid sultry stenches, of hopeless-faced women deformed by hardship, retaining of womanhood no trait save weakness, while from the windows leered girls with brows of brass. Like the starving bands of mongrel curs that infect the streets of Moslem towns, swarms of half-clad brutalized children filled the air with shrieks and curses as they fought and tumbled among the garbage that littered the court-yards.[43]

There was a hint of fear in Bellamy's remarks, and indeed some historians have alleged that fear of the poor was perhaps one subconscious motivation of the reformers. For a person who had spent only a generation in the city, the changes that had taken place must have seemed enormous and threatening—foreigners and blacks pouring into the city, massive industrial plants dominating the urban landscape, and neighborhoods of misery and despair developing near the urban center. The warnings of prominent reformers that action must be imminent were frequently laced with fear. In 1871 Charles Loring Brace, a pioneer in the treatment of juvenile delinquency, wrote *The Dangerous Classes of New York,* a book whose title described Brace's view of the poor. In his book Brace warned that if "the civilizing influence of American life fails to reach them [the poor] . . . we should see an explosion from this class which might leave this city in ashes and blood."[44]

That some reformers may indeed have been motivated by fear should not diminish the positive reforms they sought. One reaction to fear, of course, is to run. The reformers, on the contrary, stood and fought to make their city and its people better. The relationship of fear to the reform movement is important, however, in providing a major clue to why these men and women did not seek to overhaul society (though they recognized society's complicity in producing a poverty class), but rather attempted to work within the system they wanted so dearly to maintain to relieve the plight of the poor. The programs they sponsored reflect this progressive, yet conservative ideal.

Many of the ideas for the reformers' programs originally came from England, indicating the reformers' educational background. In 1869 the numerous charities of London had joined to form one large charity organization to systematize the business of charity and to bring it under the control of professional social workers. The consolidation and professionalization movement spread to this country and in 1878 charities in New Haven and Philadelphia formed Charity Organization Societies (COS). New York, Boston, and other cities soon followed. The consolidation of antebellum charities had proved to be only temporary, since by 1878 Philadelphia had nearly 800 charity groups. Unlike the antebellum consolidation, the COS did not provide relief but rather functioned as a clearing-house for the city's charities. In addition, the COS was to promote "scientific" charity "with least waste and with greatest efficiency."[45] Like steel production, charity had become a business complete with its own chamber of commerce.

A significant contribution of the COS was its employment of professional case workers. Since the COS did not dispense charity, the case worker's primary function was investigative, in the words of social work pioneer Mary E. Richmond, to bring about "better adjustments in the social relationships of individual men, women, or children."[46] The case worker would accomplish this ideal by discovering the basic reasons for a family's or an individual's poverty and then removing those causes, with financial assistance being only one of several options. As one historian has observed, the COS believed that "the very concern shown by a benevolent community would be of more value to the worthy poor than the actual material assistance dispensed."[47]

The investigations of the social workers discovered, not surprisingly, that the environment was a major cause of poverty. One obvious solution would be to disperse the poor throughout the city. Logistically this was impossible since the poor, including the working poor, constituted half of the population in some cities. Philosophically, it contradicted the basic conservatism of the reformers who did not seek to destroy but merely to modify the slum. They emphasized, therefore, the concept of neighborhood reconstruction.

The settlement house was the indispensable element in this concept. Borrowed, once again, from England, the settlement was to be the reformers' beachhead into the slum. While case workers visited slum neighborhoods occasionally, the settlement worker lived in them. The settlement house was an all-purpose community center. It was a home to those who were homeless or whose home lives had disintegrated; it was a school for those who wished to learn subjects ranging from stenography to Shakespeare; and it was a clubhouse for those who sought friendship and recreational activities. The settlement house, in short, was its own self-contained neighborhood environment, in, but not of, the slum environment.

The first and most famous settlement in this country was Chicago's Hull House, founded in 1889 by Jane Addams, a young Rockford (Illinois) College graduate. Addams had visited settlement houses in England and was convinced that the idea would work well in American cities. Like so many young, relatively affluent, women college graduates of her day, Addams was restless since the opportunities available to educated women were so limited, and she resolved to devote her energies to the newly opened field of social reform.

Hull House was a rambling old residence that had been built a generation earlier in what was then a Chicago suburb. The new settlement was adjacent to clusters of at least five immigrant groups. In the neighborhood itself, according to Addams, "the streets are inexpressibly dirty, the number of schools inadequate, factory legislation unenforced, the street-lighting bad, the paving miserable . . . and the stables defy all laws of sanitation." The area, in short, seemed to be the perfect place for a settlement. Addams set as her goal "to preserve and keep for them [the poor immigrants] whatever of value their past life contained and to bring them into contact with a better type of American."[48] Thus, the settlement house appreciated the immigrants' cultural heritage and at the same time sought to balance it by introducing them to a better environment than the one in which they lived.

Hull House was a great success and quickly became a neighborhood institution. On Saturday evenings, for example, Italians and their families were guests of the house where they came to settle legal disputes and employ Addams as an arbiter in their frequent wars of vendetta. Hull House also catered to native-born Americans, who formed a house club, the Young Citizens' Club, which discussed municipal issues. A few years after opening Hull House, Addams renovated an adjacent saloon and transformed it into a gym. She began a day nursery as well. Eventually, she even arbitrated a strike at a nearby knitting factory. Addams was careful to point out that the house's activities were not philanthropy, but rather were meant to recognize the aspirations of the poor and to provide them with the means of attaining those aspirations. Indeed, the house dispensed charity only in emergency cases. Addams felt that the settlement worked at its best for people at the subsistence level—the working poor—rather than with the more hard-core cases of poverty. This set the settlement apart from the COS, which dealt with all types of poverty, especially the most serious cases.

The settlement idea soon spread throughout the country. By 1900 there were more than one-hundred settlement houses in poor neighborhoods in all of the major cities. Settlements became active participants in neighborhood life. In addition to providing an array of services and facilities, settlement workers pressed for legislation to ameliorate the slum environment. Settlement workers were often valuable consultants to legislative bodies and some became founders of national reform organizations like the NAACP. In 1908 Jacob Riis paid the following tribute to the settlement house:

The settlement . . . cleaned the streets. It brought the mortality among the tenements' babies down to the lowest mark, and . . . it made odious the very name of slum. . . . When today we have to fight for the things that make for the city's good . . . we fight no longer for but with the people. And this is the settlement's doing.[49]

Despite their successes, the settlements were still an outside force, especially in immigrant neighborhoods. As one immigrant declared: "No outside agency can undertake to tell my people what to do."[50] Immigrant men particularly distrusted settlement workers. Also, whether foreigner or native born, the poor represented a social gap that proved difficult to bridge. The wife of a young settlement worker became friends with a woman who lived nearby. They shared a common experience in that they had both given birth on the same day, so they daily exchanged anecdotes on the progress of each baby. It soon became apparent, though, that the baby of the poor mother was not as healthy as his more well-to-do counterpart. When the settlement worker's wife suggested a particular brand of milk to improve the sick baby's health, her friend replied sadly, "Yes, but that costs too much." As the settlement worker recalled this incident, he noted with a certain amount of despair that "here at one blow was cut away all common ground between them. How could they pretend to help the family . . . when the conditions under which they were living were so different, when they were not on the same economic basis at all."[51]

Reformers realized the shortcomings of settlement houses, so they used them in conjunction with other programs that would improve the neighborhood environment more directly in the short run. Recreational facilities became a concern for neighborhood reconstructionists when investigations revealed the high densities prevalent in slum districts. Settlements and religious institutions attempted to fill this void, but could not provide the necessary outdoor activities. Reformers hoped that appropriate recreational facilities would lure the poor from the "unsavory" entertainment environment that existed in slum neighborhoods. The great urban parks, however, were located on the urban periphery and were generally beyond the access

of the poor. With space a premium in the slums, reformers pushed successfully for the attachment of a park-playground to the neighborhood public
schools.

The emphasis on recreation revealed the reformers' desires to protect
children from the negative impact of the slum environment. This concern
led to a major educational reform effort that would transform public education from an essentially educational institution to a tool for environmental
reform. The broad framework for which reformers targeted the school
system was summarized by Jacob Riis. "When the fathers and mothers meet
under the school roof as in their neighborhood house, and the children have
their games, their clubs, and their dances there, . . . that day the slum is
beaten." The neighborhood public school would therefore be similar to the
medieval church—"the visible symbol of the community's solidarity, the
transmitter of its ideals and values."[52]

To this end, reformers were responsible for inaugurating a series of
programs in the public schools. The kindergarten, another European innovation that fared well in American cities, was a turn-of-the-century "head-
start" program designed to remove the child from the tenement environment as early as possible. The purposes of the kindergarten were thus
primarily moral rather than educative. As Jacob Riis contended, the kindergarten would "rediscover . . . the natural feelings that the tenement had
smothered."[53] In addition to the kindergarten, slum schools received an
array of vocational courses to both discipline and prepare poor students for
productive adult lives. Both the kindergarten and vocational curricula were
conservative measures; the former designed to inculcate society's values at
the earliest possible age, and the latter to point slum children toward careers
in the manual trades.

The conservatism of the urban reformers probably accounts for a great
deal of their success. Few business leaders could find anything repugnant
about settlement houses or vocational curricula. The spatial isolation of the
poor remained, but several new elements had penetrated their environment
posing at least some alternatives for them. In addition, the exhaustive
investigations conducted by the reformers generated considerable new data
and information concerning the poor and their environment. Finally, their
professional and secular approaches to the problems of poverty were decided improvements over earlier attempts at dealing with the poor. Urban
poverty, of course, remained; but at least more and more people were
looking for the causes of poverty out in urban society and not within the poor
themselves.

At the very least the city was caring. As awful as conditions were in the
factories, among the blacks, and in the slums, they did not go unnoticed. The

poor were being helped, and more aid would be forthcoming in the future. Jacob Riis, in his book on the other half, expressed the idealism that infused him and his fellow reformers as they prayed that the precarious fabric of urban life would not be torn into two separate societies. "I know of but one bridge that will carry us over safe," he wrote, "a bridge founded upon justice and built of human hearts."[54]

Ward Heelers and Mornin' Glories:
Urban Politics in a Diverse Society

Another group in urban society was equally concerned with building bridges to the poor, especially to the immigrant poor, though in a much less poetic fashion. The first "reformer" an immigrant was likely to meet was the representative of the local ward boss, who, if necessary, could provide such basic survival services as food, shelter, clothing, and employment. This assistance was not without a price. The boss expected political support.

The big-city political machines of the late nineteenth and early twentieth centuries—with all their corruption—were based on votes and the ability to turn out those votes when necessary. The city boss was often loathed by the "respectable" upper and middle classes, but he provided assistance and services for millions of lowly urban dwellers who were practically ignored by the established institutions and fragmented political structure of the time. Of course, the boss used his constituents to remain in power. But it was a reciprocal relationship, and a very pragmatic one for all concerned: the boss counted on his constituents for votes and they, in turn, counted on him for food, clothing, shelter, and jobs when all else failed.

Political machines varied from city to city, some depending on the force of major personalities, others operating entirely without apparent regard for personalities. But almost all were complex structures that were efficient enough to accomplish their goals. Most machines maintained a chain-of-command structure that reached down into the precinct and even block levels. Some congested slums even boasted tenement captains. The lieutenants in this system were the precinct and ward bosses who were responsible for specific areas of the city. The functional test for all, of course, was getting out the vote. Sometimes, individual ward bosses hashed out compromises in city councils, and in some cities the ward bosses were themselves lieutenants for powerful citywide politicians. But virtually all machines reflected structure and organization among their major features. In fact, political machines usually cut through red tape and the confusion of innumerable boards and agencies to wrest a measure of stability and order from political chaos. And this was valuable to many different urban groups.

Beyond ministering to the immediate needs of their constituents, the bosses and their machines served business and financial interests by providing fire and police protection, paved streets, and low taxes and license fees and sometimes by relaxing safety- and building-code enforcement. Many businesses sought profitable franchises for public utilities—especially streetcar lines—and public construction contracts. The relationship between business and the bosses was also based on mutual self-interest, and most frequently led to bribes, inducements, promises of campaign funding, and the "boodling" that so upset reformers.

And the bosses also worked with illegitimate businesses—gambling and prostitution especially. Such activities were deeply rooted in all major cities, and they constituted, in fact, a significant portion of the urban economy. And they were patronized in varying degrees by most social classes. But it was the bosses' protection of "immorality" that earned them the undying enmity of the middle- and upper-class reform groups, as we have discussed earlier.

Fundamentally, bosses survived because they *produced*—votes, franchises, protection, assistance, whatever was needed. As Martin Lomasny, a Boston ward leader, put it: "I think that there's got to be in every ward somebody that any bloke can come to—no matter what he's done—to get help. Help, you understand; none of your law and justice, but help."[55] This was generally true whether it applied to newly arrived immigrants, gambling-house operators, or transit tycoons.

One fairly typical case, at least in the beginning, was the political organization in Kansas City. James Pendergast, born in a small Ohio town of Irish parents, found his way to Kansas City in 1876. From a job in a packing house, James rose to ownership of a hotel and saloon, purchased mostly with racetrack winnings. By 1891 he was quite successful, acquiring a new saloon and becoming active in local politics. Representing the citizens of the West Bottoms, lying in the core of the city's industrial district, Alderman Pendergast worked for city parks and low utility rates, while also protecting gambling and his own saloon interests and showering assistance and favors on friends and supporters. Jim Pendergast apparently did not indulge in illegal voting practices, and he hardly needed to. He was a strong representative of his constituency, and his favors were amply returned. He died a much beloved and respected community figure, at least among "his" people. In later years, when his younger brother Tom took over the organization, the Pendergast machine was expanded to include Kansas City and much of the surrounding area, with significant ties in state politics. And its tactics made it a notorious example of malfeasance in the reformers' lexicon.

The intensively local base of the machine is also illustrated in the case of

Chicago's first ward. There, "Bathhouse" John Coughlin and Michael "Hinky Dink" Kenna presided over a raucous and vital urban scene between 1890 and the mid-1920s. Like other local bosses in the city, they played crucial roles in electing and defeating candidates for mayor, but their main activity was protecting the interests of their constituents for their own survival—interests that included gambling, prostitution, and illegal liquor operations as well as legitimate businesses. Presidents, senators, and mayors came and went, but the political fortunes of Bathhouse John and Hinky Dink, and the conditions of the "Levee" district, were hardly affected.

The most famous big-city political machine of the era was New York's Tammany Hall, which dominated the affairs of the nation's largest city into the twentieth century. Among Tammany's most well-known sachems was Richard "Boss" Croker, who saw the organization defeated in 1894 by a group of ardent reformers—including Theodore Roosevelt, who served in the reform administration as police commissioner—and oversaw its return to power several years later. Croker decentralized Tammany's patronage, putting more favors in the hands of the district leaders. He had no qualms about the spoils system (the practice of rewarding loyal supporters with government jobs); in fact, he regarded it as a logical and effective way of dispensing rewards and incentives for good performance. "Politics," Croker once said, "are impossible without the spoils. . . . [W]e have to deal with men as they are and with things as they are."[56]

One district leader was George Washington Plunkitt, whose exploits have been preserved in William L. Riordan's *Plunkitt of Tammany Hall* (1905). In a typical day, Plunkitt bailed a saloon keeper out of jail, assisted victims of a fire, intervened in court on behalf of six drunks, paid the rent for a poor family, secured jobs for four constituents, attended Italian and Jewish funerals, presided at a meeting of election district captains, attended a church fair, bought tickets to a church excursion and a community baseball game, and attended a Jewish wedding and dance late in the evening. In every instance, his assistance and generosity were quite conspicuous. Plunkitt referred contemptuously to reformers as "mornin' glories"; their appeal, he claimed, lasted only a short part of a day, while Tammany tended to voters' needs round-the-clock, no questions asked. Taking care of one's friends was a natural and honest act in private life, Plunkitt argued; why shouldn't he do the same in public life? And he insisted on a distinction between "honest" and "dishonest" graft—a distinction many reformers would have found meaningless. According to the Tammany district leader, dishonest graft consisted of robbing the public treasury or "blackmailin' gamblers, saloon-keepers, disorderly people, etc.," but honest graft was simply taking advantage of one's position to make a living. "It's just like lookin' ahead in Wall

Street or in the coffee or cotton market. It's honest graft, and I'm lookin' for it every day in the year." Plunkitt even proposed his own epitaph: "George W. Plunkitt. He Seen His Opportunities, and He Took 'Em."[57]

Reformers damned the machine for its corruption—for graft of any sort—and there was much truth in the accusation. Perhaps the most notorious instance in American politics, now raised to the level of political folklore, was the infamous "Tweed Ring" scandals in New York City during the late 1860s and early 1870s. Led by William Meagher Tweed, Tammany Hall rose from a Democratic club to a full-fledged political machine, with power stretched into every ward of the city and even into the corridors of the state legislature. A reform campaign launched in 1870 pointed to the ring's illegal voting tactics, the widespread diversion of public funds into the hands of favored supporters, and the systematic buying off of potential opponents through government contracts and bribery. Reformers managed to get inside information to reveal the dimensions of the corruption and published it in highly subjective accounts of the ring's villainy. As the campaign caught strength, Tweed was portrayed as a wicked thief, a threat to the foundations of democracy itself. Thomas Nast's famous cartoons in *Harper's Weekly* were but one weapon in the mounting attack. Eventually, in 1871, the Tweed Ring was brought down, and Tweed himself was later sent to prison.

The Tweed machine stole anywhere from $20 million to $200 million from the public treasury, and although the authorities recovered less than $1 million of it, the reformers celebrated their victory as having saved New York City—and, indeed, American city government generally—from graft and corruption. Samuel Tilden was one of a number of prominent political figures who used the fight against Tammany to win national prominence, in Tilden's case a near-successful bid for the presidency of the country.

American municipal politics was not so easily cleansed, of course. Bosses and reformers continued their battles well into the twentieth century, and the crusade against the Tweed Ring became something of a model of the struggle between dishonest bosses and heroic reformers who promised honesty, efficiency, integrity, economy, and morality in government. In reality, matters were not so simple.

For one thing, the destitute residents in the urban core were less immediately interested in morality, integrity, and economy than they were in survival. And the bosses, in many ways, responded better to this basic need, and served a number of other important purposes in the late-nineteenth- and early-twentieth-century city as well. The political machine provided jobs and assistance to families in distress, helped immigrants adjust to American life, and created a measure of stability and order in the city. In an era when unemployment compensation, welfare benefits, and social security programs were quite primitive or—more frequently—nonexistent, the bosses' immorality existed largely by middle- and upper-class standards and tastes, just as saloons were dens of iniquity in some eyes, but they were also social centers of the working class.

Reformers were an even more varied group than bosses. The municipal-reform movement of the 1890s, which led to a national reform spirit known as *progressivism* in the first two decades of the twentieth century, was based on firm opposition to the bosses and their machines. The movement hoped to accomplish a number of suggested improvements in city government, notably fair and honest election practices, "home rule" municipal charters allowing localities greater autonomy in their own affairs, leadership by "proper" and "legitimate" representatives, and professional administration to insure economy and efficiency in the public interest. Some reformers, like Jane Addams, Jacob Riis, and Frederic C. Howe, were genuinely committed to easing the plight of the less fortunate and to changes in the social and economic system that would accomplish these goals. Their outlook, as we have seen, was in many ways quite conservative. Riis, especially, was drawn to the ideal of the small town, with its face-to-face contacts and human scale, as at least a conceptual answer to the complexities and confusion of the metropolis. Other reformers, however, were not committed to real social change, but rather to "purifying" the political system of disreputable elements and unwanted behavior and controlling the activities of the "lower classes." This branch of the reform movement saw foreign immigration as the source of many social ills by introducing alien customs into American culture and providing the basis—through ignorance and poverty—for the corrupt political machine. The solution, in their view, was to restrict immigration, especially from southern and eastern Europe, and to apply literacy tests, property qualifications, and stricter standards generally, for voting.

Many reformers also shared the belief that municipal government had fallen into evil hands, and should be restored to the care of educated, respectable leaders whose principal loyalties were to the public interest rather than to a narrow constituency. The civil-service movement set out to eliminate the spoils system by basing government service on ability and training, rather than on political connections or rewards. Efficiency and economy were also major goals, holding a much higher priority in the minds of some reformers than the efforts to meet the immediate needs of the poor. The crowding of impoverished immigrant hordes into the central districts of the larger cities was also seen as a threat to order, decency, and democracy, and many reform spokesmen suggested the decentralization of the city— along with immigration restriction—as one way of alleviating this threat of alien radicalism and discontent.

If reformers were committed to the principles of democracy, honesty, and efficiency, many were also quite concerned with maintaining their superior position in society and forcing their own particular morality and mores on other people. The bosses, for their part, were indeed often corrupt. Plunkitt's "honest" graft was graft nonetheless. And the bosses' basic goal—even though it had certain beneficial consequences—was to stay in power. The machine might be quite representative of the views of its constituents, but it had no aspirations to educate the electorate about complicated or serious political issues or to provide genuine political leadership. And the widespread cynicism regarding the political process which the bosses helped to inspire and confirm in the public mind tended to erode the rather fragile foundations of democracy.

The boss-reformer conflict is misleading in a number of other ways. Successful political movements, especially beyond the ward or precinct levels, generally involved coalitions of at least several groups—immigrants, business people, underworld figures, and even silk-stocking reformers. Circumstances differed from city to city, and the political climate could change quickly. In addition, some "bosses"—strong leaders of well-organized political "machines"—worked for change. These "reform bosses" included Tom L. Johnson of Cleveland, Samuel "Golden Rule" Jones of Toledo, and Hazen Pingree of Detroit. Johnson called for a reduction in the Cleveland streetcar fares and for the public ownership of utilities, and tended to overlook the "evils" of the saloon and the gaming table. Much of his support came from the foreign born of Cleveland's West Side. "Golden Rule" Jones instituted the eight-hour day in several city departments, increased public services, and fought for the municipal ownership of utilities. Jones was opposed by virtually every business leader and newspaper in Toledo, and just as consistently returned to office until his death in 1904. Hazen Pingree also established an effective organization on the basis of a largely immigrant, lower-class constituency, and focused his fire on the corruption of big business and excessive utility rates. Like many other reformers and machine politicians, he supported "home rule."

The methods of Pingree's machine were similar to those of machines everywhere, including threats of economic reprisal against citizens and city employees as a means of insuring their political loyalty. The use of code inspectors and city contracts to secure support was also widespread, and reform bosses were just as interested in getting out the vote as was the most notorious ward heeler. Even many of the less forward-looking big-city machines supported various reforms from time to time, like the direct election of U.S. senators. Basically, machines tended to favor those policies and programs that maintained or increased their power or term in office;

and they were often much quicker to respond to changing circumstances and public needs than reformers committed to abstract principles and theories.

In many smaller cities, local machines composed of "professional politicians" simply did not exist. Especially in the South and West, which did not experience substantial foreign immigration and industrialization, the big-city political model was far less likely to emerge. There were exceptions, however. Memphis and New Orleans in the South and San Francisco in the West did have relatively potent political organizations that practiced many tactics used by machines in order to stay in power. But these cities were all marked by significant immigration from both foreign and native sources, unlike a number of even smaller communities in this era. And these "machines" were rather carelessly, and somewhat inaccurately, compared in the local reform press with Tammany Hall and other well-known northern urban examples. In most of the smaller towns of the country outside the industrial belt, local business leaders and even the local gentry were far more likely to hold elected office and to have considerable influence in municipal affairs. In the mill towns of the South and industrial towns everywhere, the major political force was not a political machine but a corporation. And in the South, of course, the largest disadvantaged and oppressed group—blacks—was severely limited by law and custom from any effective political participation.

The dynamics of urban politics were closely related to the basic patterns of city growth and development. In the eighteenth and early nineteenth centuries—the era of the clusters and market places of the preindustrial city—urban politics was relatively unified, just as most city dwellers lived close together. Generally, the upper classes and the most powerful groups easily dominated these more tightly knit communities. Beginning in the late nineteenth century, however, as cities began to add populations and to expand over greater territory—largely with the aid of streetcar transit—communities became separated. The radial center was a city of numerous distinct areas—immigrant districts, new streetcar suburbs, east side, and west side. The ward system of political representation was a superb reflection of this spatial differentiation, with each neighborhood or district electing representatives to the municipal council. Each ward or area contained populations and institutions that were clearly identified with a particular tract of urban space. Many of the conflicts in the late-nineteenth-century city were, in fact, struggles among the various parts of the city for services, amenities, and influence. Perhaps in a larger sense, they were also conflicts between older areas of the city and newer sections created in the wake of urban expansion and growth. The newer areas stood to benefit from expanded utility services, streetcar construction, and outlying parks and boulevards, while older neighborhoods feared that they would receive little benefit and bear a disproportionate share of the costs. The radial center contained not a unified political structure but a fragmented one, reflecting the new spatial form the city was assuming.

After the turn of the century, other trends appeared in the political process. The urban core was transformed from a mixed and varied community into an increasingly commercial and administrative center, with activities that ranged over the entire metropolitan area. The central business district, with its tall office buildings and far-flung financial and real-estate operations, symbolized a new centralization of economic and political power in a time when chambers of commerce and citywide civic associations exercised influence without spatial limitations. A strong degree of localism persisted in the early twentieth century as well, of course, especially in the inner-city immigrant districts; but the new business and professional emphasis and political influence, so well expressed in the reform goals of citywide, "at large," elections rather than ward politics, presaged an important shift in the structure of municipal politics for the remainder of the century. Commercial, civic, and professional groups advocated centralized decision making to control the growing metropolis and fought the bosses because of their parochial constituent base. At the same time, they encouraged population decentralization. As a consequence, suburbs and the major economic interests of the central business district were often pitted in the political arena against the older, distinctive districts, which by 1910 or 1920 were pretty much occupied by lower-income populations.

It was not unusual that political and social reform attracted the same individuals. Reform of politics and reform of urban society were merely two avenues toward establishing a more orderly urban environment. The city-planning movement and its predecessors, despite their grounding in the urban economy, were reforms of sorts, too: spatial reforms. Despite the conservative and at times condescending policies promoted by the urban reformers, they evidently cared a great deal about their cities. They were saved, to borrow a phrase from Dreiser, "by longing for that which was better."[58] Caring was very important because it would have been easy to become enraptured by the music of economic and geographic expansion and ignore not only the spatial and political consequences of that expansion, but also the other half of urban society clamoring at the doors of the concert hall for a place in the audience. Much, of course, remained to be done. But the recognition, investigation, and attempted solution of urban problems, however narrowly conceived and carried out, were a necessary beginning.

The vast assemblage of descriptive information and data produced by professionals during these years was one of their greatest legacies. The city was a "giant magnet" not only for people, but for ideas as well. From settlement houses to skyscrapers, from urban novels to elevators, the city was at the cutting edge of American civilization. The city, in short, was America's future. Perhaps with that idea deep in their subconscious, reformers, scientists, immigrants, and business people sought to improve upon the urban creation.

By 1920 more people lived in cities than in the countryside. From an unwanted intruder into America's pastoral democracy, the city was becoming America itself. The city had arrived. Still anchored by a vigorous downtown, the city had radiated its culture, institutions, and spatial patterns into the suburbs. It seemed a perfect equilibrium: as the city's heart grew stronger, so did its extremities. But there were tears in this organic fabric that threatened to unravel the equilibrium of the radial center: poverty, the status of blacks, the conditions endured by working men and women, and the spatial segregation that seemed to create enclaves instead of a community. The future of the city, and by inference of America, would depend on how successful urban residents would be in reducing the pressure on the fragile equilibrium.

Notes

1. See Upton Sinclair, *The Jungle,* rev. ed. (New York: Signet, 1960), p. 27.

2. See Rudolph J. Vecoli, *"Contadini* in Chicago: A Critique of *The Uprooted,"* in David R. Goldfield and James B. Lane, eds., *The Enduring Ghetto: Sources and Readings* (Philadelphia: J. B. Lippincott, 1973), pp. 88–103.

3. *Ibid.,* p. 98.

4. Quoted in Bayrd Still, ed., *Urban America: A History with Documents* (Boston: Little, Brown, 1974) p. 273.

5. Emily Dinwiddie, "Housing Conditions in Philadelphia's Ghettos," in Goldfield and Lane, eds., *Enduring Ghetto,* p. 74.

6. Betty Smith, *A Tree Grows in Brooklyn* (New York: Harper & Row, 1943), pp. 23, 181.

7. *Ibid.,* p. 134.

8. *Ibid.,* p. 135.

9. *Ibid.,* p. 142.

10. Quoted in Still, ed., *Urban America,* p. 274.

11. Abraham Cahan, *The Rise of David Levinsky,* rev. ed. (New York: Harper & Row, 1966), pp. 93, 110.

12. Quoted in Herbert G. Gutman, "Work, Culture, and Society in Industrializing America, 1815–1919," *American Historical Review,* 78 (June 1973), p. 547.

13. Cahan, *Levinsky,* p. 3.

14. See Stephan Thernstrom, *Poverty and Progress: Social Mobility in a Nineteenth Century City* (New York: Atheneum, 1969), p. 136.

15. See Sam Bass Warner, Jr., *Streetcar Suburbs: The Process of Growth in Boston, 1870–1900* (New York: Atheneum, 1974).

16. Dennis Clark, *The Irish in Philadelphia: Ten Generations of Urban Experience* (Philadelphia: Temple University Press, 1973), p. 127.

17. Cahan, *Levinsky*, p. 526.

18. Quoted in Roy Lubove, *The Progressives and the Slums: Tenement House Reform in New York City 1890–1917* (Pittsburgh: University of Pittsburgh Press, 1962), p. 58.

19. Both newspapers quoted in Gutman, "Work, Culture, and Society," p. 584.

20. Quoted in Robert Rockaway, "Ethnic Conflict in an Urban Environment: The German and Russian Jew in Detroit, 1881–1914," *American Jewish Historical Quarterly,* 40 (December 1970), 150.

21. Quoted in Gilbert Osofsky, ed., *The Burden of Race: A Documentary History of Negro-White Relations in America* (New York: Harper & Row, 1967), p. 263

22. As told in Allan H. Spear, *Black Chicago: The Making of a Negro Ghetto, 1890–1920* (Chicago: University of Chicago Press, 1967), p. 137

23. *Ibid.*

24. Quoted in Still, ed., *Urban America,* p. 279.

25. Quoted in David Katzman, *Before the Ghetto: Black Detroit in the Nineteenth Century* (Urbana, Ill.: University of Illinois Press, 1973), p. 122.

26. Gilbert Osofsky, "The Enduring Ghetto," *Journal of American History,* 45 (September 1968), pp. 243–255.

27. Gilbert Osofsky, *Harlem: The Making of a Ghetto* (New York: Harper & Row, 1963), p. 40.

28. Quoted in Osofsky, "Enduring Ghetto," p. 250.

29. Quoted in Osofsky, *Harlem,* p. 43.

30. Quoted in Zane L. Miller, "Urban Blacks in the South, 1865–1920: The Richmond, Savannah, New Orleans, Louisville, and Birmingham Experience," in Leo F. Schnore, ed., *The New Urban History: Quantitative Explorations by American Historians* (Princeton, N.J.: Princeton University Press, 1975), p. 187.

31. Quoted in James B. Lane, "Unmasking the Ghetto: Jacob A. Riis and *How the Other Half Lives,*" in Goldfield and Lane, eds., *Enduring Ghetto,* p. 156.

32. Sinclair, *The Jungle,* p. 79.

33. Quoted in Lubove, *Progressives and the Slums,* p. 58.

34. *Ibid.,* p. 70.

35. Quoted in Charles N. Glaab, ed., *The American City: A Documentary History* (Homewood, Ill.: Dorsey Press, 1963), pp. 289, 296.

36. Quoted in Still, ed., *Urban America,* pp. 283–284.

37. Quoted in Lane, "Unmasking the Ghetto," p. 157.

38. Carroll D. Wright, "Housing of the Working People," in Goldfield and Lane, eds., *Enduring Ghetto,* p. 150.

39. Quoted in Still, ed., *Urban America,* p. 284.

40. Quoted in Gordon Atkins, "Health, Housing, and Poverty in New York City, 1865–1898" (Ph.D. dissertation, Columbia University, 1947), p. 230.

41. Quoted in Still, ed., *Urban America,* p. 292.

42. Dinwiddie, "Housing Conditions," in Goldfield and Lane, eds., *Enduring Ghetto,* p. 77.

43. Edward Bellamy, *Looking Backward* (New York: Amsco, 1888), p. 198.

44. Quoted in Henry Nash Smith, ed., *Popular Culture and Industrialism, 1865–1890* (New York: Anchor, 1967), p. 200.

45. Quoted in Walter Trattner, *From Poor Law to Welfare State* (New York: Free Press, 1974), p. 98.

46. Quoted in Lubove, *Progressives and the Slums,* p. 200.

47. Michael H. Frisch, *Town Into City: Springfield, Massachusetts, and the Meaning of Community, 1840–1880* (Cambridge, Mass.: Harvard University Press, 1972), p. 227.

48. Quoted in Still, ed., *Urban America,* p. 294.

49. Quoted in *ibid.,* p. 296.

50. Quoted in Allen F. Davis, *Spearheads for Reform: The Social Settlements and the Progressive Movement, 1890–1914* (New York: Oxford University Press, 1967), p. 87.

51. Quoted in *ibid.*

52. Quoted in Lubove, *Progressives and the Slums,* p. 73.

53. Quoted in *ibid.,* p. 74.

54. Quoted in Goldfield and Lane, eds., *Enduring Ghetto,* p. 12.

55. Quoted in Lincoln Steffens, *The Autobiography of Lincoln Steffens* (New York: Harcourt, Brace and Company, 1931), p. 618.

56. Quoted in Blaine A. Brownell and Warren E. Stickle, eds., *Bosses and Reformers: Urban Politics in America, 1880–1920* (Boston: Houghton Mifflin, 1973), p. 25.

57. Quoted in *ibid.,* pp. 33, 35.

58. *Sister Carrie,* rev. ed. (New York: W. W. Norton, 1970), p. 368.

IV.
VITAL FRINGE

Clusters and market places still existed in America in 1900. But the dominant urban form of the twentieth century dwarfed its predecessors in expanse, population, economic power, and complexity. The radial center, made possible by the electric streetcar and massive industrialization, grew larger and more omnipresent along the sinews of paved highways and waves of modern communications and was replaced by the vital fringe—the city of suburbs, shopping centers, and scattered communities.

In 1920 a majority (51.4 percent) of Americans lived in urban places. Some of these places were mere villages of 2,500 or so people, to be sure; but the statistics supplied further evidence of a trend that had been gaining momentum for over a century and was reflected in major population movements and a consistent decline in agricultural employment. By 1950 the city was so large and spread out and overwhelming that some observers wondered whether it was a city at all by the traditional definition. By 1970 more than 75 percent of all Americans lived in urban areas, but the urban population density was less than it had ever been, and more people lived in suburbs than in central cities. The metropolis was less a center than a region. Urban places had become an urban nation. Downtown had become no town.

The form of the vital fringe may have been new, but it was shaped by the same basic forces that had brought towns out of the wilderness: technology, new patterns of economic organization and activity, and migrations of population. Technology supplied much of the impetus and means for the formation of the twentieth-century metropolis, not only in terms of new transportation modes like the automobile and the airplane, but also in manufacturing, construction, and more efficient means of communication and marketing like the telephone, the radio, and television. Economic organization reached new heights in sophistication, concentrated in huge agglomerations that commanded untold resources and stretched worldwide. And the emphasis of the economy shifted increasingly after World War II from heavy manufacturing to new light industries and the delivery of professional and personal services to a growing consumer market.

Urbanization in the first half of the twentieth century, as in earlier eras, proceeded not by the natural increase of city populations, but by great migrations of people to urban places, both from the rural areas of America and from Europe, Asia, and Latin America. The two most significant migrations of the post-1920 era were internal—the movement of southern rural blacks to the major centers of the Northeast and Midwest, and the surge of urban dwellers to burgeoning suburbs. These migrations played major roles in the urbanization process. As in prior years, too, the post-1920 metropolis was shaped not only by anonymous social and economic forces, but by people seeking opportunity, community, escape, and survival.

The metropolis had emerged in the late nineteenth century. No longer contained by poor and inefficient transportation after 1890, the largest cities in the nation's industrial core extended over large territories penetrated by the rails of streetcar lines and commuter trains. But the radial center had an unmistakable core, and the urban periphery was a more-or-less orderly arrangement of new neighborhoods, small commercial clusters, and transit corridors. After 1915 the gasoline-powered motor vehicle provided a new means of decentralization. Metropolitan areas began to spread over many square miles, and a number of smaller cities in the South and West began to reflect the new pattern of growth at even greater rates than their counterparts in the North and East. If the radial center resembled a multipointed star, the vital fringe called to mind an inkblot—covering some natural barriers that had impeded the streetcar and the train. (See Figure I.11.)

By midcentury the metropolitan areas of some large cities actually began to overlap, creating urban regions of unprecedented dimensions. The *megalopolis* or *conurbation* composed of two or more metropolitan areas might cover hundreds and even thousands of square miles and cut across the boundaries of several states and scores of counties and other civil divisions. Perhaps the best single example is the highly urbanized region extending from Boston in the North to Washington, D.C., and Richmond, Virginia, in the South, and passing through New York City, Philadelphia, Wilmington, and Baltimore. Though periodically relieved by patches of farm land and forest, this entire coastal belt is essentially urban in many social and economic characteristics.

The central business districts of the older cities, which had once been identical to the cities themselves, became intensive commercial and administrative clusters in a diverse urban setting of scattered residential areas, outlying shopping centers, and remote industrial sites. In newer cities, experiencing their most rapid growth in the era of innovations in transportation and communications, central districts were virtually subordinated from the beginning to peripheral development. The central city was by no means gone: It remained an important, and usually the largest, node of economic activity for the metropolitan area, and it had the greatest population density. But the city had clearly grown beyond it.

The United States Bureau of the Census attempted to keep up with this urban phenomenon, wrestling continually with the basic question "What is a city?" The problem was quite obvious even early in the century, as urban places were no longer confined within political boundaries or concentrated in a relatively small space. The urban-population minimum of 2,500 in use at the turn of the century was totally inadequate as a measure of the metropolis. In 1910 government statisticians established a new *Metropolitan District* classification, which was applied to areas with central cities of at least 50,000 people and included adjacent civil divisions with a certain population density (numbers of persons per square mile). For the first time, the dimensions of the vital fringe began to be apparent in the decennial population counts. Twenty-five metropolises with central-city populations of 200,000 or more were listed in the 1910 census, and nineteen more had central areas with at least 100,000 people.

The difficulty of definition was even greater by midcentury. Population —and even population density—alone were not sufficient to distinguish "urban" from "rural," and a much larger suburban dimension had appeared, composed of settlements that were clearly part of the urban scheme yet were outside central-city boundaries and had fairly low population densities. The *Standard Metropolitan Area* (SMA) classification, introduced in 1950, was based on counties rather than on minor civil divisions (in areas outside New England), in recognition of the increasing expansion of major cities into surrounding territory. The *Standard Metropolitan Statistical Area* (SMSA) classification, developed for the 1960 census, was a more flexible measure of urban places. Generally, it required that a city, or two nearby cities, have a total population of at least 50,000, and it included in the enumeration the population of adjoining counties if those counties met certain criteria, such as a designated percentage of nonagricultural workers and of commuters to the central city or county.

Since the building blocks of the SMA and the SMSA were counties, however, a large amount of territory that was essentially rural in character was often included. The *Urbanized Area* classification, introduced in the 1950 census, attempted to deal with this problem by including the population of the central city or cities and the actual urban "fringe"—that is, nearby incorporated places (cities and towns) and areas with a certain population density. While the Urbanized Area classification is perhaps the most accurate for statistical purposes, even it does not cover with precision the actual area of urban "influence," which can be measured in a great variety of ways.

The Census Bureau continues to refine its enumeration classifications, and the task grows no easier. The distinctions among rural, urban, and suburban are even more muted and uncertain today than they were before. Modern communications and transportation have extended urban culture throughout most areas of the country. Thus, metropolitan areas might best be defined by the extent of their "commuting zones"—that is, by how far people travel to work near the central city—or by the extent of metropolitan newspaper circulation and television coverage.

Throughout most of the nineteenth century, political boundaries tended to follow population growth. As settlements and neighborhoods appeared on the urban fringe and as growth approached outlying communities, they were typically *annexed* into the central core. Thus, the land areas and populations of cities expanded, municipal governments maintained authority over most of the actual urban population, and the census attributed the "new" population of the urban area to the central city. Annexation was not automatic by any means. Some cities found it more difficult than others (usually because of restrictions set by state legislatures), and a number of cities, even in the eighteenth century, had adjoining settlements on their borders that were counted independently. But this pattern generally prevailed. Another method was *consolidation,* joining various independent political subdivisions that had, for all practical purposes, grown together. The most dramatic consolidation in American history occurred in 1898, when the major boroughs of New York City were combined (absorbing Brooklyn, which was the third largest city, after New York and Chicago, in America in 1890) into a Greater New York covering 299 square miles and containing 3 million people.

Annexations were less frequent in the major northeastern and midwestern cities in the early twentieth century, and became rare by the 1940s. As problems of the inner cities mounted, surrounding communities were reluctant to share them and even more anxious to preserve tax advantages and controls over their own land use and populations. Many cities in the South and West, though, continued to expand by annexation into and beyond midcentury, accounting for much of the population growth in modern boom towns like Houston and Phoenix; and consolidations occurred in Nashville, Tennessee (with Davidson County) and Jacksonville, Florida (with Duval County).

As cities grew beyond the political boundaries of the central core, metropolitan areas became fragmented into scores of politically independent communities. Even though new devices were developed to deal with region-wide problems (devices such as multicity authorities and cooperative service districts), this fragmentation was a major factor in the twentieth-century urban decline. Older central cities were increasingly populated by low-income, poorly educated people who demanded additional social services, at the same time that these cities suffered from a declining tax base and a loss of population and industry. The infernos that engulfed inner-city neighborhoods during the riots of the 1960s and the near-bankruptcy of New York City in the 1970s symbolized the urban dilemma and the fact that virtually no large city in America could meet its basic social and financial needs by drawing solely upon its own resources.

Another important dimension of the urban difficulties that plagued the older northeastern and midwestern cities was an economic and population shift to the southern and western urban frontiers. This shift to the "Sunbelt" (the area extending roughly from Virginia down through the Southeast and Southwest out to southern California) was not entirely new; urban growth in these regions had been greater than the national average through most of the century. But the trend accelerated after World War II, due among other things to improvements in transportation and communications technology and a decentralized service-oriented economy. In addition, a new leisure and consumer society placed great emphasis upon warmer climate and year-round recreation, and tourism, employee retirement patterns, and the businesses that followed these new markets all fueled Sunbelt growth. (See Table I.5, especially the column labeled "previous rank.") Meanwhile, New York, Boston, Pittsburgh, Cleveland, Detroit, and Chicago experienced population and business declines.

The twentieth-century metropolis was vital and dynamic on its fringe, and often decaying in its core. It was fragmented politically and socially, with responsibilities for services and decision making divided among a number of autonomous municipalities. Populations of varying income and racial and ethnic background were frequently separated over a large territory. Indeed, land uses and population groups were generally more segregated than they had ever been in the history of American cities. Urban institutions were highly bureaucratized and closely tied to the economic structure. Occupational patterns inclined toward ever more specialized professional services, with many of the unskilled relegated to a semipermanent or even permanent state of unemployment. The economy as a whole was dominated as never before by large concentrations of capital, often operating in close affiliation with the federal government and flung across the globe. The focal points of the vital fringe were increasingly, of course, located on the urban periphery—in industrial parks, shopping centers, amusement areas, and scattered residential subdivisions and occasional multifunctional planned communities. The urban core continued to serve as a symbol of metropolis and as a relatively dense administrative area and home for lower-income populations, but it was only one of a number of commercial clusters, and usually the most troubled.

Like most other broad generalizations, these have their exceptions. Many large cities have recently experienced a "reverse" migration of people back into the central core. In addition, the suburbs are not without major social and economic problems, regardless of their attempts to avoid annexation into central cities. The overall distinction between the core and the rim still exists, but it is less marked than ever.

The city achieved perhaps its ultimate, and ironic, manifestation in the years after 1920: While urban population in America is concentrated today in roughly 2 percent of the nation's total land area, American society as a whole is unquestionably urban in its culture, dominant institutions, and lifestyles. The city has become so dominant, in fact, that it seems to have lost its distinctive character. Urban, suburban, and rural places have become less distinguishable from one another, and *exurbia*—development beyond the bounds of the suburbs—has been pronounced in the 1970s. The tight clusters of the eighteenth century have become a truly national urban society by the last quarter of the twentieth.

The very size and power of the metropolis have cast its failures in high relief. Ever-present urban ironies seem more potent now than ever. The city harbors incredible possibilities and ominous dangers for American life, and the limitations on possibility are perhaps more troubling today since they are not so much technological as social and economic and, ultimately, political in the broadest sense of the term.

Frederic C. Howe, one of the most prolific writers on the early-twentieth-century city, wrestled with urban ironies and helped to set some of the basic themes for considering the city's impact on American life throughout the modern era. In *The City: The Hope of Democracy* (1905), Howe declared that the "modern city marks an epoch in our civilization," a revolution "in industry, politics, society, and life itself." The city was "El Dorado, the promised land which fires the imagination," a place where "there is the chance, and life, movement, and recreation even in failure." But the city also had a less positive side. "The city has replaced simplicity, industrial freedom, and equality of fortune," Howe wrote, "with complexity, dependence, poverty, and misery close beside a barbaric luxury like unto that of ancient Rome . . . . The city exacts an awful price for the gain it has given us, a price that is being paid in human life, suffering, and the decay of virtue and the family."[1]

Most of these problems can no longer be attributed to "the city" as a specific entity. Indeed, they are endemic to American life. Through most of the twentieth century the problems of growth and decay, fragmented decision making, new technology and environmental disaster, progress and poverty were not confined to cities, for the cities had become, in a very real sense, the nation.

Notes

1. Frederic C. Howe, *The City: The Hope of Democracy* (New York: Scribner, 1905), pp. 9, 25, 32.

11.
Urban Society:
Cells and Fortresses

New Morals, New Music, New Negroes,
New Heroes, Old Values

In the 1920s, the country's first decade as an urban nation, national moods and events came to a focus within urban society. The decade, ushered in as an era of "normalcy," was anything but normal. Americans were simultaneously exhilarated by the victory of World War I and disillusioned by the peace, buoyed by the prosperity generated by the war effort and disappointed by the recession that followed it. In addition, they were buffeted by the great ethnic and racial changes that had come to a climax by 1920. The volatile mixture created by these diverse elements took urban society, and America, on a wild and sometimes frightful rollercoaster ride before, as an F. Scott Fitzgerald character stated, "everything wore out" in the depression thirties.[1] This is not to imply that urban society departed on a new course in the 1920s. The basic aspects of social segregation remained. It was just that some traditional urban social trends were twisted into weird shapes by the volatility of the times.

Prohibition provides one example of the perhaps illogical conclusion of progressive reform. Though the antiliquor movement had rural origins, middle-class urban Protestants supported the campaign as well. They looked upon alcohol as an inevitable accompaniment and contribution to poverty and political corruption—two of the reformers' primary targets. Prohibition stopped neither poverty nor corruption and only made drinking more adventurous and probably more popular in the cities. The speakeasy, which became a popular institution among the growing numbers of urban middle-class men and women, typified the easy access to illicit liquor.

The speakeasy also demonstrated the cavalier attitude with which some urban residents viewed the law. Indeed, speakeasy profits frequently went to support perhaps the most booming business of the twenties: organized crime. Criminal activity in urban society was, of course, nothing new. Prohibition provided expanded opportunities for a number of professional criminals who, by the 1920s, were adopting modern business techniques and technology much like legitimate corporations. They did not, of course, engage in advertising, though they did leave calling cards in the forms of bombs and bullets.

Chicago was one of the most flourishing centers of organized crime. The city's excellent communications and transportation systems as well as its proximity to its raw material source in Canada accounted, in part, for its distinction. Chicago proved to be a city of opportunity for the Irish, Italian, and Jewish immigrants who chose to be upwardly mobile through the ladder of organized crime. Though hazardous, crime did indeed pay for ambitious young immigrants. Al Capone, at the pinnacle of the Chicago crime hierarchy, was earning $100 million a year by the end of the decade. Like many prominent firms of the era, the Capone organization opened suburban branches outside of Chicago. With crime and politics as the only quick ways to success, it is not surprising that immigrant groups dominated both fields, frequently with close connections.

Organized crime proved adaptable. Though Prohibition provided it with its first mass market, the end of the dry era in 1933 did not end organized criminal activity. Vice, gambling, and narcotics—two old rackets and one new—generated sufficient income to keep the various organizations afloat during depression and war.

The efficiency of organized crime underscored a traditional urban axiom: Concerted action for a particular goal is profitable. The fact that civic clubs like the Elks, Kiwanis, and Lions clubs enjoyed record membership was more a tribute to their promotion of psychic income than real income. If the city had become America, it had also become pluralistic, chaotic, confusing, and foreign to those who had resided there for only a generation. Just think of it: In 1890 the city was relatively small, limited by the range of the horse-drawn railway; immigrant populations from Europe and the South had not yet begun to make themselves noticeable in large numbers; and the structural city presented a fairly even skyline. By 1920 electric trolleys were skimming out to the suburbs, while automobiles, crazed machines that they were, inundated every urban street; the majority population in a dozen major cities was foreign born or black; and business buildings hulked over all. Change, of course, is the essence of urbanization. Each generation must cope with and respond to change. But it must have been especially difficult for some in 1920, since the change had been so rapid and so extensive. Old-timers are notorious for "remembering when." When "when" was last year or the year before that, change was rapid indeed.

The uncertainties were probably heightened by a seeming breakdown in morals, of which the popularity of speakeasies was merely one symptom. The psychology of Sigmund Freud, which depicted sexual restraint as the root of neuroses, achieved widespread popularity both in promulgation and in practice. The young high school or college couple might not have been able to distinguish between Freud and Fitzgerald, but the portable living room, the automobile, enabled them to follow both Freud's psychological precepts and Fitzgerald's depictions of urban lifestyles.

The urbanization of America meant, in the words of one observer, an "urbanization of American morals."[2] The lurid urban tales that had enthralled readers in the 1850s now came alive on the silver screen for everyone. *Alimony,* a movie that boasted "brilliant men, beautiful jazz babies, champagne baths, midnight revels, petting parties in the purple dawn, all ending in one terrific smashing climax that makes you gasp,"[3] captured urban audiences—composed primarily of women and children, incidentally. One can only wonder at the gasps emitted by audiences viewing such pictures as *Sinners in Silk* and *Women Who Give.*

The popularity of motion pictures like *Alimony* reflected a more open morality, while the popularity of motion pictures generally indicated the fruition of a mass culture. Industrialization had raised the standard of living and had helped to broaden the base of the middle class. Technology had made possible more leisure time for middle-class men and women. Even skilled workers shared some of the benefits of mechanization, with reduced hours and higher wages made possible by the huge profits enjoyed by corporations through most of the decade. Finally, the massive concentrations of population in the cities made possible the marketing and distribution of a mass culture.

Urban residents were not only the recipients of mass culture but active participants in it as well, and they left an indelible imprint on various art forms. Vaudeville was not especially an urban art form, though obviously it was possible only where crowds of people could congregate. Small towns were frequent sites for traveling vaudeville shows, but the entertainment was derived from the leading vaudeville repertoires in the major cities. For comedy and song, few surpassed the popularity of Fanny Brice, a product of New York's ethnic cauldron, the Lower East Side. Her numbers, which included such standards as "Second Hand Rose," became part of vaudeville shows across the country, even down to the heavy Yiddish accent Brice affected. It is impossible to estimate how many vaudeville performers sang from one knee in blackface, but Al Jolson, son of immigrant Jewish parents from Washington, D.C., was probably the most imitated performer of his day. In such lyrics as "my heart strings are tangled around Alabammy," Jolson sang about the sunny South as if he were a displaced native longing for home, but the vaudeville audiences in New York, Boston, and Chicago had about as much familiarity with the region as Jolson did. To the audience, the South was exotic, warm, mannerly, and traditional, while the urban North was often cold, indifferent, and insensitive to tradition. The blackface merely added to this nostalgia.

The urban vaudevillians enjoyed laughing. Indeed, a sense of humor was one of the major self-help devices in the immigrant neighborhoods. In vaudeville, the laughs were typically on the performers themselves. Stories about how lowly immigrants or other "little people" outsmarted "the authorities" were especially enjoyable for audiences. The comedy teams of Weber and Fields and Clayton, Jackson, and Durante were probably best at this social commentary with a laugh. The motion picture industry with Charlie Chaplin, Harold Lloyd, and Buster Keaton borrowed freely from vaudeville's comedy routines to make a hero out of the common urban man. Mack Sennett's Keystone Cops were probably the most popular representations of inept and stupid authorities. While the entire country enjoyed these and similar films, urban audiences particularly could identify with the downtrodden, often abused, but usually vindicated characters. In the 1930s, the legacy of social comedy passed on to the Marx Brothers—also products of urban immigrant neighborhoods.

The recording industry was another mass cultural creation of the 1920s that was influenced by urban America's first decade of statistical dominance. The swelling of the urban population provided a vast market for recordings, and technological advancements in the field produced nationwide hits recorded, marketed, and first played in eastern urban centers. The "Charleston," originally recorded in 1925 by the California Ramblers, a group that included Red Nichols and Tommy and Jimmy Dorsey, became probably the greatest record success of the 1920s and eventually came to symbolize the decade's affinity for dancing and liquor. All three—the record, the dance, and the alcohol—were launched from the city.

When urban Americans were not dancing to the Charleston or to the music of vocalists like Bing Crosby and Eddie Cantor, they were listening to a variety of popular or "Tin Pan Alley" music with a decidedly urban flavor. Jazz, one of the few distinctively American music forms, emerged from the bawdy houses in New Orleans' French Quarter and traveled first to St. Louis and Chicago, and then to New York to become the musical craze of the 1920s. When the first important commercial recording was made in 1917 by Nick La Rocca and his Original Dixieland Jass Band, the music was denounced as immoral because of the freewheeling Dixieland beat and its brothel origins. By the early 1920s, however, Dixieland had gone "uptown" and such legitimate orchestras as Paul Whiteman's performed jazz to rapt urban audiences. Jazz also inspired another urban immigrant son, George Gershwin, whose "Rhapsody in Blue" coupled jazz with earlier classical and romantic styles.

The fact that jazz's greatest early commercial successes were due, in part, to white musicians and composers should not obscure the black urban origins of jazz. Indeed, jazz and urban audiences provided blacks with their first major entree to commercial musical success. Lionel Hampton and Louis Armstrong, for example, began their great careers in the 1920s. The queen of the blues, the more soulful, sorrowful side of jazz, was undoubtedly Bessie Smith. Her mid-twenties rendition of "Yellow Dog Blues" evoked all of the personal heartache and loneliness of the black experience. One could recognize a sense of fatalism and dejection in her rich, deep tones.

Fatalism and dejection, even for urban blacks, were not the prevailing emotions of the twenties. The capital of Negro despair, Harlem, became, in fact, a glittering mecca for whites in the twenties. Its bright lights shouted out news of the best jazz, the best dances, and the best entertainers in the country. The growing appreciation for black culture among white audiences was reflected in the growing cultural pride among blacks themselves.

By the 1920s the first generation of southern black immigrants had settled into northern urban ghettos. Isolated and rejected by white society, blacks looked within themselves and their neighborhoods for emotional and economic sustenance, much as their white European predecessors had done. The emphasis on race pride and group solidarity was exemplified by the "New Negro," a phrase popularized by black writer Alain Locke in 1921. The New Negro was "self-respecting, educated, prosperous, race-proud, self dependent, [and] deserving and demanding full citizenship."[4] He or she was the new image for the urban black.

The manifestations of this race pride and self-dependence were most evident in the cultural outpourings of black writers, musicians, and entertainers. Because Harlem was the black cultural mecca, the movement was called the Harlem Renaissance. In addition to the contributions to jazz, dancing, and vaudeville, the Harlem Renaissance produced some notable literary works that reflected the new urban habitat of the New Negro. Claude McKay, for example, one of the more talented products of the

Renaissance, revealed not only a new race pride, but also a new militancy born of the disappointments of blacks after their move to the northern "promised land." In the wake of the bloody post–World War I race riots, McKay wrote his most famous poem, "If We Must Die":

If we must die, I say let us nobly die,
So that our precious blood may not be shed in vain; then even the monsters we defy
Shall be constrained to honor us though dead! . . .
Like men we'll face the murderous, cowardly pack,
Pressed to the wall, dying, but fighting back![5]

McKay always sought to rouse the black masses from their torpor of defeat. In his later poems and novels, he carefully studied and portrayed Negro folk life from Marseilles in France to the rent parties in Harlem. The interest in black culture and mores was evident in the writings of Alain Locke, who wrote enthusiastically about the "Negro Contributions to America" and suggested that "the main line of Negro development must necessarily be artistic, cultural, moral, and spiritual."[6] Only in the city, of course, could this new development be attained.

For the mass of urban blacks, the Harlem Renaissance meant something quite different. The appeals of Alain Locke were optimistic, but were based on a misunderstanding of the average urban black's pessimism resulting from poor living and working conditions. The mass version of race pride and group solidarity came in the form of the ideas of another West Indian, Marcus Garvey. This "Black Moses" dreamed of a new black empire in Africa peopled, in part, by American blacks. The initial success of the Garvey movement was a measure of the urban black hopelessness. Its ultimate failure reflected the helplessness of the lowly ghetto resident.

Garvey's organization, the Universal Negro Improvement Association (UNIA), promoted black culture and race pride. The black, red, and green flags flying from ghetto tenement windows, portraits of a black Jesus and a black Virgin Mary hanging on the walls, and visions of a redeemed Africa playing in the minds of poor ghetto residents were some of the memorabilia of the Garvey dream. Garvey's explanation was as simple as Locke's: "We are organized not to hate other men, but to lift ourselves, and to demand respect of all humanity."[7] Following these precepts millions of black Americans poured millions of dollars into such UNIA projects as hotels, steamship lines, hospitals, and commercial enterprises. The ultimate goal of these endeavors was to establish a haven for American blacks in Africa. This was the hope that came from the despair of the urban ghetto. Jealous rival black leaders, nervous public officials, and Garvey's own mismanagement doomed his enterprises and his dream. The government eventually deported him, and the momentary flicker of self-respect and hope he brought to the ghetto was extinguished.

As the black masses receded again into anonymity and desperation, the glittering aspect of the Harlem Renaissance returned to center stage, if in fact it had ever left. When whites flocked to Harlem, they saw not the poverty of black life, but rather the lights and excitement of an exotic culture: dancers, musicians, and singers, but rarely individuals. Black writers were responsible for this stereotype, too, though a white author, Carl Van Vechten, probably captured the white public's image of the New Negro best in his novel *Nigger Heaven.* It was a guidebook for white visitors to "the barbaric rhythms of Negro jazz, the intoxicating dances, and the wild abandon of cabaret life after midnight."[8]

Harlem continued to serve as a seedbed for American popular music into the 1960s with the Apollo Theater as the cultural focal point. Ironically, rhythm and blues, which in the 1940s transplanted jazz as the indigenous black ghetto musical expression, was similarly appropriated by white musicians. By the time Buddy Holly and the Crickets became the first white group to perform at the Apollo in 1957, rock and roll (the white designation for rhythm and blues) was a national phenomenon with its black urban roots largely ignored. Tragically soon, Holly and his music were gone, and some time later so was the Apollo.

The day the music died there were few mourners. The image of happy Harlem was, of course, no less than the image of the happy plantation, a superficial one. The New Negro movement, in general, failed to resolve the basic conflicts for urban blacks, who, despite all the talk of race pride, strove desperately to emulate and to enter the white world. Mary Love, an exponent in *Nigger Heaven* of the New Negro philosophy, said dejectedly that "her race spent more money on hair-straightening and skin-lightening preparations than they did on food and clothing."[9]

The striving for black identity while trying to be white lent a pathetic and hopeless atmosphere to the black ghetto. Neither effort seemed to be of effective help: The lot of the urban black did not improve, and the inadequacy of the environment was only made more clear during the decade. The ghetto had become a prison and each dwelling a cell or, as black leader W. E. B. Du Bois called it, "a dark cave."[10] In the meantime, urban Americans enjoyed themselves with their new music and lavished affection on their new heroes. The blacks would have to relinquish their hopes for another era.

While lights and music blared from Harlem, a new sound burst forth farther uptown in the Bronx. The noise reverberating off the new concrete and steel of Yankee Stadium signaled the arrival of baseball, another of the new mass entertainment events of the twenties, as the national pastime.

Baseball had, of course, received national recognition before the 1920s. Such stars as Christy Mathewson, Honus Wagner, and Napoleon Lajoie provided turn-of-the-century fans with exciting sports entertainment. City streets and parks echoed with bats and balls as children emulated their heroes of the diamond. But during the twenties baseball became a mass phenomenon. New stadiums including the palatial Yankee Stadium, completed in 1923, and new stars testified to the growing popularity of the sport. The new heroes were not necessarily the pitchers or the singles hitters anymore; they were the home run hitters. City dwellers packed the stadiums to get a glimpse of the latest longball sensation and cheer with growing intensity for the team representing their city. Urban rivalry, so long a concern of rival elites, now reached the hearts and voices of the general public.

Babe Ruth typified the new sports hero. Rising from poverty and neglect in Baltimore, he became the king of the home run hitters, the Sultan of Swat for the New York Yankees. Anchoring the famed Murderers' Row batting order, Ruth hit an incredible sixty home runs during the 1927 baseball season. His lifestyle earned him as much publicity as his hitting. Brash, generous, swaggering, and fond of eating and drinking, Ruth fit into the lifestyle of the 1920s very well. When a reporter asked him in depression-ridden 1930 if he felt concerned that as a baseball player he was making more than President Hoover, Ruth retorted, "Why not? I had a better year."[11]

The cheers for new sports heroes rolled over cities throughout the country. They cheered for Gene Tunney—145,000 of them in Chicago's Soldier Field—as he knocked out Jack Dempsey. They cheered for Red Grange as he galloped like a ghost across the football fields of the Midwest. They cheered for Knute Rockne and for Notre Dame's Four Horsemen. They cheered for Bill Tilden as he sent another forehand careening down the line.

They also cheered for William Simmons as he lit a kerosene-soaked cross atop Stone Mountain, just outside of Atlanta. The restless search for heroes and the coming together in clubs and theaters was as much a search for order and for traditional values, as it was for entertainment. The Ku Klux Klan with its flowing silk paraphernalia, elaborate rituals, and fiery night skies was certainly entertaining for those who sought refuge within the Invisible Empire. It was another social club, much like the Elks. This social club, however, promised action: action against the changes that had taken place in the cities.

The urban manifestation of a phenomenon that had traditionally been viewed as limited to rural areas and small towns says as much about the centrality of cities to American society as about the frustrations within those cities. The Klan knew no sectional boundaries. The largest single Klan organization existed in Chicago, and midwestern cities collectively had more members than any other region. The black, the immigrant, the new morality: wherever there was change or something different, the Klan rose to combat it. The most active Klan memberships were, not surprisingly, in those cities that had experienced the most rapid growth since the early years of the twentieth century: Chicago, Detroit, Memphis, Dayton, Youngstown, Dallas, and Houston. The men and women who belonged to the Klan were typically long-time residents who remembered what their city had once been when it was their city.

The Klansmen and women were not wealthy. They frequently lived in working-class neighborhoods on the edges of expanding black or immigrant districts. They felt trapped. Unable to afford the move to the periphery or to the suburbs, they felt threatened by what they thought to be an impending invasion. "Fear of change," wrote historian Kenneth T. Jackson, "not vindictiveness or cruelty was the basic motivation of the urban Klansman."[12] When it became apparent by the late 1920s that the Klan could not deliver on its promise to squelch the aspirations of the urban newcomers, the organization slowly faded.

Others lashed out more effectively against change. The race riots during and after World War I were the most overt manifestations of white hostility toward black residential and economic aspirations. The Red Scare of 1919 was a national hysteria, born of disillusionment, to rid the country of suspected subversives. Most of the persecuted were urban immigrants. Finally, Congress, in a series of laws passed throughout the decade, closed the golden door and severely restricted immigration, especially from the southern and eastern European countries that had provided the millions of pioneers since the turn of the century.

Restricting immigration was a collective turning inward, an attempt to grasp a lost innocence that somehow change had shattered. The decade was as schizophrenic as the urban society that dominated it. There were new morals, new music, New Negroes, and new heroes, yet there was little that was really new. Women may have raised their skirts, bobbed their hair, and even bellied up to speakeasy bars, yet the Carries and the Dulcies abounded. The New Negro, while generating some genuine creative talents, was more ideal than real, and shattered quickly with the onset of the depression. Audiences laughed at and cried with the immigrant entertainers, but vigorously supported attempts to bar their friends and relatives from ever partaking in the American dream.

Novelists, perceptive social critics that they were, were not dazzled by the blaring movie marquees, the stadium lights, or the jazz babies. Even the values of the past had become counterfeited by the ephemeral causes of the present: Prohibition, the Ku Klux Klan, and fundamentalist Protestant religion with urban evangelists preaching "Salvation and Five Per Cent," as though the Bible came out of a Wall Street ticker tape. Sinclair Lewis wrote about the shallow piety of the medium-sized city, and F. Scott Fitzgerald dealt with the emptiness and excess of urban and suburban life: stark, yet revealing contrasts to the gaiety of the twenties.

It would not be fair to close our discussion of this remarkable decade without observing that, for the first time, millions of Americans *enjoyed* their cities. The mass culture, whatever its reflection of deeper values, touched all segments and indeed emanated from all segments of urban life. The sight of a Ruthian clout clearing the right-field fence, the sound of Jolson belting out a Dixie melody, and the sights and sounds of Harlem and Broadway were shared by a broad spectrum of the urban population. For a time, one could forget.

The party ended in 1930, and the hangover was excruciating. That urban America still went to ball-parks and attended vaudeville and motion-picture shows was not only an indication of the pervasiveness of these mass cultural forms, but also a reflection of the dull, dreary, and often heart-rending lives led by city dwellers in the thirties.

Old Frustrations and Old Divisions

The freshness of the twenties quickly wilted in the thirties. The old fears and frustrations of joblessness and starvation, apparently conquered by the prosperity following World War I, reappeared in massive proportions. One estimate held that a quarter of a million persons were starving to death in Philadelphia during 1932, while Chicago had an unemployment rate over 40 percent. The specter of violence and memories of the riots of the late nineteenth century, when workers had been pitted against the upper and middle classes, haunted local officials. But timely assistance from the federal government and the acceptance of labor unions like the Congress of Industrial Organizations (CIO) seemed to defuse a potentially dangerous situation, though sporadic violence occurred throughout the decade.

More serious was the psychological impact of unemployment on individuals and families. The generation that grew up in the thirties included our present-day leaders. What effect did deprivation and unemployment have on their values and outlook? Was the free spending of the 1960s in part a reaction to the fact that free spending in the 1930s seemed to lift the country's spirit? And did the great insecurity of the depression decade make security the end in itself for the sixties, with little regard for idealism or the occasional insecurity of bold or unpopular decisions? The responses to these questions are obviously difficult, and are highly individual, but it is certain that protection and security became a major motivating force in urban society after World War II. The individual family and local institutions were similarly stressed. While it may require a leap of faith to go from the young man or woman selling apples on the street corner to that same person sitting in a suburban home securely surrounded by television, appliances, and family, there may be some psychological parallels. This is not to criticize either, but merely to raise the possibility, even the probability, that the psychological wounds of depression and war may still be with us today.

For urban blacks, that growing and increasingly separate part of urban society, these decades brought more than psychological wounds. Emotionally, blacks continued to be plagued by what Ralph Ellison, in his sensitive 1947 novel *Invisible Man,* termed the "twoness" of black existence: the drive for black identity and the striving to be an American in a white-dominated society. This division not only troubled the black masses, but splintered the black leadership as well. W. E. B. Du Bois broke with the NAACP and advocated a policy of "organized and deliberate self-segregation," specifically in the form of all-black economic cooperatives. He denounced integration as an unattainable goal and counseled blacks not to waste their time seeking acceptance by white society. "No, by God," he urged, "stand erect in a mud-puddle and tell the white world to go to hell, rather than lick boots in a parlor."[13]

Of course, urban blacks, confined to ghettos, had very little choice but to fall back on themselves as the less shrill voices of the New Negro movement had reminded them in the 1920s. But Du Bois's hopes for a new economic order were unrealistic. A writer in *The Nation* asked Du Bois how he hoped to advance blacks economically in a segregated society. "Is Wall Street colored? Is finance capital high yaller?"[14] To make Du Bois's call even more utopian, the relief statistics of the thirties demonstrated that the depression hit hardest at those on the lowest rung of urban society—the blacks. More than half of black families in the cities were on relief, compared to a national urban rate of 10 to 13 percent for whites. In some southern cities, such as Norfolk and Charlotte, blacks comprised four-fifths of the relief rolls. An ungrammatical, but poignant letter from a little black girl in Houston to President Roosevelt underscored the statistical situation in more human terms:

I know you will be surprised to hear from us but we are two little Negro sisters 9 and 7 years old an it is time for Santa Clause to come an our parents are poor and dis able to give us. My Dad doesn't have day work an he is an ex service man will you please tell Santa to come to see us we want even have food.[15]

As in times of slavery, religion proved to be one of the few solaces for the urban black. In the local church, the poor Negro could assume positions of leadership, express thoughts and ideas, and hope for a better life in the next world. A new sect that rejected Christianity appeared in the 1930s. Wallace D. Fard, a Detroit street peddler, established the Temple of Islam to attract blacks from Christianity to the true religion, the Nation of Islam. Fard's successor, Elijah Mohammed (Robert Poole), transformed the small, local organization into a national movement. The Black Muslims became one of the ghetto's leading self-help groups. Their philosophy, similar to that of the colonial Puritans, stressed strong family and community ties, hard work, strict dietary and Sabbath observances, and an uncompromising belief in themselves as the chosen people. For a rejected and dejected black urban community, adrift in a sea of helplessness and despair, the Muslims offered order, discipline, and self-respect. Malcolm X, one of the Muslims' more famous members, was a petty criminal who converted to Islam in his prison cell. In his *Autobiography* he related how, as a youth, he conked (straightened) his hair and sought out the material possessions that were measures of success in the white world—automobiles and clothes. The Muslims, however, helped him to perceive his own identity, his own worth, and the value of work and prayer.

The Nation of Islam, which adopted some of the principles of the New Negro and Du Bois's separatist philosophy, remained too demanding for the majority of black urban residents. When each day was a struggle for simple survival, the Muslim's emphasis on self-help responded more to an ideal than to the debilitating reality of the urban black condition.

The fatalism that marked life in that increasingly distinctive spatial entity known as the ghetto did not inhibit some blacks from actively protesting the conditions of their discriminatory urban life. Harlem, which housed more blacks than any other black ghetto in the country, took the lead, especially through prominent church leaders like Adam Clayton Powell, Jr., who later went on to represent Harlem in Congress. Commanding pickets at such diverse locations as the 1939 World's Fair in New York, drugstores in Harlem, and the local bus company, Powell successfully pressured these employers to hire more blacks.

The events of World War II, however, demonstrated that American prejudice was still very much intact with the black frequently as its target. As in World War I, massive migrations of blacks to industrial cities of the North and Midwest, job and wage discrimination, poor housing, and an escalating war with neighboring whites characterized the black experiences in the Second World War. Although the establishment of the Fair Employment Practices Commission (FEPC) at the insistence of black labor leader A. Philip

Randolph (and after a threatened march on Washington) reduced job discrimination in the war plants, residential differences increased. During the 1940s there were literally hundreds of incidents of violence against blacks who moved into all-white neighborhoods. The competition over jobs and housing finally erupted into riots in Detroit and New York during the summer of 1943. Though hostility smoldered in dozens of other cities during the war, these were the only cities where it surfaced into widespread violence.

During this period, new immigrants, attracted by employment, began to enter American cities. The Latin Americans were merely the latest in the long line of newcomers to American cities, but their racial differences and

Figure 11.1   Mexican Barrio, Los Angeles, 1936

The restrictive immigration legislation of the twenties and the depression of the thirties slowed European immigration considerably. Black migration from the South continued, but émigrés from Latin America—especially from Mexico—were the newest group of arrivals to U.S. cities. In terms of residential and employment patterns, they resembled the blacks, and, with the additional handicap of a language barrier, they shared with the blacks the discrimination of white America. (Library of Congress)

their competition for jobs and housing made them as odious to the white urban population as the blacks were. In 1943, the same summer as the Detroit and New York riots, restless sailors in Los Angeles, avenging an attack by a Mexican youth gang on one of their own, roamed for several nights through the Chicano *barrio* (neighborhood) attacking every Mexican boy they could find, while the police stood idly by. The names and the accents were different, but this merely underscored the continued drift of urban society into two separate racial entities. (See Figure 11.1.)

Suburban Fortresses and City Cells

The years immediately following World War II witnessed an acceleration of the trend toward two separate racial societies, this time on a much broader spatial scale than had existed before. The combinations of government policies, personal preferences, and mass-production technology in the housing industry stimulated the abandonment of the city. It was an overwhelmingly white exodus primarily because even at the prevailing modest prices, home ownership was an economic impossibility for most urban blacks. Then, too, suburban jurisdictions, learning from the big cities, incorporated the current racial beliefs through more open, but nonetheless equally effective, exclusionary zoning. The spatial composition of most suburban communities militated against black incursion: large lot sizes, few if any provisions for multifamily dwellings, and square-footage minimums. Although such devices are under legal attack today, they remain in force in most suburban jurisdictions, and it is by no means certain that they will have to be excised from local plans in the foreseeable future. The suburbs, in short, surrounded themselves with impenetrable legal barriers designed to preserve racial and income (often one and the same) homogeneity.

For white residents of urban or older peripheral neighborhoods, the exclusionary devices common to the vital fringe were useless in their already built-up neighborhoods. Many of these neighborhoods were remnants of larger ethnic enclaves reduced by the movement to the suburbs in the 1940s and 1950s. The pattern of life in these areas was that of what Herbert Gans called an "urban village"—a small, virtually autonomous community with its own daily rhythms and institutions.[16] As in the small town, everyone knew everyone else. It was a street society, where the sidewalks were typically crowded with residents chatting or walking to the local stores where they shopped daily as much to talk with friends as to purchase fresh produce. The intrusion of a stranger into the midst of the village residents was duly noted and usually tolerated so long as the outsider was passing through. But if the stranger threatened to stay and to bring other strangers with different

customs, cultures, and above all, race, then village battlements were
mounted and the integrity of the village was maintained.

With this view in mind, the fierce antagonism to new and different residents common to transitional neighborhoods in northern cities (where the
urban villages predominate) becomes understandable. The psychological
attachment to space ran deep in these communities, and separation from the
space, whether by the intrusions of a freeway or of blacks or Hispanics, was
likely to cause severe emotional disruption for many residents. Also,
local institutions like schools elicited similar attachments. In these villages,
schools are not merely educational facilities, they are community institutions
as well. They are used for meetings and for recreation. Just as it would be
inconceivable to hire a minister of a different ethnic background to tend the
local house of worship, so it would be difficult to separate the community
from its local school. When city officials compared the ferocity with which
residents of the South Boston urban village opposed the busing of students
from outside the community to local schools with milder reactions in some
supposedly racist southern cities, they were not aware of the urban-village
psychology of the neighborhood residents.

These urban villages, especially those adjacent to black or Hispanic areas,
are the urban combat zones of the postwar era. The angry taunts and
sporadic violence of white ethnic villagers in such a Chicago neighborhood
shocked Martin Luther King, Jr., who claimed that he had not encountered
such animosity even in the darkest days of Selma and Birmingham in the
early 1960s.

While some villages like South Boston have successfully maintained their
whiteness, others have become dispersed, their residents leaving for areas on
the vital fringe seeking the accustomed spatial separation from the strangers. But even fortress suburbia, especially in the older areas, can show
cracks occasionally. In 1971, when New York City began a low-income
housing project in white middle-class Forest Hills in the residential borough
of Queens, angry residents successfully halted the project. Although they
objected partly because the projected housing was clumsily designed and
would have thrown additional burdens on an already tax-weary community,
the incident revealed something of the inner psychology of the fortress
residents. Michael Tabor, a reporter from Cambridge, Massachusetts, observed the protesters and noted that the main reason behind their objections
was "fear—perhaps even justifiable fear. They have moved out of two,
three, four or more neighborhoods before coming to Forest Hills. They have
watched blacks, Puerto Ricans, and welfare families move in and have seen
their neighborhoods deteriorate."[17] Though there were good reasons for
this deterioration quite apart from any inherent faults in the minorities

Figure 11.2   Black Ghetto, Philadelphia, 1951
(National Archives)

themselves, the Forest Hills residents were not about to launch sociological studies to determine why their neighborhoods declined when it already seemed evident to them.

In Rosedale, New York, another community on the fringe between city and suburb, the fortress mentality persisted through the 1970s for the same reasons. The words of the lower middle-class and middle-class residents depict an almost pathetic adulthood of running and fear. Rosedale was typical of inner suburban communities and urban villages in that it marked a coming together of diverse white ethnic groups for a common purpose of preserving and protecting the neighborhood as it was. As one resident noted, "We've got Jews, we've got Italians, we've got Slovaks. You know, a melting pot." Their fierce pride and protectiveness is evident in a comment by one resident: "It took me eight years to save money to buy a house. . . . And I'm not gonna just say, 'Here, it's yours.' I'm not givin' in to anybody and I'm not gonna run 'cause there's no where to run today." Fatigued by "running," the residents of Rosedale and similar communities are determined to make their stand there: "I'm gonna stay and fight because I can't be

Figure 11.3   White Neighborhood, Philadelphia, 1951
Two separate societies. (National Archives)

pushed anymore. They pushed me outta East New York; I'm not gonna be
pushed again. I'm too old to move right now, I'm gonna make my stand. I'm
stayin'."[18]

So for blacks, the fulfillment of the suburban dream seems far off.
Though increasing numbers of blacks were moving into the suburbs by the
mid-1970s, many were appearing in these zones of emergence, these combat
zones that more likely would become spatial extensions of the central-city
ghetto. The corollary of the suburban fortress, then, is the ghetto prison.
Blacks cannot escape because there is no place to go.

For ghetto-bound blacks, the alternatives have not always seemed so slim.
Indeed, the most amazing fact of black urban existence has been the resil-
ience and the continued hopefulness of some, though by no means all, ghetto
residents. In the mid-1950s and early 1960s it did in fact seem that a new era
for the urban black could be approaching.

The most dramatic changes occurred in southern cities where racial
segregation had been most entrenched, though the sharp spatial distinctions
that characterized residential areas in northern cities were not as evident.

Beginning with the Montgomery bus boycott in 1955, the Reverend Martin Luther King, Jr., and his Southern Christian Leadership Conference attacked segregated urban society throughout the South. Eventually, the urban-desegregation movement came to encompass everything from sitting-in at lunch counters to lengthy marches for voting rights. Just as white urban northerners protected their neighborhoods, sometimes violently, some southern urban whites resorted to brutality to preserve their way of life. Birmingham, in particular, became the focal point for the civil rights struggle in the early 1960s. Beginning with the assault on the Freedom Riders in 1961, and culminating in the bombing of a black church in which four young girls were killed, the events in Birmingham laid bare the close connection between the local officials, the police, and such organizations as the Ku Klux Klan.

The protests led by Dr. King and groups like the Student Nonviolent Coordinating Committee (SNCC) touched a responsive chord outside the South. For here were groups of black and white men and women risking verbal and physical abuse to advance the dream of an integrated society in a nonviolent way. Even more impressive were their successes in integrating public facilities and in providing a foundation for voter registration. It was equally encouraging that significant numbers of whites joined southern urban blacks to overthrow the rigid segregation of the southern city. On a national scale, the nonviolent protests led to the passage of the 1964 Civil Rights Act that secured integration in public accommodations. It seemed as though a new era was beginning for the urban black. In northern cities, blacks hoped that the good will generated by the civil rights movement and the positive gains made under legislation would improve ghetto conditions.

But this was to be a false hope. Little change occurred in the black ghetto. If anything, conditions were getting worse. The desegregation of lunch counters, movie theaters, and public transit, while genuine victories in southern cities, had little relevance in the ghettos of the North where the daily battles to survive, to eat, to live in decent housing took precedence over eating hamburgers with whites. For more than a generation blacks had been caged in northern ghettos, and those neighborhoods had developed a pathology all of their own, unlike the more temporary slum quarters of the European immigrants.

The physical pathology of the postwar ghetto was its most evident feature. The old buildings, teeming with rats and plagued by falling plaster, indifferent plumbing, and ancient heating systems, resemble the tenements Jacob Riis toured almost a century ago. Garbage piles up in the streets, and many apartment windows have no screens or are boarded up. The new buildings, the results of federal urban policy, are scarcely much better. They are ill-designed, poorly maintained high-rise ghettos. As black author James Baldwin wrote, "The projects . . . are hated. . . . The projects are hideous . . . , there being a law . . . that popular housing shall be as cheerless as a prison. They are lumped all over Harlem, colorless, bleak, high, and revolting."[19]

The ghetto is ugly. Its land-use patterns and spatial dimensions tell a story of inferiority and neglect. The parks, if there are parks, are strewn with broken glass and poorly maintained. There are few, if any, cultural facilities in the ghetto, few museums, art galleries, and legitimate theaters, perhaps only a library. What the ghetto has in great quantity, black psychologist Kenneth Clark wrote, is "hundreds of bars, hundreds of churches, and scores of fortune tellers."[20] This is hardly a land-use pattern from which to build a viable economic or social community.

The psychological impact of ghetto life, though more subtle than its visible physical debilities, is nonetheless equally serious. The vision of the ghetto as a prison appears frequently in the language of both residents and observers. In contrasting her former Alabama home with her present ghetto residence in Boston, a black woman confided, "Up here they have you in a cage. There's no place to go, and all I do is stay in the building." This sense of physical confinement is a mental constraint as well. Journalist Richard Hammer wrote that for the people in Harlem in the early 1960s the ghetto's "walls are invisible; they are inside the mind, built by the people who live on the block and by society outside. But the walls are as real as if they were made by mortar and stone."[21]

Behind these ghetto walls are defeated people, searching for their identity as men and women because the outside society does not see them as individuals. As Du Bois wrote in his book *Dusk of Dawn* sixty years ago: "It gradually penetrates the minds of the prisoners that the people passing do not hear; that some thick sheet of invisible but horribly tangible plate glass is between them and the world."[22] The inconsequence of their being leads inevitably to a sense of fatalism, a loss of hope. Through television and radio they see what the other world is like. Unlike Jacob Riis's "other half," who rarely knew about the lifestyles of their more fortunate urban brethren, the residents of the contemporary ghetto know the types of lives they are missing and cannot attain. As one Harlem resident says, "A lot of times, when I'm working, I become as despondent as hell and I feel like crying. I'm not a man, none of us are men! I don't own anything."[23] Sometimes it is even tiring to be frustrated and to wonder about who you are. A black Boston woman viewed her life as a daily struggle, where survival was victory: "When I go to bed at night I tell myself I've done good to stay alive and keep the kids alive, and if they'll just wake up in the morning, and me too, well then, we can worry about that, all the rest, come tomorrow."[24]

Adverse values and practices developed in this adverse environment: fatalism instead of ambition, truancy instead of education, bars instead of libraries. The "hustle" replaces the job because if and when there is a job, it is likely to be much less remunerative than the hustle. As one Harlem gang member retorted when asked why he did not get legitimate employment: ". . . go downtown and get a job? Oh, come on. . . . I make $40 to $50 a day selling pot. You want me to go down to the garment district and push one of those trucks through the street and at the end of the week take home $40 or $50 if I'm lucky?"[25]

Given these conditions and the heightened, but false, expectations brought on by civil rights victories and legislation, it was not surprising that numbers of ghetto residents revolted in the mid-1960s. The young—teenagers and young adults—were especially active in the riots of that period. They had not yet assumed the fatalism of their elders but were making a stand against a society that viewed them as invisible. They became visible enough during the sixties.

The immediate causes of the riots were inconsequential incidents that occurred almost on a daily basis. Most of these precipitating incidents involved the police—the visible force and presence of white society in the ghetto. But the roots of frustration and bitterness lay deep within the accumulated burdens of ghetto life. From July 18, 1964, when violence erupted in Harlem, through the aftermath of the Martin Luther King, Jr., assassination in the spring of 1968, 75 major urban riots occurred in all sections of the country, but primarily in the ghettos of the Northeast and Midwest. There were 83 deaths, 82 percent of these deaths occurring in Detroit and Newark alone. All but 10 percent of the fatalities were blacks, a fact which highlighted the futility of these disturbances regardless of the conditions which brought the violence to the surface.

Almost all of the looting and property damage occurred within the ghetto, the majority being white-owned businesses, though a few black businesses and residences were burnt out by the rioters. The net effect of this was to increase insurance rates, accelerate commercial disinvestment, and leave the ghetto with fewer shopping alternatives than it had before. The hope for a black-owned ghetto emerging from the rubble was as elusive as Du Bois's plan for economic cooperatives, and for the same reasons. For most of the young blacks who had participated in the riots, the temporary exhilaration and pride gave way to life as usual behind ghetto walls. For older ghetto residents, initial shame and fear surrendered to the fatalism characteristic of ghetto veterans.

The greatest impact of the riots occurred in the white community, both public and private. The invisible men and women had become visible and had menacingly rattled their cages. Though additional civil rights legislation was one of the results, the report of the special commission appointed by President Johnson to investigate the disturbances was perhaps most instructive. With former Illinois governor Otto Kerner at its head, the commission placed the blame for the riots on white racism. Specifically, the Kerner Commission noted "pervasive discrimination and segregation in employment, education, and housing, which have resulted in the continuing exclusion of great numbers of Negroes from the benefits of economic progress."[26]

But looking to the eradication of white racism as the solution to the black urban condition seemed to some observers to be a very long-term process during which time over numerous long, hot summers the ghetto might explode on the urban scene. Further, the attempt to rectify ghetto life involved so many different programs that the price tag (which the commission did not mention) would be unacceptable to the American taxpayer. Finally, the commission correctly pinpointed the ghetto as an environment of despair, but generally neglected to analyze the possibilities of ghetto enrichment and self-help: a rich, if largely unfulfilled, legacy from the New Negro to Du Bois to the Muslims.

It was soon evident that self-help would be the only realistic policy to pursue. As if to underscore the commission's view that white racism was a major cause of the black ghetto, many whites became even more intransigent toward their black neighbors. This "white backlash" included a national law-and-order campaign, the presidential candidacy of Alabama governor George Wallace (who ran strongly in the contested transitional neighborhoods of the urban North), and the protective attitudes of Rosedale and Forest Hills residents. Some whites, of course, responded more positively to the riots. Police departments were briefed in community relations, and local black leaders elicited quicker responses from city hall, especially in the areas of sanitation and police services.

The most positive responses came from blacks themselves. The riots of the 1960s were different from the violence a half-century earlier in places like Chicago and East St. Louis. In the earlier encounters whites typically were the aggressors and blacks the victims. During the 1960s, the target was not so much race as it was property. The Detroit riot, the most severe of all the decade's disturbances, was, in fact, an integrated affair with poor whites and poor blacks enjoying looting and burning together. Whatever the inner meaning of these distinctions between two eras of rioting, in the 1960s at least, blacks were on the offensive, and they attacked the whites where it hurt the most: the pocketbook. If this initiative and energy were transferred to more constructive purposes, the ghetto could in fact become a more positive environment.

In viewing the last decade of black ghetto life, it seems that whatever progress has occurred in these communities has occurred through self-help. Though Du Bois's ideal of economic independence is as far from reality today as it was in the 1930s, there is a "New Negro" spirit abroad in the ghetto. The cries of "Black Power" and "Black is Beautiful" were early constructive steps in establishing identity and pride, especially among the young. As one young poet from the Watts Workshop, established by local whites and blacks after the 1965 riot, wrote: "You become a man when you stop all of those faces from coming out of your mouth and begin shaping your lips to sing the recognizable features of your own past, *and what you know is true.*"[27]

In addition to improving the psychological ghetto, efforts are under way to improve the physical community. Now that the confused and sometimes disastrously broad federal programs have generally subsided, local residents can concentrate on smaller-scale, more realistic projects. In black Roxbury (Boston), for example, a group of black professionals came together in the early 1970s to form the Roxbury Action Program (RAP) designed to purchase and rehabilitate ghetto structures so that residents could live in safe and clean housing. In addition, the group plans landscaping and other improvements to make the ghetto beautiful. In Washington, D.C., minority contractors are now engaged in rebuilding parts of the areas devastated by the 1968 riot. Most major cities, in fact, have black groups engaged in the physical improvement of the ghetto.

While blacks may still be invisible to many whites, their growing political power has made them a political force in numerous cities. This is understandable from sheer weight of numbers. In such cities as Newark, Baltimore, Washington, Charleston, Savannah, Atlanta, Detroit, Gary, and New Orleans, blacks constitute close to or over one-half of the population. Since the riots of the mid-sixties, black mayors have been elected in Cleveland, Gary, Detroit, Washington, Newark, Los Angeles, and even in deep South cities like Atlanta and New Orleans. Black mayors have not initiated revolutionary reforms, nor have they brought heaven to the ghetto. Working within the financial and political constraints binding all big-city mayors, the black mayors have made city hall more responsive to ghetto problems and have generated a feeling of optimism where none had existed before. Local neighborhood projects get full support and encouragement from the mayor's office.

In the area of education, self-help is becoming more prevalent as blacks realize that success and education are inseparable. The new emphasis on education is encouraging because it means that concern over immediate problems such as food, shelter, and employment is not overwhelming the blacks' planning for more future-oriented goals. In the mid-1970s, the Reverend Jesse Jackson, a veteran of the Southern Christian Leadership Conference, began an assault on the intellectual poverty of the ghetto. Some of his rhetoric recalls the early days of the Jewish and Italian ghettos and the way the first generation of immigrants sacrificed itself so that the next could improve. He preaches the value of sacrifice and asks why, if blacks can run faster, shoot straighter, and jump higher on inadequate diets, broken homes, and poor housing, can't they read better under those same conditions. His admonition is that blacks should not use the conditions of ghetto life as an excuse for failure, but rather as hurdles to be bounded over on the way to success. As he puts it: "You may not be responsible for being down, but you are responsible for getting up."[28]

A good example of self-help comes from New York's Puerto Rican ghetto, Spanish Harlem. The Hispanic urban ghettos share the same pathology as the black ghettos. The testimonials of residents, many of whom have arrived since World War II, evince the same disillusionment and frustration. The Hispanic ghettos, outwardly gay with bright lights and lively music, are inwardly despairing. (Puerto Rican author Piri Thomas, writing a decade ago, compared the Latin ghetto to "a great big dirty Christmas tree with lights but no fuckin' presents."[29]) The Puerto Ricans and the Chicanos, as the newest immigrants, share the lowest economic and social rungs of the ladder with the blacks, and like the blacks they are groping for identity by emphasizing Spanish culture and language. Also like the blacks, they have developed local self-help groups. Perhaps the most famous is the Young Lords of Spanish Harlem, a street gang who turned anger and violence into constructive community-building efforts. They first burst on the public consciousness late in the 1960s by tossing garbage into the middle of Spanish Harlem streets to protest the city's poor sanitation service to the area. Garbage collection improved. With a highly disciplined organization that allows no drugs or crime, they have begun breakfast programs, clothing drives, and have prodded local officials to perform health and sanitation services promptly and competently.

The creative ghetto or barrio can only create from its own resources, which remain very limited. Blacks point to increasing numbers of their race in professional occupations who potentially can have a significant impact on ghetto pathology, as the Roxbury Action Program demonstrates. It is not clear, however, whether the increasing number of upwardly mobile blacks and Chicanos will return to the ghetto to share their abilities and resources. Many of them worked hard to escape the ghetto in the first place. The problem with the ghetto-enrichment formula is that it is limited by the poverty of the ghetto. There are more possibilities for the young black or Latino today, but the old prison pathology remains.

The creativity of the ghetto is, nevertheless, like a thousand candles. "And the light and warmth of these candles may help redeem and regenerate the core of the ghetto, that decomposed inner city waiting either for a phoenix to rise from the ashes, or for bigger and more terrible fires."[30] Will these candles melt the fortresses and cells metropolitan society has erected? As urban America moves to an era beyond the fringe, this is one of the questions that awaits it.

Notes

1. This phrase from "Babylon Revisited" (1930) is quoted in Frederick J. Hoffman, "The Temper of the Twenties," in Joan Hoff Wilson, ed., *The Twenties: The Critical Issues* (Boston: Little, Brown, 1972), p. 112.

2. Gilman M. Ostrander, "The Revolution in Morals," in Joan Hoff Wilson, *The Twenties*, p. 139.

3. *Ibid.*, p. 138.

4. Quoted in August Meier, *Negro Thought in America, 1880–1915* (Ann Arbor: University of Michigan Press, 1966), p. 259.

5. Quoted in Wayne Cooper, "Claude McKay and the New Negro of the 1920's," *Phylon*, 25 (Fall 1964), 297–306. From *Selected Poems of Claude McKay*, copyright 1953 by Twayne Publishers, Inc. Reprinted with the permission of Twayne Publishers, A Division of G. K. Hall & Co., Boston.

6. Quoted in Gilbert Osofsky, ed., *The Burden of Race: A Documentary History of Negro-White Relations in America* (New York: Harper & Row, 1967), p. 322.

7. Quoted in A. J. Garvey, ed., *The Philosophy and Opinions of Marcus Garvey* (New York: Macmillan, 1968), p. 74.

8. Quoted in Eugene Arden, "The Early Harlem," *Phylon*, 20 (Spring 1959), 27.

9. Quoted in *ibid.*

10. Quoted in Gunnar Myrdal, "Foreword," in Kenneth B. Clark, *Dark Ghetto: Dilemmas of Social Power* (New York: Harper & Row, 1967), p. ix.

11. Quoted in Robert W. Creamer, "Colossus of the Game," *Sports Illustrated*, 40 (April 1, 1974), p. 47.

12. Kenneth T. Jackson, *The Ku Klux Klan in the City, 1915–1930* (New York: Oxford University Press, 1967), p. 242.

13. Quoted in Osofsky, ed., *Burden of Race*, p. 344.

14. Quoted in *ibid.*, p. 346.

15. Quoted in *ibid.*, p. 412.

16. See Herbert J. Gans, *The Urban Villagers: Group and Class in the Life of Italian-Americans* (New York: Free Press, 1962).

17. Quoted in Bayrd Still, ed., *Urban America: A History with Documents* (Boston: Little, Brown, 1974), p. 439.

18. Quoted in "Rosedale: The Way It Is," *Bill Moyer's Journal,* transcription of PBS television show aired January 18, 1976.

19. Quoted in David R. Goldfield and James B. Lane, eds., *The Enduring Ghetto: Sources and Readings* (Philadelphia: Lippincott, 1973), p. 120.

20. Kenneth Clark, *Dark Ghetto: Dilemmas of Social Power* (New York: Harper & Row, 1965), p. 27.

21. Statements about Boston and Harlem are quoted in Goldfield and Lane, eds., *Enduring Ghetto,* pp. 14, 65.

22. Quoted in Clark, *Dark Ghetto,* p. ix.

23. Quoted in *ibid.,* p. 1.

24. Quoted in Goldfield and Lane, eds., *Enduring Ghetto,* p. 106.

25. Quoted in Clark, *Dark Ghetto,* p. 13.

26. Quoted in Still, ed., *Urban America,* p. 414.

27. Quoted in Goldfield and Lane, eds., *Enduring Ghetto,* p. 226.

28. Jesse Jackson, CBS News, *60 Minutes,* December 4, 1977.

29. Quoted in Goldfield and Lane, eds., *Enduring Ghetto,* p. 11.

30. Quoted in *ibid.,* p. 228.

12.
Urban Economy:
Technology and Efficiency

Economic and technological forces were as significant in the development
of urban America since 1920 as they are complex and difficult to explain
precisely. Furthermore, they are very closely related: technological capability has tremendous impact on the size and character of markets and on the
costs of labor and production. But the consequences of these forces are as
obvious in the modern city as they are anywhere else.

Bigger Is Better:
Cities in the National Economy

The corporation emerged in the late nineteenth century as a vehicle for
consolidating huge capital resources and a variety of related economic
activities—usually within the same industry—under a single overall authority, to control supply, price, distribution, and competition. The trend toward concentrated economic power became even more pronounced after
1920, through the formation of larger holding companies and corporate
mergers. Federal and state regulations of business and industry were extended during and after the 1930s, but they did not impede the movement
toward bigness and major corporate dominance of the national economy.
After World War II, fewer corporations controlled more of the nation's
total wealth and productivity, and new variants of economic consolidation
appeared.

A logical extension of the corporate framework was the *conglomerate,* composed of numerous enterprises in a variety of areas—ranging, for example, from textiles to spark plugs to medical instruments. A number of traditional corporations also began branching out by acquiring and investing in other industries. Finally, corporate enterprise led to the creation of the *multinational corporation,* the ultimate in power and scope, conducting operations in many countries, shifting capital reserves to achieve the best tax advantage, extracting raw materials from one area, processing them with cheap labor in another, and selling them in a world market. The largest multinational corporations, especially in the energy field, came to resemble sovereign states more than companies. They are among the largest economic entities in the world today.

Corporate giants altered the skylines of the largest cities with their headquarters buildings; provided a rich lode for urban banks, investment companies, tax lawyers, advertising agencies, communications media, and consulting firms; and created unprecedented networks of interurban communication by shifting their employees from one area to another. Their powers and interests extended well beyond the local area and even into other countries, and their direct or indirect participation in local, state, and national politics was sometimes massive. In short, the corporate giants of the late twentieth century exercised far-flung influence on American urban life, affecting areas from working conditions to tax rates, from factory locations to major construction projects. When allied with major city banks, some corporations had more authority over the shape and health of the metropolis—through their residential investment, the use of their extensive land holdings, and the relocation of their plants and facilities—than any local elected public body.

Cities were also affected as the character of the national economy shifted from heavy industry (steel, automobiles) to light, high-technology industries (electronics, computers, chemicals), consumer-goods manufacturing (appliances, household furnishings, sports equipment, personal products), and professional and personal services (medicine, insurance, travel bureaus, hotels). The newer industries were often less labor intensive (that is, they employed fewer workers) and were frequently spatially decentralized, with branch offices in many cities across the country. This pattern encouraged the growth of cities that had formerly been outside the economic mainstream—Houston, Atlanta, Denver, and Los Angeles. The new economic trends supported the continuing regionalization of the national economy.

The nation's industrial core included the northeastern states and most of the Midwest, and through transcontinental rail links began to serve an economic hinterland that included the entire country in the early twentieth century. Cities in this hinterland—especially in the South and Southwest—were, however, usually subordinate to the major manufacturing centers, processing raw materials for northern urban industries and relying on northern industries and banks for a good deal of local investment.

This pattern continued into the twentieth century, though by the 1920s the hinterland had begun to develop and become less dependent on the urban North. The South gained new white residents, though rising losses of rural blacks to the urban North blunted overall regional population growth—but southern cities were growing rapidly. In the West, population increased significantly, especially in the cities.

The Great Depression of the 1930s strained the national economy, and all cities felt its effects. But the damage was especially severe in the major industrial centers. Labor-intensive industries like steel and automobiles were stricken, and thousands of workers had to be cut back or laid off. This was as true in Birmingham, Alabama—the "hardest hit city in the nation"[1]—as it was in Pittsburgh, Pennsylvania. Smaller cities that were oriented to commerce or agriculture were affected too, but not as severely. These cities had been, perhaps, less well-off to begin with. (An agricultural depression had existed, after all, through much of the 1920s.) However, they were also less industrially developed and thus less susceptible to the consequences of massive capitalist disaster. State capitals like Austin, Texas, for example, were quite well off by comparison with Chicago or Philadelphia, and some cities in or near the Texas oil fields paradoxically experienced something of a boom during the 1930s. Norfolk, Virginia, had its soup lines too, but these did not appear until they were common sights in the urban North.

The mobilization for World War II brought the country out of the depression. Local economies that were able to survive under New Deal assistance programs often thrived with the wartime market demands created by the federal government. Major industrial centers revived with the receipt of large orders for war material and equipment. Other cities benefited from the location of new defense installations, port facilities, and military camps. Though the most dramatic recoveries occurred in those cities that had been hardest hit by the depression (mainly, in the industrial belt), a number of towns in the South and West received their first military installations and defense industries, or found existing facilities expanded significantly, in a trend that prefigured some very dramatic regional economic shifts in the postwar period.

Millions of returning GIs led a new resurgence of consumer demand, pent-up by economic depression and wartime rationing. New families wanted new houses, new cars, better jobs, and more education. While many New Deal programs had been phased out just before or during the war, others continued as an accepted part of American life, providing federal regulation and assistance—and indirect government subsidy—in a variety of areas, housing, transportation, and urban redevelopment among them. Even during the administrations of President Dwight D. Eisenhower during the 1950s, when conservative Republicans were in power in Washington, massive federal outlays continued and increased in national defense sectors. The Korean conflict and the intensifying Cold War with the Soviet Union kept millions of dollars pouring into armaments industries and related businesses, with considerable impact upon individual cities and regional urban economic patterns.

By the 1950s a process of *regional succession* in the national economy had become apparent, and it accelerated in the 1970s. The South, Southwest, and Far West—regions that had previously served as a vast economic hinterland of the industrial core, providing the major northeastern and midwestern cities with raw materials, labor, and new markets—increasingly began to siphon people, resources, and economic capacity away from these older, and now declining, regions. The process was by no means uniform. Some northern cities continued to grow, especially in their suburban areas, and the major financial and industrial centers generally maintained their dominance. But a number of observers pointed to the dramatic growth and development of the "southern rim" or Sunbelt—a region extending roughly from Virginia down through the Southeast and Southwest and out to southern California. (See Figure 12.1.)

Figure 12.1   The Sunbelt
This is one of the more common conceptions of the Sunbelt. Despite the region's general prosperity, the conception conceals many variations within it.

Technology supported both the regionalization of the national economy and the vitality of the fringe. The twentieth-century city is virtually inconceivable without electricity, the telephone, the automobile, and the airplane. Each of these innovations expanded urban possibilities and, taken together, constitute the technological framework for the vital fringe. They opened up new industries, created jobs, generated consumer demand, and caused significant shifts in the nation's economic life and in the form of its cities. Even the indirect consequences of these technologies amounted to economic growth measured in the billions of dollars.

But technology did not create the vital fringe. It provided new and significant *means* for the implementation of patterns that had already existed in American culture—greater individual mobility, economic expansion, and spatial decentralization. It was not so much technology as the uses to which technology was put that reshaped the American city. And yet once certain technological systems became dominant, they tended to limit individual choices as well as to expand them. The American city was increasingly shaped so that automobiles and telephones and electrical power were essential to participation in urban society, for example. And industries that were unable or unwilling to adopt certain technologies often failed. The important point is that technology was shaped by existing trends and by human aspirations and needs, while at the same time it shaped those trends and needs in new directions.

National Urban Technology

Electricity was *the* major new power source of the late nineteenth century, with applications in the cities ranging from running elevators to lighting streets and powering industrial machinery. The impact of electricity on transportation alone—through streetcars—was far-reaching. Electricity also quickly began to replace kerosene and, to a lesser extent, natural gas as a dominant residential energy source, and it was a boon to suburbs and rural areas. It also made possible a number of other innovations, like the telephone, the radio, and television. It was even considered seriously as a fuel for motor vehicles until the internal combustion engine proved to be more convenient.

Electrification of the nation's cities was well under way by the turn of the century. A maze of overhead wires stretched along tall poles was a familiar sight in the downtown sections and became a principal target for those who wished to beautify urban America. During the 1910s and 1920s, the major effort was expended on extending electrification farther into the countryside—especially to the expanding suburbs—and on devising a coordinated system of electrical-power distribution to serve metropolitan complexes. Both the streetcar and the provision of residential power opened new land on the urban outskirts for development, creating new markets in real estate and construction. As the century progressed, homes provided with electricity were also immediate candidates for radios and televisions and a growing array of other electrical appliances that constituted one of the most rapidly growing and persistent consumer-goods industries in the country.

Electrical engineers anticipated increasing demands for power, and during the 1920s a number of schemes were on the drawing boards for gigantic systems of power connections, concentrated especially along the eastern seaboard and in the industrial belt. In periods of peak demand, sharing of electricity among various urban markets helped stave off temporary shortages and the "brownouts" and "blackouts" that threatened major urban regions after World War II. Perhaps the major overall impact of electricity on urban America was the availability of a cheap and plentiful power source that stimulated new industries and commerce, better communications, and spatial decentralization.

After the mid-twentieth century the proliferation of household appliances and electrical gadgets—and particularly home and office air conditioning—created unprecedented demands for electrical power, just as the fuels (like petroleum) used to generate electricity were becoming more scarce and costly. Utility companies in the largest metropolitan areas were often forced to cut back during peak summer hours, and natural disasters and unanticipated failures in the distribution system led to dramatic blackouts. After decades of greater and greater usage of electrical power, and the resources used to generate it, urban America had become dependent. Cities that had developed on the premise of cheap, plentiful energy were slow to adjust. In fact, the options for adjustment were quite limited without fundamental changes in the city itself. It is difficult to imagine, for example, Houston without air conditioning or Los Angeles without automobiles.

Alexander Graham Bell's invention of the telephone in 1876 led to a revolution in communications that had significant implications for the twentieth-century city. Still something of a novelty in the 1890s, telephones contributed substantially to the efficiency of the great urban skyscrapers that multiplied vertical distances between workers and activities. Steady improvement in the device and reductions in its basic costs made telephones more of a necessity than a convenience. Better communications, like improved transportation, facilitated decentralized commercial activities and new suburban development, and spread the social and cultural influence of the city into the countryside.

By the 1970s telephone lines and microwave transmission paths were used for a huge variety of communications. An array of new devices enable telephone circuits to carry illustrations, photographs, and other visual material over long distances, and to link remote terminals with central computer facilities. Satellite-communications technology permits instantaneous international transmissions, and holds possibilities for a variety of new applications. The present phone system, when coupled with television consoles, fulfills a dream of many futurists, who predicted that sophisticated electronic communications would someday make concentrations of people—perhaps even cities as we know them—obsolete and unnecessary. Whether this comes to pass or not, the telephone makes it less essential for the day-to-day person-to-person contact that vitalized the city before the twentieth century.

Radio and television are the other major communications systems that have profoundly influenced American culture and have helped to produce an urban society, while at the same time reducing the need for one of the city's major attributes—a location to facilitate the exchange of ideas and information. The radio had its heyday between the 1920s and the 1950s. By the mid-twenties, the inexpensive crystal set was a constant companion of many children, and the larger radio console was a fixture in many living rooms. The early music and talk shows were followed by phonograph recordings, situation comedies, dramatic presentations, and even "live" broadcasts of great orchestras from cultural emporia like Boston and New York. By 1924 even political conventions were radio fare. The radio was a major step toward the "mass-media" culture of the late twentieth century, transmitting norms, styles, and tastes to a national audience. It was, and remains, a basic component of the instantaneous communications network that blankets the nation and indeed much of the world. Television, developed experimentally in the early years of the century, became a mass phenomenon in the 1950s. Soon the TV had replaced the radio as the main home-entertainment medium. Television involved more than a simple extension of the possibilities of radio. We are still, in fact, discovering ways in which everything from voting habits to child behavior is influenced by television and TV programming.

The large corporation in the large city dominated the new broadcasting industry. New York, as the nation's communications center for more than a century, became the logical headquarters of national radio and television networks. The major business and industrial corporations were also nearby, providing advertising dollars in exchange for the dissemination of their commercial messages throughout the country. Network headquarters in New York, and to a lesser extent in Los Angeles, determined both the programming and the advertising their affiliates in other cities would receive. Only in 1976 did network affiliates achieve some independence in program selection. The broadcasting industry had established its own urban hierarchy, which included adjacent rural areas as well. It has become, probably, one of the nation's major urbanizing forces.

While messages traveled with facility over lines and airwaves, the increasing regionalization of the economy required more travel by corporation personnel. There was still a great deal of business to be done by face-to-face encounter. The airplane facilitated the trend toward corporate regionalization. It was the railroad of the twentieth century in terms of economic and spatial impact. Most major and minor cities had some sort of airstrip by the end of the 1920s, and air-mail service was inaugurated during that decade between most major cities. Chambers of commerce saw, even at this early date, some new possibilities for business and trade, and usually promoted the further development of air-travel facilities. After World War II, and many improvements in aircraft design and equipment, the airplane became a primary common carrier of both passengers and freight. Travel times between major cities were cut dramatically, enabling businessmen virtually to commute to far-flung ventures and branch offices. In the 1960s and 1970s the private-plane market boomed, to the point that private air traffic had to be separated from heavier commercial traffic.

The aircraft industry was a significant source of jobs for skilled and semiskilled workers, and it brought millions of private and federal dollars into areas with large aircraft production plants. Some cities, in fact, became as dependent on this new industry as Pittsburgh was upon steel; Seattle, for example, where the Boeing Company has its headquarters, is dependent on the aircraft industry. And virtually every city, large and small, contained one or more airport facilities—facilities that demanded large land areas and, very often, the active involvement of local and state governments in their construction and maintenance. In the 1940s and 1950s airports tended to be located fairly close to the urban core. But with larger aircraft, more passengers, and a huge increase in the number of flights, the need for additional land quickly became apparent. Newer airports were located generally farther and farther into the urban fringe. The John F. Kennedy and John Foster Dulles international airports, serving New York and Washington, D.C., respectively, were built many miles from the city center, though they soon became surrounded by residential areas. The newest terminals, like the one in Kansas City, are located in virtually rural locations, with not a skyscraper in sight. The ultimate modern airport, in terms of size and location, is set midway between Dallas and Fort Worth, Texas, in a territory larger than Manhattan Island, linked to two major cities by a limited-access freeway.

The Texas-sized airport is an interesting case of spatial overkill. Its amorphous sprawl is exceeded only by its ugliness, certainly in contrast with two other major airports, the graceful Dulles and the rustic Kansas City. It is not a pedestrian airport: One is totally dependent on motor transport, and many a passenger has wished for an automobile in which to negotiate the airport's vast interior space to make a connection. Airlines dislike the place, because the spaced-out construction increases personnel costs. The airport's greatest impact has been in generating a land bonanza in the area, with everything from fast-food emporiums to luxury apartment houses springing up from the farm fields. It has accelerated the decentralizing tendency of the metropolitan area, just as the old railroad depots were a centralizing influence. The airport is an appropriate symbol for no town.

The similarity between the airplane and the railroad goes further than their spatial impact. Airline travel, like rail travel, requires service between relatively fixed points. The network of airline connections demands large regional airports that serve scores of smaller facilities. The crowded terminals in Atlanta and Chicago, the busiest in the United States, handling hundreds of flights daily, are reminiscent of the surging crowds in turn-of-the-century Grand Central Station. And such large facilities, even if remotely located within the vital fringe, often wrench the urban physical and social fabric. New airports and airport extensions require the displacement of hundreds of households and beset remaining communities with noise and dropping property values. Perhaps the superb irony of modern transportation is that the crush of ground traffic around the major airports not only gluts nearby neighborhoods, but also often entails a journey to the airport that takes more time than the plane trip to a distant city.

No transportation form, however, can match the impact of the automobile, especially in its effect on urban life. The gasoline-powered motor vehicle was invented in Europe, but it struck such a responsive chord among Americans that the United States became far and away the leading car culture in the world. The first successful American auto was probably built by Charles E. and J. Frank Duryea of Springfield, Massachusetts, in 1893, during a decade marked by the first primitive car races and a proliferation of vehicle manufacturers. By the turn of the century some 8,000 motorcars were registered throughout the country.

The major hindrance to the automobile's popularity in the early years of its development was its cost, which was simply too high for the great majority of people. In 1908 Henry Ford introduced his Model T, a car designed for the assembly line and the "common man." The Model T was by no means fancy, and it came in only one color, basic black; but it was within the financial means of the average family. As a result of mass-production techniques, the Model T runabout sold for $345 in 1916—a year in which almost 735,000 units were produced. By May 1927, over 15 million "Tin Lizzys" had rolled off the assembly lines, and the price had dropped to $290.

By 1910 there were almost 469,000 automobiles in America. Ten years later there were more than 8 million. During the 1920s automobile ownership became a mass movement, as scores of new models appeared and customers (and dealers) could buy on credit. Within a single generation, the motor vehicle had advanced from the curiosity of a few begoggled enthusiasts to a common household item. Auto registrations exceeded 27 million in 1930—about one car for every five people in the country—and continued to increase during the depression. When the Soviet Union pirated the 1940 film *Grapes of Wrath,* based on John Steinbeck's poignant portrait of the migration of Oklahoma dust bowlers to California, they advertised it as the decline of capitalism. Russian audiences, however, were more impressed by the fact that the Okies, poor as they were, undertook their odyssey in automobiles. The authorities quickly withdrew the film from circulation.

The depression of the 1930s posed the first major test of the auto's persistence. When the depression was over, it was apparent that a new, permanent fixture had been added to American life. Even in the throes of economic disaster, people held onto their cars if it was at all possible. Gasoline rationing and wartime uses of steel blunted auto use and manufacturing during World War II, but in the late 1940s the surge was on again as people returning from the armed forces started new families and moved to the suburbs. Production and sales boomed in the 1950s as model styles changed annually and intensive marketing by the few large firms that now controlled the industry—General Motors, Ford, and Chrysler—and public demand led to two-, three-, and even four-car families. By 1973 annual automobile sales totaled 11.4 million.

The consequences of the automobile's popularity were felt all over America. Motorcars especially appealed to farmers, who had now found a new power tool. (Model Ts, for example, could be converted into tractors and also used as stationary engines to drive other machinery.) Possession of an automobile also offered the farmer a way of lessening rural isolation and getting produce to market. But the auto also had dramatic implications for American cities.

The impact of the motor vehicle alone on the economy was enormous. More than five hundred automobile manufacturing plants of varying sizes existed at the turn of the century, and these had dwindled to a handful by 1950, with the industry concentrated in Michigan, especially in the suburbs of Detroit. But vehicle-assembly plants, parts manufacturers, raw-materials suppliers, and associated businesses were scattered across the nation: few major cities lacked some portion of the automobile industry. Mass production of automobiles not only provided jobs and economic benefits in areas with vehicle plants, but also generated huge demands for raw and processed materials—steel and other metals, wood, canvas, and rubber—that boosted urban economies from Maine to California. Automobile dealers proliferated, adding scores of new retail businesses to local economies. And related businesses, both wholesale and retail, sprang up. Garages, filling stations, repair shops, tire stores, parts establishments, and even "automobile laundries" cropped up all over the city—many of them located along "automobile rows" in and around the urban core.

In some ways, the auto's impact was even more pronounced in cities outside the industrial core. In Atlanta, for example, the number of auto dealers rose from 4 in 1908 to 80 in 1920, and auto-related businesses numbered 236. One estimate, for 1917, put the total Atlanta bank clearings attributable to automobile retailing at $50 million. Measured in building rentals, new construction, and new jobs, the dimensions of the impact became even larger. And Atlanta's Robert W. Woodruff, later chairman of the Coca-Cola Company, got his beginnings in the auto business.

The indirect economic consequences of the motor vehicle were equally impressive and far-reaching. Roadhouses, highway campgrounds, and the earliest "auto hotels" depended largely on the motor vehicle trade. Perhaps even more important, the new territory that the automobile opened for development stimulated real-estate sales, construction and insurance businesses, and led to new public outlays for utilities, streets, and other facilities. All auto businesses were hit hard by the depression, but the post–World War II revival was dramatic, to the point that the auto industry drove the entire national economy. In 1970 auto businesses accounted for more than a tenth of the nation's Gross National Product, and one of every six American workers was connected in some way with the industry. The motor vehicle brought bad times to some businesses—harness makers, stables, and carriage shops—but the overall result was a tremendous boost to the national economy and to the economies of cities.

The motor vehicle became the chief competitor of urban mass-transit systems, especially in smaller cities that did not have elaborate streetcar networks in the 1920s. Nationally, the peak of streetcar patronage was reached in the early 1920s and, except for a few years during World War II, declined consistently thereafter. New York City now accounts for about 40 percent of all mass-transit passengers in the entire nation. The auto was not solely to blame for this shift. Streetcar companies were usually privately owned and frequently overcapitalized, badly managed, and overextended. The economic pressures of the 1930s would have brought many of them to ruin in any case. But the auto doubtless accelerated the trend during the twenties, and provided a ready alternative to streetcar service when the companies began to falter.

Suburbanization did not originate with the automobile. The electric streetcar provided the first major momentum for peripheral urban development. But the auto gradually added a new dimension: *lateral mobility*, as contrasted with radial mobility. The auto had the capacity to move wherever decent roads existed and often well beyond or between the fixed paths of streetcar transit. The full potential of the motor vehicle could be realized, then, only with good roads and highways. A national network of federal highways was under construction during the 1920s, and a number of improvements were made in local streets; but the years after World War II ushered in the building of major circumferential highways that circled large cities, opening up new land and far-flung industrial sites and residential subdivisions. The interstate highway system, approved by Congress in 1956, ensured a principal national transportation network oriented to the motor vehicle, cutting travel times between cities, creating new outlying land-use possibilities, redirecting patterns of local growth, and providing peripheral industries with viable alternatives to railroad service.

The consequences of the automobile's popularity for social patterns and lifestyles have also been significant, though less easily measured. In the 1920s the motor vehicle seemed to some a license for immoral behavior, drawing families away from church and out into the country on Sunday drives, and young couples into the rumble seat on unchaperoned dates. Along with the motion picture, the motorcar was an invitation to recreation outside the home and fit nicely into the world of flappers and hip flasks. And the auto had a reputation for fast getaways well beyond Bonnie and Clyde, especially since many police forces in the early twenties were equipped mainly with bicycles.

Many of these images of the motor vehicle persisted into the 1950s and

1960s, though by then concern had shifted to other things—the high auto accident and death toll and the threat of environmental pollution, for example. Ironically, the motor vehicle had been welcomed in the early twentieth century because it was quite *un*polluting, when compared with the horse. Cities were suddenly called upon to provide acres of new parking space and to widen and extend downtown streets, but they were relieved of the burden of streetcleaning after animal horsepower. Though accident rates actually declined relative to numbers of auto trips, the increase in the number of trips brought higher and higher total death tolls on streets and highways, reaching levels associated more with wartime than with domestic travel.

Increasing reliance on auto travel led to the development of new lifestyles, symbolized by the two-car garage, limited-access highways, and drive-in facilities of all descriptions—banks, restaurants, movies, and even mortuaries. Just take a look at any peripheral strip development around a city today, and you will observe how dependent it is on the automobile. The signs and lights blink out drive-in fast food, drive-in banks, auto dealerships, service stations, a car wash, and eventually, a shopping center. A repeat of the Arab oil embargo of 1973 would create many more problems than merely disgruntled drivers.

The phenomenon of neighbors who hardly knew one another but maintained far-flung contacts with acquaintances throughout the city was attributable in part to the ease of mobility afforded by the car. Various auto models presumably signaled the image the owner wished to create, and the automobile became a symbol of everything from political opinions to corporate status, upward mobility, and sex appeal. New gadgets like the citizens' band radio and luxury interiors—and commuting times in large cities of up to three hours a day—rendered the automobile literally a home away from home.

The American romance with the car was not, however, entirely blind. The motor vehicle appealed to Americans because it enabled them to do things they wanted to do. Mobility, always prized in American culture, now had new dimensions, and as the price of cars dropped, a measure of equality entered in as well. Independence from fixed schedules was a major advantage of the auto over mass transit. All evidence suggests in the 1970s that Americans can be weaned away from their automobiles only at the cost of considerable inconvenience and great expense. And, like other technological innovations, the vehicle that opened up new choices in the beginning has now become a necessity.

The automobile was a highly standardizing force, affecting all American cities at about the same time in very similar ways. But its impact varied somewhat from city to city, simply because all cities were not alike and they had been in various stages of growth at the time of the appearance of the automobile. Older, established urban areas like New York, Boston, Pittsburgh, and Chicago maintained much of their previous form—along dense traffic corridors initially etched by streetcar lines. But new, smaller cities—like Los Angeles, Atlanta, and Dallas—experienced their greatest growth rates during the auto era of the 1920s and after. Their configurations were not as dense, and reliance on the car and truck for transportation led to a more even distribution of population over a greater area. Even older cities felt the auto's impact: Route 128 in Boston, for example, was a principal circumferential road that pulled businesses and residential communities out to the urban rim. But younger cities were literally molded according to the dictates of the motor vehicle. By the 1950s, in fact, many of them were so dispersed that fixed rail transit was no longer a realistic transportation alternative. "No town" was "auto town."

Regardless of city age or size, the automobile enhanced the trend toward decentralization. Like the streetcar before it, the auto facilitated the great migration to the suburbs. The suburban realm is a world of scattered, low- to medium-density settlement that not only fits in well with the automobile, but also demands it. But the suburb is much more than a creature of transportation technology. It has come to characterize the American lifestyle. Metropolitan America is now, in fact, primarily suburban America, with central cities containing less than half the country's urban population. Suburbs now contain 13 million more people than the central cities they surround.

The Suburban Migration: Searching
for a Lost Eden Through a Windshield

Growth in the suburbs—defined as places within metropolitan areas located outside the limits of the central cities—has been associated particularly with population losses after midcentury in the major cities of the Northeast and Midwest. (See Table 12.1.) Between 1950 and 1970 the cities of New York and Chicago lost population, while their suburban rings grew, respectively, by 117 and 195 percent. Detroit's population fell by almost 20 percent, and its suburbs expanded by 206 percent. This trend was also evident in Boston, Washington, Cleveland, St. Louis, Minneapolis, Pittsburgh, Baltimore, and a number of other cities. Some central cities continued to add population, though this was often due to continued annexations in the South and West. (See Figure 12.2.) The growth of suburban rings was, however, in all cases greater than that of the cities they

Table 12.1   Central-City-Area Population as a Proportion of Total SMSA
Population, 1900, 1930, 1960, 1970, 1973 (1.00 equals total SMSA population)

Region and SMSA	1900	1930	1960	1970	1973
East					
Bridgeport	0.80	0.69	0.46	0.40	0.38
Hartford	0.52	0.52	0.29	0.23	0.22
Washington, D.C.	0.67	0.68	0.36	0.26	0.24
Baltimore	0.70	0.75	0.52	0.43	0.41
Boston	0.42	0.36	0.26	0.23	0.22
Springfield	0.62	0.66	0.58	0.52	0.51
Worcester	0.65	0.71	0.56	0.51	0.49
Jersey City	0.53	0.45	0.45	0.42	0.42
Newark	0.47	0.35	0.23	0.20	0.19
Paterson	0.59	0.37	0.23	0.20	0.20
Albany	0.47	0.56	0.42	0.35	0.33
Buffalo	0.69	0.62	0.40	0.34	0.31
New York	0.90	0.86	0.72	0.68	0.67
Rochester	0.48	0.60	0.43	0.33	0.31
Syracuse	0.38	0.52	0.38	0.30	0.28
Philadelphia	0.68	0.62	0.46	0.40	0.38
Pittsburgh	0.41	0.33	0.25	0.21	0.20
Providence	0.57	0.48	0.43	0.37	0.35
Mean	0.59	0.56	0.41	0.36	0.34
Standard deviation	0.14	0.15	0.13	0.13	0.12
Midwest					
Chicago	0.81	0.75	0.57	0.50	0.45
Fort Wayne	0.58	0.78	0.69	0.63	0.64
Gary	0.38	0.98	0.60	0.52	0.51
Indianapolis	0.47	0.63	0.51	0.67	0.64
Des Moines	0.75	0.82	0.78	0.70	0.67
Wichita	0.37	0.64	0.66	0.71	0.69
Detroit	0.66	0.72	0.44	0.35	0.33
Flint	0.18	0.65	0.47	0.38	0.35
Grand Rapids	0.51	0.57	0.38	0.36	0.34
Minneapolis	0.79	0.83	0.53	0.41	0.36
Kansas City	0.47	0.57	0.43	0.40	0.38
St. Louis	0.67	0.57	0.35	0.26	0.23
Omaha	0.50	0.68	0.65	0.64	0.64
Akron	0.43	0.65	0.47	0.40	0.38
Cincinnati	0.52	0.53	0.39	0.32	0.30
Cleveland	0.76	0.69	0.45	0.36	0.33
Columbus	0.57	0.70	0.62	0.58	0.57
Dayton	0.37	0.52	0.36	0.28	0.25
Toledo	0.55	0.64	0.50	0.55	0.53
Youngstown	0.45	0.58	0.44	0.37	0.35
Madison	0.27	0.51	0.57	0.59	0.56
Milwaukee	0.70	0.70	0.57	0.51	0.48
Mean	0.53	0.67	0.52	0.48	0.45
Standard deviation	0.17	0.11	0.11	0.13	0.14
South					
Birmingham	0.21	0.50	0.47	0.40	0.39
Mobile	0.50	0.46	0.53	0.50	0.48
Jacksonville	0.71	0.83	0.44	1.00	1.00

Table 12.1 (*Continued*)

Region and SMSA	1900	1930	1960	1970	1973
South (*continued*)					
Miami	0.80	0.77	0.31	0.26	0.25
Tampa	0.33	0.65	0.59	0.48	0.43
Atlanta	0.45	0.58	0.47	0.35	0.30
Columbus	0.28	0.45	0.53	0.64	0.72
Louisville	0.69	0.73	0.53	0.43	0.39
Baton Rouge	0.35	0.45	0.66	0.58	0.94
New Orleans	0.89	0.87	0.69	0.56	0.52
Shreveport	0.23	0.50	0.58	0.61	0.60
Jackson	0.10	0.45	0.65	0.59	0.59
Charlotte	0.32	0.64	0.63	0.58	0.65
Oklahoma City	0.17	0.67	0.63	0.57	0.54
Tulsa	—	0.47	0.62	0.69	0.68
Knoxville	0.29	0.50	0.30	0.43	0.43
Memphis	0.60	0.74	0.73	0.80	0.83
Nashville	0.65	0.69	0.36	0.82	0.76
Austin	0.46	0.67	0.88	0.85	0.84
Corpus Christi	0.38	0.36	0.63	0.71	0.71
Dallas	0.16	0.51	0.60	0.54	0.50
El Paso	0.64	0.77	0.88	0.89	0.90
Fort Worth	0.31	0.70	0.62	0.51	0.47
Houston	0.37	0.63	0.66	0.62	0.60
San Antonio	0.58	0.72	0.82	0.75	0.81
Norfolk	0.50	0.76	0.72	0.61	0.56
Richmond	0.55	0.71	0.50	0.48	0.44
Mean	0.43	0.62	0.59	0.60	0.61
Standard deviation	0.22	0.13	0.14	0.17	0.19
West					
Phoenix	0.28	0.31	0.66	0.60	0.56
Tucson	0.88	0.58	0.80	0.74	0.72
Anaheim	0.30	0.34	0.40	0.31	0.29
Fresno	0.32	0.36	0.36	0.40	0.39
Los Angeles	0.61	0.62	0.46	0.45	0.44
Sacramento	0.38	0.49	0.30	0.31	0.30
San Bernardino	0.32	0.37	0.27	0.26	0.27
San Diego	0.51	0.70	0.55	0.51	0.51
San Francisco	0.78	0.70	0.41	0.34	0.32
San Jose	0.36	0.40	0.31	0.41	0.45
Denver	0.72	0.74	0.53	0.41	0.37
Honolulu	0.67	0.67	0.58	0.51	0.48
Albuquerque	0.21	0.58	0.76	0.77	0.77
Portland	0.60	0.66	0.45	0.37	0.35
Salt Lake City	0.62	0.67	0.42	0.31	0.28
Seattle	0.60	0.67	0.50	0.41	0.39
Spokane	0.63	0.76	0.65	0.59	0.57
Tacoma	0.67	0.65	0.45	0.37	0.38
Mean	0.53	0.57	0.49	0.45	0.44
Standard deviation	0.19	0.15	0.15	0.14	0.14
Total mean	0.51	0.61	0.51	0.49	0.47
Standard deviation	0.19	0.14	0.15	0.17	0.18

Source: Advisory Commission on Intergovernmental Relations, *Trends in Metropolitan America* (Washington, D.C., 1977).

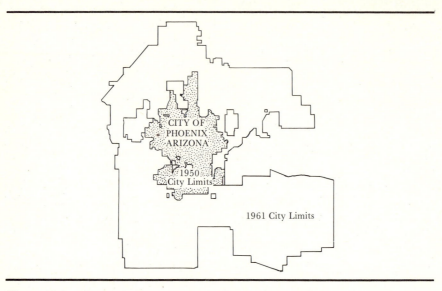

Figure 12.2   Phoenix and Her Annexation Empire, 1961

After 1950, Sunbelt cities experienced growth primarily through annexation, an option not open to older cities in other regions. (From *Sick Cities* by Milton Gordon. © 1963, Macmillan Publishing Company, Inc.)

surrounded. Los Angeles's population rose by about 43 percent in the two decades after midcentury, but its suburbs grew by more than 141 percent and contained two million more people than the central city in 1970. The two major Texas cities—Dallas and Houston—had central-city growth rates of 94 and 107 percent, respectively, but suburban growth rates of 370 and 330 percent. And not only were most urban dwellers found in the vital fringe: By 1970 the majority of urban jobs were also located outside central cities.

Much of the impetus for suburbanization came from the desire and the ability of the urban middle and upper class to live in less crowded neighborhoods. After 1920 a more-or-less typical pattern was evident: Older residential areas near the city core were abandoned by affluent citizens for new streetcar and auto suburbs, and their houses passed into the hands of middle- or working-class people, who in turn left them to less well-to-do groups. Urban sociologists described this in the 1920s as a pattern of concentric rings, with the wealthiest groups living farthest away from the city center in exclusive suburban enclaves, middle- and working-class groups inhabiting more modest residential areas closer to downtown, and the lowest-income groups huddled in the dense and often deteriorating neighborhoods of the urban core. As housing was often passed down to successively lower-income populations, it was usually converted for financial reasons from single-family to multifamily use and frequently allowed to deteriorate by speculative landlords who held the property for profit and in hopes that it would one day be sold at a higher price for commercial or industrial use. As cities continued to expand, especially in the automobile era, the residential-succession process saw affluent groups moving into ever more distant settlements and middle-income citizens entering the formerly exclusive suburbs closer in to the central city.

This process worked to the advantage of upper-income groups, who could benefit from lower land costs on the periphery and afford the greater transportation costs involved, and also for many middle-income citizens who had at least enough resources to buy homes in decent neighborhoods. A number of the descendents of the foreign immigrants of the late nineteenth and early twentieth centuries also found their way into the suburbs, often leaving behind their ethnic associations. But low-income groups were successively exploited by this process. They were usually forced to rely on rental dwellings, with the rent set at the highest rate the market would bear. Even when they could afford to buy their own homes, however, they often received less housing for their money than more affluent groups and found it difficult to keep these dwellings in repair. As suburbanization proceeded, in fact, the gap between rich and poor—not only in income but in quality of life—actually grew greater. And blacks were universally met with barriers of intense racial prejudice, in addition to those of economics. Their suburban migration has been limited until recently, and their movement even into nearby middle- or working-class white neighborhoods has often been violently resisted.

New settlements in the relatively open spaces on the urban fringe lowered the overall population density, even in downtown sections that were increasingly converted to commercial uses. Income and educational levels of the population tended to rise, as levels of density fell with distance from the city center. The urban population became increasingly segregated by race, income, land-use patterns, housing types, and lifestyle. The day of the cluster and the market place, with their cluttered mixture of activities and inhabitants, was over.

Suburbs came in a variety of shapes, sizes, and forms. The bedroom subdivisions of the upper middle class, where endless arrays of split-level houses line repetitive cul-de-sacs and where station wagons, children, daily trips to and from the commuter station, and weekend battles with creeping crabgrass were a way of life, became a stereotype of the 1950s. Much of this image was plainly inaccurate, fashioned by critics of the apparent conformity of modern American life. The main point is that suburbs were not all alike. They ranged from Cambridge, Massachusetts (older than most American cities), through heavily industrialized Hoboken in New Jersey, to fashionable Shaker Heights in Ohio, Larchmont in New York, and Beverly Hills in California. While some suburbs were populated predominantly by blacks, most were lily-white, or close to it. Some—like Pullman in Illinois and Fairfield in Alabama—had arisen as small towns or industrial centers that only later found themselves close to the city's edge. Others were planned as exclusive enclaves, with houses set upon estate-sized lots and all but small, acceptable businesses prohibited entirely.

The most significant years of suburbanization occurred in the two decades following World War II. A variety of factors combined to direct migration to the suburbs after 1945. First, there were the conditions in the cities: the rising taxes, declining services, increasing numbers of minorities, and a declining quality of life. Second, the suburbs appeared to offer everything the cities were coming to lack: space, racial and economic homogeneity, home ownership, low taxes, and quality education. It was like finding Eden on a quarter-acre plot.

The characteristics of the migrants themselves were a second factor favoring the suburbs. They were in their twenties, married, and with young children. They thought in terms of the future. Who would quarrel with that, considering what the past had been? The suburb was their vision of the future because it was clean and new and did not remind them of their urban past—the past of depression and war. Above all, their vision of the future included a prominent place for their children. "For the sake of the children" was an often-repeated justification for the move out to the suburbs. The children's education, their recreation, their safety—these were perhaps the greatest attractions of the suburbs.

The federal government, in its effort to maintain wartime prosperity in the postwar era, subsidized the migration by enabling home buyers to qualify for VA or FHA mortgage loans. The great advantage over previous methods of home buying was that now, with little or no money down, a young couple could move into their dream house immediately. In the 1950s the Interstate Highway Act provided another suburban boost by facilitating commuting at little cost to suburban residents.

Finally, two of the major economic forces of the twentieth century—advanced technology and corporate consolidation—made suburbia affordable for many people. In the late nineteenth and early twentieth centuries small builders and landholders—like the 9,000 lot owners in suburban Boston—had dominated the suburban market. After World War II the large builder supported by an extensive corporate enterprise came to dominate the home-building market, which was predominantly the subur-

Figure 12.3   Suburban Housing: Mass Production Works on Behalf of the Masses.
(© William A. Garnett)

ban market. In 1949, for example, large firms (those that built more than a hundred houses per year and employed over a hundred people) built 54 percent of all houses in the country. By 1955 that figure stood at 78 percent.

Abraham Levitt and Sons were the Henry Fords of the housing industry and demonstrated the benefits of mass production as applied to building construction. In 1947 Levitt purchased 1,400 acres of Long Island potato farms thirty miles from New York City. Utilizing prefabrication, employing his own work force, manufacturing and supplying his own materials (lumber, for example, came from Levitt's own company and was cut from his own timber with his own equipment to his own specifications), and coordinating work forces and materials with precision, Levitt, by 1948, was producing 35 houses per day and 150 houses per week. (See Figure 12.3.) A new house was completed every fifteen minutes. With the federal government supplying Levitt and other large builders with billions of dollars in credit and insured loans up to 95 percent of the value of the house, Levitt was able to offer his own financing to prospective buyers. His homes sold just about as fast as he could build them.

The houses in several Levittowns in the Northeast sold for $7,990, or more than $1,500 less than the nearest competitor's houses. All of Levitt's houses were small, detached, single-family homes, Cape Cod in style and centrally located on a small lot. It became fashionable to refer to these structures as "ticky-tacky," but they were well-constructed, and variety had never been a characteristic of suburban architecture in any case, whether there were 9,000 builders or just one. A visit to any Levittown today shows neat, tree-lined streets with small but solid houses that have been given some individuality by additions to the original house or by owners' varying the facade. Most important, the Levittowns enabled thousands of blue-collar families to fulfill their dreams of home and land ownership—dreams that previously had been primarily confined to middle- and upper-income groups. For $56 a month, with no down payment, a GI could move into a house equipped with a fireplace, electric range and refrigerator, washer, and even a television—at no extra cost. It was cheaper than renting an apartment in the city, and the federal government made home ownership even more attractive through tax incentives.

The urban economy inevitably followed the urban population. Industries seeking space, better access to transportation (the motor truck), tax advantages, and proximity to a skilled labor pool moved to the fringe. But the most visible economic defection from the city was the suburban shopping center. As suburbs developed, commercial shopping centers followed the outward drift of customers. In the early twentieth century, suburban

Figure 12.4   The Shopping Mall at Levittown, Pennsylvania, 1948
(National Archives)

business growth had often followed the patterns of neighborhood commercial centers, with two or three stores clustered at an intersection. Increasingly, they located along major thoroughfares for streetcars and autos, creating "string streets" of commerce surrounded by residential communities. Eventually, shopping centers—groups of stores within parking lots—emerged, first in Baltimore in 1907 and then in a number of other areas, particularly Los Angeles. A fancy shopping complex in Kansas City's Country Club District presaged a pattern to be followed widely after World War II, when shopping centers cropped up by the hundreds across the land. (See Figure 12.4.) By 1970 it was not unusual for people to live *and* work in the suburbs, commuting from one outlying residential community to another along six- and eight-lane beltways and avoiding the congested central business district entirely except for occasional specialized entertainment or shopping. (The congestion of the downtown area is shown in Figure 12.5.)

The stereotype of suburbia inhabited by men in gray flannel suits and housewives condemned to a life dominated by spoiled children and meaningless garden clubs was an image with some truth; but it was precisely as accurate a picture of American suburbia generally as the aristocratic club rooms of London were typical of all England. The fact is that most urban

Figure 12.5   The Shopping Mall of Downtown Philadelphia, Market and Twelfth
Streets, 1950
The suburban shopping mall shown in the figure on the preceding page offered
most of the variety of consumer goods and none of the headaches of the downtown
retail area. (National Archives)

Americans now live outside central cities. Suburbanites do tend to be
whiter, wealthier, and better educated than dwellers in the central core, but
suburbs are becoming more and more representative of urban America,
and cannot be stereotyped. Many American downtowns contain their "gold
coasts" of posh apartment houses and condominium complexes, and suburbs include the working class and the poor.

The process of suburbanization, in addition to its economic impact, exposed three political realities: first, that public policy can indeed enhance
demographic and economic redistribution; second, that urban government
had failed to cope with the problems of urban society; third, that the
suburban trend had regional implications, though the region itself was
politically fragmented. Politics and public policy had helped to make the
fringe vital.

Notes

1. See Blaine A. Brownell, "Birmingham, Alabama: New South City in the 1920s," *Journal of
Southern History*, 38 (February 1972), 30.

13.
Urban Politics and Public Policy:
With Friends Like These . . .

The political process continued to be dominated in many urban areas by strong political organizations, and in others by highly influential commercial groups. The cumulative impact of the various "reform" movements of the late nineteenth and early twentieth centuries was carried over into the 1920s and subsequent decades, and changes in the composition of the electorate presaged the rising importance of new issues and concerns. While established interest groups remained highly influential in the urban decision-making process, the backdrop of public policy was quite varied and complex.

New Political Technology and Old Results:
The Search for Order

During the 1920s the big-city political machines continued to operate in more-or-less classic fashion, with a solid voter base in immigrant communities. They were less prevalent in the South and West, partly because foreign immigration and industrialization had not touched cities in these regions as deeply. Political organizations resembling the northern big-city model existed in San Francisco, New Orleans, and Memphis, and their power was maintained through getting out the vote and wielding gifts, assistance, and patronage. But they were also influenced by business groups, reflecting the persistent power of the commercial elite in less industrialized areas. The Choctaw organization in New Orleans, for example, boasted a membership roll containing many names from the roster of the Association of Commerce. In smaller towns and cities, prominent citizens from established families—and not "professional politicians"—were likely to hold major political offices and determine local policies.

But the boss and the machine remained highly important and had a remarkable capacity to adjust to new circumstances. As the "reform" movements of the late nineteenth and early twentieth centuries gained momentum and continued, even after a number of setbacks, to challenge traditional political organizations, the bosses attempted to stay in power. In some cases, this meant devastating the reformers at the polls through fraud and even violence. More typically, it meant adopting—at least publicly— some of the reformers' ideas and goals, particularly those that gave more autonomy to local governments. Bosses were not hesitant to advocate effi- ciency and economy, so long as they continued in power. They even launched an occasional campaign against vice and gambling to reassure middle- and upper-class voters. Already, some machine leaders had begun to widen their political base, building beyond the inner-city ethnic blocks to include business people and suburbanites. The boss and the urban machine were, in other words, committed first of all to survival, and they did a remarkable job of it even into the 1930s and 1940s.

The political organization that James Pendergast had fashioned in the West Bottoms and North End of Kansas City in the 1880s and 1890s as- sumed entirely new dimensions in the twentieth century. When James's younger brother Tom assumed control of the organization in 1909, he began to introduce a variety of illegal voting tactics and strong-arm methods, and he extended the organization's influence into middle-class residential areas, established alliances with local Republicans, attracted support from the business community, and achieved political supremacy in all of Kansas City by 1925. Seven years later he became boss of Missouri politics as well, dominating not only the city hall but the governor's man- sion.

New York City's Tammany Hall continued as the nation's most well- known political machine. While its strength still rested on tightly organized neighborhoods and precincts and a finely tuned flow of patronage and favors, Tammany was clearly responding to new conditions in a way that Boss Plunkitt would have found strange in all but method. Under the leadership of Charles Francis Murphy, Tammany brought to national prominence two of the most notable liberal reformers of the twentieth century—Alfred E. Smith and Robert F. Wagner—and supported a variety of measures including the regulation of banking and insurance companies, a strengthening of the tenement house laws, and the public ownership of utilities. Although Tammany maintained its traditional lack of interest in moralistic reforms, it supported woman suffrage, the direct election of U.S. Senators, the direct primary, and "home rule." In addition, it succeeded in expanding state and city services, creating a public employment office, and establishing old-age pensions and a six-day work week.

Robert F. Wagner rose to prominence on the shoulders of Tammany and became a key member of the U.S. Senate during the New Deal era, fashioning a wide variety of progressive legislation, especially in labor and social security. Al Smith, whose boyhood was spent on city streets near the Fulton Fish Market, was elected Governor of New York and carried the Democratic presidential banner in the hard-fought election of 1928. Though he lost to Herbert Hoover, Smith drew the support of many intellectuals, the inner-city ethnic blocs, and labor unions, thus helping to build the highly effective New Deal coalition that swept Franklin D. Roosevelt into office in 1932 and kept him there for three more terms.

New York City slipped away from Tammany's control during the 1930s, however. James J. Walker, the city's flashy Tammany-backed mayor in the late twenties and early thirties, was removed from office in 1933. Jimmy once said that "there comes a time in politics when a man must rise above principle." And that time came often for Jimmy. Fiorello La Guardia, whose Jewish great-grandmother, Italian father, and Episcopal religion enabled just about everybody in New York except the Irish and blacks to identify with him, succeeded Walker on a Fusion-Republican ticket. Flamboyant Fiorello, who read comic strips over the radio during a newspaper strike and fulfilled a boyhood dream by riding with firefighters to fires, was a master of ethnic-bloc politics, having a strong ethnic background himself. A major leader of the big-city liberals, La Guardia maintained close ties with the Roosevelt administrations in Washington. La Guardia built a personal constituency, not a political organization, however, and he had little lasting impact on New York City politics, though Tammany would never again wield the tight-fisted power it had once enjoyed in the nation's largest city.

The huge relief programs of the New Deal seemed certain to undermine the appeal of the urban political machine. Now, city dwellers and other Americans could look to Washington, rather than to the local ward boss, for jobs, unemployment assistance, food in time of need, and old-age benefits. The boss presumably no longer had a monopoly on resources to meet the needs of his constituents. In fact, however, the most highly organized machines thrived on these new federal programs. The sources of assistance may have shifted significantly to Washington, but distribution of these resources frequently remained in the hands of the local political machines. Among other reasons, the national administration was loathe to by-pass, and thus alienate, the very organizations that could be counted on to carry their precincts by large majorities in federal elections.

The Pendergast machine, for example, was actually strengthened by New Deal programs. Tom Pendergast was invariably consulted on political appointments involving Kansas City and Missouri, and his machine dispensed federal largesse, increasing the powers of the ward bosses. The downfall of the Pendergast organization proceeded not from the New Deal, but from the excesses of the machine itself—specifically, a series of prominent election scandals in 1936 that brought to public light the entrenched corruption of one of the most successful and notorious political machines in American history.

After World War II, the traditional urban political machine existed in relatively few cities. The best example of its persistence undoubtedly was the Chicago organization headed, into the 1970s, by Mayor Richard J. Daley. Now that Daley is gone, internal squabbling and unattended urban problems are beginning to erode the machine's grip on Chicago politics. In New York and most other big cities, relatively loose coalitions of interest groups—including some old-style precinct leaders, but also rising bureaucrats and ethnic spokespeople—dominate the scene. The boss and the machine had changed, so much so that many of their basic nineteenth-century features passed away over time. The older ethnic constituencies began to disperse increasingly in the twentieth century, ties with Washington became more important than those with the State House, and mass-media electioneering and political polling forced a new style of politics based on images and catch phrases. The demise of some machines and the transformation of others was also due to increasing pressures from "reform" forces, who objected to the traditional organization's power, its questionable ethical standards, its reliance upon poor and uneducated citizens, and its laxity on moral issues.

Actually, the urban reform movements that reached a sustained pitch in the 1890s and the early twentieth century lost momentum after World War I and seemed buried, at least at the national level, beneath the complacency of the postwar decade. But many reform themes continued into the 1920s, particularly at the local level.

The drive for economy, efficiency, and "proper" methods of urban government continued, and in the 1920s scores of small and medium-sized cities converted to the city-commission and city-manager forms of municipal government. City leaders, especially business leaders, saw the need for centralized administration such as existed in the major corporations but was lacking in the ward-based type of city government. The political implications of spatial segregation were not to their liking. The city-commission form of government, inaugurated by flood-ravaged Galveston, Texas, in 1900 as an emergency experiment, became by the 1920s the choice of local government for more than a hundred communities, most of them small cities. The commission combined both legislative and administrative functions and was elected at large rather than on a ward basis. Ultimately, the commission neither provided a significant increase in efficiency nor proved immune to machine politics, as Boss Ed Crump demonstrated in Memphis.

The city-manager system of municipal government, the other major administrative reform of the early twentieth century, first appeared in the small Shenandoah Valley city of Staunton, Virginia, in 1908. The city manager was a nonpartisan technician charged with administering the city. Usually, the city council would hire the manager, frequently from outside the community. The elected mayor became a ceremonial figure. The watershed for the city-manager idea occurred when a flood-inundated Dayton, Ohio, chose a city manager to organize cleanup and construction in 1910. The success of the city manager in directing mop-up and rebuilding activities inspired numerous smaller cities and some larger ones like Cleveland and Kansas City to adopt the plan. Once again, it was difficult in the larger cities to keep the city manager apart from politics, and the system remains today primarily a small-city phenomenon.

Regardless of the form of local government, ties between government and major economic interests became tighter, and older political machines in the larger cities grew to rely as much on support from big business as they did on voter turnout in order to survive. Demands for additional urban services were incessant, in new subdivisions as well as in older areas previously lacking paved streets, sewerage, and street lighting. Increases in urban scale and complexity and the dimensions of urban problems, along with the new emphasis on trained public servants, created larger and larger municipal bureaucracies. While the delivery of services was generally more "businesslike" and perhaps a good deal less corrupt, the new bureaucracies were in some ways less responsive to individual human problems than the ward boss had been. Accountability to the public was increasingly abstract, and some city agencies—especially police departments—awkwardly attempted to mediate among various racial and income groups increasingly separated in space and socioeconomic status. At a time when urban problems were mounting, urban politics, despite the experiments, was both less able and less willing to attack them.

To compound the difficulty, an old political problem grew worse. Increasingly, municipalities were pitted against state legislatures that curtailed local taxing authority, prevented or discouraged annexation, neglected serious urban ills in the distribution of state funds, and otherwise

meddled in local business. State legislatures—even in the more industrialized North—tended to be dominated by rural interests, and increasingly by rural and suburban coalitions. Legally, cities had always been creatures of state government, deriving their jurisdictions and authority from
state legislatures. A major urban reform of the early twentieth century was
"home rule," whereby legislatures would approve new municipal charters
allowing cities a much greater degree of autonomy over their own affairs.
Even when such charters existed, however, the political power of cities was
generally less at the state level than their populations would warrant,
primarily because rural districts were disproportionately represented in
state assemblies. In Tennessee in 1960, for example, a legislator from a
rural county in the state's House of Representatives represented 3,154
persons. A legislator from an urban area in the state represented 78,000
persons. This meant that a voter in a rural county had twenty-five times as
much influence as a voter in an urban county. In 1962 the Supreme Court
declared in *Baker* vs. *Carr* that federal courts have the power to investigate
legislative apportionments, thus effectively establishing the "one man, one
vote" principle. The U.S. Supreme Court's landmark decision largely
eliminated malapportionment, but by that time a number of cities were
actually losing population, and rural-suburban coalitions were still often
opposed to the wishes and interests of larger municipalities. As one political
observer noted, urban government is of the cities, by the state legislature,
for the suburbs.

The new forms of local administration, the campaign for municipal ownership of utilities, and the fight for home rule were all attempts to order
what had become a complex and an immense urban environment. Indeed,
the ecological theories of urban growth that emerged from the Chicago
sociologists in the 1920s may be viewed as the intellectuals' reassurance that
even amidst this seeming chaos, there was an order, a pattern to urban
growth. It was a pattern that had evolved "naturally." Yet given the passion
of the times for order and efficiency, it was not surprising that a group of
professional experts appeared on the scene to tamper with nature. These
reformers did not seek to channel their desires for stability into the activities of the Kiwanis, the Klan, or Prohibition. They formed a more exclusive and more professional but equally orderly movement called American
city planning. Backed up by their own professional organization, American
city planners ventured into the 1920s, drawing pens in hand, ready to
conquer urban space.

City Planning: The Politics of Space

The development of professional city planning paralleled in many ways the
shifts in the municipal reform movements of the time. The vision of a

healthy, orderly, prosperous city as a result of wide-ranging and far-reaching social change that had inspired many of the settlement house workers, "progressives," and planners around the turn of the century became less clear and forceful in the 1920s. The emphasis changed to one of efficiency, functionalism, and "practical" change (that is, change that could readily be accepted by established social and economic interests). *Professional* planning was thus rooted not in utopian schemes and basic social change but in the more limited spheres of physical design and construction permitted by established groups and acceptable to the urban leadership. Planners generally accepted this role out of a desire to be practically useful and to find a niche for themselves in the existing scheme of things. In the words of the Los Angeles County Regional Planning Commission in 1929:

Planning is an amplification of those fundamental principles which have always been practiced in engineering, namely, the accumulation of data, the reduction to formulae, the application to design, and the accomplishment of predetermined objectives.[1]

There were, of course, exceptions to these general trends. The hope for healthy and pleasing cities remained, even if the planning approach was increasingly limited and piecemeal; and a number of planners still recalled the ambition of Daniel Burnham's call to "make no little plans."[2] And while the majority of planners searched for a proper professional role and more precise techniques, some remained in the broader reform mold. The Regional Planning Association of America (RPAA) advanced ideas in the 1920s about the shape of the urban future that differed from simple linear projections of existing trends. One of the organization's founders, Lewis Mumford, was also its most articulate spokesman. In a number of books and articles—including *Sticks and Stones* (1924) and *The Culture of Cities* (1938)—Mumford advocated the Garden City proposals that Ebenezer Howard had espoused at the turn of the century. Mumford and his RPAA colleagues believed that cities should be repositories of culture and arenas for individual fulfillment, and should be fashioned to human scale. The giant, confused, and polluted cities of the industrial era, congested and demeaning, were affronts to human possibility.

Mumford was quick to recognize and eager to welcome the trends toward urban decentralization. Cities of the future would be regional cities, cast over a wide area, and not the tightly packed warrens of the late nineteenth century. Planning was a key to realizing the potential of these trends—primarily in the intelligent development of new towns limited in size, linked efficiently with other towns through roads and mass transit, and containing industries and work places as well as residences. The regional city of tomorrow would thus be composed of humane and manageable clusters, each providing access to the entire area in addition to uncongested living spaces and jobs close to home. Thus, the delicate social fabric of neighborhoods would be protected in an age of increased urban scale.

Mumford and the RPAA had virtually no influence on the planning movement of the time, and their suggestions have received more serious attention in the 1970s than they did in the 1920s and 1930s. They reflected, among other things, a utopian flavor increasingly out of fashion among planners after 1910 and a clear realization of the many relationships between physical configurations and socioeconomic conditions that had limited relevance for professionals embarked on physical designs that posed no fundamental changes in existing arrangements and institutions. Most American city planners were simply marching to different drummers during the 1920s and 1930s.

The most important innovation of the "professional" planning movement, perhaps, was the so-called *comprehensive plan*, which was designed to take every major urban factor, from transportation to housing and civic art, into account. Scores of comprehensive plans were made for large and medium-sized American cities during the 1920s. In virtually every case the emphasis was on two principal elements—the major street system and zoning. These were priorities for commercial and civic leaders, who dominated the planning movement at the local level, and questions of esthetic design and housing improvement were usually relegated to a few paragraphs if they were included at all.

Major street plans invariably received a great deal of attention. Street planning provided planners with an excellent opportunity to demonstrate their special skills in solving a noncontroversial problem of great concern to urban business leaders. In most American cities, the streets were too narrow for rising loads of automobile traffic. Streets are the blood vessels of the city, many planners kept saying; and local leaders, picking up on their metaphor, perceived street widening, extension, and improvement as vital to the commercial health and growth of the city. Professional planners promised to update urban streets and render them more capable of bearing greater traffic volumes without crumbling under the strain.

Zoning was equally important in comprehensive plans. By 1930 most large and medium-sized communities had adopted zoning statutes, even if they did not have formal planning departments or comprehensive plans. The typical zoning ordinance divided cities into industrial, commercial, and residential areas (usually with subclassifications for single-family and multifamily use). Some ordinances also included restrictions on building heights and regulations for lot sizes, building set-backs, and the width of side yards. Most zoning plans limited high-rise businesses and intensive commercial activity to the downtown section, restricted a variety of other commercial uses to major thoroughfares and some local streets and street corners, and provided for various residential uses in the interior and outlying blocks. Apartments were encouraged closer to the downtown section. Industries were set apart in areas already developed for such uses, often outside the central districts and along the major rail lines. Zoning was used for other purposes too, including racial segregation, and it did not so much create a new spatial configuration for American cities as it gave permanence and legitimacy to existing patterns and trends.

Another important approach adopted by most planners during the period was *regional planning*, which recognized the interdependence of the communities that comprised metropolitan regions. The most elaborate effort in this direction was the *Regional Plan of New York and Its Environs*, initiated in 1921 by the Russell Sage Foundation and some prominent business leaders. Based upon elaborate surveys and recommendations by teams of architects, planners, engineers, sociologists, and other specialists, the plan called for the location of new industries in the region outside of New York City, for residential communities for workers located near the factories, and for business subcenters scattered throughout the area; it also included plans for a regionwide network of trunk highways and interlacing streets. The scope of the New York Regional Plan was indeed impressive, and the detailed recommendations, the varied expertise of the staff and consultants, and the expense (over $1 million) made it a national model of such efforts for years to come. Regional plans were also undertaken in other cities, including Los Angeles and Chicago, and they all reflected considerable sharing of information and of basic approaches. The comprehensive plan was the most typical of the professional efforts made during the early twentieth century, but the regional plan was recognized as the most extensive and ambitious.

Planning made great strides through the 1920s, both in techniques and in developing relationships with local governments, even though it did not achieve a full-fledged professional status or become an influential and regular part of municipal establishments. But many of the contributions of planning during these years were flawed and were not entirely beneficial in their impact on American urban space. For one thing, comprehensive plans were not comprehensive; as we have seen, streets and zoning received most of the attention, while housing and most social issues were ignored, and most proposals in the realm of civic art simply decorated the planning reports. The emphases were not necessarily the choices of the planners themselves, but of the commercial and civic groups who were the major clients of planning consultants.

Regional planning recognized the reality and interdependence of the metropolis, the way in which central cities and suburbs and nearby rural areas were socially and economically joined in the modern urban region. In the proposals of Lewis Mumford and the RPAA, regional planning was a way of reordering the city for explicit social goals. But most regional planning was innovative only in the scope of its coverage. The basic underlying premises were conventional, and the goals were to maintain the economic viability of the city and its basic social and economic patterns by adapting to changing circumstances. The New York Regional Plan, for example, attempted to preserve the economic vitality of New York City and make the surrounding metropolitan region suitable for additional industrial growth through decentralization of new economic activities. The elaborate system of highways and transportation links was intended not to create new ways of living and working, but rather to maintain New York's dominance of the region and to combat the congestion and transportation inefficiency that threatened to choke off the area's future growth. The plan posed no break with existing economic arrangements and no alternatives to the distribution of economic power, and it failed to address a number of issues that quickly assumed critical importance, such as the proliferation of autonomous governments in the region that fragmented metropolitan decision making and hindered the delivery of public services. Like many other planning efforts of the time, regional planning generally accepted the status quo and projected its trends and patterns into the future.

Though government controls over urban development had always been minimal in the United States, especially when compared with the practices in other industrial nations, the metropolis of the 1970s did not simply spring from the consequences of unregulated and capricious social, economic, and technological forces. It was, in some important respects, planned in the early twentieth century, primarily by commercial-civic and other major interest groups and by the professional planners who prepared proposals under their general influence and at their request. This planning process was by no means confined to formal surveys, reports, proposals, and drawings; it mainly entailed a number of land-use decisions based upon certain more-or-less shared notions of what the city should be and what it should become. Such notions also provided a basis for most comprehensive and regional plans of the time, as well as for zoning ordinances and more specific legislation and proposals.

Urban leaders—especially those with a major economic stake in the downtown areas—desired cities that had both a strong and vital business and administrative core and an expanding periphery; they wanted both continued centralization of economic activities and decentralization of population. In this view, the modern city should be a strong center surrounded by vital expansion. It would also be divided into specialized areas of economic function and land use dispersed over a broad territory, with the various parts working logically for continued growth and prosperity. This vision promised continued growth with no changes in the existing economic or leadership structure, and population decentralization without deterioration of the urban core. One of the keys to realizing this concept was transportation, for only through efficient transport could the scattered activities and populations, along with the center and the much larger area that surrounded it, be held together. Thus, planners and their clients drew up zoning laws that divided the city into designated functional areas and devised elaborate street and highway systems that linked the center with the growing urban fringe.

Elements of this vision eventually proved naive or unworkable. Even the automobile, for example, was limited in its capacity to connect increasingly dispersed functions in a continually more fragmented metropolis, and suburbanization on the scale experienced after World War II had many tragic consequences for the central cities. Many professional planners, beginning to have second thoughts about this "metropolitan idea," warned of the dangers of decentralization and touted the virtues of mixed rather than separated land uses and the necessity for adequate mass-transit systems. The important point is that the mid-twentieth-century metropolis was not simply an unwanted and vagrant phenomenon. Indeed, its beginnings can be detected in the comprehensive and regional plans of the 1920s and in many of the urban policies adopted by the federal government during and after the Great Depression of the 1930s.

Cities Become National Policy: Depression and War

Policies of the federal government affected cities and the patterns of urban development from the earliest years of the republic. The location of military posts; the paths of internal improvements like turnpikes, canals, and railroads; the construction of docks, storage facilities, and harbors; and extensions of postal service—all these decisions helped to determine the fate of many localities.

These federal projects and activities were intended to benefit the general welfare and were not specifically designed to aid cities. They were not, in other words, part of a federal urban policy. In fact, Washington and the nation's local governments studiously ignored each other through most of American history. Cities struggled in the nineteenth century not for federal dollars but for relief from meddling and usually unsympathetic state governments, which provided the sole legal basis for municipalities and made myriad decisions that influenced the everyday lives of urban dwellers—from restrictions on city budgets to the patterns of streets and services. A major demand of the municipal-reform movements during the 1890s and early twentieth century was home rule, allowing cities to control their own destiny under new charters from the state legislatures. This approach had limited success in the early years of the twentieth century, but local reformers continued to seek greater independence and expanded powers for towns and cities during the 1920s.

The arrival of economic depression rendered most of these political questions virtually meaningless. The dimensions of financial crisis were so far-reaching that local governments quickly exhausted their resources and stood almost helpless before the onslaught. Depressions were not new to the American experience, of course, but the Great Depression following the New York stock market crash in 1929 was unprecedented in its depth, and it demanded unprecedented measures. And the call for home rule was drowned out by cries for help.

Perhaps the most important long-term impact of the depression on cities was the formation of a new pattern of relationships between the federal government and local governments. Beginning with the New Deal, the neglect of local affairs by Washington officials and agencies ended forever. Since that time, the ties between federal and local governments have been extensive, even though this partnership has often been confusing and the policies involved have sometimes been counterproductive.

The years immediately after World War I were ones of economic adjustment. A business recession lasted until the early years of the 1920s punctuated by a series of labor disputes and a pronounced shortage of decent housing in virtually all cities. As the economic "boom" of the twenties got under way, some tell-tale signs of crisis to come lay just below the surface. Employment among unskilled workers sagged, wage levels barely kept pace with prices and production, and speculative investments in the stock market and in real estate often went sour. Meanwhile, cities enjoyed rising tax revenues and confidently floated large new bond issues. Even after the stock market crash, government leaders, major financiers, and countless newspapers predicted that the economy would soon rebound. These hopes were soon dashed. The wind had gone out of the sails of prosperity, and the ship itself listed badly, buffeted by thousands of business failures and bank closings.

The cycle of the economic downturn was tragic and seemingly unbreak-
able. As businesses sank, workers were laid off or fired. Bankrupt businesses and unemployed workers paid no taxes, and the coffers of city
treasuries and local charity drives quickly emptied. In most cities real property assessments plummeted, tax revenues fell by anywhere from 25 to 50
percent (and even more in some places), and the debt service on municipal
bonds—many floated during the prosperous twenties—ate up increasingly
large proportions of city budgets, rising as high as 70 percent or more in
some cities. With little market for new bonds, state limits on bonding authority, and an already burdensome bonded debt, municipalities had piti-
fully few choices. As cities and school boards ran out of money, they too
were forced to lay off or dismiss many police, firefighters, teachers, sanitation workers, clerks, and other public employees. City payrolls were slashed
by 50 percent and more, and many programs—especially city planning and
public works—were virtually eliminated. And all of the unemployed joined
the ranks of the sick, the elderly, and the disabled in making tremendous
demands on public agencies just as those agencies were becoming less and
less able to offer help than ever before.

Municipalities had turned early to state governments for aid. But politically sensitive governors and rural-dominated state legislatures were not
very sympathetic, and often blamed the cities for spending themselves into
bankruptcy. Banks were of even less help. Their first priority was to protect
their investments, and they made loans conditional on balanced municipal
budgets or exacted a high price for the renegotiation of existing notes. So
local officials looked to a new source for assistance and sought in
Washington what they had failed to find elsewhere.

The federal government was aware of the mounting seriousness of the
situation but responded very hesitantly at first in hopes that the downturn
would eventually bottom out. Indeed, some government economists looked
upon the crisis as an inevitable and necessary adjustment of the business
cycle. President Herbert Hoover was a capable man with a record for
efficiency and humanitarianism. He also had a proven interest in urban
affairs, especially in the areas of planning and zoning. But Hoover and
many other Republicans and conservative Democrats were adverse to federal intervention of any kind in local affairs, and especially to large-scale
government relief programs that would, they reasoned, only foster dependence and lethargy among the recipients. There was also no way to ensure
that monies distributed directly to needy citizens would be spent wisely in
accomplishing economic recovery.

Consequently, the Hoover administration's programs were quite limited
and largely ineffective. They were devised mainly to assist corporations and

banks rather than the mass of citizens. The Emergency Relief and Construction Act of 1932 provided only $1.5 billion to deal with the economic crisis, and only $300 million of that was allocated for emergency relief loans. Detroit alone was spending up to $2 million a month for relief. Projects funded under the act had to be self-liquidating and, even more important, required the approval of state governors, which was often not forthcoming. The Reconstruction Finance Corporation (RFC) established by the act was an inadequate response, and very few of its benefits reached the individual citizens who were thrown into the maw of poverty and uncertainty. As 1933 approached, the nation was drifting ever deeper into depression and municipalities were becoming desperate.

The presidential campaign of 1932 had the expected outcome. Public confidence in Hoover and the Republicans had fallen almost as low as the stock market. The time seemed momentous for change. Franklin D. Roosevelt, Governor of New York and Hoover's opponent, hardly sounded like a national savior. His platform pledged a balanced budget, his public statements were not very specific on programs or policy, and for political reasons (and his own inclinations) he emphasized rural problems and needs more than urban ones. But Roosevelt hardly needed to convince voters by arguing the issues. His main goal was to hold together the strong coalition that was forming in his behalf—including intellectuals, the traditionally Democratic South, labor unions, and masses of voters in the urban North. Roosevelt won handily, building upon the urban political strength tapped by Al Smith in 1928.

Roosevelt's actions during his first days in office were dramatic. Immediately after his inauguration on March 3, 1933, he declared a national bank holiday, delaying the runs on banks across the country that threatened to drive them under, and he used the breathing spell to build public confidence and propose new legislation to provide security for deposits. The first hundred days of Roosevelt's term produced an unprecedented flood of legislation in a Congress eager to act against the economic crisis. The National Industrial Recovery Act (NIRA), passed in 1933, provided for low-interest loans and outright grants for municipal projects, which did not have to be self-liquidating. The Public Works Administration (PWA) funneled millions of dollars into various city construction projects, including schools, auditoriums, sewage treatment plants, streets, and transportation facilities. The appropriations were always less than cities needed, but the PWA did reduce the marked physical deterioration of the nation's urban areas that had begun with the onset of depression.

The New Deal also tackled the problem of relief, not only by providing additional funds for public welfare but also through new work-relief programs, enthusiastically requested by the nation's mayors, designed to create useful work for the unemployed, complete worthwhile public projects, and fuel the economy. The Civil Works Administration (CWA), enacted in 1933, lasted barely four months, but it was the first clearly urban-oriented legislation of the New Deal. It boosted the hopes of beleaguered local officials and provided a useful precedent for subsequent urban programs. The Works Progress Administration (WPA), created in 1935, provided a more significant boon for cities. More than half of all WPA grants were made in the nation's fifty largest cities through state directors of the WPA program. The WPA added considerably to the physical city by constructing 500,000 miles of roads and streets, 500,000 sewerage connections, and 110,000 public buildings as well as completing countless beautification projects. But the WPA was never intended to be permanent, even though it continued through the rest of the decade. In the eyes of the Roosevelt administration, it was an emergency measure. Appropriations were made from year to year, and cities could not effectively prepare long-range budgets or make maximum use of the funds. Also, at best, WPA provided jobs for no more than one-third of the nation's unemployed. In 1939 Congress cut Roosevelt's request for work-relief appropriations, while at the same time funding farm subsidy programs at higher levels. During World War II, WPA was terminated.

A variety of other New Deal measures were also significant for American urban areas. The Social Security Act (1935) provided a pension program for millions of urban workers (though domestic, part-time, and certain other categories of workers were not included until revisions of the law in later years); the National Labor Board, established in 1933, mediated strikes and helped build a much more secure foundation for organized labor; and the Wagner National Labor Relations Act—named for its leading sponsor, Senator Robert F. Wagner of New York—guaranteed labor's right to organize and bargain collectively and prohibited firms from imposing company unions.

A number of New Deal agencies dealt with the cities in other ways, primarily by collecting and analyzing a wealth of data on demographic and economic trends in the country's urban areas. The CWA's Real Property Inventory revealed much useful information about the state of urban housing, and the investigations of the National Resources Board were particularly thoughtful. Many of the academic urbanologists brought to Washington to participate in this data gathering and evaluation helped to shift the government's concern much more in urban directions.

The Resettlement Administration (RA), initiated in 1935, carried out one of Roosevelt's pet ideas: reducing the problems of urban life by bringing urban dwellers into the country, where they settled in "greenbelt" towns. It was Roosevelt's own conception of the vital fringe. The greenbelt communities were to be limited to about 10,000 people, provided with basic social and educational facilities and decent housing, and surrounded with a belt of open land to control sprawl and its consequences. The RA envisioned the construction of many of these new towns, but only three were ever built—outside of Washington, Cincinnati, and Milwaukee. The program encountered problems of excessive construction costs and, most importantly, a determined congressional opposition to any government efforts which would interfere with the private construction and real-estate business. Like previous administration efforts to establish subsistence farm communities, the RA's greenbelt program made very little impact on cities or on urban planning and policy. In fact, rather than being self-sufficient "garden cities" on the British model, the greenbelt towns were little more than carefully designed suburbs. The RA itself was scrapped by Congress in 1938.

The New Deal also took some steps toward improving the nation's housing. The Federal Housing Act of 1934 and the public works sections of the NIRA both promoted new housing construction, though the Federal Housing Administration, created under the 1934 act, was from the beginning oriented toward the support of the private construction and real-estate industry. And the United States Housing Act of 1937, which finally received the President's support after heavy lobbying by urban interests, provided a strong foundation for federal action for public housing and placed direct federal-municipal ties on a permanent basis.

The range of New Deal programs to aid the cities was extensive, and their impact was considerable. As New York's mayor, Fiorello La Guardia, said, "If it weren't for the federal aid, I don't know what any of us could have done."[3] But federal assistance to the cities during the 1930s was hardly perfect or sufficient to deal with the full dimensions of the urban economic and social crisis.

Despite all the New Deal's activity on new urban fronts, its overall impact was nevertheless often limited. Roosevelt had a much better grasp of rural problems and issues, and for political reasons he often played to the rural galleries. Thus, his administration succeeded in establishing new farm subsidy programs, rural conservation plans, and the most sweeping New Deal legislation of all—the Tennessee Valley Authority. The Departments of Agriculture and the Interior provided large bureaucratic centers for the pursuit of rural interests in Washington and helped to coordinate agricultural programs and policies. Legislation affecting the cities was often, however, directed not at urban problems per se, but at broad national problems—like unemployment—that happened to be especially severe in cities. In addition, many of the construction and work-relief programs that assisted the cities were not designed to attack deep-rooted urban conditions over the long term, but rather to boost the economy by putting more money into circulation and getting people off the dole. The New Deal, in other words, did not develop or follow a coherent urban policy, and urban interests continued to play second fiddle to the more organized rural lobbies in the halls and offices of Washington.

Beyond the efforts necessary to boost the economy, Roosevelt was not committed to revolutionary social and economic change. He wanted to get the traditional American system functioning again and to provide stability and prosperity by dealing with those problems that had to have immediate solutions. The capitalistic economic system was not to be destroyed, but saved. Roosevelt also remained convinced that a balanced budget was the ultimate goal, and he fueled the economy reluctantly and out of necessity rather than out of conviction. Most programs of the New Deal were stop-gap measures to deal with immediate and temporary difficulties, and usually they fell far short of meeting the true dimensions of national need, especially in the cities. Unemployment was erased not by the New Deal (some eight to ten million people were still unemployed in 1939), but by the mobilization of World War II. And once American involvement in that conflict was under way, many programs (like WPA) were scrapped. But the New Deal did fashion a new pattern of relationships between the federal government and local areas that was extremely significant for the future; Roosevelt's was the most urban-oriented national administration in American history to that time; and it set ample precedents for new national initiatives in the areas of urban housing, transportation, and public welfare. The New Deal also signaled the advent of new American values that were much more appropriate to the collective, urban realities of the modern era than to the individualistic and largely rural ethic of the past. And the crisis of the 1930s also brought forth a new coalition of urban interests that made the problems and desires of cities very familiar to national policymakers in later years.

Even as the economic crisis deepened in the early 1930s, most state governors were loathe to admit the failure of state and local governments to contend with the situation or to call for radical alternatives. The nation's mayors, however, were not so timid. Their options were limited very quickly, and while waging war on the banks to keep some meat on barebones budgets, struggling to maintain even meager levels of urban services, and encountering angry crowds of unemployed workers in the streets or on the steps of city hall, they were willing to experiment.

Since municipal officials had traditionally been concerned with economy, efficiency, and home rule before 1930, existing municipal coalitions were not suited to the demands of new times. The National Municipal League, dating from 1894, remained committed to the principle of home rule, with no outside interference in local affairs from either the state or federal quarter. The International City Managers Association was composed of professional urban executives, but it was primarily an information clearinghouse. The American Municipal Association, established in 1924, was also mainly a "nonpartisan" and information-sharing body, composed of state municipal leagues rather than individual cities. None of these organizations met the needs of mayors determined to develop a strong voice in Washington.

Detroit's mayor Frank Murphy emerged as the most important early leader of efforts to organize an effective coalition of urban interests. The nation's motor city was especially hard-hit by the economic crisis, and it also had a history of providing a broad range of urban welfare services, which were, of course, almost made impossible in the early 1930s. Murphy discussed the need for action with other municipal leaders in Michigan and throughout the country. He called a national meeting of mayors in 1932, a gathering that included the chief executives from twenty-nine cities, and called for federal aid and a Washington declaration of war against unemployment and depression. A more significant outgrowth of this initial effort was the creation in 1933 of the permanent United States Conference of Mayors (USCM), an organization limited to mayors of cities with 50,000 or more people. Cities were represented directly, rather than through state associations, and the USCM was conceived from the beginning as a potent lobby with a policy focus. The message it took to Washington was not home rule and states' rights, but the immediate necessity for extensive federal-municipal cooperation.

USCM representatives put pressure on the White House and the Congress for work-relief programs, and they steadfastly supported WPA until its demise. They lobbied intensively, but in vain, for effective federal legislation to refund municipal debts or permit a moratorium on debt service payments during the economic emergency. They constantly presented facts on the inadequacy of appropriations under existing programs to deal with urban deterioration and misery, and they held their own in some instances with the long-entrenched lobbies in real estate, banking, and agriculture.

Beyond these specific activities, the USCM represented another important result of the depression—the permanent organization of the nation's larger municipalities to fight for urban interests and seek support from the federal government. Other urban organizations that joined this coalition in later years often held different policy views, so that the joint urban effort was still quite fragmented when compared to the unity of other powerful lobbies. And the USCM generally had its hands full with a few major projects like WPA, and could not effectively operate across the broad range of urban difficulties and needs. But the new urban lobby led by the formation of the USCM helped to shape the federal-municipal relationship that would, in turn, have a large role in shaping the cities in the last half of the twentieth century. The impact of this relationship is revealed in the areas of urban housing and transportation.

Housing and Urban Redevelopment: A Policy Gone Astray

Urban reformers since the nineteenth century had complained about the disease and immorality resulting from inadequate housing. Jacob Riis's dramatic photographs of the noxious, squalid tenements and water-filled basements of New York City highlighted campaigns for change that usually focused on stricter building codes to prohibit the construction of unsafe and unsanitary hovels and force the improvement of existing dwellings. But this approach dealt with the symptoms of the problem, not the causes. The fact is that the private American housing industry had not provided decent housing for millions of low-income Americans. Slums were often profitable, while decent low-income housing was not.

In the early 1930s the state of America's urban housing was still scandalous. The CWA Real Property surveys indicated that almost one-third of all housing units in the nation's cities were substandard. Some limited state programs to correct housing deficiencies in the early twentieth century, the construction of some housing units for workers during World War I by the federal government, and the establishment of minimum building standards by local government were the only precedents for governmental action in the housing area by the beginning of the 1930s. Housing was obviously a serious problem; but it had been traditionally looked upon in America as a local and individual problem.

The depression, however, made housing a problem for wide segments of the population, including many middle-income people. The construction industry was in a shambles, and few people had enough money to purchase houses through conventional bank loans, which required high down payments. The Federal Housing Administration (FHA) was created in 1934 to provide government guarantees for private mortgages and thus enable families to invest in houses and at the same time provide a market for the construction industry. Since its inception, FHA has guaranteed billions of dollars in mortgages and encouraged the construction of thousands of homes and the rehabilitation of others. But FHA assisted the construction industry and people in the middle- and upper-income brackets primarily. The poor and many minority groups were hardly served at all, and in many cases FHA even worsened their plight.

FHA operated like a private business. Loans were guaranteed only when they met certain financial criteria. Houses in run-down areas and applicants without sufficient funds were considered poor risks. Consequently, FHA assistance went overwhelmingly to new housing developments in the suburbs. The major debilities which cities suffered from the private economy—where money was funneled into areas of greatest profit rather than into those of greatest social need—were merely compounded by FHA, which declared vast tracts of America's inner cities ineligible for government mortgage insurance, and "red-lined" these areas on their property maps just as private financial institutions did. In addition, FHA followed accepted real-estate practices by refusing to insure mortgages in racially integrated neighborhoods and even warning against racial mixing.

In 1940, mortgage insurance was made available for older homes for the first time, but the amount of money used for this purpose was small. This encouragement of the rehabilitation of inner-city housing stock was ineffective. In the 1960s, largely in response to the "urban crisis" and the civil rights movement—and decisions of the U.S. Supreme Court—FHA eliminated many of its discriminatory provisions against minorities and inner cities. However, for most of the years of its existence the actions of this government agency had widened social and economic inequalities in the nation's cities.

Some reformers were quick to point out these deficiencies of FHA and to call for government construction of low-income housing units. Their efforts found additional public support during the depression and resulted in the construction of some public-housing projects under WPA and the passage of the Housing Act of 1937, which created the United States Housing Authority (USHA) and committed the federal government to public housing on a permanent basis. President Roosevelt was not a public-housing advocate, and he agreed to support the measure reluctantly. An increasingly conservative Congress was even less fond of the idea. Thus, USHA was able to build fewer than 100,000 new units by World War II, and received no additional appropriations until 1948.

The resistance to public housing was led by the National Association of Real Estate Boards (NAREB), which was joined by the U.S. Chamber of Commerce, various banking associations, and other private-interest groups. Public housing represented to them a socialistic interference of the government in free enterprise, and they worked avidly to have the entire program scrapped. Government aid was, in their view, more beneficial when extended to private businesses. The favorite project of the NAREB involved broad government subsidy for private redevelopment of "blighted" (that is, unprofitable) tracts in the inner cities. What the real-estate industry wanted was nothing less than the power of eminent domain (the ability to acquire private property for public uses), government authority to clear a tract, and government subsidies for clearing and redeveloping the land for private profit. NAREB pointed out the benefits of this approach for the public weal: It would add to the municipal tax base, clear away acres of decrepit dwellings, and help to revivify declining downtown areas. But the organization apparently saw nothing contradictory between its redevelopment proposals and its firm opposition to what it called socialistic public housing.

The redevelopment interests were potent enough to block extensions of public housing, and the public-housing interests had the votes to maintain their program and prevent legislation authorizing redevelopment. Action on both fronts was thus stalled for years. Professional urban planners, led by the American Institute of Planners, complicated matters further. They liked the idea of redevelopment, but they wanted a very broad-scale effort to reshape urban America, with attention to the suburbs as well as the inner cities and with few limitations on the alternatives that could be considered or implemented under federal legislation. The planners tended to favor the redevelopment proposals and believed that a sole emphasis on housing neglected the larger urban framework.

Finally, after repeated public hearings and behind-the-scenes negotiations, the Housing Act of 1949 passed Congress and was signed into law by President Truman. The act provided for expanded public-housing programs and also for redevelopment—with the federal government supplying subsidies to defray the cost of private redevelopment and authorizing $500 million over a five-year period. The legislation provided a sop to planning interests by requiring "a general plan for the development of the locality as a whole" as a condition of local eligibility for federal funds. Generally, the law was weighted toward housing. Areas cleared for redevelopment had to be used for "predominantly residential" purposes, and the act's preamble stated that the government's intent was "to realize as soon as feasible the goal of a decent home and a suitable living environment for every American family." The act provided no funds for relocating families displaced by redevelopment, however; this task was left to local communities.

Planning historian Mel Scott wrote that with the passage of the Housing Act of 1949, "Congress had at last recognized the importance of cities to the national welfare."[4] The results do not support the

Figure 13.1   Urban Renewal—Urban Removal. (Frank Chalmers/*Winnipeg Tribune*)

Figure 13.2   Herbert H. Lehman Village in New York City, 1963

A low-rent high-rise that typified the massive, cheerless, institutional structures built with federal funds in the 1950s and 1960s. (National Archives)

hope of that statement. Between 1950 and 1960 more homes were destroyed than were built; those homes that were destroyed were primarily low-rent dwellings; and most of the structures built were high-rent homes. Add to this the psychological heartaches of dislocation (as illustrated in Figure 13.1), the permanent demise of numerous small businesses, and the hideousness of many of the structures that sprouted on cleared land, and the actual as opposed to the intended impact of the 1949 Housing Act and its 1954 companion become clearer. (See also Figure 13.2.)

The inability of the Congress and federal administrators to foresee the destructive consequences of their urban policies was even more evident in the implementation of an urban transportation policy.

Urban Transportation Policies:
Cities Taken for a Ride

Even a short automobile journey in 1910 usually resembled a safari into the wilderness, especially in bad weather. The nation's roads were so poor that even horses and wagons found them impassable at certain times of the year. Many urban streets were in similar condition. As the number of motor vehicles increased, however, the demand for good roads also grew, supported by farmers (who wanted better access to markets and urban amenities), chambers of commerce and other business groups (who saw the economic advantages of faster travel and tourism), and the early cluster of motorcar interests (including manufacturers, dealers, auto-owners, oil companies, and construction firms). When downtown traffic congestion rose during the 1920s, merchants called for improved city streets and expanded parking facilities.

In the early twentieth century roads were the responsibility of states and localities. Meeting the demands of the automobile in any real sense, however, meant virtually the complete renovation of existing streets and the construction of a new road system in cities and throughout the countryside. Most states decided very early that much of the money for such projects would be generated through taxes on automobile operators and their vehicles. These user taxes—including levies on gasoline and operator's license and registration fees—were usually earmarked for special "trust funds" dedicated to highway construction and repairs. Since most state governments were dominated by rural interests, however, most of these monies were expended on the rural road system, with urban areas bearing a much higher proportion of street costs. In 1916 the federal government passed the first legislation providing national assistance for roads and highways in the auto era—the Federal Highway Act—but city streets and highways were specifically exempted from the legislation. The entire bill was associated with improved postal service in rural areas, and the program was administered by the Department of Agriculture. Through the 1920s, most cities undertook extensive street construction and improvement, funded through combinations of state funds and new municipal bond issues. When the depression struck, however, good roads were among the first victims.

Roads and highways were often among the urban projects funded through the public-works and work-relief programs of the New Deal (though rural roads still received the most attention), and a variety of New Deal agencies—especially WPA—conducted transportation studies and drew up plans for municipalities throughout the country. The public romance with the motorcar persisted even during economic crisis, and the officials in Washington became increasingly aware of the car's crucial role in urban policy.

The Federal Bureau of Public Roads took up the urban cause in the 1940s and called for new highways to relieve the traffic congestion choking the central business districts. The Highway Act of 1944, reflecting a compromise with rural interests, did recognize the legitimacy of urban needs, but only 25 percent of federal road funds were allocated for cities. The act also authorized a new national system of highways, though appropriations for this project were not forthcoming until passage of the Highway Act of 1956, which initiated the Interstate Highway System on the basis of 90 percent federal and 10 percent state funding. A massive engineering effort, the interstate highway system contained a crucial contradiction. Initially proposed as a means of alleviating downtown traffic congestion, the 1956 act emphasized high-speed travel between cities, often bypassing downtown areas entirely or slicing awkwardly through them. The justification for the interstate system was, in fact, not the relief of traffic congestion but a better transportation network for national defense. Furthermore, the act contained no emphasis on urban planning and provided no coordination whatsoever with other major federal or state programs in housing and urban renewal.

The primary effect of the Interstate Highway Act was to reinforce the spatial trend toward the vital fringe. The limited-access highways expanded the range of the automobile and encouraged dispersed settlement. In fact, when suburbanites explained where they lived, the name of the town was frequently an afterthought; the important piece of information was the exit on the expressway. Besides determining the boundaries of residential growth, the ribbon highways, like the trolley tracks that preceded them, generated commercial and industrial uses. The Capital Beltway, an interstate road circling Washington, D.C., ten miles out, which was completed in 1964, sprouted numerous "beltway industries" drawn by the easy access to the motor truck. The beltway has been helpful in bolstering the tax base of primarily residential suburban communities.

The interstate's boost to suburban settlement contrasted sharply with its spatial impact on the city. The interstate, frequently an elevated structure, was a voracious devourer of city space. (See Figure 13.3.) Neighborhoods were leveled or cut in half by its hulking concrete and steel structures. The interstate system, in fact, became a leading policy tool in the federal urban renewal effort. Unfortunately, the limited housing options of the displaced poor-black and white-ethnic population were thus reduced even further, and in some cases, their familiar neighborhoods were destroyed

Figure 13.3   St. Louis Interstate Network
A tangle of concrete and steel where a neighborhood once stood, the expressway
gobbles up huge chunks of urban real estate and cuts the city off from the recreational and scenic possibilities of the Mississippi River. (David R. Goldfield)

forever. By the 1970s, urban residents were rebelling against this attack on
their residential space. In Boston and San Francisco, local groups were
successful in halting construction of interstate projects.

Some of the urban spatial depredations of the interstate might be for-
given if they had alleviated downtown traffic congestion and provided
some economic sustenance to downtown merchants. Interstates, however,
have generally disgorged massive amounts of traffic onto narrow downtown streets, creating even greater congestion and making downtown
shopping even more of a chore.

The federal emphasis on the highway also meant an emphasis on the
auto. Commuter train service deteriorated, and railroads lobbied
Congress—with some success—for permission to cut their unprofitable
passenger schedules. This trend worried many business people and planners, since the entire rail transportation system seemed in jeopardy; and
some cities even explored the possibility of constructing new rail transit
systems. But the federal government was not generous with assistance. The

largest transportation subsidies went overwhelmingly to highways, and the revenues collected from gasoline and automobile taxes were denied for mass transportation until some small appropriations were permitted in the late 1960s.

Federal urban policy has therefore not been especially beneficial for the cities. As one historian commented,

The values federal officials adopted in fulfilling their responsibilities were those of the taxpayer, the banker, the home-owner, and the automobile driver. This is only natural in a democratic society since the government should reflect the dominant mood of the country, and these were the pre-eminent values. Unfortunately for the cities, these beliefs were antithetical to the urban way of life.[5]

In fact, it would probably be more accurate to talk in terms of federal suburban policy. The urban conflagrations of the 1960s, perhaps more than anything else, awakened policymakers to the shortcomings of earlier programs. By the 1970s new policy orientations began to appear. Ironically, it was also the time when the long-favored suburbs began to experience some urban problems of their own as the nation began to move beyond the fringe.

Notes

1. Quoted in Mel Scott, *American City Planning Since 1890* (Berkeley: University of California Press, 1971), p. 208.

2. Quoted in Thomas S. Hines, *Burnham of Chicago: Architect and Planner* (New York: Oxford University Press, 1974), p. xvii.

3. Quoted in Mark I. Gelfand, *A Nation of Cities: The Federal Government and Urban America, 1933–1965* (New York: Oxford University Press, 1975), p. 46.

4. Scott, *American City Planning Since 1890*, p. 464.

5. Gelfand, *A Nation of Cities*, p. 235.

14.
Beyond the Fringe:
Downtown and No Town

The United States Census has cataloged major population shifts twice in this century. In 1920 the census showed that the nation of farmers had capitulated to the siren song of the city. We were an urban nation. In 1970 the census recorded the resurrection of the arcadian ideal. We had become a suburban nation. When Americans are counted in 1980, it is unlikely that a major announcement comparable to those resulting from the 1920 and 1970 census will be forthcoming. The latter census years reflected, after all, population movements that had been accumulating for decades. The 1980 census will demonstrate, however, that the restless American nation is carrying its odyssey beyond the fringe to the countryside and to newer cities. The fringe itself will no longer be so vital.

The Urbanization of Suburbia

A generation has grown up in the suburbs. The almost missionary fervor that accompanied the move out from the city has not been transferred to the new generation. The epithets that scholars hurled at the suburbs—sterile, dull, conformist, confining—are now being repeated by the offspring of the first pioneers. The vast majority of those moving beyond the fringe to exurbia, as the new territory is called, come from the suburbs. In what amounts to a further stretching and decentralization of the metropolitan area, exurbia offers newcomers what most suburbs lack—open spaces, cheaper land, and a simpler lifestyle. If these attractions sound vaguely familiar, it is because these were the attractions of the original suburbs. The strength of the lure of exurbia is a measure of what the suburbs have lost.

The wide-eyed innocence of life in the post–World War II suburb is gone. The reality of urban problems has begun to be felt. For the older, inner suburbs a stable, if not declining, tax base coupled with increased service costs accelerated by a growing elderly and poor population has necessitated a period of financial retrenchment. Even for the more affluent outer suburbs such as Suffolk County, New York, and Fairfax County, Virginia, penny-pinching, job cutbacks, and school closings have become commonplace.

The property tax has soared to keep pace with service demands, especially in the area of education. The highly touted suburban school systems that were one of the major attractions for migrating urbanites are in trouble themselves. In some systems teacher morale is as low as the pay raises of recent years. It is difficult to imagine a teacher in Montgomery County, Maryland, who makes a starting salary of $11,000 a year trying to find housing in a suburb where the median family income is above $20,000. The quality of suburban education has come under fire as well. With a plethora of new technology, curricula, and methodologies, the suburban school was supposed to launch a new era in education. It is evident now that the high expectations for the suburban education systems have not been realized.

Finally, suburban society, under greater stress now than previously, has begun to show the strain. Crime and drugs have invaded the suburban Eden. The criminal activity, primarily crimes against property, is not a spillover from the central city. While the school systems were struggling to produce scholars, the production of drug and alcohol users and abusers was taking place with much less publicity but with greater frequency. The appearance of drug rehabilitation centers and counseling programs in the suburbs is not only an overdue admission of this problem, but also a further burden on tight suburban treasuries.

If the period from 1945 to 1970 could be termed the era of suburban growth, then it is likely that the 1970s will be known as the decade of suburban stabilization. The massive migrations from the city that fueled suburban growth after World War II have slowed to a trickle. Numerous inner suburbs, in fact, are beginning to experience outmigration. Diminished population growth inevitably signals slower industrial and retail expansion as well. Even that suburban bellwether, the shopping center, has been overbuilt, in false anticipation of a continuing burgeoning of the population. For some inner suburbs, it is more appropriate to talk of decline rather than of stabilization as the process of urbanization and its attendant problems overtakes them. Declining populations, eroding tax bases, aging capital facilities, and social and racial disorders have invariably caught the small and ill-prepared inner suburban jurisdictions by surprise. The movement to exurbia may not necessarily be an escape from these problems, but geographically, the areas beyond the fringe are far away from the same problems from which an earlier generation sought refuge in the suburbs.

The problems of suburbs, especially of the inner suburbs, demonstrate that these communities are not distinct entities, but are in fact extensions of the city. The spillover of black and Hispanic populations into contiguous suburban neighborhoods in metropolitan areas as diverse as New York, Washington, Denver, and San Antonio offers further support for this view. The inner suburban ring is evolving into a racial battleground in much the same manner as transitional urban neighborhoods were buffeted by racial antagonisms in the 1960s. The Rosedales may, in fact, become the racial tinderboxes of tomorrow. The Carter administration, in recognition of growing inner-suburban blight, has broadened its federal aid target areas from "distressed cities" to "distressed communities." Indeed, the present administration is considering the formulation of a suburban policy for the 1980s.

The trend toward suburban stabilization is supported by national demographic trends that point away from the suburban lifestyle. The demographic patterns that facilitated suburban growth have changed. Young families with small children were typical of the households that left the city for the suburb. Today, however, more women are opting for careers instead of marriage. If and when they get married, these women frequently postpone childbearing, thereby limiting the number of offspring. In addition, more young men and women today are deciding not to have children at all. The results of these demographic trends are that there are more and smaller households and fewer reasons to be tied to a house or a community. A single man or woman and an adult-oriented couple have needs that are different from the young child-oriented families of yesteryear.

The suburb, with its predominance of single-family homes, its open spaces, and its organized activities for youngsters is not equipped to fulfill the needs of the single and adult-oriented population who comprise nearly one out of two households in some metropolitan areas. The city, on the other hand, with its larger stock of rental units, its cultural and entertainment facilities, and the stability of its professional employment base in service-oriented activities such as government, finance, and insurance seems to be a more appropriate location for the new single and adult-oriented households. That many of these individuals are choosing the exurban alternative is not necessarily a rejection of the city, since some exurban settlements such as Westlake Village in southern 'California and Reston in northern Virginia have urban cluster development.

The urbanization and stabilization of suburbia relate directly to the urban future as the demographic trends imply. The close connection between suburban and urban destinies is even more evident in the evolution of contemporary federal policy. The federal government helped to subsidize the post–World War II suburban migration. These subsidies are still intact, but their impact has diminished considerably. Moreover, new federal policies have evolved that, in contrast with earlier policies, may have a more beneficial effect on cities.

The Federal Housing Administration (FHA), which enabled young middle-income families to invest in a suburban home, still bolsters the single-family-home market. It is a market, however, with reduced supply (housing) and considerably reduced effective demand (individuals able to afford new homes). With new suburban homes selling for as much as $125,000 to $150,000, the new type of household is virtually priced out of the market. When young marrieds do take the plunge into homeownership, they frequently become "house poor" with upwards of 40 percent of their income going to support their new home.

The federal subsidy of road construction, especially through the Interstate Highway Act of 1956, still, of course, exists. The highway was and remains the suburb's umbilical cord and is a necessity for economic and demographic growth. Despite the growing national awareness of energy shortages, there has not been a corresponding diminution in the use of the automobile—the technology that facilitated the suburban movement. One thing is certain, however: The costs attendant upon maintaining one and, in the suburbs, frequently two automobiles are of increasing concern to newly formed households. The new public transit systems in the San Francisco, Washington, D.C., and Atlanta metropolitan areas are public expressions of these concerns, but the full impact of energy costs is yet to be felt. Eventually, decisions on household and even industrial location may be made with energy considerations as an important part of the decision-making equation. If that occurs with any degree of regularity, the outer suburbs will stagnate.

Finally, the federal tax advantages of homeownership remain, but they are more than offset by the high costs of homeownership for a good portion of the single and adult-oriented population. In addition, the growing number of condominiums, frequently located in urban centers or in urban environments, provide comparable tax relief to residents.

If events have reduced the federal government's role as suburban booster, they have also minimized the negative impact of federal policy on the cities. The major federal urban policy—providing housing—sped the city toward its precipitous decline in the 1960s. From the Housing Act of 1949 through the various adjustments of the 1960s, the emphasis remained on housing production rather than on providing social services. This focus created high-rise ghettos in the inner city populated by both stable and antisocial families thrown together with predictable results. As housing reformer Catherine Bauer noted with considerable regret in 1957: "Life in the usual public housing project just is not the way most American families want to live."[1] Federal policy did not re-create the neighborhoods it had destroyed, it merely created buildings. If, as one planner has commented, "neighborhood confidence must be the cornerstone of housing policy," then "city after city inadvertently sacrificed this priceless commodity in the game to obtain federal assistance."[2]

Ironically, as federal housing policy evolved in the 1930s, the concept of neighborhood preservation and housing assistance for the working poor, rather than for the hardcore poor, was an important ideal in the developing program. Depression necessities and, later, the impact of other federal policies such as freeway construction through poor neighborhoods pushed the federal focus to the worst neighborhoods, the poorest people, and production of units rather than of livable dwellings.

By the mid-1960s there was a growing consensus that federal urban policy should be re-examined. Concepts evidently had not changed much since the days of Lawrence Veiller, and some of the prevailing environmentalist viewpoints went even further back than that. The creation of the cabinet-level Department of Housing and Urban Development (HUD) in 1965 was a recognition of the deteriorating urban condition that the civil disturbances of mid-decade had brought into sharp relief. The Model Cities program, inaugurated in 1966, attempted to rectify errant federal urban policy by shifting emphasis almost entirely to social, as opposed to physical, programs. The woefully underfunded effort targeted particular neighborhoods, usually the most impoverished areas, where results, if any, would not be apparent for quite some time.

Since most of the target neighborhoods under the Model Cities program have not changed appreciably, nor has the poverty of the residents, it has been common to label the program a failure. What we do not know, however, is whether the residents of these areas in the late 1960s were able to take advantage of the grants to obtain some skills and leave the ghetto. Many of those residents are gone now, making success-failure assessments a much more complex matter than merely looking at the physical neighborhood and its present inhabitants. Model Cities may well have provided opportunities to some ghetto residents even if it did not change the environment itself.

The Model Cities program, in its emphasis on neighborhood conservation and local initiative, presaged the new era of federal urban policy inaugurated by the Community Development Act of 1974. The Act, heralded as the "new federalism" by the Nixon administration, combined all existing grant programs into one block grant. The recipient communities are given virtually a free rein to apply the money where local officials think it can best be used, thus eliminating the albatross of tying federal funds to the worst and hence least salvageable neighborhoods. Grants are allocated on the basis of a formula that takes into account population, overcrowdedness, age of housing stock, and poverty (counted twice). Conservation and rehabilitation rather than destruction and production are encouraged. (See Figure 14.1.)

Critics of the Community Development Block Grant (CDBG) approach contend that local officials have too much latitude and accordingly ignore

Figure 14.1 Neighborhood Preservation in the Inner City—Washington, D.C., 1975

Community development legislation allows cities the flexibility to apply block-grant funds to a variety of neighborhood projects, from rehabilitating structures to planting trees. The emphasis is on recycling the old rather than on creating the new. (David R. Goldfield)

the poorest neighborhoods in favor of moderate- and even upper-income areas. Indeed, figures demonstrate that this trend away from the traditional recipients of federal assistance has increased every year the program has been in existence. They also point to the political pressures faced by local officials as neighborhoods clamor for available CDBG funds. This has resulted in a "showering" effect whereby the grant is dispersed throughout the city, leaving only small portions to a given area. Given the finite funds appropriated, comprehensive neighborhood plans are virtually impossible to implement.

Despite these inequities, the CDBG program may prove helpful in the long run. Its emphasis on conservation and on salvageable neighborhoods seems more realistic than Great Society goals to eliminate slums and poverty. There is no housing shortage in most of America's large cities. Row upon row of vacant, abandoned dwellings, occasionally interspersed with empty lots, line city blocks. The contemporary image of the city is in many respects a picture of what the city once was, rather than what it has become. Massive population depletions in northeastern and midwestern cities have left empty spaces in once-dense center cities. Some cities, in fact, are approaching suburban densities. The thinned-out cities are now, ironically, applying suburban solutions to their new, depleted status: preserving and exalting the residential community and revitalizing the economic base with policies borrowed from suburban jurisdictions.

The Suburbanization of the Cities:
Back to the Basics

The CDBG may develop as a suitable federal policy to face the new urban reality of the shrinking city. Urban neighborhoods, bisected by freeways, encrusted with blight, and ignored by city hall may receive the greatest benefit from the new turn in federal events. The selectivity implied in the CDBG program could, in the long run, be a major asset to neighborhood recovery.

The *triage* concept adapted by Chicago urbanist Anthony Downs from wartime terminology and applied to the more contemporary urban war captures the spirit of the new federal policy. Triage divides neighborhoods into three categories: those areas that can recuperate or maintain themselves, those neighborhoods that need major surgery with a dim prognosis even then, and those areas that, with the application of treatment (funds), will survive. It is the last type of neighborhood that Downs foresees receiving the bulk of the CDBG money.

Of course this raises the appropriate question of what is to be done for the poorest people in the poorest neighborhoods. Heavy doses of money and good will have not brought about significant gains in the past. Planners now are beginning to talk about the so-called hardcore poor—those beyond immediate rehabilitation—and neighborhoods that are beyond redemption. While this might strike some as callous, others argue that neither the funds nor the expertise is available to attack these individuals or areas with the type of long-term commitment that is necessary. The CDBG approach does, however, provide some hope for residents of these moribund neighborhoods.

The CDBG plan demands that each jurisdiction (city, suburb, and county) prepare a housing-assistance plan to accompany all block-grant applications. If such a plan fails to provide for a reasonable number of low-income units, then any jurisdiction or regional body within that SMSA may challenge that community's entire application. The courts have already upheld the procedure in a case involving Hartford, Connecticut, and seven surrounding municipalities. If the surrounding communities wish to receive the block grant, they must provide for low-income housing. This provision (called the A-95 review process) has the potential for distributing the poor more evenly through the metropolitan area. At the least, cities will no longer have to build public housing, thereby increasing the segregation and poverty within their midst. For already financially troubled suburbs, the prospect of losing federal funds is not a happy one.

The CDBG plan may have another, more indirect impact on urban America. Its emphasis on local initiative demands greater creativity at city hall. The role of the local entrepreneur in shaping urban destiny was well known in the nineteenth century but was buried under weighty federal and city bureaucracies in the twentieth century. The new federal policy minimizes red tape, and hence bureaucracy, and enables local leaders to apply funds to fit the unique situation of their city. Equally important, the program provides yearly funding of not very large sums of money. While this might seem a drawback at first glance, it encourages smaller scale, back-to-basics projects rather than grandiose comprehensive schemes that either never materialize, thereby falsely raising expectations, or become obsolete before they are completed. The modest sums accorded to cities encourage leaders to develop new sources within the community, especially in the private sector. "Only the city can help itself" may yet be the motto of the newer federalism.

The emphasis on local initiative and imagination is the cornerstone of the Carter administration urban policy. As HUD Secretary Patricia Roberts

Harris put it: "The keynote of the urban policy we are developing is self-help for the cities and their neighborhoods."[3] The implication is that the federal government, which since the 1930s has played the role of initiator, will continue the role of facilitator begun in the Nixon administration. President Carter's conflicting goals of fiscal conservatism and of aiding his black and urban supporters; the internal conflicts within his own administration between HUD and the Department of Commerce over which agency is to assume the policy lead for urban economic development; divisions between mayors and governors over the role of the states in implementing urban policy; and regional conflicts over the relative sectional benefits of federal-aid programs—all of these factors make major federal urban-policy initiatives unlikely. In short, political realities ensure a more modest federal urban-policy profile. The diminishing role of the federal government both encourages and necessitates the back-to-basics movement and the increasing public-private sector cooperation at the local level.

The opportunities that this situation presents can best be realized in the neighborhoods. The CDBG has precipitated a new flexibility with regard to neighborhood revitalization projects. Federal funds are being utilized (*leveraged,* in the government's terminology) to subsidize interest rates on loans provided by banks to homeowners in marginal neighborhoods. Grant money can also be deposited in cooperating banks in return for liberalized loan policies for repairs in certain neighborhoods. Cities can purchase, with federal funds, tax-delinquent properties and then offer them for sale at $1 per property in return for the buyer's promise to rehabilitate the structure and remain in that dwelling for a specified length of time. *Urban homesteading,* as this process is called, began in Wilmington, Delaware, in the early 1970s and has now spread to dozens of other cities. Finally, in recognition of the fact that "people buy neighborhoods, not shelter," cities are investing their grants in capital facilities, landscaping, and a general upgrading of services in the area.[4]

The uses of CDBG funds in neighborhood conservation are beginning to reverse perhaps the primary cause of urban decline: disinvestment. In the case of residential neighborhoods, banks had refused to lend mortgage or repair money for a variety of reasons ranging from racial prejudice to just plain ignorance of the nature of the housing stock. *Red-lining,* as this practice is called, proved, in many cases, to be a self-fulfilling prophecy in pushing a neighborhood into the condition the bankers predicted it would go when they justified their rejection of loan applications. Now, however, this situation has changed. It is not that bankers have suddenly become public-spirited (though there is certainly that element in some cities), but rather that these loan ventures into stable, if old and not very pretty, neighborhoods have been profitable. With risks diminished by local or federal guarantee of loans in some instances, the banker has little to lose in reinvesting. The city, in turn, bolsters its tax base, and the residents maintain their neighborhood. One of the more hopeful features of this process is the renewed partnership of local government and the business community to further urban prosperity, an aspect missing from the Model Cities program. As opposed to the nineteenth-century partnership, however, this new liaison is effecting broader social reforms.

The neighborhood revival precipitated by the public and private sectors' cooperation has another encouraging aspect. The urban neighborhood, as the focus of public policy, is becoming a sought-after location for the new type of household, especially in those cities that have successfully maintained finance, real-estate, and government employment bases. Areas like Capitol Hill in Washington, D.C., and the Fan District in Richmond have been transformed from decay to their original grace and charm, through private efforts. The citizens of these and similar areas are the singles and adult-oriented couples advancing so rapidly in numbers and influence on the metropolitan scene. The advantages of these neighborhoods in terms of the suitability of the housing stock and access to work, public transportation, and entertainment are precisely those lifestyle attributes not offered by suburbia or exurbia.

The spatial implications of the private redevelopment movement are potentially significant. Inner-city neighborhoods, initially the residence of affluent citizens, ultimately became the location of the poor and minority neighborhoods. While some cities have traditionally maintained pockets of wealth in inner-city areas—Boston's Beacon Hill, for example—the center and the neighborhoods adjacent to it have become the least desirable residential locations. Since the middle-income professional is the most common participant in private redevelopment, the spatial cast of some cities may be changing. Lower-income groups are being pushed toward the periphery and into the inner suburbs, while middle-income residents refurbish old units near the city center. Washington, D.C., is already evincing this urban European and early American spatial configuration.

While local officials count tax revenues from previously poor neighborhoods in disbelief that a housing market has blossomed where none had existed before, they are mindful of some discordant notes in the symphony of neighborhood revitalization. When a neighborhood and its housing stock suddenly become attractive to private investors, current residents, mostly poor and mostly black or Hispanic, will eventually be forced to leave due to rising taxes. This process, known as *gentrification*, places city officials in a dilemma. On the one hand, the return of the middle-class homeowner to the city is very encouraging; on the other hand, the displacement of the poor replicates the most insensitive aspects of earlier federal policy. Since gentrification is carried on within the private market, local government intervention is all the more difficult. Yet there are alternatives, or at least modifications, to the process of gentrification.

Leopold Adler II initiated the Savannah Landmark Rehabilitation Project in the late 1960s. The aim of the project was to preserve a 45-block area near downtown known as the Victorian District. Gentrification was already under way in adjacent areas, and it appeared that the predominantly black tenants of the district would ultimately be pushed out. With federal subsidies and private funding the project is planning to purchase and restore 600 of the 1,200 structures in the district, and then rent them back to poor tenants at affordable rents. Similar private-action groups exist in Pittsburgh, Cincinnati, and Roxbury, Massachusetts.

The hammer is not the only sound heard in urban neighborhoods today. Voices are heard in the neighborhood, not fighting city hall, but rather helping city hall decide what is best for the neighborhood. The fact that the city has shrunk in the past two decades does not necessarily make it a more intimate place in which to live or an easier place to govern. The massive bureaucracies built up over the years in cities have inhibited the flow of services to neighborhoods and have deadened the responsiveness of city hall to neighborhood problems. Migrants to the suburbs invariably stated that they looked forward to greater participation in the decision-making process than they had experienced in their abandoned urban neighborhoods.

Neighborhood residents, mistreated by insensitive federal and local policies, or ignored altogether, have been organizing since the 1960s. Cities are finding that government by neighborhood not only is not threatening, but is also an improvement over the bureaucratic disarray that prevailed earlier. Accordingly, the Washington, D.C., home rule charter in 1973 provided for the creation of Advisory Neighborhood Councils; the new charter for Detroit mandated a commission to prepare proposals for neighborhood government; Atlanta has decentralized its planning function by creating neighborhood planning offices; and New York City has established the Office of Neighborhood Government (ONG) to facilitate service delivery to the city's neighborhoods.

These movements toward decentralization—and toward a system resembling the strong ward system that the old-time bosses loved and reformers abhorred (and ultimately killed)—do not mean abdication of responsibility or function at the top of urban administration. To the contrary, these efforts are occurring in cities that possess strong executives. These are attempts to involve neighborhoods in the decision-making process. In turn, residents will identify with their neighborhood, and a stronger sense of community reminiscent of the close-knit ethnic communities of the late nineteenth century will develop. Further, city fathers hope that the so-called rat problem can be solved through decentralization. The "rat problem" illustrates the bureaucratic inefficiency common to most cities: If a rat is discovered in an apartment, it is the responsibility of the housing authority; if it runs into a restaurant, the health department takes jurisdiction; and if it goes outside and dies in an alley, it is the province of public works. Bureaucratic overlap, inefficiency, and waste are chronic conditions of urban administration. If the neighborhood is the unit of social survival for the troubled city, it may also be its political salvation as well.

The neighborhood is even more than that. It is the prototype for urban recovery. The themes of back to basics and public-private cooperation being played so well on neighborhood streets are now being heard in other parts of the city. These are the sounds of a city unwilling to admit that its present condition is its future.

The downtown was the hub of urban life two centuries ago. Commerce bustled on its streets, nascent industry clung to its periphery, and residences clustered near its major thoroughfares. Time advanced and cities grew, until downtown became the province mainly of retail commerce and secondarily of entertainment. The diminution in its variety was not accompanied by a decrease in downtown's economic influence. It attracted people and investment not only from adjacent neighborhoods, but frequently from the region as well. The retail magnetism of downtown in the older northeastern and midwestern cities is now considerably reduced. The suburban shopping center has, in effect, moved downtown to the suburbs and is one important factor in the decline of the city center. Disinvestment in neighborhoods and disinvestment in downtown went hand in hand. Rehabilitating a downtown, though, is considerably more difficult than rehabilitating a house. Yet in familiar public-private partnership, cities are once again beginning to flex their economic muscle.

In the continuing irony of city-suburb relations, the suburban shopping center, once the bane of downtown, is now the model for downtown revival. Triggered by organized merchants, suburban shopping malls have been re-created in the hearts of American cities. (See Figure 14.2) The Crown Center in Kansas City, the Embarcadero Center in San Francisco, and Peachtree Center in Atlanta, with tremendous infusions of private capital enticed by tax breaks and low-interest loans, duplicate the even climate, pedestrian ambience, and ample parking of the suburban mall. Even more than their suburban counterparts, these mixed-use developments are multipurpose centers. In addition to the usual array of shops, both exotic and

Figure 14.2   The Crystal Court at Nicollet Mall, Minneapolis, 1974
Part of a current nationwide attempt to restore the historic magnetism of downtown by constructing suburbanlike shopping malls on the downtown periphery. (David R. Goldfield)

mundane, they include hotels, theaters, and restaurants. The centers approach the variety of the historic downtowns with the added convenience of the suburban shopping mall.

In an older part of downtown, by the waterfront or railroad depot, abandoned warehouses, twisted railroad tracks, and empty piers signal a malaise similar to the one that has gripped the retail center. The truck and superhighway have made these doleful districts obsolete. Tax incentives, land, and easier access to materials and labor have pushed industry to the suburbs. But cities are concocting a variety of plans to return these forsaken properties at least to the tax rolls, if not to their original land uses. Minneapolis, for example, is creating urban industrial parks, offering land and tax incentives to manufacturers in much the same way that suburban jurisdictions attracted industry in the 1950s. San Antonio transformed its decaying riverfront in downtown into a pleasant, landscaped river walk and lured restaurants and hotels to build alongside it. The Paseo del Rio with its outdoor cafes, paddle boats, and meandering walkway gives the heart of the city a distinctly European flavor, and it vies with the Alamo as a tourist attraction. Finally, Baltimore's rotting Inner Harbor has been facelifted into an urban open space with parks, playgrounds, an aquarium, and the frigate *Constellation* as the main attractions. These projects demonstrate that some of the worn-out areas of the city are excellent candidates for reusable space. Perhaps similar innovation can be applied to some empty residential areas in our cities. Returning downtown and the waterfront to pedestrians in particular and to people in general is one positive way of planning for the urban future by re-creating the spatial elements of the past.

If the story of the urban future were to end here, we would indeed be facing a rosy prospect, especially compared with the doldrums of the recent past. But cities have never had it easy in the past, so it is probable that the struggle not only for prosperity but also for sheer survival will be difficult. Behind those shiny new skyscrapers lie disturbing reminders of the obstacles to recovery. Detroit's ambitiously named Renaissance Center, looming like a modern fortress above the Detroit River, is probably the flashiest of the mixed-use developments. It is surrounded, however, by a sea of decay, despair, and violence reflecting a city that has lost one-quarter of its employment base over the past two decades and almost all of its major retail activity. The Renaissance Center is a monument to public and private enterprise, but clearly more is necessary in Detroit than a new skyline.

The reinvestment process that began in the neighborhoods and extended to downtown is a key step in the recovery process, but it must be accompanied by more vigorous leadership in city hall. Specifically, policies must be geared to the realities of urban shrinkage by encouraging shrinkage in the city administration. It is in this area that urban leaders need to be most creative in the pattern of their nineteenth-century predecessors. It is no coincidence that those cities that have adjusted best to their new demographic and economic size have had the most vigorous mayors.

Pittsburgh is an interesting example, because this city that once glowed in perpetual twilight shared all of the ills of the declining industrial North in the early 1970s. The city's population declined by one-third between 1950 and 1975—one of the greatest decreases in the country—and the workings of urban renewal demolished five dwelling units for every one that was built, spreading blight and misery over a wide swath of urban real estate. When Pete Flaherty took over a mayor in 1970, he froze hiring, eliminated 900 jobs, restricted overtime, and transformed a projected $2 million deficit into a $3.7 million surplus. In the seven years of his administration he cut the city work force by nearly 30 percent, theorizing that a smaller city required a smaller work force. He was tough with municipal unions, even to the point of hauling garbage himself during a sanitation strike, but his re-election indicated widespread public support for his policies. Despite this austerity (or perhaps because of it), Pittsburgh's downtown Golden Triangle has taken on the character of a nineteenth-century city center. As one visitor marveled: "A rich fabric of old and new, it is alive, safe, complete, and above all, marvelously compact."[5] Add to that, cobblestone streets, electric trolleys, and "inclines" (Pittsburgh's version of the cable car), and the picture is of old San Francisco, rather than of a struggling industrial city.

Flaherty's vision of the new, smaller city has been shared by equally imaginative mayors such as Baltimore's William Schaefer, New Orleans's Ernest Morial, and New York's Edward Koch. They are looking at tax structures, employment statistics, and crime-prevention programs. They believe that the best deterrent to crime is a strong neighborhood, but they are also pushing for tougher sentencing, especially for juveniles, who commit much of urban crime. They are also aware that a sound financial approach to urban administration will help to regain the confidence of business leaders, who will not only stay in the smaller city but may reinvest in its future as well. This is really what cutback planning should mean: planning not in defeat but in the realization that smaller, in the long run, may actually be better.

The Rise of No Town:
A New Type of City

The focus here has been on the older cities of the Northeast and Midwest because it is in these regions that the urban malaise is most serious. Certainly the statistics depict a grim condition. Since 1960, northeastern cities have lost nearly 14 percent of their manufacturing jobs, while the nation as a whole gained by nearly 9 percent. In population, some cities in these regions have experienced an absolute decline in the first half of the 1970s. In fact, in every major metropolitan area in these regions more people have left than have migrated into the SMSA. (See Table 14.1.) This represents quite a difference from the earlier position of these cities, which for many decades had seemed giant magnets, drawing in people and industry. Only net natural increase (births over deaths) prevented some areas from showing an absolute population loss. The Minneapolis–St. Paul region eked out a 2.3 percent population increase between 1970 and 1974, the largest for any SMSA in the Northeast and Midwest. All of the growth occurred in the suburbs. The city of Minneapolis, for example, has lost 30 percent of its population since 1950.

These figures coupled with the resultant loss in tax base and consumer purchasing power created the financial instability mentioned earlier. The attempts by political and economic leaders to encourage reinvestment indicate an appreciation of this difficult situation. Still, for most cities, it will be a long uphill battle. As the president of Cleveland's city council stated: "We're going to survive, but it is going to be very, very hard."[6]

While the cities of the Northeast and Midwest immerse themselves in the newer federalism, in neighborhood and downtown redevelopment, and in sound financial management, their brethren in the South and West face a different kind of urban future. Spatially, these are the cities of the future. Perhaps one reason why urbanists focus almost exclusively on the cities of the North results from their incredulity that Houston, Orlando, Phoenix, and Los Angeles are in fact cities in the traditional sense of having a defined downtown, distinct residential communities, and occasional open spaces. These cities are, in this view, no towns. Drives through these cities seem endless, and that is the point. They can be appreciated only through the windshield of an automobile. Newer cities, raised to adulthood in the automobile age, they exhibit the spatially dispersed patterns of their upbringing. While critics might call them nothing more than super suburbs and jokingly dare anyone to locate downtown Los Angeles, these Sunbelt metropolises are indeed cities.

One of the themes of this book has been that the spatial structure of cities changes over time. The newer cities have a new and different configuration, but not an entirely new or very different one. The basic spatial characteristics of the older cities are evident in the new: an identifiable core with several major commercial nodes or nuclei along major arteries extending toward the periphery (for example, Peachtree Center in Atlanta and peripheral Phipps Plaza), and distinct residential neighborhoods segregated by income

Table 14.1 Population and Net Migration for the Twenty Largest Metropolitan Areas: 1960 to 1974

Region and Area	Population[a]			Change 1960–1970		Change 1970–1974		Net Migration	
	1960	1970	1974	Number	Percent	Number	Percent	1960–1970	1970–1974
Northeast									
New York	15,779	17,494	17,181	1,715	10.9	−313	−1.8	301	−635
Philadelphia	5,024	5,628	5,642	604	12.0	14	0.2	98	−105
Boston	3,457	3,849	3,918	392	11.3	69	1.8	61	−2
Pittsburgh	2,405	2,401	2,334	−4	−0.2	67	−2.8	−166	−89
North Central									
Chicago	6,795	7,611	7,615	816	12.0	4	0.0	−6	−242
Detroit	4,122	4,669	4,684	547	13.3	15	0.3	15	−151
Cleveland	2,732	3,000	2,921	268	9.3	−19	−0.6	−36	−159
St. Louis	2,144	2,411	2,371	267	12.5	−40	−1.7	24	−105
Minneapolis–St. Paul	1,598	1,965	2,011	367	23.0	46	2.3	118	−26
Cincinnati	1,468	1,611	1,618	143	9.7	7	0.4	−33	−43
Milwaukee	1,421	1,575	1,589	154	10.8	14	0.9	−29	−30
South									
Washington, D.C.	2,097	2,909	3,015	812	38.7	106	3.6	429	−14
Dallas–Ft. Worth	1,738	2,378	2,499	640	36.8	121	5.1	368	10
Houston	1,571	2,169	2,402	598	38.1	233	10.7	328	116
Miami	1,269	1,888	2,223	619	48.8	335	17.7	512	312
Baltimore	1,804	2,071	2,140	267	14.8	69	3.3	54	22
Atlanta	1,169	1,596	1,775	427	36.5	179	11.2	233	102
West									
Los Angeles	7,752	9,983	10,231	2,231	28.8	248	2.5	1,172	−84
San Francisco	3,492	4,424	4,585	932	26.7	161	3.6	489	45
Seattle	1,429	1,837	1,794	408	28.6	−43	−2.3	235	−91

[a]Population numbers are in thousands.

Source: U.S. Bureau of the Census, Current Population Reports, Series P-25, No. 640, "Estimates of the Population of States with Components of Change, 1970 to 1975" (Washington, D.C., 1976).

level and race, generally becoming whiter and more affluent the farther away they are from the core. (The residential patterns of Denver and Portland, Oregon, are indistinguishable from the spatial residential configurations of older eastern cities.) The only spatial difference is the extension of these patterns over considerably wider areas in southern and western cities. Even here, however, were it not for the ease with which annexation occurs in these cities, there would hardly be a difference at all. Many southern and western cities have captured their suburbs. These cities, therefore, have densities equal to or even less than those of many suburbs in the North and Midwest. Declining densities, incidentally, are also characteristic of the older cities as emigration, abandonment, and renewal have thinned out populations and structures. In short, dispersed cities may eventually become the prevailing urban form unless energy constraints intervene. Even in an energy-scarce environment, however, the greater importance of moving information rather than people—a major characteristic of the postindustrial age—will not necessarily preclude a dispersed arrangement.

And Americans, of course, are finding these newer, more dispersed cities more to their liking. The cities of the South and the West with their newer industrial infrastructures, their proximity to superhighways, and their receptivity to growth have drained the cities of the North. At a time when national population growth and economic growth are small, these Sunbelt areas have been booming. These changes have been even more dramatic since 1970, especially in the South. Among major metropolitan areas, Miami and Houston have been the fastest-growing regions in the nation. This population shift is significant because of the multiplier effect it has on local urban economies. More people mean more building construction, which, in turn, triggers subsidiary service industries involving insurers, mortgage bankers, furniture vendors, and fabricators. Further, the movement in the Sunbelt is to the cities and the nearby suburbs. Exurbia is primarily a phenomenon of the older regions. This massive intermetropolitan shift of people and of economic power may ultimately demonstrate that people were not turned off by cities, but rather that the cities in which they resided were unable to fulfill the needs of modern society. The Sunbelt cities evidently are more attuned to current economic realities.

The shift to the Sunbelt will eventually alter the national urban system. New York, once the undisputed center of the urban network, will continue as a primary city, but its financial power will be shared with Washington and its retail power shared with Atlanta, Dallas, and Los Angeles. While these cities have traditionally been leaders in their regions, they are beginning to assume a national role as economic power shifts in their direction. The South is beginning to evidence a national urban prominence, which is anchored by Atlanta in the east and Dallas and Houston in the west, in much the same way as New York and Chicago used to and to some extent still do function as giant bookends for the northern urban system. The dream of the antebellum southerners of economic parity has become a reality, and, in an ultimate irony, it is now the northern cities that are clamoring for sectional equilibrium.

The feeling of Sunbelt cities is different, too. Cities can of course be counted, analyzed, and written about, but, above all, they must be experienced. Sure, such places as Renaissance Center create an excitement all their own, but in walking beyond the new skyline of the struggling metropolises one feels, in the words of one observer, "an atmosphere of sepulchral menace."[7] Take a walk through downtown Atlanta, on the other hand, and for sheer exuberance and chutzpah it is difficult to beat. In the early 1970s architect John Portman introduced downtown Atlanta to show business with the dazzling twenty-story Hyatt-Regency Hotel, replete with space-ship elevators and capped with a revolving dome. Downtown has occupied center stage ever since. Peachtree Center soon hovered around the Hyatt, and a few blocks away a seventy-story glass silo became the tallest hotel in the world with a half-acre lagoon for a lobby, where gondoliers glide by with liquid potations. Y'all know this is not Venice, but it is a put-on everyone enjoys. A nearby hotel, not to be outdone, comes equipped with an ice skating rink, where, fortunately, there is no drinking permitted. Overdone, perhaps, but fun, oh yes.

There are, however, clouds hovering over the Sunbelt cities. In the West, Los Angeles is beginning to lose population for the first time in its history, and San Francisco is barely holding its own. The picturesque city by the bay is experiencing some financial problems that have been plaguing less naturally well-endowed cities in the East. The Bay Area Rapid Transit (BART) train system has so far been a financial fiasco after spending its first years as a technological disgrace with computer-controlled doors opening while trains were whizzing along at 70 miles per hour and those same computers "forgetting" to stop a train until it plunged from its elevated tracks. One cynic remarked that if the sky ever fell, California would be the most logical place.

How an increase in the price of gasoline to $1 per gallon will affect the freeway civilization of smog-enshrouded Los Angeles is not certain. If Pittsburgh may be referred to as old San Francisco, then Los Angeles is old Pittsburgh, at least as far as air quality is concerned. The freeways feeding the city have already been the scene of a memorable 108-car pileup in 1969 when fog and smog reduced visibility to nearly zero. In addition, the uncertain future of the aerospace industry is casting apprehension over urban southern California. Finally, the ravages of too much or too little water are beginning to cut into the once-carefree lives of western urban residents.

In southern cities, where most of the national urban growth has occurred since 1970, there are problems of a different type. As antebellum planners were quick to discover, rapid growth had to be made rational to be effective. While cities like Miami, Atlanta, and Birmingham have adopted decentralization plans that focus on neighborhoods, other cities have tempted chaos by failing to improve communications as they expand. In Houston, for example, the Hispanic community has been especially incensed about inadequate and insensitive police services. Yet local channels for resolving such conflicts are not available. Planning in some cities continues to follow the 1920s pattern of streets and zoning (Houston does not even have zoning) to the general exclusion of social planning. While great strides have been made in race relations, for example, the service differentials between black and white neighborhoods are greater in southern cities than in cities elsewhere. As northern cities could point out, the combination of police insensitivity and official neglect is a volatile mixture.

The optimism generated by rapid growth can occasionally lead to overconfidence, as Atlantans have discovered. Beneath the architecture of entertainment abounding in downtown lies a shaky financial structure. Developers overbuilt in the early 1970s and are now suffering the consequences. Office space remains unoccupied, a large office-residential complex has plunged into bankruptcy, and several financial institutions that bankrolled the ill-timed expansion are in trouble. The economic and demographic decline common in northern cities is appearing in the New South's glamor metropolis.

The Atlanta experience underscores the fact that growth is not eternal. As capital facilities and physical plants age, public expenditures and outmigration of industries may both increase. Those attractive tax-incentive programs that lured industry south and west are nearing the end of their time limit in some states. There is no reason why opportunistic industries should show loyalty to southern and western communities any more than they displayed attachments to their former locations in the North.

Then there are the usual urban problems of poor housing, poverty, and crime that are characteristics of the urban condition everywhere, including the Sunbelt. The South still is, after all, the poorest section of the country in terms of per capita income, and the poverty in places like Mobile, Alabama, and Jackson, Mississippi, is as abject as anywhere. This only points out that in the midst of the Sunbelt ballyhoo, we are, after all, talking about cities, even if their spatial forms and latitudes are distinctive. The term *Sunbelt* tends to obscure the distinctions within the area. There are greater differences among the cities in the region than among the various regions.

Despite these problems, it seems clear that the movement of people and jobs to Sunbelt cities will continue through the early 1980s. While policies in northern cities, described earlier, may slow this movement to some degree, the shift of urban dominance to the South and Southwest—previously the most rural areas of the country—is inevitable. It is important to reiterate that this momentous shift is not a rejection of the city, though the suburban and later the exurban movements have perhaps obscured this fact. It is simply the process that George Sternlieb has called "repositioned urban growth."[8]

While the spaced-out nature of some of the cities may jar our spatial notion of cities, it is only fair to point out that this newest urban form is merely the logical spatial conclusion of a decentralization process begun nearly two centuries ago. In the 1930s architect Frank Lloyd Wright prepared a plan for what he called "Broadacre City." (See Figure 14.3.) The city was a linear development that stretched almost endlessly along a superhighway and featured open spaces, neat homes, cultural facilities, and commercial activity in rather low density. Contemporaries scoffed at this plan and wondered how it could even be called a city. They claimed that it was clearly an aberration from an otherwise brilliant architect who should have stuck to designing structures rather than communities. Yet in a more complex sense, of course, this is what many of our newer Sunbelt cities are like. Wright believed that Broadacre City would be a healthier, more natural urban environment for residents, and he may be correct.

Geographer Brian J. L. Berry has called this trend of dispersed urban settlements "urbanization without cities."[9] Older cities have thinned out, their suburbs have become more dense, and newer cities have become spatially dispersed. We may in fact be entering an era when urban forms stretch like wheat fields beyond the horizon and entire regions, from Pensacola to Dallas or from Boston to Miami, for example, are transformed into this spaced-out existence. (See Figure 14.4.) Before we become overwhelmed by this urban, or semiurban similitude, it is important to note that the cities will retain their distinctiveness as they always have; that you will be able to discern whether you are in Phoenix or Indianapolis; and that whatever they call the city in the future, its diversity, its happiness, its culture, its employment, and even its miseries will still be there to attract and distract residents and

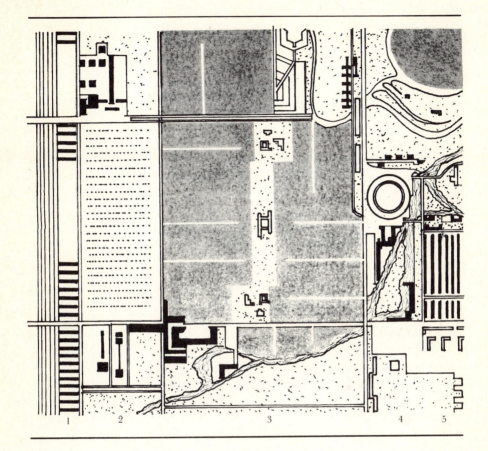

Figure 14.3   Broadacre City in a Plan of 1932

Frank Lloyd Wright's vision of the city of the future included five large sections parallel to a superhighway and a regional rail system (far left). Section 1 contains small factories and roadside markets. Section 2 consists of community-owned small farms. Section 3, the largest section, is residential, broken primarily into one-acre lots. Section 4 is for civic and cultural uses. Section 5 is a green belt interspersed with more expensive houses. This last section was no more than two miles from the highway. The plan predicted residential development near highways, decentralization of industry, and segregated land uses strung along the highway for miles of urbanlike development, or no town. (Broadacre City [F. L. Wright], in Thomas A. Reiner, *The Place of the Ideal Community in Urban Planning* © 1963 University of Pennsylvania Press. Adapted by Reiner from several Wright drawings.)

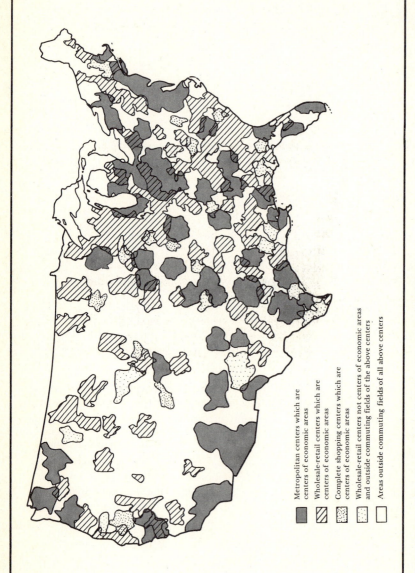

Metropolitan centers which are
centers of economic areas

Wholesale-retail centers which are
centers of economic areas

Complete shopping centers which are
centers of economic areas

Wholesale-retail centers not centers of economic areas
and outside commuting fields of the above centers

Areas outside commuting fields of all above centers

Figure 14.4   The Formation of Urban Regions, 1970

The national urban hierarchy (based on economic function) in 1970 not only continued the regionalization of the national economy, but spread the urban influence across much of the continent. Note the megalopolitan pattern of the northeastern, Great Lakes, Gulf Coast, and southern California areas. (Reprinted with permission from *Growth Centers in the American Urban System*, copyright 1973, Ballinger Publishing Company) visitors. In fact, what Berry may actually be saying is that the city has stretched out so far that it is difficult to separate city from suburb from countryside as they all blend into one another. To put it another way, the city and the nation are synonymous, which is the reason that the solution to urban problems is, in effect, a solution to our national ills.

Thrive, cities—bring your freight, bring your shows, ample and sufficient rivers,
Expand, being than which none else is perhaps more spiritual,
Keep your places, objects than which none else is more lasting.
. . . .
We fathom you not—we love you—there is perfection in you also,
You furnish your parts toward eternity,
Great or small, you furnish your parts toward the soul.

Walt Whitman, "Crossing Brooklyn Ferry"

Notes

1. Catherine Bauer, "The Dreary Deadlock of Public Housing," *The Architectural Forum,* May 1, 1957, pp. 140–141.

2. Rolf Goetze, *Building Neighborhood Confidence: A Humanistic Strategy for Urban Housing* (Cambridge, Mass.: Ballinger, 1976), p. 9.

3. Patricia Roberts Harris, "Helping the Cities—and Those Within," *Washington Post,* February 16, 1976.

4. Roger Montgomery, review of *Neighborhood Change: Lessons in the Dynamics of Urban Decay* by Charles L. Leven, *Journal of the American Institute of Planners,* 43 (October 1977), 411.

5. Gurney Breckenfeld, "It's Up to the Cities to Save Themselves," *Fortune,* 95 (March 1977), 197.

6. Quoted in *ibid.*

7. *Ibid.*

8. George Sternlieb and James W. Hughes, "New Regional and Metropolitan Realities of America," *Journal of the American Institute of Planners,* 43 (July 1977), 239.

9. See Brian J. L. Berry, "The Counterurbanization Process: Urban America Since 1970," in Berry, ed., *Urbanization and Counterurbanization,* vol. 11, Urban Affairs Annual Reviews (Beverly Hills, Calif.: Sage Publications, 1976), 24.

Suggestions for Further Reading

Introduction.
The City: People, Space, and Time

Beginning points for the study of American urbanization are two books that are not about American cities only: Lewis Mumford, *The City in History: Its Origins, Its Transformations, and Its Prospects* (New York: Harcourt, Brace & World, 1961), which relates the impact of technology on the urban form and on the urban resident from ancient times to the twentieth century, and Adna F. Weber, *The Growth of Cities in the Nineteenth Century: A Study in Statistics* (New York: Macmillan, 1899), which was probably the first major urban study to appreciate the importance of space, technology, and population trends as the foundations of urban growth analysis. While both books discuss American cities, their approach includes an examination of cities worldwide, adding an important comparative perspective to the student's introduction to the American city.

General historical surveys of the American city include Howard P. Chudacoff, *The Evolution of American Urban Society* (Englewood Cliffs, N.J.: Prentice-Hall, 1975); Charles N. Glaab and A. Theodore Brown, *A History of Urban America*, rev. ed. (New York: Macmillan, 1976); and Zane L. Miller, *The Urbanization of Modern America: A Brief History* (New York: Harcourt Brace Jovanovich, 1973).

The evolution of the American urban system is the subject of several studies including Daniel J. Elazar, *Cities of the Prairie: The Metropolitan Frontier and American Politics* (New York: Basic Books, 1970), which focuses on seventeen cities in the Midwest; Blaine A. Brownell and David R. Goldfield, eds., *The City in Southern History* (Port Washington, N.Y.: Kennikat Press, 1977) deals with southern cities. Other studies dealing with the evolution of American cities include: Eric E. Lampard, "The Evolving System of Cities in the United States: Urbanization and Economic Developments," in Harvey S. Perloff and Loudon Wingo, Jr., eds., *Issues in Urban Economics* (Baltimore: Johns Hopkins Press, 1968), pp. 81–139; Allan R. Pred, *The Spatial Dynamics of U.S. Urban-Industrial Growth, 1800–1914* (Cambridge, Mass.: MIT Press, 1966); James E. Vance, Jr., "Cities in the Shaping of the American Nation," *The Journal of Geography,* 75 (January 1976), 41–52.

Two good introductions to the evolution of urban space are Larry S. Bourne, ed., *Internal Structure of the City: Readings on Space and Environment* (New York: Oxford University Press, 1971) and Leo F. Schnore, ed., *The New Urban History: Quantitative Explorations by American Historians* (Princeton, N.J.: Princeton University Press, 1975). On some of the more specific aspects of urban space see Wayne Andrews, *Architecture, Ambition, and Americans: A Social History of American Architecture* (New York: Free Press, 1964), which, together with Vincent Scully's *American Architecture and Urbanism* (New York: Praeger, 1969), provides an easily understood survey of the city's built environment, the spatial relationship of those structures, and their reflections of and impact on urban society. Peter G. Goheen, "Interpreting the American City: Some Historical Perspectives," *The Geographical Review,* 64 (July 1974), 362–384; Leon Moses and Harold F. Williamson, "The Location of Economic Activities in Cities," *American Economic Review,* 57 (May 1967), 211–222; Sam Bass Warner, Jr., *Private City: Philadelphia in Three Periods of Its Growth* (Philadelphia: University of Pennsylvania Press, 1968); and Warner, *The Urban Wilderness: A History of the American City* (New York: Harper & Row, 1972) emphasize the relationship between economics, technology, and the internal structure of the city.

Other useful studies of space and urban society include Tamara K. Hareven, "The Historical Study of the Family in Urban Society," *Journal of Urban History,* 1 (May 1975), 259–265; Homer Hoyt, *The Structure and Growth of Residential Neighborhoods in American Cities* (Washington, D.C.: Federal Housing Administration, 1939); Robert E. Park, Ernest W. Burgess, and Roderick D. McKenzie, eds., *The City* (Chicago: University of Chicago Press, 1925); John W. Reps, *The Making of Urban America: A History of City Planning in the United States* (Princeton, N.J.: Princeton University Press, 1965), a superb survey of the early plans for America's major, minor and nonexistent cities from the colonial period until World War I; and Leo F. Schnore, *The Urban Scene: Human Ecology and Demography* (New York: Free Press, 1965).

Part I.
Genesis

Any study of colonial urban life and development should begin with Carl Bridenbaugh's classic works, *Cities in the Wilderness: The First Century of Urban Life in America, 1625–1742* (New York: Ronald Press, 1938) and *Cities in Revolt: Urban Life in America, 1743–1776* (New York: Capricorn, 1955). A number of books by John W. Reps—especially *Town Planning in Frontier America* (Princeton, N.J.: Princeton University Press, 1969)—provide a detailed analysis of the design and physical structure of colonial cities and indicate their indebtedness to many European patterns.

Studies of New England towns have been especially prominent and numerous for the colonial era. These include Sumner Chilton Powell, *Puritan Village: The Formation of New England Towns* (Garden City, N.Y.: Doubleday, 1965); Kenneth A.

Lockridge, *A New England Town: The First Hundred Years: Dedham, Massachusetts, 1636–1736* (New York: W. W. Norton, 1970); Darrett B. Rutman, *Winthrop's Boston: Portrait of a Puritan Town, 1630–1649* (Chapel Hill, N.C.: University of North Carolina Press, 1965); Michael Zuckerman, *Peaceable Kingdoms: New England Towns in the Eighteenth Century* (New York: Vintage, 1970); William Haller, Jr., *The Puritan Frontier: Town-Planting in New England Colonial Development, 1630–1660* (New York: Columbia University Press, 1951); Philip T. Greven, Jr., *Four Generations: Population, Land, and Family in Colonial Andover, Massachusetts* (Ithaca, N.Y.: Cornell University Press, 1970); and G. B. Warden, *Boston: 1689–1776* (Boston: Little, Brown, 1970). Sam Bass Warner, Jr.'s *Private City: Philadelphia in Three Periods of Its Growth* (Philadelphia: University of Pennsylvania Press, 1968) contains a section on the eighteenth century and information useful in studying colonial cities in general. The dynamics of town development in the South are explored in Carville Earle and Ronald Hoffman, "The Urban South: The First Two Centuries," in Blaine A. Brownell and David R. Goldfield, eds., *The City in Southern History: The Growth of Urban Civilization in the South* (New York: Kennikat Press, 1977); and John C. Rainbolt, "The Absence of Towns in Seventeenth-Century Virginia," *Journal of Southern History,* 35 (August 1969), 343–360. Blake McKelvey's *American Urbanization: A Comparative History* (Glenview, Ill.: Scott, Foresman, 1973) compares American towns and cities with those in England, Europe, and Latin America in the seventeenth and eighteenth centuries.

Useful works on the colonial urban economy include: Bernard Bailyn, *The New England Merchants in the Seventeenth Century* (Cambridge, Mass.: MIT Press, 1955); Arthur L. Jensen, *The Maritime Commerce of Colonial Philadelphia* (Madison, Wisc.: State Historical Society of Wisconsin, 1963); Edward C. Papenfuse, *In Pursuit of Profit: The Annapolis Merchants in the American Revolution, 1763–1805* (Baltimore: Johns Hopkins Press, 1975); Joseph A. Ernst and H. Roy Merrens, "'Camden's Turrets Pierce the Skies!': The Urban Process in the Southern Colonies During the Eighteenth Century," *William and Mary Quarterly,* 30, 3rd series (October 1973), 549–574; Richard Walsh, *Charleston's Sons of Liberty: A Study of Artisans, 1763–1789* (Columbia, S.C.: University of South Carolina Press, 1959); and Charles S. Olton, "Philadelphia's Mechanics in the First Decade of Revolution, 1765–1775." *Journal of American History,* 59 (September 1972), 311–326.

Perhaps the best single volume on colonial urban society is Jackson Turner Main's *The Social Structure of Revolutionary America* (Princeton, N.J.: Princeton University Press, 1965), even though it does not focus solely on cities. Also important are: James A. Henretta, "Economic Development and Social Structure in Colonial Boston," *William and Mary Quarterly,* 22, 3rd series (January 1965), 75–92; John Demos, *A Little Commonwealth: Family Life in Plymouth Colony* (New York: Oxford University Press, 1970); Elizabeth A. Dexter, *Colonial Women of Affairs: Women in Business and Professions in America Before 1776* (Boston: Houghton Mifflin, 1931); and Raymond A. Mohl, "Poverty in Early America, A Reappraisal: The Case of Eighteenth Century New York City," *New York History,* 50 (January 1969), 5–27.

Two recent works explore the relationships between urban socioeconomic patterns and political activity in the colonial era: Edward M. Cook, Jr., *The Fathers of the Towns: Leadership and Community Structure in Eighteenth-Century New England* (Baltimore: Johns Hopkins Press, 1976), and Thomas J. Archdeacon, *New York City, 1664–1710: Conquest and Change* (Ithaca, N.Y.: Cornell University Press, 1976).

John C. Teaford's brief but informative book *The Municipal Revolution in America: Origins of Modern Urban Government, 1650–1825* (Chicago: University of Chicago Press, 1975) contains much of interest on the period before the Revolution.

Very little has been written about urban facilities and services, though the works of Bridenbaugh contain a wealth of material on the subject. Also see James Richardson, *The New York Police, Colonial Times to 1901* (New York: Oxford University Press, 1970). Thomas J. Wertenbaker's *The Golden Age of Colonial Culture* (New York: New York University Press, 1942) is a very brief but enjoyable survey of cultural developments in Boston, New York, Philadelphia, Annapolis, Williamsburg, and Charleston.

Two studies on a portion of the middle colonies have uncovered a society generally lacking in community spirit, possessing a great degree of transiency and a variety of ethnicity, and dominated by the profit motive—antitheses of the well-documented New England experience: See James T. Lemon, *The Best Poor Man's Country: A Geographical Study of Early Southeastern Pennsylvania* (Baltimore: Johns Hopkins Press, 1972) and Stephanie Grauman Wolf, *Urban Village: Population, Community, and Family Structure in Germantown, Pennsylvania, 1683–1800* (Princeton, N.J.: Princeton University Press, 1977). It remains to be seen whether these traits persisted throughout the middle colonies.

Part II.
Market Place

Several books and essays provide excellent insight into the process of urban growth in an era during which small towns were transformed into thriving cities. The analyses of urbanization include Richard D. Brown, "The Emergence of Urban Society in Rural Massachusetts, 1760–1820," *Journal of American History,* 61 (June 1974), 29–51; Michael P. Conzen's *Frontier Farming in an Urban Shadow: The Influence of Madison's Proximity on the Agricultural Development of Blooming Grove, Wisconsin* (Madison, Wisc.: State Historical Society of Wisconsin, 1971), which provides an interesting discussion of the impact of urbanization on rural communities; Leonard P. Curry, "Urbanization and Urbanism in the Old South: A Comparative View," *Journal of Southern History,* 40 (February 1974), 43–60; Bayrd Still, "Patterns of Mid-Nineteenth Century Urbanization in the Middle West," *Mississippi Valley Historical Review,* 28 (September 1941), 187–206; and Richard C. Wade, *The Urban Frontier: Pioneer Life in Early Pittsburgh, Cincinnati, Lexington, Louisville, and St. Louis* (Chicago: University of Chicago Press, 1964). Studies of individual cities that deal with questions of urbanization are Stuart M. Blumin, *The Urban Threshold: Growth and Change in a Nineteenth-Century American Community* (Chicago: University of Chicago Press, 1976); Michael H. Frisch, *Town Into City: Springfield, Massachusetts, and the Meaning of Community, 1840–1880* (Cambridge, Mass.: Harvard University Press, 1972), probably the best single-city urbanization analysis to date; Roger W. Lotchin, *San Francisco, 1846–1856: From Hamlet to City* (New York: Oxford University Press, 1974); and Kenneth W. Wheeler, *To Wear a City's Crown: The Beginnings of Urban Growth in Texas, 1836–1865* (Cambridge, Mass.: Harvard University Press, 1968).

The literature involving the development of the commercial urban economy and its eventual meshing with the national economy centered at New York includes

Wyatt W. Belcher, *The Economic Rivalry Between St. Louis and Chicago, 1850–1880* (New York: Columbia University Press, 1947); Thomas C. Cochran, "The Business Revolution," *American Historical Review,* 79 (December 1974), 1449–1466; David R. Goldfield, *Urban Growth in the Age of Sectionalism: Virginia, 1847–1861* (Baton Rouge, La.: Louisiana State University Press, 1977); Douglas C. North, *The Economic Growth of the United States, 1790–1860* (Englewood Cliffs, N.J.: Prentice-Hall, 1961); Allan R. Pred, *Urban Growth and the Circulation of Information: The U.S. System of Cities, 1790–1840* (Cambridge, Mass.: MIT Press, 1973); Merl E. Reed, *New Orleans and the Railroads: The Struggle for Commercial Empire, 1830–1860* (Baton Rouge, La.: Louisiana State University Press, 1966); Julius Rubin, *Canal or Railroad? Imitation and Innovation in the Response to the Erie Canal in Philadelphia, Baltimore, and Boston* (Philadelphia: American Philosophical Society, 1961); and Louis B. Schmidt, "Internal Commerce and the Development of the National Economy before 1860," *Journal of Political Economy,* 47 (December 1939), 798–822.

The rich fabric of urban society in the marketplace era has inspired numerous studies on various aspects of that society. Works on immigrant life include: Kathleen Neils Conzen, *Immigrant Milwaukee, 1836–1860: Accommodation and Community in a Frontier City* (Cambridge, Mass.: Harvard University Press, 1976) and Robert Ernst, *Immigrant Life in New York City, 1825–1863* (New York: King's Crown Press, 1949). Studies dealing with the black experience include: Ira Berlin, *Slaves Without Masters: The Free Negro in the Antebellum South* (New York: Pantheon, 1974); Claudia D. Goldin, *Urban Slavery in the American South, 1820–1860: A Quantitative History* (Chicago: University of Chicago Press, 1976); Leon F. Litwack, *North of Slavery: The Negro in the Free States, 1790–1860* (Chicago: University of Chicago Press, 1961); Robert S. Starobin, *Industrial Slavery in the Old South* (New York: Oxford University Press, 1969); Richard C. Wade, *Slavery in the Cities: The South, 1820–1860* (New York: Oxford University Press, 1964). Works on labor include: John Coolidge, *Mill and Mansion: A Study of Architecture and Society in Lowell, Massachusetts* (New York: Columbia University Press, 1942); David Montgomery, "The Working Classes of the Pre-Industrial American City, 1780–1830," *Labor History,* 9 (Winter 1968), 5–22. Books describing poverty are Robert H. Bremner, *From the Depths: The Discovery of Poverty in the United States* (New York: New York University Press, 1956) and Raymond A. Mohl, *Poverty in New York, 1783–1825* (New York: Oxford University Press, 1971). Studies of social and geographic mobility include: Peter R. Knights, *The Plain People of Boston, 1830–1860: A Study in City Growth* (New York: Oxford University Press, 1971); Edward Pessen, "The Social Configuration of the Antebellum City: An Historical and Theoretical Inquiry," *Journal of Urban History,* 2 (May 1976), 267–306; Stephan Thernstrom, *Poverty and Progress: Social Mobility in a Nineteenth-Century City* (Cambridge, Mass.: Harvard University Press, 1964); and Thernstrom and Richard Sennett, *Nineteenth-Century Cities: Essays in the New Urban History* (New Haven: Yale University Press, 1969), which contains several essays on social mobility and cities.

On the spatial manifestations of urban society see especially Charles Lockwood, *Manhattan Moves Uptown: An Illustrated History* (Boston: Houghton Mifflin, 1976); Allan R. Pred, *The Spatial Dynamics of U.S. Urban-Industrial Growth, 1800–1914* (Cambridge, Mass.: MIT Press, 1966); George R. Taylor, "The Beginnings of Mass Transportation in Urban America," *Smithsonian Journal of History,* 1 (Summer 1966), 35–50 and (Autumn 1966), 31–54; and David Ward, *Cities and Immigrants: A*

Geography of Change in Nineteenth-Century America (New York: Oxford University Press, 1971).

Several works cover the development of local government and the provision of urban services. On the important question of police and public order, see Michael Feldberg, *The Philadelphia Riots of 1844: A Study in Ethnic Conflict* (Westport, Ct.: Greenwood Press, 1975); David Grimsted, "Rioting in its Jacksonian Setting," *American Historical Review,* 77 (April 1972), 361–397; Theodore M. Hammett, "Two Mobs of Jacksonian Boston: Ideology and Interest," *Journal of American History,* 62 (March 1976), 845–868; Roger C. Lane, *Policing the City: Boston, 1822–1885* (Cambridge, Mass.: Harvard University Press, 1967); and James F. Richardson, *The New York Police: Colonial Times to 1901* (New York: Oxford University Press, 1970). On the adoption of public responsibility for health services see John Duffy, *A History of Public Health in New York City, 1625–1866* (New York: Russell Sage Foundation, 1968); David R. Goldfield, "The Business of Health Planning: Disease Prevention in the Old South," *Journal of Southern History,* 42 (November 1976), 557–570; and Charles E. Rosenberg, *The Cholera Years: The U.S. in 1832, 1849, and 1866* (Chicago: University of Chicago Press, 1962). On a related topic, water service, see Nelson M. Blake, *Water for Cities: A History of the Urban Water Supply Problem in the U.S.* (Syracuse: Syracuse University Press, 1958). On social services see M.J. Heale, "From City Fathers to Social Critics: Humanitarianism and Government in New York, 1790–1860," *Journal of American History,* 63 (June 1976), 21–41. On environmental services see Albert Fein, *Frederick Law Olmsted and the American Environmental Tradition* (New York: Braziller, 1972). On the growth of local government in general see Robert A. McCaughey, "From Town to City: Boston in the 1820s," *Political Science Quarterly,* 87 (June 1973), 191–213; Edward Pessen, "Who Governed the Nation's Cities in the 'Era of the Common Man'?" *Political Science Quarterly,* 87 (December 1972), 591–614; and Jon C. Teaford, *The Municipal Revolution in America: Origins of Modern Urban Government, 1650–1825* (Chicago: University of Chicago Press, 1975).

The manner in which Americans came to view the nineteenth-century city is the theme of several books, including Thomas Bender, *Toward An Urban Vision: Ideas and Institutions in Nineteenth-Century America* (Lexington, Ky.: Kentucky University Press, 1975); Kevin Lynch, *The Image of the City* (Cambridge, Mass.: MIT Press, 1960); Anselm Strauss, *Images of the American City* (Glencoe, Ill.: Free Press, 1961); and Morton White and Lucia White, *The Intellectual Versus the City: From Thomas Jefferson to Frank Lloyd Wright* (Cambridge, Mass.: Harvard University Press, 1962).

Part III.
Radial Center

Most of the literature concerning the rapid spatial expansion of the city that was characteristic of the period deals with the impact of transportation technology on the city's spatial configuration. The works include Carl W. Condit, *The Railroad and the City: A Technological and Urbanistic History of Cincinnati* (Columbus, Ohio: Ohio State University Press, 1977); Robert M. Fogelson, *The Fragmented Metropolis: Los Angeles, 1850–1930* (Cambridge, Mass.: Harvard University Press, 1967); Clay McShane, *Technology and Reform: Street Railways and the Growth of Milwaukee, 1887–1900* (Madison, Wisc.: State Historical Society of Wisconsin, 1974); Joel A. Tarr, *Transportation Innovation and Changing Spatial Patterns: Pittsburgh, 1850–1910* (Pittsburgh: Carnegie

Mellon University, 1972); Sam Bass Warner, Jr., *Streetcar Suburbs: The Process of Growth in Boston, 1870–1900* (New York: Atheneum, 1974); and Olivier Zunz, "Technology and Society in an Urban Environment; The Case of the Third Avenue El," *Journal of Interdisciplinary History,* 3 (Summer 1972), 89–101. On the radiant-center aspects of the spatial equilibrium see David F. Burg, *Chicago's White City of 1893* (Lexington, Ky.: Kentucky University Press, 1976); the excellent volumes on architecture, technology, and society in Chicago by Carl W. Condit: *Chicago, 1910–29: Building, Planning, and Urban Technology* (Chicago: University of Chicago Press, 1973) and *Chicago, 1930–70: Building, Planning, and Urban Technology* (1974); and Jon A. Peterson, "The City Beautiful Movement: Forgotten Origins and Lost Meanings," *Journal of Urban History,* 2 (August 1976), 415–434.

On the period's economic, especially industrial, expansion, see Gunther Barth, *Instant Cities: Urbanization and the Rise of San Francisco and Denver* (New York: Oxford University Press, 1975), which deals with entrepreneurial activity on the urban frontier; Charles N. Glaab, *Kansas City and the Railroads: Community Policy in the Growth of a Regional Metropolis* (Madison, Wisc.: State Historical Society of Wisconsin, 1962); Peter G. Goheen, "Industrialization and the Growth of Cities in Nineteenth-Century America," *American Studies,* 14 (Spring 1973), 49–65; Carol E. Hoffecker, *Wilmington, Delaware: Portrait of an Industrial City, 1830–1910* (Charlottesville, Va.: University Press of Virginia, 1974); and Robert H. Wiebe, *The Search for Order, 1877–1920* (New York: Hill and Wang, 1967).

The transformation of urban labor generated by the new economic order was the subject of numerous contemporary novels and more recent historical accounts including Edward Bellamy, *Looking Backward* (New York: Amsco, 1888); Stuart D. Brandes, *American Welfare Capitalism, 1880–1949* (Chicago: University of Chicago Press, 1976); Stanley Buder, *Pullman: An Experiment in Industrial Order and Community Planning, 1880–1930* (New York: Oxford University Press, 1967); Herbert G. Gutman, "Work, Culture, and Society in Industrializing America, 1815–1919," *American Historical Review,* 78 (June 1973), 531–588; Samuel P. Hays, *The Response to Industrialism: 1885–1914* (Chicago: University of Chicago Press, 1957); Susan J. Kleinberg, "Technology and Women's Work: The Lives of Working Class Women in Pittsburgh, 1870–1900," *Labor History,* 17 (Winter 1976), 58–72; Gerd Korman, *Industrialization, Immigrants, and Americanizers: The View from Milwaukee, 1866–1921* (Madison, Wisc.: State Historical Society of Wisconsin, 1967); Daniel Nelson, *Managers and Workers: Origins of the New Factory System in the United States, 1880–1929* (Madison, Wisc.: University of Wisconsin Press, 1975); Neil L. Shumsky, "San Francisco's Workingmen Respond to the Modern City," *California Historical Quarterly* (Spring 1976), 46–57; and Upton Sinclair, *The Jungle* rev. ed. (New York: Signet, 1973; originally published 1906).

The literature on immigrant life in urban America is extensive. Some of the more helpful general studies include: Milton Gordon, *Assimilation in American Life: The Role of Race, Religion and National Origins* (New York: Oxford University Press, 1964); Oscar Handlin, *The Uprooted* (Boston: Little, Brown, 1951); and John Higham, *Strangers in the Land: Patterns of American Nativism, 1860–1925* (New York: Atheneum, 1963), which recounts the organization of anti-immigrant sentiment.

Studies that are concerned with particular immigrant groups or a specific city include: Abraham Cahan, *The Rise of David Levinsky* (New York: Harper & Brothers, 1917); Dennis Clark, *The Irish in Philadelphia: Ten Generations of Urban Experience*

(Philadelphia: Temple University Press, 1973); Dean R. Esslinger, *Immigrants and the City: Ethnicity and Mobility in a Nineteenth-Century Midwestern Community* (New York: Kennikat Press, 1975); Irving Howe, *World of Our Fathers* (New York: Harcourt Brace Jovanovich, 1976); Thomas Kessner, *The Golden Door: Italian and Jewish Immigrant Mobility in New York City, 1880–1915* (New York: Oxford University Press, 1977); Humbert S. Nelli, *The Italians in Chicago, 1860–1920: A Study in Ethnic Mobility* (New York: Oxford University Press, 1970); Moses Rischin, *The Promised City: New York's Jews, 1870–1914* (Cambridge, Mass: Harvard University Press, 1962); Betty Smith, *A Tree Grows in Brooklyn* (New York: Harper & Row, 1943); and Olivier Zunz, "The Organization of the American City in the Late Nineteenth Century: Ethnic Structure and Spatial Arrangements in Detroit," *Journal of Urban History,* 3 (August 1977), 443–465.

The material on urban blacks is also voluminous, and has increased in recent years. The student should begin with the following: August Meier and Elliot Rudwick, *From Plantation to Ghetto* (New York: Hill and Wang, 1966) and Gilbert Osofsky, "The Enduring Ghetto," *Journal of American History,* 55 (September 1968), 243–255. More specific studies include Nathan I. Huggins, *Harlem Renaissance* (New York: Oxford University Press, 1971); David M. Katzman, *Before the Ghetto: Black Detroit in the Nineteenth Century* (Urbana, Ill.: University of Illinois Press, 1973); Kenneth L. Kusmer, *A Ghetto Takes Shape: Black Cleveland, 1870–1930* (Urbana, Ill.: University of Illinois Press, 1976); Gilbert Osofsky, *Harlem: The Making of a Ghetto: Negro New York, 1890–1930* (New York: Harper & Row, 1966); Howard N. Rabinowitz, *Race Relations in the Urban South, 1865–1890* (New York: Oxford University Press, 1978); and William Tuttle, Jr., *Race Riot: Chicago in the Red Summer of 1919* (New York: Atheneum, 1970).

On social mobility, or the lack of it, during the period see Howard P. Chudacoff, *Mobile Americans: Residential and Social Mobility in Omaha, 1880–1920* (New York: Oxford University Press, 1973); Stephen Crane, *Maggie: A Girl of the Streets,* rev. ed. (New York: Fawcett, 1960); Richard Sennett, *Families Against the City: Middle Class Homes of Industrial Chicago, 1872–1890* (Cambridge, Mass.: Harvard University Press, 1970); and Stephan Thernstrom, *The Other Bostonians: Poverty and Progress in the American Metropolis, 1880–1970* (Cambridge, Mass.: Harvard University Press, 1973).

The increasing concern over urban poverty and its relief during the radial-center era is reflected in Allen F. Davis, *Spearheads for Reform: The Social Settlements and the Progressive Movement, 1890–1914* (New York: Oxford University Press, 1967); Joseph M. Hawes, *Children in Urban Society: Juvenile Delinquency in Nineteenth-Century America* (New York: Oxford University Press, 1971); Nathan I. Huggins, *Protestants against Poverty: Boston's Charities, 1870–1900* (Westport, Ct.: Greenwood Press, 1970); James B. Lane, *Jacob A. Riis and the American City* (Port Washington, N.Y.: Kennikat Press, 1975); and Roy Lubove, *The Progressives and the Slums: Tenement House Reform in New York City, 1890–1917* (Pittsburgh: University of Pittsburgh Press, 1962).

The social conscience reflected in the stepped-up war on poverty or at least on its purported causes was also evident in the development of public education. Studies of public education during this era include: Ronald D. Cohen, "Urban Schooling in the Gilded Age and After," *Journal of Urban History,* 2 (August 1976), 499–506; Maxine Seller, "The Education of Immigrant Children in Buffalo, New York, 1890–1916," *New York History* 57 (April 1976), 183–99; and Selwyn K. Troen, *The Public and the*

Schools: Shaping the St. Louis System, 1838–1920 (Columbia, Mo.: University of Missouri Press, 1975).

The colorful struggle for political power between bosses and reformers is recounted in Lyle W. Dorsett, *The Pendergast Machine* (New York: Oxford University Press, 1968); Melvin G. Holli, *Reform in Detroit: Hazen S. Pingree and Urban Politics* (New York: Oxford University Press, 1969); Joy J. Jackson, *New Orleans in the Gilded Age: Politics and Urban Progress, 1860–1896* (Baton Rouge, La.: Louisiana State University Press, 1969); Seymour Mandelbaum, *Boss Tweed's New York* (New York: Wiley, 1965); Zane Miller, *Boss Cox's Cincinnati, Urban Politics in the Progressive Era* (New York: Oxford University Press, 1968); Jerome Mushkat, *Tammany: The Evolution of a Political Machine, 1789–1865* (Syracuse: Syracuse University Press, 1971); and William L. Riordan, *Plunkitt of Tammany Hall* (New York: McClure, Philipps & Co., 1905).

Part IV.
Vital Fringe

The volume of materials available on American cities in the twentieth century is enormous. An early, and still useful, survey is Blake McKelvey, *The Emergence of Metropolitan America, 1915–1966* (New Brunswick, N.J.: Rutgers University Press, 1968).

The emotional cauldron that characterized urban society at the beginning of the period is captured well in Kenneth T. Jackson's *The Ku Klux Klan in the City, 1915–1930* (New York: Oxford University Press, 1967) and Mark Haller's "Organized Crime in Urban Society: Chicago in the Twentieth Century," *Journal of Social History,* 5 (Winter 1971), 21–34. For some of the reasons why the cauldron continues to boil today, see Kenneth B. Clark, *Dark Ghetto: Dilemmas of Social Power* (New York: Harper & Row, 1965); St. Clair Drake and Horace R. Cayton, *Black Metropolis: A Study of Negro Life in a Northern City,* 2 vols. (New York: Harper & Row, 1962); Ralph Ellison, *Invisible Man* (New York: Random House, 1952); Leo Grebler, *et al., The Mexican-American People* (New York: Free Press, 1970); Lee Rainwater, *Behind Ghetto Walls: Black Families in a Federal Slum* (Chicago: Aldine, 1970); *The Report of the National Advisory Commission on Civil Disorders* (New York: Bantam Books, 1968); and Karl E. Taeuber and Alma F. Taeuber, *Negroes in American Cities: Residential Segregation and Neighborhood Change* (New York: Atheneum, 1969).

On some aspects of automobile technology and American cities, see John B. Rae, *The Road and the Car in American Life* (Cambridge, Mass.: MIT Press, 1971); James J. Flink, *The Car Culture* (Cambridge, Mass.: MIT Press, 1975); Carl W. Condit, *Chicago, 1930–70: Building, Planning, and Urban Technology* (Chicago: University of Chicago Press, 1974); and Blaine A. Brownell, "A Symbol of Modernity: Attitudes Toward the Automobile in Southern Cities in the 1920s," *American Quarterly,* 24 (March 1972), 20–44.

The suburbs, which expanded with the aid of technology and affluence, have drawn increasing attention. The significance of suburban development was recognized some time ago in Harlan Paul Douglass, *The Suburban Trend* (New York: Century, 1925). Also see Herbert J. Gans, *The Levittowners* (New York: Pantheon, 1967); Kenneth T. Jackson, "The Crabgrass Frontier: 150 Years of Suburban

Growth in America," in Raymond A. Mohl and James F. Richardson, eds., *The Urban Experience: Themes in American History* (Belmont, Calif.: Wadsworth, 1973), pp. 196–221; David R. Goldfield, "The Limits of Suburban Growth," *Urban Affairs Quarterly,* 12 (September 1976), 83–102; Louis H. Masotti and Jeffrey K. Hadden, eds., *The Urbanization of the Suburbs* (Beverly Hills: Sage, 1973); and Seymour I. Toll, *Zoned American* (New York: Grossman, 1969). Two interesting studies of the ideological framework for the suburban movement are Leo Marx, *The Machine in the Garden: Technology and the Pastoral Ideal in America* (New York: Oxford University Press, 1964) and Scott Donaldson, *The Suburban Myth* (New York: Columbia University Press, 1969). A study of the interactions among urban expansion, technology, and attitudes toward the urban community is Blaine A. Brownell, *The Urban Ethos in the South, 1920–1930* (Baton Rouge: Louisiana State University Press, 1975).

The best single study of the growing involvement of the federal government in urban affairs is Mark I. Gelfand's *A Nation of Cities: The Federal Government and Urban America, 1933–1965* (New York: Oxford University Press, 1975). Also see Joseph L. Arnold, *The New Deal in the Suburbs: A History of the Greenbelt Town Program, 1935–1954* (Columbus, Ohio: Ohio State University Press, 1971); Paul K. Conkin, *Tomorrow a New World: The New Deal Community Program* (Ithaca, N.Y.: Cornell University Press, 1959); the Urbanism Committee to the National Resources Committee, *Our Cities: Their Role in the National Economy* (Washington, D.C.: Government Printing Office, 1937); Scott Greer, *Urban Renewal and American Cities: The Dilemma of Democratic Institutions* (Indianapolis: Bobbs-Merrill, 1965); and Frances Fox Piven and Richard A. Cloward, *Regulating the Poor: The Functions of Public Welfare* (New York: Random House, 1971).

Studies of local government functions and malfunctions in an intergovernmental era include Robert A. Caro, *The Power Broker: Robert Moses and the Fall of New York* (New York: Random House, 1974); Robert E. Dahl, *Who Governs? Democracy and Power in an American City* (New Haven: Yale University Press, 1961). On the continuing saga of bosses and reformers, see Michael P. McCarthy, "On Bosses, Reformers, and Urban Growth: Some Suggestions for a Political Typology of American Cities," *Journal of Urban History,* 4 (November 1977), 29–38; Arthur Mann, *La Guardia Comes to Power: 1933* (Chicago: University of Chicago Press, 1965); Mike Royko, *Boss: Richard J. Daley of Chicago* (New York: New American Library, 1971); and Bruce M. Stave, *The New Deal and the Last Hurrah: Pittsburgh Machine Politics* (Pittsburgh: University of Pittsburgh Press, 1970).

On city planning see Joseph L. Arnold, "City Planning in America," in Raymond A. Mohl and James F. Richardson, eds., *The Urban Experience: Themes in American History* (Belmont, Calif.: Wadsworth, 1973), pp. 14–43; Lloyd Rodwin, *Nations and Cities: A Comparison of Strategies for Urban Growth* (Boston: Houghton Mifflin, 1970); Thomas S. Hines, *Burnham of Chicago: Architect and Planner* (New York: Oxford University Press, 1974); Mel Scott, *American City Planning Since 1890* (Berkeley, Calif.: University of California Press, 1969); and Blaine A. Brownell, "The Commercial-Civic Elite and City Planning in Atlanta, Memphis, and New Orleans in the 1920s," *Journal of Southern History,* 41 (August 1975), 339–368.

The urban future is and has been the subject of a flood of books and articles, especially since the 1960s. Some of the most provocative include Edward C. Banfield, *The Unheavenly City: The Nature and Future of Our Urban Crisis* (Boston: Little, Brown, 1968); Gurney Breckenfeld, "It's Up to the Cities to Save Themselves,"

Fortune, 95 (March 1977), 194–206; Jane Jacobs, *The Death and Life of Great American Cities* (New York: Vintage, 1963); and Norton E. Long, "A Marshall Plan for Cities?" *Public Interest*, 46 (Winter 1977), 48–58. For a radical analysis of the nature of the urban crisis, see David Harvey, *Social Justice and the City* (Baltimore: Johns Hopkins Press, 1973).

The new spatial arrangements of cities, regions, and the urban nation are analyzed in Brian J. L. Berry, *Growth Centers in the American Urban System*, 2 vols. (Cambridge, Mass.: Ballinger, 1973); Jean Gottmann, *Megalopolis: The Urbanized Northeastern Seaboard of the United States* (Cambridge, Mass.: MIT Press, 1961); Stephen Grabow, "Frank Lloyd Wright and the American City: The Broadacres Debate," *Journal of the American Institute of Planners*, 43 (April 1977), 115–135; A. H. Hawley, *The Changing Shape of Metropolitan America: Deconcentration Since 1920* (Glencoe, Ill.: Free Press, 1956); and George Sternlieb and James W. Hughes, "New Regional and Metropolitan Realities of America," *Journal of the American Institute of Planners*, 43 (July 1977), 237. For a review of developments in the urban South, see Blaine A. Brownell, "The Urban South Comes of Age, 1900–1940," and Edward F. Haas, "The Southern Metropolis, 1940–1976," in Blaine A. Brownell and David R. Goldfield, eds., *The City in Southern History: The Growth of Urban Civilization in the South* (Port Washington, N.Y.: Kennikat Press, 1977), pp. 123–158 and 159–191.

The importance of neighborhood preservation as a foundation for urban policy is made especially clear in Roger S. Ahlbrandt, Jr., and Paul C. Brophy, *Neighborhood Revitalization* (Lexington, Mass.: D. C. Heath, 1975) and Victor Bach, "The New Federalism in Community Development," *Social Policy*, 7 (January/February 1977), 32–38. Walter I. Firey's *Land Use in Central Boston* (Cambridge, Mass.: Harvard University Press, 1947) was one of the earliest studies to demonstrate the deep emotional attachments of residents to their neighborhoods. Also see Rolf Goetze, *Building Neighborhood Confidence: Humanistic Strategy for Urban Housing* (Cambridge, Mass.: Ballinger, 1976); David R. Goldfield, "Historic Planning and Redevelopment in Minneapolis," *Journal of the American Institute of Planners*, 42 (January 1976), 76–86; and John Mudd, "Beyond Community Control: A Neighborhood Strategy for City Government," *Publius*, 6 (Fall 1976), 113–135.

INDEX

Abilene, Kansas, 208
Adams, John, 92
Addams, Jane, 234, 282, 289
Adler, Felix, 277
Albany, New York, 65, 185
Alexandria, Virginia, 55, 56, 170, 185
American Institute of Planners, 219, 375
American Medical Association, 175
Annapolis, Maryland, 35, 46, 79
Apprenticeship, 58, 59, 67
Architecture
  and building materials, 29, 84, 86–88, 146
  and building technology, 212, 320
  cultural influences on, 87–88, 146
  "dumbbell" tenement, 275–76, 278
  row house, 87, 88, 146–47, 278, 279
    (illus.)
  skyscraper, 212–14, 337
  suburban, 204–05
  wealth and, 88, 89, 146–47
Artisans
  decline of, 60, 150–51, 163
  earnings of, 143, 181
  immigrants as, 154
  percentage of population as, 53, 58
  in social structure, 59–60, 66, 150, 159
  urban location of, 38, 58–59
  See also Industry; Labor; Social order/
    patterns
Atlanta, Georgia, 210, 333, 340, 342, 392,
    401
  blacks in, 263, 328

Peachtree Center, 393, 397, 400
regional supremacy of, 200, 399–400
and transportation, 208, 345, 385
Augusta, Georgia, 103, 123
Austin, Texas, 334
Automobile, *see* Transportation
Axial design, 26, 35–36

Backcountry, *see* Hinterlands
Baldwin, James, 325
Baltimore, Maryland, 36, 95, 193, 219, 298,
    345, 353
  blacks in, 157, 328
  industry in, 224, 225, 228
  labor and labor problems in, 157, 178,
    238
  as mercantile city, 36, 44, 111, 116, 128
    and wheat trade, 56, 113, 115
  parks, 185, 188, 395
Baptists, *see* Protestantism
Baseball, 313–14
Bauer, Catherine, 386
Bell, Alexander, Graham, 337
Bellamy, Edward, 280
Berkeley, California, 188
Berry, Brian J. L., 402, 405
Bienville, Jean Baptiste, sieur de, 27–28
Birmingham, Alabama, 223, 227, 244, 334,
    401
  blacks in, 263, 321, 324
Black Muslims, 318

Blacks
   Africans as ethnic group, 62, 63
   antagonisms toward, 73, 83, 85, 155–56,
       158, 178–79, 180, 264, 265–67, 291,
       315, 318–22, 349, 384, 401
   civil rights of, 155, 157–59, 265, 269–70,
       324
   cultural influence of, 311–13, 315
   distribution of, 199, 259–62, 297, 309, 328
   and housing, 88, 158, 203, 391
       ghetto, 20, 265–70, 312, 322 (illus.),
           323, 324–30
       in suburbs, 320–23, 349, 350, 384
   in labor force, see Labor
   in the North, 73, 85, 155–59, 178, 199,
       325–29
       and migration to, 259, 261–68, 270,
           297, 311–13, 318–19, 334
   in politics, 328
   poverty of, 71, 98, 157–58, 270, 317–18
   segregation of, see Segregation
   self-help institutions for, 267–70, 312,
       317, 318, 324, 327–30
   social/occupational mobility of,
       156–57, 262–63
   urban compared to rural, 155, 261,
       270–71, 284
   West Indian, 62, 267
   See also Slavery and slave trade
Bosses (political), 285–91, 355–59, 392
Boston, Massachusetts, 29, 32, 46, 70, 81,
       160, 224, 286, 298, 402
   blacks in, 62, 158, 321, 325
   Boston Common, 33, 88
   central business district (downtown), 152
       expansion of, 211 (illus.)
   churches and religion in, 33, 68, 69, 75, 77
   as cultural center, 91, 92, 93, 338
   as dominant New England city, 33, 38, 39,
       56
   immigration into, 71, 153, 257
   as mercantile city, 44–56 passim, 75, 89,
       128, 130, 139
       and Revolution, 94, 95
   population of, 199, 303, 345
   social problems in, 72, 82, 84, 85, 175,
       178, 180, 280
   social services in, 71, 75, 84, 85, 281
   street pattern (and crowding) of, 26, 87,
       89, 108, 185–86, 187 (illus.), 345
   suburbs of, 33, 45, 143, 144, 152, 203,
       204, 257, 345, 350
   transportation in, 143, 144, 145, 345, 380
   wealth in, 65, 160, 391
   zoning in, 219
Brace, Charles Loring, 280
Bradford, William, 22
Bradstreet, Anne, 92
"Broadacre City," 402, 403 (illus.)

Brooklyn, New York, 145, 302
Bryant, William Cullen, 186
Buffalo, New York, 115, 223, 238, 244, 278
Building materials, see Architecture
Burgess, Ernest W., 9, 12
Burnaby, Andrew, 87
Burnham, Daniel H., 214, 216, 361
Business
   and corporate management, 119, 224–27,
       332–33, 338–39, 350–51
   government regulation of, 168, 333
   See also Industry; Trade

Cabot, John, 25
Cahan, Abraham, 256, 258
Cairo, Illinois, 113
California
   railroads in, 209
   See also individual cities
Cambridge, Massachusetts, 33, 45, 91, 350
   Mt. Auburn Cemetery, 185–86, 187 (illus.)
Camden, South Carolina, 54–55, 56
Canada, 25, 27, 95, 156, 308
Canals, see Transportation
Capone, Al, 308
Carolinas, the, 36, 42–43, 51, 54.
       See also individual cities
Carter administration, 384, 389, 390
Catholicism, 68, 161, 183
   and anti-Catholic violence, 178, 179, 180
   of immigrants, 247, 252, 255
   See also Religion
Cemeteries, 185–86, 187 (illus.)
Census, U.S. Bureau of, 130, 299–301, 382.
       See also Population
Central America, 27
Central business district, see "Downtown"
Central city, see "Downtown"
Central Park (New York), 33, 186, 188
Central place theory, 2, 4, 5, 55
Champlain, Samuel de, 25
Charleston, South Carolina, 38, 78, 185
   architecture and building materials in, 86,
       88, 89
   blacks in, 156, 158, 328
   as cultural center, 91, 92, 93
   as mercantile city, 36, 43, 44, 49, 50–56
       (passim), 59, 128, 130, 140
   slavery in, 36, 52, 60, 62, 65, 72, 85
   social problems in, 72, 82, 85
   social services in, 71, 85
Charlestown, Maryland, 56
Chesapeake area settlements, 35–36, 43, 46,
       62. See also individual cities
Chicago, 103, 139, 208, 235, 278, 302, 303,
       311, 360, 400
   blacks in, 261–62, 266–69, 321, 327
   fire in, 198

foreign-born in, 153, 246–47, 258–59, 282, 308
growth of, 162, 198, 199, 200, 203, 315
  vs. decline, 345
industry, labor and working conditions, 222, 224–25, 227, 229, 231, 232, 238–39
land values, 103, 212
politics, 287, 358
regional supremacy of, 4, 16, 18, 116–17, 131, 200
spatial development and design of, 10, 105, 146, 193, 216–17, 345, 363
stockyards, 224 (illus.)
and transportation, 116–17, 118, 129, 131, 340, 345
unemployment (1932), 316, 334
World's Fair (Columbian Exposition, 1893), 214, 215 (illus.)
Chicago *Defender* (black newspaper), 261, 262, 268
Chicago School, 212
Chicago Times, 258
Child labor, 67, 227, 231–32
Christaller, Walter, 2–4
Cincinnati, Ohio, 160, 162, 171, 177, 392
  blacks evicted from, 155–56, 178
  grid pattern in, 104–05
  industry and trade of, 110, 124–25, 131, 174, 239
  as port, 15, 103, 104, 114
City(ies)
  as America's future, 293
  definitions of, 20
  location of, *see* Location of cities
  planning and growth, *see* Urbanization/ urban growth; Urban planning
  primate, 4, 15, 56
  suburbanization of, 388–96
  three types of Spanish, 27
  as "way of life," 189–95
  See also Ecology; Suburb(s); Urban forms; Urban hierarchy
"City Beautiful," 214–17
"City Efficient," 217–21
Civil War, 192, 223
  approach of, 131, 133, 158
Clark, Dennis, 257
Clark, George Rogers, 103
Clark, Kenneth, 325
Class, social, *see* Social order/patterns
Cleveland, Ohio, 146, 167, 203, 397
  blacks in, 261, 262, 264, 328
  and industry, 123, 222, 228
  politics in, 290, 359
  population of, 200, 303, 345
Clinton, DeWitt, 114
Cluster (urban form), 13–15, 20, 23, 39, 82, 291, 296, 349, 362

and clustering of ethnic groups, 154, 250–53 (*see also* Immigrants)
proximity to work and, *see* Labor
College of William and Mary, 35, 91
Colonization
  and cultural influence, *see* Culture(s)
  Dutch, 34, 42, 63
  English, 29–37, 38–39, 41–43, 58, 62, 63
  and European models for urban areas, *see* Europe
  and trade, 42–43, 48 (illus.) (*see also* Trade)
  urban transition in, 23–24, 39
  westward expansion of, 37
Colorado Springs, Colorado, 209
Columbian Exposition (World's Fair, 1893), 214, 215 (illus.)
Communications, *see* Technology
Community
  consensual, 75, 83, 85, 180
  political, 73–80 (*see also* Government, local)
  religion and, *see* Religion
Community Development Block Grant (CDBG), 387–90
Commuters, *see* Transportation
Competition, *see* Trade; Urbanization/urban growth
Concentric zone theory, 10–11, 12, 13, 348
  and Puritan idea of community, 30
Congregationalism, *see* Protestantism
Connecticut, 32, 75. *See also individual cities*
Constitution, U.S., 96
Cooper, James Fenimore, 190
Corporations, *see* Business
Costs
  health, 172, 174
  homeownership, 385
  industrial production, 223, 224
  land, in suburbs, 203–04
  of street cleaning and paving, 170–72
  transportation, *see* Transportation
Cotton trade, 128, 129, 131, 261
"Cotton triangle," 129. *See also* Cotton trade
Crane, Stephen, 232, 277
Crime, *see* Social problems
Culture(s)
  abandonment of, 258
  mass, 309–13, 315–16, 338 (*see also* Entertainment)
  Old World, transmission of, 39, 62, 87–90, 92, 94, 146, 244, 246–50, 252, 254, 255–56, 258
  Puritan, 62, 91
  See also Architecture; Printing and publishing
Currency and credit, *see* Economics

Daley, Richard J., 358
Dallas, Texas, 315, 340, 345, 348, 399–400, 402

Dayton, Ohio, 315, 359
Dedham, Massachusetts, 76–77
Democratic Party, 131, 288, 367, 368
Denver, Colorado, 103, 104, 131, 178, 333,
    384, 399
Depression, Great (1930), *see* Great
    Depression
Depressions, *see* Economics
Detroit, Michigan, 27, 290, 315, 392, 395
    blacks in, 156, 157, 178, 261, 262, 263,
        265, 319, 320, 326, 327, 328
    economic crisis in, 368, 372
    ethnic groups in, 250–51, 259, 262
    industry in, 223, 342
    population of, 199, 200, 303, 345
Dinwiddie, Emily, 249, 278
Disease, *see* Social problems
"District city" (of Christaller), 4
Dodge City, Kansas, 208
Dorchester, Massachusetts, 143, 204
Douglas, Stephen A., 131–32
Downs, Anthony, 388
"Downtown"
    as city center, 14, 208, 212, 292
        vs. suburbs, 20, 141–42, 151–52, 225,
            296, 299, 353, 393
    economic expansion and segregation of,
        15, 18, 99, 134–35, 141, 159, 163,
        210–12
    employment opportunities in, 151–52,
        154, 227, 250
    as financial center, 140, 141, 142, 147,
        200, 210
    as residential area, 141–42, 151–52, 227
    revival of, 20, 393, 395, 396
Dreiser, Theodore, 198, 199, 235–36, 292
Du Bois, W. E. B., 270, 313, 317, 318, 325
    326, 327, 328
"Dumbbell" tenement, 275–76, 278
Duryea, Charles E., and J. Frank, 340
Dutch, 47, 49, 50, 51, 262
    colonization by, 34, 42, 63
    cultural influence of, 87, 88

Ecology, 9–13
    and environmental reform, 276–85
    and environmental services, 184–89, 194
    pollution and, *see* Social problems
Economics
    automobile and, 342 (*see also*
        Transportation)
    and city loction, 5–8, 15
    of colonies, 23, 42, 53
    consumer-oriented economy, 89, 138–39,
        150, 210, 334–35, 336, 337
    corporations and, 332–33
    currency and credit, 52–53, 60, 122, 129

and depressions, 52, 53, 60, 366
    Great Depression (1930), 334, 341, 365,
        366–72, 373, 378
    Panic of 1837, 103, 183
and economic development, 194, 257–58,
    297
    government support of, 168–69
the merchant and, 57–58 (*see also*
    Merchants)
and urban hierarchy/regional succession,
    16–17, 122–23, 335
See also Industry; Trade; Wealth
Education
    blacks and, 159, 265, 269, 329
    and busing, 321
    immigrants and, 253–57
    public, 181, 183–84, 188–89, 284
    religion and, 69, 91
    and social class, 162, 184
    in suburbs, 383
Eisenhower, Dwight D., 335
Electricity, *see* Technology
Electric Streetcar, *see* Trolley
Elevator, 212, 336
Elkton, Maryland, 56
Ellsworth, Kansas, 208
Emerson, Ralph Waldo, 123, 191
England, 120
    Church of, 29, 68 (*see also* Religion)
    colonial resentment toward, 60, 73, 94–95
        (*see also* Revolutionary War)
    exploration and colonization by, 29–37,
        38–39, 41–43, 58, 62, 63
    influence of
        on colonial government, 62, 71, 73–75,
            78, 80
        on U.S. reform movements, 281
    Poor Law (1601) of, 71
    and trade with colonies, 42–60 passim, 63,
        94–95, 128
Entertainment
    jazz, 310–11
    motion pictures, 266, 269, 309, 310, 316,
        343
    sports, 313–14, 316
    vaudeville, 309–10, 316
Entrepreneurs, 110–11, 113, 134, 140–42,
    389
    and architecture, 213–14
    and social services, 179, 183
    and specialization, 138
    and transportation technology, 116–19,
        124–27, 208–10
Environment, *see* Ecology
Erie Canal, 114–15, 128. *See also*
    Transportation
Ethnicity and racial diversity, 15. *See also*
    Blacks; Culture(s); Immigrants

Europe, influence of, 68, 118, 238
    on architecture, 87–88, 146
    on government, 73–75, 79–80, 82
    on settlement patterns, 13–14, 22, 25–29,
        33–37, 81
    on urban planning, 215, 218–19
    See also Culture(s); Immigrants; Trade
European wars, 53, 60, 63, 94, 110, 128, 244
Exurbia, *see* Suburb(s)

Factor (trading agent), 51–52, 58, 128
Family
    industrialization and, 230
    in slums, 273, 283–84
    as social unit, 67–68, 70, 246, 253
    and status, 66, 79
Farming
    automobile and, 341–42
    as basis of society, 92
    "downtown," 15
    and railroads, 119
    regulations of, 125, 127
    and settlement patterns, 15, 30, 32, 35,
        37, 41–42
    subsistence, 70, 261, 370
    and urban market, 32, 44, 53, 110, 144–45
    See also Hinterlands; Land uses; Trade
Fire(s)
    in Boston (1600s, 1700s), 82
    in Charleston, 82
    in Chicago, 198
    dangers of, 23, 82–83
    and fire regulations and control, 15, 33,
        84, 85, 86, 176–77, 286
    See also Social problems
Fitzgerald, F. Scott, 307, 309, 316
Fitzhugh, George, 126, 131
Florida, 41, 113. *See also individual cities*
Ford, Henry, 341
Forest Hills, New York, 221, 321–22, 327
Forts and fortresses, 27. *See also* Wall(s)
Fort Worth, Texas, 340
Foster, George G., 189–90
France
    exploration and colonization by, 25,
        27–28, 47
    and French West Indies, 49, 50
    Huguenots from, 62, 63
    influence of, on American urban areas,
        14, 25, 27–28
Franklin, Benjamin, 44, 63, 69, 84, 91, 92, 93
Fredericksburg, Virginia, 55, 56
Freud, Sigmund, 309
Frisch, Michael, 168
Fur trade, 46, 50, 52, 54, 55

Galveston, Texas, 359
Gans, Herbert, 320

Garbage and waste disposal (sanitation), *see*
    Social problems
"Garden city," 220–21, 361, 370
Garment industry, 223–24
Garvey, Marcus, 312
Gary, Elbert, 226
Gary, Indiana, 226–27, 328
Geography
    and trade, 110, 114, 128 (*see also*
        Transportation)
    and urban growth, 10, 15, 19, 42–43,
        54–55, 104, 110, 199
Georgia, 36, 51, 128. *See also individual cities*
German city planning, 218–19
Ghetto, *see* Blacks; Housing; Immigrants
Goheen, Peter, 205
Gold rush, 104, 105
Gompers, Samuel, 237–38
Goodyear, Charles, 122
Government, federal
    aid by, during Depression, 367–73 (*see also*
        Economics; New Deal)
    and business regulation, 168, 333
    and fringe/suburban development, 20,
        350, 351, 384–88
    and government spending, 335
    and housing, 373–75, 377
    and urban development and decline, 364,
        365–66, 369–73, 378–81, 385–93
    and westward expansion, 101
    See also Laws and legislation
Government, local
    and environmental services, 184–89, 194
    European/English influence on, 62, 71,
        73–75, 78–80, 82
    federal aid to, 367–73
    mayors, 131, 167–68, 172, 328, 357, 370,
        372, 396
    merchants and, 15, 98
    municipal incorporation, 74, 78–79, 359,
        366
    New England town, 66, 74–78, 79
    and social services, 180–84 (*see also* Social
        problems)
    trade regulations, 74, 75, 78, 79–80, 86,
        168
    and urban growth, 166–80, 355–60,
        389–93, 395–96
    and voting, 74, 79, 155, 169, 261, 324,
        355
    See also Politics
"Great Awakening," 68–69. *See also* Religion
Great Depression, 334, 341, 365, 366–72,
    373, 378. *See also* New Deal
"Greenbelt" towns, 369–70
Greensboro, North Carolina, 227
Gridiron pattern
    in colonial towns, 25, 26, 27

Gridiron pattern, in colonial towns, *cont'd.*
　Boston, 89, 108, 185–86, 187 (illus.)
　New Orleans, 28 (illus.)
　New York, 35, 108
　Philadelphia, 33, 34 (illus.), 101,
　　104–05, 107
　in suburbs, 204
　in western towns, 102, 106, 108
　　Chicago, 105, 193
　　Cincinnati, 104–05
　　Salt Lake City, 101
　　San Francisco, 105, 106 (illus.)
Griffith, David W., 266, 269
Griscom, Dr. John C., 149, 175
Gulf Coast, 27, 36, 128

Hammer, Richard, 325
Hancock, Thomas, 50
Harlem, 264–65, 270, 311–13, 318, 325,
　326, 329
Harlem Renaissance, 311–13
Harris, Chauncy D., 12
Harris, Patricia Roberts, 389–90
Harrison, Peter, 88
Hartford, Connecticut, 389
Harvard University, 91, 121, 162
Havre de Grace, Maryland, 56
Hawthorne, Nathaniel, 30
Health (vs. disease), *see* Social problems
Henretta, James, 65, 66
Henry, O., 234, 236
"Hexagons," *see* Hinterlands
Highways, *see* Transportation
Hinterlands
　and backcountry urbanization, 54–57, 334
　colonial, 37, 54, 55
　as "hexagons," 2, 3
　Midwestern, in mid-19th century, 7
　and trade, 48, 54–57, 109–10, 127 (*see also*
　　Trade)
　See also Farming
Holland, *see* Dutch
Holly, Buddy, 313
Holyoke, Massachusetts, 122, 123
Hoover, Herbert, 314, 357, 367–68
Hopkins, Mark, 213
Horowitz, Louis J., 213
Horse-drawn street railway, 144, 145, 206.
　See also Transportation
Housing
　boarding houses and taverns, 69–70, 72,
　　148, 158, 161
　commercial land use vs., *see* Land uses
　corporate enterprise and, 350–51
　Federal Housing Administration (FHA)
　　and, 373–74, 385
　ghetto, 20, 154, 250–52, 263–70, 312, 322
　　(illus.), 323, 324–30, 386 (*see also*
　　Cluster [urban form])

immigrant, *see* Immigrants
　legislation, 275, 278, 370, 374, 375, 377,
　　386–87
　low-income, 12, 324, 349, 373, 377 (illus.),
　　389, 392
　proximity of, to work, *see* Labor
　public, 374–75, 389
　reform, 18, 276–85
　and rents, 87, 148, 149, 206, 265, 268,
　　392
　shortage/overcrowding as social problem,
　　83, 86, 87, 88, 142, 274–75, 289, 366
　　(*see also* Social problems)
　slum, 149, 158, 159, 194, 264, 273,
　　274–84, 285, 324, 373
　socioeconomic status and, 18, 149, 391
　spatial development and, 11–12, 87–88
　See also Architecture
Housing and Urban Development (HUD),
　Department of, 386, 389–90
Houston, Texas, 178, 302, 315, 317, 333,
　337, 348, 397, 401
　regional supremacy of, 200, 399, 400
Howard, Ebenezer, 220–21, 361
Howe, Frederic C., 289, 305, 306
Hoyt, Homer, 11–12
Huguenots, 62, 63
Hull House (Chicago), 282

Immigrants, 285
　antagonism toward, 258–59, 289
　vs. blacks, 266
　Chinese, 218–19
　colonial, 32, 83
　Czech, 251
　German, 49, 54, 62, 63, 68, 153–55, 157,
　　158, 246, 247, 254
　and "ghetto" (ethnic) neighborhoods, 154,
　　250–52
　and housing, 142, 143, 149, 155, 203, 205,
　　259
　influx of, 18, 20, 62–63, 71, 98, 153–55,
　　156, 199, 240, 243–50, 297, 307–08
　　restricted, 244, 266, 315
　Irish, 122, 153, 154, 157, 158, 178,
　　183–84, 257, 258, 262–63, 273, 308
　Italian, 246–58 passim, 262, 282, 308, 329
　Jewish, *see* Jews, the
　in labor force, *see* Labor
　Mexican (Chicano), 319–20, 330, 401
　organizations and societies of, 155, 246,
　　251–53, 270
　Polish, 247, 250–51, 252, 254, 255, 257,
　　262–63
　in population, 62, 153–54, 244, 245
　　(table), 249, 251, 308–09
　and religion, 247, 252, 255, 256
　Russian, 247, 251, 252, 253, 256, 258

Scotch-Irish, 49, 54, 62, 63, 68
social/occupational mobility of, 184, 247,
  257–58, 259, 262
as "strangers" (in New England), 62, 71
See also Culture(s)
Indianapolis, Indiana, 219, 238, 402
Indians, 100
feared and repressed, 83, 85
hostility and attacks of, 32, 54, 101, 110
Indigo trade, 43, 50, 52, 55
Industry
and the artisan, 150–51 (*see also* Artisans)
automobile, 342 (*see also* Transportation)
clothing, 223–24
and economy of industrial cities, 16–17,
  122–23, 297, 333–34
and industrial waste and pollution, 222,
  227, 228 (*see also* Social problems)
location of, 135, 138, 141, 152, 219
  on periphery, 12, 18, 351, 395
meat, 224–25
and preindustrial city, 11, 227
processing industries, 119–23
railroads and, 119–20
rural vs. urban, 120–23
shipbuilding, 48, 50, 53, 55, 135, 136
  (illus.)
steel, 222–23, 333, 334
technology and, *see* Technology
textile, 121–22
and working conditions, 228–40
See also Business; Labor; Merchants;
  Trade
International Harvester, 230, 239, 240
Ipswich, Massachusetts, 32
Ireland, towns of, as American model, 14, 25
Irving, Washington, 190

Jackson, Andrew, 179
and Jacksonian Age, 113, 116, 138, 167,
  169
Jackson, Rev. Jesse, 329
Jackson, Kenneth T., 315
Jackson, Mississippi, 402
Jacksonville, Florida, 14, 302
Jamestown, Virginia, 14, 25, 29, 35, 41
Jefferson, Thomas, 65, 92, 107, 191
Jenney, William L., 212
Jews, 154, 219, 258, 259, 308
and education, 253–57 passim
as ethnic/religious group, 63, 68, 161,
  247–49, 252, 256
in ghettos, 250, 251, 329
Johnson, Lyndon B., 327
Jones, Rev. Hugh, 35

Kansas, 103, 126, 208
Kansas City, Missouri, 126, 131, 340, 353, 393
politics, 286, 356, 358, 359

Kellogg, Paul U., 230
Kerner, Otto, and Kerner Commission, 327
King, Martin Luther, Jr., 321, 324, 326
Ku Klux Klan, 266, 314–15, 316, 324, 360

Labor
apprenticeship, 58, 59, 67
black, 156–57, 158, 261–63, 268, 318–19
child, 67, 227, 231–32
division of, 58
and "downtown" employment opportunities, 151–52, 154, 227, 250 (*see also*
  Transportation)
and employee-employer hostility and
  strikes, 151, 179, 180, 226, 227,
  236–40, 258, 263, 282, 366, 396
female, 121–22, 189–90, 227, 231, 232–36
immigrant, 122, 130, 154, 225, 230,
  236–37, 243, 244, 258, 261, 282
  vs. blacks, 157, 262
legislation, 231, 282, 369
and proximity to work (vs. occupational
  segregation), 87, 142–43, 146–47,
  151–53, 154, 158, 225–30 passim,
  234, 250, 274, 353
and unemployment, 71, 236–37, 316–17,
  334, 366–69, 370, 371
unions, 163, 237, 253, 263, 316, 396
unskilled and semiskilled, 60, 64–65, 71,
  143, 150–51, 156–57, 159, 181
wages and earnings, 143, 144, 181, 207,
  227, 228–29, 231, 234, 235, 236, 238,
  240, 309, 366
working conditions, 228–40
See also Artisans; Industry; Slavery and
  slave trade
La Guardia, Fiorello, 357, 370
Lancaster, Pennsylvania, 54–55
Land ownership, 118
by blacks, 157
communal, 27, 30, 74
and land values, 87, 103, 206, 212, 218,
  219, 275
and rents, *see* Housing
and residency, 30, 74, 79
social hierarchy and, 30, 63–65 (*see also*
  Social order/patterns)
and speculation, 101–04, 117, 203–04,
  206, 208, 264
Land uses
commercial vs. residential, 44–45, 86–89,
  99, 141–42, 148, 202–03, 206, 362–63
  (*see also* Housing; Suburb(s); Urban
  planning)
"downtown," in early communities,
  14–15, 98–99, 134–35
environmental services (parks), *see* Parks

Land uses, *cont'd.*
  industrial, 227–28
    New York City, 135, 223–24
  and "liberty lands," 41 (*see also* Farming)
  multiple-nuclei theory of, 12–13
  for office buildings, 212
  segregated, *see* Segregation
  See also Industry; Spatial organization
Law enforcement, *see* Social problems
Laws and legislation
  concerning blacks, 157, 291
  and business regulation, 168
  civil rights, 265, 269, 324
  economic (during depression), 368–69,
    370, 372
  English Poor Law (1601), 71
  health, 175
  Highway Acts, 350, 378–79, 385
  housing, 275, 278, 370, 374, 375, 377,
    386–87
  immigration, 315
  labor, 231, 282, 369
  and law enforcement, *see* Social problems
  social reform (Pennsylvania), 163
  tree ordinances, 185
  urban planning
    Laws of the Indies, 26–27
    in Virginia, 35, 43
Laws of the Indies, 26–27
Leavenworth, Kansas, 126
L'Enfant, Pierre, 107, 216
Levitt, Abraham, and Levittowns, 352, 351
    (illus.)
Lewis, Sinclair, 316
Lexington, Kentucky, 114, 176
Lima, Peru, 39
Lincoln, Abraham, 131–32
Liverpool, England, 92, 93, 128, 129
Living standards, 59, 206, 228–35. *See also*
    Labor; Social order/patterns
Location of cities
  coastal/waterfront, *see* Waterfront
  economics and, 5–8, 15
  related to size and function, 2
  trade and, 15, 37, 38–39, 43–51
Locke, Alain, 311, 312
London, 34, 39, 56, 91, 92, 93, 281
  post-fire (1666) plans for, copied, 33, 35,
    88
  St. James's Square (1684), 37
London Company, *see* Virginia Company of
    London
London Town, Maryland, 46–47
Long Island, 145, 351
Los Angeles, California, 319, 320, 328, 333,
    339, 353, 399
  population, 200, 348, 400
  and transportation, 209, 337, 345,
    397, 400

  and urban planning, 361, 363
Louisiana, 68, 117. *See also* New Orleans,
    Louisiana
Louisiana Purchase, 28, 110, 113
Louisville, Kentucky, 106, 132, 154, 178
  Cave Hill Cemetery in, 186
  established, 103–04
  and industry, 113, 123
Lowell, Massachusetts, 121–22, 123
  public schools, 183–84
Lubove, Roy, 20, 221

McKay, Claude, 311–12
McMillan, James, 216
Machine politics, *see* Bosses (political),
    Tammany Hall
Mafia, 246
Main, Jackson Turner, 66, 71
Malcolm X, 318
Market area, markets, *see* Merchants; Trade
Market place (urban form), 16 (illus.),
    23–24, 39, 95, 98–99, 291, 296, 349
  and city as "way of life," 189–95
  "engineers," *see* Entrepreneurs
  national, 127–33
  technology, *see* Technology
Martinsville, West Virginia, 238
Maryland, 47, 68, 113. *See also individual
    cities*
Massachusetts, 75, 199. *See also individual
    cities*
Massachusetts Bay, 29, 30, 32, 84, 91, 95. *See
    also* Boston, Massachusetts
Maverick, Samuel, 33
Mayors, 131, 167–68, 172, 328, 357, 370,
    372, 396
Medicine, 93
  and disease, *see* Social problems
Megalopolis, 298, 402, 404 (illus.)
Melville, Herman, 188
Memphis, Tennessee, 113, 131, 132, 203,
    315
  politics, 291, 355, 359
Merchants
  and American Revolution, 95
  and English mercantilism, *see* England
  and entrepreneurship, *see* Entrepreneurs
  and local industry, 119–20, 150
  and markets, market days, 57
  organizations of, 53, 120, 124, 126–27,
    163
  and retail stores, 109, 138–40, 159, 210
  and shopping centers, 352, 353, 354
    (illus.), 383, 393, 394 (illus.), 395
  in social structure, 64–67, 159
  and urban growth, 15, 47–54, 57–58
  Western urban, 109–10
  See also Industry; Trade

Mexico City (1750), 39
Miami, Florida, 399, 401, 402
Midwest, 7, 333
  blacks in, 259, 297, 326
  population distribution in, 199, 345, 397
Migration, *see* Blacks; Immigrants; suburb(s)
Milwaukee, Wisconsin
  foreign-born in, 153, 154, 155, 244
  industry, 223, 230, 239
Minneapolis, Minnesota, 345, 394 (illus.),
    395, 397
Mission (Spanish), 27
Mississippi Delta, 27–28
Mobile, Alabama, 14, 27, 132, 156, 193, 401
  and industry and trade, 123, 131
Mobility
  geographic, 15, 18, 164, 250, 343, 344 (*see
    also* Transportation)
  social/occupational, *see* Social order/
    patterns
Model Cities program, 386–87, 391
Modesto, California, 218
Mohl, Raymond A., 71, 72
Monterey, California, 27
Montgomery, Alabama, 324
Montreal, Canada, 27
Moore, Thomas, 107
Mormons, the, 100–01
Mortality rate, 83, 273
Motion pictures, *see* Entertainment
Mt. Auburn Cemetery, 185–86, 187 (illus.)
Multiple-nuclei theory, 12–13
Mumford, Lewis, 361–62, 364

NAACP (National Association for the
    Advancement of Colored People),
    266, 269, 283, 317
Nashville, Tennessee, 105, 302
Nast, Thomas, 288
Natchez, Tennessee, 113, 131, 156, 193
Nation, The, 317
National Housing Association, 279
Nativism, 63
"Natural areas," 9, 10 (illus.)
Naugatuck, Connecticut, 122
Nauvoo, Illinois, 100, 101
Negro Convention Movement, 159. *See also*
    Blacks
New Amsterdam, 14, 34, 46, 63. *See also*
    New York City
Newark, New Jersey, 326, 328
"New Athens," 102
Newburyport, Massachusetts, 65
Newcourt, Richard, 33
New Deal, 334–35, 357, 358, 366, 368–71
  and WPA, 369, 371, 373, 374, 378
New England
  blacks in, 155

and church or meetinghouse as central
    point, 29–30, 33, 68
  culture in, 90–93
  English settlements in, 29–33, 41
  family importance in, 67–68
  industrial technology/growth and, 15, 122
  land allotment in, 27, 30, 63–64, 74, 79
  river towns in, 55
  "strangers" (immigrants) in, 62, 71
  town government in, 66, 75–78, 79
  See also individual cities, states
Newfoundland, colonial trade with, 54
New Haven, Connecticut, 46, 48, 55, 281
New Jersey, 78, 145, 199
New London, Connecticut, 32
New Orleans, Louisiana, 27–28, 132, 140,
    154, 193, 311
  blacks in, 156, 328
  commercial importance of, 28, 103, 109,
    113, 114, 116, 117–18, 130, 131
  Greenwood Cemetery, 186
  plans of, 28 (illus.), 105
  politics, 291, 355–56
  social problems in, 173, 177
Newport, Rhode Island, 38, 44, 48, 56, 60,
    62, 91
  architecture and building materials, 86,
    88, 89
New York City, 46, 70, 84, 95, 185, 208, 298,
    303
  architecture and building materials, 86,
    87, 89, 213, 377 (illus.)
  blacks in (and Harlem), 263–70 passim,
    311–13, 318–29 passim
  Central Park, 33, 186, 188
  as cultural center, 91, 92, 93, 215, 338
  described by popular writers, 189, 190,
    192, 193
  dominance of, 5, 15, 16, 18, 35, 38–39,
    114, 127–31, 160, 200, 339, 364, 399,
    400
  ethnic/religious groups in, 63, 68, 153,
    246, 248–49, 250, 255, 256, 258, 321,
    329
  European influence on, 14, 34, 215, 219
  Fifth Avenue, 146, 161, 210, 219, 249
    (illus.)
  as financial center, 128–29, 140
  government, 78, 79, 392
  grid pattern in, 35, 108
  industrial land use in, 135, 223–24
  labor and labor problems in, 236, 239
  Lower East Side, 248 (illus.), 309
  as mercantile city, 44, 49, 51, 53, 56, 57,
    95, 114–15, 124, 125, 127–31, 139
  Municipal Art Society, 215
  politics (Tammany Hall), 287–88, 291,
    356–57, 358
  population, *see* Population

New York City, *cont'd.*
  public and private charity/welfare, 71–72,
    182, 281
  Regional Plan, 363, 364
  slavery in, 60, 62
  slums, 149, 264, 273, 274–78, 373
  social class in, 160, 162
  social problems in, 72, 73, 173, 174–78
    passim, 180, 192
  streets (and street-cleaning), 35, 171, 172,
    209
  suburbs, 143, 145, 221, 302, 321–23, 327,
    350, 351, 384
  taxable wealth in (1700s), 66
  transportation in (and commuters to),
    143, 144–45, 151, 339, 343, 345
New York Post, 186
New York State, 69, 78, 114–15, 155, 199.
  See also individual cities
New York Times, 139, 258
Nixon administration, 387, 390
Nolen, John, 218, 219
Norfolk, Virginia, 55, 56, 130, 171, 173,
  183, 317, 334
North Carolina, 42
Norton, Rev. John, 30
"No town"
  as "auto town," 345
  "downtown" as, 296
  spatial organization of, 20, 397

Occupational segregation (vs. proximity to
  work), *see* Labor
O'Farrell, Jasper, 105
Oglethorpe, James, 36–37, 41–42
Oklahoma land rush, 208
Olmsted, Frederick Law, 186, 188, 195, 204
Olmsted, Frederick Law, Jr., 216
Omaha, Nebraska, 203, 250–51, 264
Omnibus (horse-drawn), 143–44, 145, 206,
  308. *See also* Transportation
Organizations and groups
  black self-help, *see* Blacks
  charity, 281
  ethnic/immigrant, 155, 246, 251–53, 271, 329
  merchant, 53, 120, 124, 126–27, 163
  municipal, 372–73
  social, 160, 163
Orlando, Florida, 397
Osofsky, Gilbert, 266
Ovington, Mary White, 269

Pacific coast population distribution, 199
Panic of 1837, 103, 183
Park, Robert E., 9, 269
Parks, 189, 194, 208, 283–84, 395
  Boston, Common, 33, 88
  Central Park (New York), 33, 186, 188
  in Philadelphia plan, 33–34

Pedestrians
  emphasis on, revived, 20
  and proximity to work, *see* Labor
  See also Transportation
Pendergast, James, and Tom, 286, 356, 358
Penn, William, 36, 42, 49, 62
  Philadelphia plan of, 33, 41, 44, 87, 104
Pennsylvania colony and state, 33, 36, 68, 78
  and transportation, 113, 115, 118
  See also individual cities
Pennsylvania Gazette, 93
Pensacola, Flroida, 27, 402
Pessen, Edward, 169
Petersburg, Virginia, 55, 132
Philadelphia, Pennsylvania, 62, 70, 95, 193,
  199, 229, 298, 354 (illus.)
  architecture and building materials, 86,
    87, 88–89, 146, 147 (illus.), 278, 279
    (illus.)
  blacks in, 60, 158, 322 (illus.)
    compared to white neighborhood, 323
    (illus.)
  commuters in (1829–62), 151, 152 (illus.),
    153 (illus.)
  as cultural center, 91, 92, 93
  as dominant colonial center, 33–34, 38–39,
    115
  government, 78, 79
  immigrants in, 49, 62, 63, 158, 178,
    250–51, 257
  Laurel Hill Cemetery, 186
  as mercantile city, 44–51 (passim), 56, 58,
    60, 115, 128, 130, 139, 140
    effect of Revolution on, 95
  social problems in, 84, 172–73, 178–82
    passim, 281, 316, 334
  suburbs, 141, 164
  taxable wealth in (1770), 65
  and transportation to West, 115, 117
  urban (grid) pattern of, 33, 34, 41, 101,
    104–5, 107
  water supply, 84, 176
  Working Men's Party, 163
Philip II, king of Spain, 26
Phoenix, Arizona, 302, 348 (illus.), 397, 402
Pilgrims, 29. *See also* Plymouth, Massachusetts
Pittsburgh, Pennsylvania, 27, 101, 105, 334,
  392
  foreign-born and blacks in, 247, 257, 261
  industry and trade in, 109, 110, 124, 222,
    228, 229, 230, 238, 339
  population, *see* Population
  and transportation, 15, 103, 111, 115,
    206, 207, 345, 396
Planning, *see* Urban planning
Plantation
  as Puritan settlement unit, 29
  Southern, and urban growth, 43, 55
Plaza, 27, 29

Plunkitt, George Washington, 287–88, 290, 386
Plymouth, Massachusetts, 14, 22, 25, 29
Police and law enforcement, *see* Social
　　problems
Politics
　blacks in, 328
　immigrants and, 308, 355
　and political technology, 166–80, 355–60
　ward bosses and, 285–91, 355–59, 392
　See also Government, local; Tammany Hall
Pollution, *see* Social problems
Population
　artisans among, 53, 58
　Baltimore (1776), 36
　Birmingham, 223
　blacks in, 199, 259–62, 309, 328
　Brooklyn, New York (1820, 1860), 145, 302
　Census Bureau classifications of (SMA,
　　SMSA), 299–301, 389, 397
　cluster, 23
　decentralization, 202–03, 289, 292, 298,
　　303, 338, 340, 345, 361, 365, 401, 402
　　(*see also* Suburb[s])
　density, 142, 144, 274–75, 300, 305, 349,
　　388, 399, 402
　distribution, 2, 4, 20, 199–200, 293, 296,
　　345–48, 397–400, 402
　growth
　　and housing shortages, 87 (*see also*
　　　Housing)
　　of new settlements in New England, 30,
　　　32–33, 38–39, 41
　　and urban government, 66, 167–68
　　　(*see also* Government, local;
　　　Urbanization/urban growth)
　immigrant, 62, 153–54, 244, 245 (table),
　　249, 251, 308–9
　Lima, Peru (1750), 39
　Lowell, Massachusetts, 121
　Mexico City (1750), 39
　mobility of, *see* Mobility
　New York City, 142, 144, 199, 200,
　　274–75, 303, 345
　patterns, *see* Spatial organization
　Pittsburgh, 199, 206, 303, 345, 396
　poverty statistics, 71
　rank order of cities, *see* Rank order
　slaves among, 60, 62
　suburban, 203, 345–48, 383–84
　and taxable wealth (1687–1771), 65, 66
　westward trend of, 37–39
　Williamsburg, 35
Portland, Oregon, 399
Portman, John, 400
Portsmouth, New Hampshire, 65
Portugal, 25
Poverty, *see* Social problems
Powell, Adam Clayton, Jr., 318
Presbyterianism, *see* Protestantism

Presidio, 27
Press
　colonial, 90, 93, 95
　immigrant, 256
　and land speculation, 103
　merchants and, 125–26, 139
　negro, 159, 261, 262, 268
　and urban growth, 126
　See also Printing and publishing
Primate cities, 4, 15, 56. *See also* Urban
　　hierarchy
Printing and publishing, 121
　colonial, 90–92, 93
　and land use, 135, 137 (illus.)
　See also Press
Professions, *see* Social order/patterns
Prohibition, *see* Social problems
Protestantism, 69, 183, 307, 316
　and anti-Catholicism, 178, 179, 180
　Baptists, 68, 26
　Church of England, 29, 68
　Congregationalism and Presbyterianism,
　　68, 161. *See also* Quakers; Religion
Providence, Rhode Island, 32
"Psychology of scarcity," 168
Pueblo, 26, 27
Puerto Ricans, 321, 329
Pullman, Florence, 268
Pullman, George H., and Pullman, Illinois,
　　226–27, 238, 350
Puritans, 42, 62, 72, 85, 89, 91, 92, 104
　and Puritan community, 29–30, 75, 77, 81,
　　83

Quakers, 68, 90
　and trade, 42, 49
　See also Pennsylvania colony and state
Quebec, Canada, founded, 27

Racial diversity, 15. *See also* Blacks;
　　Culture(s); Immigrants
Radial center (urban form), 10, 11–12,
　　16–17, 18 (illus.), 198–200, 291–92,
　　296, 298
　Annapolis plan, 35
　and radial suburbs, 202–14, 218, 221
Railroad(s)
　Baltimore and Ohio, 115
　Central, 118
　Central Pacific, 213
　commuter, 144–45, 151, 298, 380
　Denver and Rio Grande, 209
　"divinity" of, 116
　era of, in America, 115–20, 121, 124–27,
　　130–31, 135, 208–09
　financing of, 115, 118–19, 123, 129, 140,
　　168, 169, 194
　and horse-drawn or street railway, 144,
　　145, 206, 308

Railroad(s), *cont'd.*
  Illinois Central, 261
  and industry, 222, 223
  New Orleans and Nashville, 117
  and residential development, 4, 12, 209, 340
  strikes, 238, 239
  transcontinental, 333
  Union Pacific, 209
  See also Transportation
Raleigh, North Carolina, 34
Ramsey, David, 191
Randolph, A. Philip, 318–19
Rank order
  and rank-size relations of U.S. cities
      (1800–1950), 6 (illus.)
  and rank-size rule, 4
  scales, 5 (illus.)
  stability, 5
  of twenty largest U.S. cities, 14–19
      (tables), 398 (table)
  and urban hierarchy, 16 (*see also* Urban
      hierarchy)
  See also Population
Reform movements, *see* Social reform
Regionalization, 361
  and regional power of suburb, 19, 292
  and urban hierarchy, 16, 18, 404 (illus.)
Regional Planning Association of America
      (RPAA), 361, 362, 363. *See also* Urban
      planning
Relationships
  colonial urbanization-trade, 47–51
  price-distance, as economic factor, 5–8
  spatial theories of (concentric zone, sector/
      wedge, multiple nuclei), 10–13, 30, 348
Religion
  and blacks, 158, 267, 270, 318
  and church as focal point of town or city,
      29–30, 33, 68
  and church-state separation, 77
  and city as "ungodly," 191–92
  and commerce as "goddess of Christian-
      ity," 101, 110
  community based on, 29–30, 32, 68, 75,
      76–77, 81, 83
  denominationalism, 68, 161, 267
  and "divinity" of railroads, 116
  and education, 69, 91
  "Great Awakening" in, 68–69
  immigrants and, *see* Immigrants
  and religious persecution, 62, 100
  and social class, 161–63
  See also Catholicism; Protestantism
Renaissance, 25
Rents, *see* Housing
Republican Party, 131–32, 265, 335, 336,
      367–68
Residential neighborhoods, *see* Housing;
      Suburb(s)

Revenues, city, 167, 169, 366, 367, 391. *See
      also* Taxation
Revolutionary War
  approach of, 60, 73, 85, 92, 93
  declaration and effect of, 94–96, 101, 113,
      128
Rhode Island, 32, 199
Rice trade, 43, 50, 52, 55
Richmond, Virginia, 154, 193, 203, 206,
      298, 391
  and industry, 123, 129
  as port, 15, 55, 56, 130
Riis, Jacob A., 232, 271–75 passim, 283–85
      passim, 289, 324, 325, 373
Riordan, William L., 287–88
River transportation, *see* Transportation
Roanoke, Virginia, 25
Roosevelt, Franklin D., 317, 357, 368–71,
      374
Roosevelt, Theodore, 287
Rosenwald, Julius, 269
Row houses, 87, 88, 146–47, 278, 279 (illus.)
Roxbury, Massachusetts, 45, 143, 204, 392
  and Roxbury Action Program (RAP), 328,
      329
Russell Sage Foundation, 221, 363

St. Augustine, Florida, 25
St. Louis, Missouri, 103, 128, 157, 178, 179,
      311, 345
  European influence on, 14, 27
  Interstate Network, 380 (illus.)
  regional supremacy of, 16
  social problems in, 171, 173, 176
  street plan of, 105, 106
  transportation and, 113, 116–17, 145–46
Salt Lake City, Utah, 104
  plans for, 100–01, 107
San Antonio, Texas, 384, 395
San Diego, California, 27
San Francisco, California, 27, 101, 161, 178,
      193, 213, 393
  grid pattern in, 105, 106 (illus.)
  land speculation, 103
  politics, 291, 355
  regional supremacy of, 16, 200
  suburbs, 164, 203
  and transportation, 380, 385, 400
Sanitation, *see* Social problems
Santa Barbara, California, 27
Santa Fe, California, 27
Santo Domingo, 26
Savannah, Georgia, 69, 88, 169, 174, 328
  Landmark Rehabilitation Project, 392
  Oglethorpe's design for, 36–37, 41–42
  and railroad, 118, 130
Saybrook, Connecticut, 32
Schlesinger, Arthur M., Sr., 199

Science and medicine, 93. *See also* Social
    problems; Technology
Scott, Mel, 375
Seattle, Washington, 339
Sector/wedge theory, 11–12, 13
Segregation
    occupational, vs. proximity to work, *see*
        Labor
    poverty and, 20, 277, 280, 284 (*see also*
        Social problems)
    racial, 158, 261, 263–68, 270, 311,
        323–24, 327, 349, 399 (*see also* Blacks)
    spatial, 18, 134–35, 138–39, 159, 164, 205,
        219, 237, 238, 265, 268, 304, 311,
        358, 397, 399 (*see also* Housing;
        Suburb[s])
Settlement houses, 281–84. *See also* Social
    reform
Seven Years' War, 53, 60, 94
Shattuck, Lemuel, 175
Ships and shipbuilding, *see* Industry;
    Transportation
Shopping centers, *see* Merchants
Sinclair, Upton, 224, 225, 229, 232, 243, 273
"Skunksburgh," 103
Skyscrapers, 212–14, 337
Slavery and slave trade, 43, 65, 67, 118, 130,
    155, 156–58
    and abolitionism, 178–79, 180, 181
    artisans as slaveholders, 60
    in Charleston, S.C., 36, 52, 60, 62, 65, 72,
        85
    indentured servitude, 43, 64, 67
    in Philadelphia, New York, and Boston,
        60, 62
    prohibition of (by Oglethorpe), 36
    and slave revolt, 72, 73
    See also Blacks
SMA, SMSA, 300, 389, 397
Smith, Alfred E., 356, 357, 368
Smith, Betty, 234, 236, 253–54
Smith, Joseph, 100
Social order/patterns
    agriculture and, 92
    artisians in, *see* Artisans
    blacks in, 157–58 (*see also* Blacks)
    the church and, 161 (*see also* Religion)
    consensual, *see* Community
    education and, 162, 184
    European influence on, 63–67, 73, 79
    family and, *see* Family
    and immigrant "ghetto" neighborhoods,
        154, 250–52 (*see also* Housing)
    land ownership and, 30, 63–65, 77
    and mob violence, 179 (*see also* Social
        problems)
    professionals in, 64–65, 66, 159
    prosperity/wealth and, 59–60, 64–67, 79,
        88, 89, 146–51 passim, 159, 162

    religion and, 161–63
    and social/occupational mobility, 18, 162
        of artisans, 59–60, 66, 150
        of blacks, 156–57, 262–63
        of immigrants, 184, 247, 257–58, 259,
        262
    spatial organization and, *see* Spatial
        organization
    the tavern and, 69–70
    and transition of neighborhoods (from
        class to class), 12
Socialist Party, 269
Social problems, 70, 306
    alleviation of, *see* Social services
    crime and vice, 72, 82, 83, 177–78, 180,
        192, 232, 235–36, 246, 268, 273–74,
        286, 287, 290, 308–09, 383
    disease, 82–86 passim, 171–76, 274
    disorder and violence, 72–73, 82–86,
        155–56, 177–80, 238–39, 247,
        266–67, 273, 280, 303, 319–20,
        326–28, 381
    drunkenness and alcoholism, 72–73, 85,
        161, 180–81, 273, 274
        and Prohibition, 307–08, 316, 360
    fire, *see* Fire(s)
    graft and corruption, 287–90, 307
    housing and, *see* Housing
    law enforcement and police, 72, 84, 85,
        177–80 passim, 186, 238, 286, 326,
        327, 343, 359, 401
    pollution, 84, 176, 189, 228, 400
    poverty, 70–72, 82, 83, 86, 98, 157–58,
        174, 180–84, 189, 194, 270, 271–85,
        307, 317–18, 389, 401
        and "deserving poor," 181, 183
    racism, *see* Blacks; Indians; Segregation
    sanitation (garbage and waste disposal),
        23, 82, 84, 171–72, 176, 189, 194,
        228, 324, 329, 359, 396
    transportation inadequacy,
        see Transportation
    unemployment, *see* Labor
    urban congestion, 220
    water supply, 82, 84, 86, 175–76, 189, 194,
        401
    working conditions, *see* Labor
Social reform, 18, 391
    administrative, 359, 366
    housing, 276–85
    legislation for, 163
    politics and, 285–91
    in urban planning, 191, 194, 292, 360–65,
        373
    See also Social problems
Social Security Act, 369
Social services
    black vs. white, 401
    colonial, 71, 75, 84, 85

Social services, *cont'd.*
  local government and, 180–84, 188–89,
      194, 278–79, 303, 389
  for the poor, 180–84, 189, 194, 275–85,
      389
  political reform and, 285–91
  settlement houses, 281–84
Society(ies), *see* Organizations and groups;
      Urban society
South America, 25, 27
South Carolina, 78. *See also individual cities*
Spain, 25, 26–28, 39, 50, 68
Spatial organization
  and church/meetinghouse as focal point,
      see Religion
  of cluster, *see* Cluster (urban form)
  colonial, 37–39, 66–67
  decentralization in, *see* Population
  dispersed arrangement, 397, 399, 402
  and environmental services, 184–89, 194
  highways and, 379–80
  industrialization and, 226–28 (*see also* In-
      dustry)
  linear, 4, 44
  of market place, *see* Market place (urban
      form)
  and megalopolis, 298, 402, 404 (illus.)
  physical/geographical barriers and, *see*
      Geography
  and proximity to work, *see* Labor
  radial, *see* Radial center (urban form)
  segregation in, *see* Segregation
  social order/patterns and, 9–13, 14, 18,
      20, 98–99, 142, 146–51, 159–60,
      162–64, 207, 391
  traditional vs. "no town," 20, 397
  transportation and, 145–46, 228 (*see also*
      Transportation)
  urban forms, four basic, 13–20
  of vital fringe, *see* Vital fringe (urban form)
  and waterfront as focal point, *see*
      Waterfront
  zoning in, *see* Urban planning
Specialization, *see* Trade
Speculation, *see* Land ownership
Sports, *see* Entertainment
Sprague, Frank, 205
Springfield, Massachusetts, 122, 213
Springfield, Ohio, 215
Stamp Act, 94. *See also* Taxation
Standard Metropolitan Area, 300
Standard Metropolitan Statistical Area, 300,
      389, 397
Status, *see* Social order/patterns
Staunton, Virginia, 359
Stead, William T., 235
Steam technology, 15, 120. *See also*
      Railroad(s); Technology;
      Transportation

Steel industry, 222–23, 333, 334
Steinbeck, John, 341
Steiner, Edward, 249
Sternlieb, George, 402
Streetcars, *see* Transportation, Trolley
Streets, 365
  care and improvement of, 170–72, 189,
      286, 359, 362, 363
  and colonial seaports as "street cities," 57
  grid pattern of, *see* Gridiron pattern
  inadequacy of, 82, 83–84, 378
  lighting of, 189, 194, 209–10, 359
  See also Transportation
Suburb(s)
  annexation of, 164, 301–02, 305, 348
      (illus.)
  of Boston, *see* Boston
  commercial nuclei in, 20
  and commuters, *see* Transportation
  development and growth of, 202–05, 296
  and exurbia, 305, 382–83, 384–85, 391,
      399, 402
  first American, 37
  "greenbelt," 369–70
  highway development and, 379, 385
  move to, 44, 45, 141–46 passim, 203, 205,
      218, 225, 297, 345–54, 392
    and "reverse migration," 304, 383
    white vs. black, 320–23, 349, 350, 384
  of New York, *see* New York City
  population of, 203, 345–48, 383–84
  radial, 202–14, 218, 221
  regional power of, 20, 292
  as semirural slums, 143, 149
  shopping centers in, *see* Merchants
  social problems of, 305, 383–84
  as "urban dream," 200, 352
  urbanization of, 382–88
Subways, 205, 264
Sudbury, Massachusetts, plan of, 31 (illus.)
Sumner, Charles, 116
"Sunbelt," 303, 335, 397, 399–400, 401–02
Supreme Court, U.S., 360, 374

Tabor, Michael, 321
Tacoma, Washington, 209
Tallahassee, Florida, 34
Tammany Hall, 287–88, 291, 356–57
Taverns, 69–70, 72, 161
Taxation, 286
  and automobile/gasoline taxes, 378, 381
  and the church, 68, 75
  and education, 183
  Parliamentary, of colonies, 60, 94–95
  property tax, 167, 169, 367, 383, 391
  and relief of poor, 71
  and taxable welath (1687–1771), 65, 66
Technology, 189, 194
  building, 212, 320

communications, 39, 124, 297, 303, 309–11, 336, 337–39
electrical, 205–06, 208, 209–10, 212, 223, 296, 308, 336–37, 343
elevator, 212, 336
industrial/marketplace, 15, 113–23, 223, 224–25, 296, 336 (*see also* Industry)
and leisure time, 309
political, *see* Politics
transportation, *see* Transportation
Tennessee
representation in, 360
See also individual cities
Tennessee Valley Authority (TVA), 370
Texas
cattle trade in, 208
See also individual cities
Textile mills, 121–22, 231. *See also* Industry
Thernstrom, Stephan, 257
Thomas, Piri, 329
Thoreau, Henry David, 191
Tilden, Samuel, 288
Tobacco, 36, 43, 46–47, 52, 55, 112 (illus.), 123
Toledo, Ohio, 290
Topography
and trade, 110, 114, 115
and urban growth, 19, 104–05
See also Geography; Transportation
Trade
Atlantic/European, 45–54, 56, 58–60, 63, 110, 128–30, 141 (*see also* England)
backcountry/hinterland, 48, 54–57, 109–10, 127
and city location, 15, 37, 38–39, 43–51
colonial urbanization relationship to, 47–51
and commerce as "goddess of Christianity," 101, 110
and commercial vs. residential land use, *see* Land uses
competition in, 119, 150, 224
cotton, 128, 129, 131, 261
the factor and, 51–52, 58, 128
fur, 46, 50, 52, 54, 55
geography and, 110, 114, 128
government regulation of, 74, 75, 78, 79–80, 86, 168
quarantine and, 173–74
reciprocal, 120
rice, wheat, indigo, 36, 43, 49–52, 55, 56
slave, *see* Slavery and slave trade
specialization in, 51–52, 58–60, 129–30, 135, 138, 139, 150
territories (market areas), 6, 7 (illus.), 8 (illus.)
tobacco, 36, 43, 46–47, 52, 55, 112 (illus.), 123
topography and, 110, 114, 115

urban network of, 131, 132 (illus.), 133
the waterfront and, *see* Waterfront
West Indies, 48–51, 54, 59
See also Business; Economics; Farming; Merchants; Transportation
Transportation
air, 336, 339–40, 401
automobile, 11, 12, 297, 298, 308, 336, 340–45, 362, 365, 378, 379, 380, 385, 397 (*see also* highways and, *below*)
BART system (San Francisco), 400
cable car, 205, 227, 396
canal, 114–15, 116–17, 118, 119, 128
financing of, 168, 169
and city size, 15, 291
commuter, 143–45, 151, 152 (illus.), 153 (illus.), 226, 228, 298, 301, 380
costs of goods, 6–8, 110, 113, 125
costs of public transit, 143, 144, 145, 151, 204, 207, 227, 290, 349, 385
highways and, 4, 12, 54, 111–13, 343, 345, 350, 363, 365, 378–81, 385, 395, 399, 400, 402 (*see also* Streets)
inadequacy of, 82, 87, 109–10, 143–44
omnibus (horse-drawn), 143–44, 145, 206, 308
vs. proximity to work, *see* Labor
river, 44, 54–56, 109, 114, 130
shipbuilding industry and, *see* Industry
and spatial/radial expansion, 4, 10, 12, 18, 19–20, 37, 39, 87, 98, 143–48, 202, 205–08, 297–98
steamboats and ferries, 113–14, 116, 128, 145
street railway (horse-drawn), 144, 145, 206
subway, 205, 264
trolley/electric streetcar, 202, 205–08, 227, 291, 296, 298, 308, 336–37, 343, 345, 396
in urban planning, 365, 378–81
See also Railroad(s); Trade
Trolley (electric streetcar), 202, 205–08, 227, 291, 296, 298, 308, 336–37, 343, 345, 396
Truman, Harry S., 375
Twain, Mark, 143, 192
Tweed, William Meagher, 288

Ullman, Edward L., 12
Unemployment, *see* Labor
University of Chicago, 9
Urban ecology, *see* Ecology
Urban forms, four basic (cluster, market place, radial center, vital fringe), 13–20. *See also individual forms*
Urban hierarchy, 160
of Christaller, 3–4
in colonial Virginia, 55–56

Urban hierarchy, *cont'd.*
  economics and, 16–17, 122–23
  regionalization and, 16, 18, 404 (illus.)
  and "urban imperialism," 56
  See also Rank order
Urbanization/urban growth
  in backcountry, 54–57 (*see also*
      Hinterlands)
  change as essence of, 309
  and city as "way of life," 189–95
  colonial patterns of, 37–39, 66–67
  competition as factor in, 96, 124–27, 135,
      291–92
  consolidation (annexation) in, 164,
      301–02, 305, 348 (illus.)
  corporations and, 226–27, 332–33
  cyclical nature of, 46
  entrepreneurs and, *see* Entrepreneurs
  government (local) and, 166–80,
      355–60, 389–93, 395–96
  industrialization and, 120, 225 (*see also*
      Industry)
  and megalopolis, 298, 402, 404 (illus.)
  migration and, 297 (*see also* Immigrants)
  the press and, 126
  private redevelopment in, 391–94
  reciprocal trade and, 120
  and residential neighborhoods, 44–45,
      86–89 (*see also* Housing)
  rival models of, 11 (illus.)
  1790–1870 rate of, 98
  spatial, *see* Spatial organization
  specialization and, 17–19, 59, 138
  of suburbs, 382–88 (*see also* Suburb[s])
  topography and, 19, 104–05
  trade and, *see* Trade
  and urban failure, 45–46
  and urbanization as "controlling factor,"
      199
  and urban population statistics, 199–200
  use of land in, *see* Land uses
  wealth and, 66–67 (*see also* Wealth)
  westward, 208–09
  and world urbanization process, 14
  See also Population
Urbanized Area (census classification),
    300–01
Urban network, *see* Trade
Urban planning
  and "City Beautiful," "City Efficient,"
      214–21
  "comprehensive," 362–63, 365
  German, influence of, 218–19
  government and, 364, 365–66, 369–73,
      378–81, 385–93
  laws and legislation, 26–27, 35, 43
  regional, 361, 363–64, 365
  Resettlement Administration (RA) and,
      369–70

speculation and, 104
traditional ideas of, 29
urban reform and, 191, 194, 292, 360–65,
    373
zoning, 218, 219, 320, 362–63, 364–65,
    401
Urban society, 307–30. *See also* Blacks;
    Culture(s); Entertainment; Social
    problems; Suburb(s)

Van Vechten, Carl, 313
Vaux, Calvert, 186
Veiller, Lawrence, 278–79, 386
Vice, *see* Social problems
Violence, *see* Social problems
Virginia, 54, 118
  colonial, urban hierarchy in, 55–56
  town planning laws in, 35, 43
  See also individual cities
Virginia Company of London, 29, 35, 41
Vital fringe (urban form), 18–20, 296–306,
    336, 354, 379
  "greenbelt" towns, 369–70
  See also Suburb(s)
Voting, *see* Government, local

Wabash, Indiana, 210
Wagner, Robert F., 256–57, 369
Wales, 25, 62
Wall(s)
  as distinguishing feature, 26
  and fortress construction, 14, 22, 25, 28,
      29, 34–35, 36
Wallace, George, 327
Wall Street, 35, 140–41
Waltham, Massachusetts, 121
Ward system, 36–37, 168, 392. *See also*
    Politics
Ware, James E., 275
Warner, Sam Bass, Jr., 204, 257
Washington, Booker T., 267, 269
Washington, D.C., 193, 298, 339, 345, 387
    (illus.), 391, 392
  blacks in, 263, 328, 384
  location and plans of, 104, 106–08, 216,
      217 (illus.)
  and transportation, 379, 385
  violence in, 178, 179
Washington, George, 107, 191
Waterfront
  and coastal cities, 15, 37, 38–39, 43–51,
      86, 128
  as focal point, 34, 44, 87, 89, 124, 133,
      134, 140, 141
  as industrial/nonresidential location, 135,
      138, 147, 154
  and trade, 43–51, 54–56, 57, 59, 69–70,
      86, 89, 128
Water supply, *see* Social problems

Wealth, 177, 391
  and abandonment of culture, 258
  and outward/radial expansion, 18, 19, 202
  and retail specialization, 138–39
  and slaveholding, 60 (*see also* Slavery and
    slave trade)
  and social status, *see* Social order/patterns
  taxable (1687–1771), 65, 66
Weber, Adna F., 206
Wedge theory, *see* Sector/wedge theory
West Indies
  immigrants from, 62, 267
  trade with, 48–51, 54, 59
Wheat trade, 36, 49–50, 51, 55–56, 113, 115
Wheeling, West Virginia, 114
White, Alfred T., 277
Whitman, Walt, 123, 190, 193–94, 405
Williams, Fannie Barrier, 262
Williams, Roger, 32, 68
Williamsburg, Virginia, 46, 70, 79, 91
  axial design of, 26, 35–36
Wilmington, Delaware, 298, 390
Wine Islands, 49, 50, 54
Winthrop, John, 29, 33, 72, 77, 100, 192,
    243, 259
Winthrop, John, Jr., 32
Women
  in labor force, 121–22, 189–90, 227, 231,
    232–36

  and women's rights, 181
Woodruff, Robert W., 342
Woolworth, Frank and Woolworth Building,
    213
Worcester, Massachusetts, 155
Working Men's Party (Philadelphia), 163
World's Fair (Columbian Exposition, 1893),
    214, 215 (illus.)
World urbanization process, 14
World War I
  employment during, 262, 263
World War II
  blacks in, 318–19
  economic effect of, 334–35, 341, 343, 371
WPA (Works Progress Administration), *see*
    New Deal
Wright, Carroll, 206, 277
Wright, Frank Lloyd, 402

YMCA, YWCA, 268–69
Young, Brigham, 100, 101, 104, 107, 192,
    243, 259
Youngstown, Ohio, 315
"Y" projects, 268–69

Zoning, *see* Urban planning

ABCDEFGHIJ–H–8210/79